Dialogue, Skill and Tacit Knowledge

Dialogue, Skill and Tacit Knowledge

Edited by
Bo Göranzon,
Maria Hammarén
and
Richard Ennals

John Wiley & Sons, Ltd

Other Wiley Editorial Offices

John Wiley & Sons Inc., 111 River Street, Hoboken, NJ 07030, USA

Jossey-Bass, 989 Market Street, San Francisco, CA 94103-1741, USA

Wiley-VCH Verlag GmbH, Boschstr. 12, D-69469 Weinheim, Germany

John Wiley & Sons Australia Ltd, 42 McDougall Street, Milton, Queensland 4064, Australia

John Wiley & Sons (Asia) Pte Ltd, 2 Clementi Loop #02-01, Jin Xing Distripark, Singapore 129809

John Wiley & Sons Canada Ltd, 22 Worcester Road, Etobicoke, Ontario, Canada M9W 1L1

Wiley also publishes its books in a variety of electronic formats. Some content that appears in print may not be
available in electronic books.

Library of Congress Cataloging-in-Publication Data

Dialogue, skill and tacit knowledge / edited by Bo Göranzon, Maria Hammarén, and Richard Ennals
    p. cm.
  Includes index.
  ISBN-13: 978-0-470-01921-4 (hard : alk. paper)
  ISBN-10: 0-470-01921-2 (hard : alk. paper)
  1. Knowledge, Theory of.   2. Tacit knowledge.   3. Dialogue analysis.   4. Knowledge management.
  5. Organizational learning.   6. Interdisciplinary approach to knowledge.   I. Göranzon, Bo, 1941–
  II. Hammarén, Maria.   III. Ennals, J. R. (John Richard), 1951–

  BD161.D43 2006
  001—dc22

                                                                           2005025137

British Library Cataloguing in Publication Data

A catalogue record for this book is available from the British Library

ISBN 13 978-0-470-01921-4 (HB)
ISBN 10 0-470-01921-2 (HB)

Typeset in 10/12pt Garamond by Integra Software Services Pvt. Ltd, Pondicherry, India
Printed and bound in Great Britain by TJ International Ltd, Padstow, Cornwall, UK
This book is printed on acid-free paper responsibly manufactured from sustainable forestry
in which at least two trees are planted for each one used for paper production.

Contents

Contents

List of Contributors

Göran Backlund is a manager and senior consultant at Combitech Systems, a knowledge based company specialised in embedded computer systems development, owned by the SAAB Group, Sweden. His assignments concern leadership and knowledge development for technical organisations. He is also a PhD student at the Royal Institute of Technology (KTH) in Stockholm, Department of Skill and Technology.

Karl Dunér is a director at the Royal Dramatic Theatre in Stockholm.

Lucas Ekeroth has a Master of Science at the Royal Institute of Technology in Stockholm.

Richard Ennals is Professor at the Centre for Working Life Research, Kingston University, and a Visiting Professor at the Swedish Royal Institute of Technology, the Norwegian University of Science and Technology, and Mykolas Romeris University in Lithuania.

Niclas Fock is Business Area Manager at Combitech Systems in Linköping. He is responsible for knowledge development at Combitech Systems and is also a PhD student at the Royal Institute of Technology in Stockholm, Department of Skill and Technology.

Bo Göranzon is Professor of Skill and Technology at the Royal Institute of Technology, Stockholm and artistic director of the Dialogue Seminar at the Royal Dramatic Theatre, Stockholm.

Maria Hammarén is a researcher at the Department of Skill and Technology at the Royal Institute of Technology, Stockholm. In her doctoral dissertation, 'Clues in Transformation: On Creating a Reflective Practice' (1999) she outlines the Dialogue Seminar Method as developed in collaboration with the company Combitech Systems and co-researcher Bo Göranzon.

Mats Hanson is vice-rector at the Royal Institute of Technology, Stockholm.

Christer Hoberg is Chief Executive Officer of Saab Combitech Systems, and engaged in collaborative research with the Department of Skill and Technology at the Royal Institute of Technology.

Allan Janik is Professor at the Brenner Archiv, Innsbruck, and has long been engaged in research on aspects of Wittgenstein's philosophy.

Kjell S. Johannessen is Professor of Philosophy at the University of Bergen, Norway. Since the early 1970s he has been engaged in research on various aspects of Wittgenstein's philosophy.

Erland Josephson is a distinguished actor and a former artistic director at the Royal Dramatic Theatre in Stockholm.

Øyvind Pålshaugen is Research Director at the Work Research Institute in Oslo.

Adrian Ratkic is a researcher at the Department of Skill and Technology at the Royal Institute of Technology, Stockholm.

John Shotter is Emeritus Professor at the University of New Hampshire, USA.

Jan Sjunnesson is a manager and senior consultant at Combitech Systems. His assignments concern leadership and knowledge development for technical organisations. He is also a PhD student at the Royal Institute of Technology (KTH) in Stockholm, Department of Skill and Technology.

Peter Tillberg is a research student in the Department of Skill and Technology at the Royal Institute of Technology.

The Department of Skill and Techology is a part of the School of Engineering and Management, Royal Institute of Technology, Stockholm, Sweden.

Introduction

Richard Ennals

Practical Needs of Learning Organisations

It is common for companies to claim to be learning organisations, without explaining what this means in practice. Conclusions from practice are confounding academic orthodoxy, and opening the way for real sustainable benefits for participating organisations. Reflection on experience can be more effective than reliance on theories from social science. In all the rhetoric about 'knowledge society', there has been little discussion of what is meant by 'knowledge'. In this book, based on practical cases, we offer a way forward.

Problems of Knowledge

It has become increasingly evident that conventional approaches to business and technology have failed to come to terms with fundamental problems of knowledge. This presents practical difficulties, amid all the rhetoric about knowledge society and knowledge economy. It had been imagined by many that knowledge could be commodified, and made available for commercial exploitation, without dependence on the continued presence of the experts whose knowledge had been elicited for use in expert systems. How can companies address this challenge in practice?

As knowledge has been seen as increasingly important as a driver for economic development, research has exposed the limits of what can be achieved by conventional means. Since 1987, collaborative research led by Bo Göranzon, and involving Maria Hammarén and Richard Ennals, has been tackling Skill, Technology, Culture and Communication. Starting by demystifying the claims of artificial intelligence, and working closely with companies, a new foundation has been developed, based on practical philosophy, and with dialogue at the centre of activities. Learning is seen as arising from encounters with differences.

Preparatory Dialogue

The three editors have collaborated since 1987, in the context of a succession of projects in the research field 'Skill and Technology', and supported by the award-winning Dialogue Seminar, based at the Royal Dramatic Theatre in Stockholm. The core ideas were set out at the 1988 conference 'Culture, Language and Artificial Intelligence', and published in a series of six volumes, edited by Bo Göranzon, published by Springer Verlag, London 1988–95:

- *Knowledge, Skill and Artificial Intelligence*, eds Bo Göranzon and Ingela Josefson. 1988.
- *Artificial Intelligence, Culture and Language: On Education and Work*, eds Bo Göranzon and Magnus Florin. 1990.
- *Dialogue and Technology: Art and Knowledge*, eds Bo Göranzon and Magnus Florin. 1991.
- *Skill and Education: Reflection and Experience*, eds Bo Göranzon and Magnus Florin. 1992.
- *The Practical Intellect: Computers and Skills*, Bo Göranzon. 1992.
- *Skill, Technology and Enlightenment: On Practical Philosophy*, ed. Bo Göranzon. 1995.

In Stockholm, the collaboration involved the Royal Dramatic Theatre, the Swedish National Institute for Working Life, and the Swedish Royal Institute of Technology, providing an encounter between different perspectives in knowledge. A succession of seminars and conferences with international partners followed, including a seminar and conference series at Kingston University. Since 2000, the doctoral programme in 'Skill and Technology', which used the six volumes as a teaching resource, has enabled the dialogue to continue and mature, with philosophical insights used as tools to reflect on practice. A series of practical cases have been developed. The doctoral students are also practitioners, experienced senior managers. The expertise of the team has matured, as a second generation of leaders are now involved. There are courses with major companies such as Combitech Systems, Sony Ericsson, Volvo and Electrolux.

The present book builds on those foundations, and this long period of dialogue, but is almost entirely comprised of new case study material and reflections. It is intended to help companies and other organisations to address problems of knowledge, and to support the new doctoral programme 'Managing Reflective Practice', and related programmes which are now developing around the world, and in particular in Europe. Many of the participants in these courses are also engaged in full-time professional practice, and the challenge is to facilitate reflection. Management is reinvented as the orchestration of reflection.

At the core of the book is a concern for epistemology. There has been a deep-seated concern among the contributors that major mistakes have been made in the treatment of knowledge, in many high profile programmes which have tended to emphasise the role of technology. As was argued at the 1988 conference, the attempt to represent the full richness of expert knowledge in explicit form was doomed to failure, and based on a misunderstanding of the nature of knowledge. Only a fraction of expert knowledge can be codified and expressed in explicit form, as facts and rules. Another layer of implicit knowledge is not usually represented, but may exist in the form of accepted procedures which can be elicited and formalised using available methods. This leaves the submerged iceberg of tacit knowledge, which is not reliably accessible by traditional analytical approaches, or 'drilling down'.

In this book we explore the significance of tacit knowledge, and consider accounts of how access has been gained, through analogical thinking. Principal among these is the 'Dialogue Seminar Method', which has been developed and applied by the first two editors. Case study accounts are provided, together with guidance for those wishing to use it. After so many years of collaborative endeavour, there is now a body of experience, and many documented cases of organisations whose cultures have been transformed by the 'Dialogue Seminar Method'.

Each chapter in the book stands alone, and is accompanied by specific references and notes. However, there are numerous links and cross-references between the chapters, for example as particular cases are considered from different perspectives. These connections are illuminated by the subject and name indexes.

Part 1. Dialogue and Skill

It is often assumed that a single model of knowledge will cover the range of different fields of study, and indeed such a view underpins positivist social science, suggesting consistency with the natural sciences. The use of computers has highlighted glaring deficiencies in this view, as is explored by Bo Göranzon, in 'The Practice of the Use of Computers: A Paradoxical Encounter between Different Traditions of Knowledge'.

For those who come from backgrounds in the natural sciences, it is possible to fall into the trap of seeing language, and writing, as used only for descriptive purposes. Maria Hammarén, reflecting on her own long experience of practice as a journalist, opens up a broader perspective, in 'Writing as a Method of Reflection'.

Adrian Ratkic, of the Royal Institute of Technology, introduces the new programme which has resulted, in 'The Dialogue Seminar as a foundation for research on skill'. Bo Göranzon and Maria Hammarén offer guidelines to 'The Methodology of the Dialogue Seminar', to enable others to take the approach forward in practice.

Part 2. Theatre and Work

The theatre has provided an arena in which the ideas have been brought together, rehearsed and presented. We have developed the concept of 'performing knowledge', with the central image of the actor as a model for professional skill. The scene is set by the distinguished actor and director Erland Josephson, in 'A Dwelling Place for Past and Living Voices, Passions and Characters'.

The philosopher Allan Janik presents theatre as offering fundamental insights into knowledge, in 'Theatre and Knowledge'.

Part 3. Case Studies

Interesting case studies are not enough in themselves. What was required was sustained engagement with committed organisations, who through their practice and reflections demonstrate the transforming impact of dialogue on their culture. Niclas Fock presents the case of his company, in 'Dialogue Seminar as a tool: experiences from Combitech Systems'.

The Chief Executive Officer of the company has been a key research leader, and has championed the transformational process, as well as publishing a successful book in Swedish on the experience. Christer Hoberg explains his approach in 'Maximum Complexity'.

The collaboration between the Royal Institute of Technology and Combitech Systems has led to major changes in approaches to systems engineering, as is described by Göran Backlund and Jan Sjunnesson in 'Better Systems Engineering with Dialogue'.

The same philosophical perspective, and insights into skill, has applications across the range of sectors, as is demonstrated by Peter Tillberg, with a military background, in his 'Some aspects of military practices and officers' professional skills'.

Meanwhile, at the Royal Institute of Technology, fresh approaches are being taken to multidisciplinary work, as expounded by Karl Dunér, Lucas Ekeroth and Mats Hanson, in 'Science and Art '.

Part 4. Dialogue Seminar as Reflective Practice

Bridging the gap between theory and practice has been a constant concern for Bo Göranzon, who links the philosophical perspectives on tacit knowledge with practical concerns for risk and decision making, in 'Tacit Knowledge and Risks'.

We emerge with new firm ground. With renewed philosophical vigour, Maria Hammarén returns to reflections on writing, in 'Skill, Story-telling and Language'.

It is not enough to be pleased about the success of a particular local favoured method. The Dialogue Seminar has been subjected to critical analysis by leading philosophers and researchers. Øyvind Pålshaugen revisits the work of Wittgenstein, solving what has been a mystery for many frustrated readers of the 'Tractatus Logico-Philosophicus', by revealing, in Wittgenstein's own words, that there had been two volumes, only one of which could be written. The chapter 'Reading and Writing as Performing Arts: at work' was first presented at a conference on 'Performing Knowledge', in Stockholm, which brought together the worlds of philosophical theory and the practice of working life.

These links are clarified in a chapter by Kjell S. Johannessen, 'Knowledge and Reflective Practice', which legitimates the epistemological underpinnings of the Dialogue Seminar method.

The argument is taken further by John Shotter, who has considerable experience of dialogue conferences and their applications in regional development as well as diverse social contexts, as he explains in 'Dialogue, Depth and Life Inside Responsive Orders'.

Part 5. Tacit Knowledge and Literature

Tacit knowledge has been a matter for academic debate for decades, but the challenge has of course been to make explicit the issues that have been so hard to understand. The Norwegian philosopher Kjell S. Johannessen provides a lucid introduction to the field in 'Rule Following, Intransitive Understanding and Tacit Knowledge'.

After years of working in Scandinavian theatre, Allan Janik tackles the challenge of assessing the importance of Ibsen, in 'Henrik Ibsen: Why we need him more than ever.'

6. Conclusions

Richard Ennals broadens the context of discussion, and identifies new potential applications of the Dialogue Seminar Method to current practical case study work in action research, workplace innovation and regional development, in 'Theatre and Workplace Actors'.

In the final chapter, 'Training in Analogical Thinking: The Dialogue Seminar Method', Bo Göranzon, Maria Hammarén and Adrian Ratkic paint a broad picture, setting the scene for the next generation of cases.

This has been a long and demanding journey, during which we have crossed many borders, bridged many gaps, and encountered many outstanding performers of knowledge. We hope that our readers will wish to join us in the process of dialogue, and bring their own distinctive contributions.

1 The Practice of the Use of Computers: A Paradoxical Encounter between Different Traditions of Knowledge

Bo Göranzon

Fundamental to the design of knowledge-based systems is the understanding of the nature of knowledge and the problems involved in computerising it. This chapter deals with these issues and draws a distinction between three different categories of knowledge: propositional knowledge, skill or practical knowledge and knowledge of familiarity. In the present debate on 'Information Society', there is a clear tendency to overemphasise the theoretical knowledge at the expense of practical knowledge thereby completely ignoring the knowledge of familiarity. It is argued that different forms of theoretical knowledge are required for the design of current computer technology and the study of the practice of computer usage. The concept of dialogue, and the concept of 'To Follow a Rule', are therefore fundamental to the understanding of the practice of computer usage.

Paradoxical Views of Knowledge in the Age of Enlightenment

In the modern sense, applied mathematics was the creation of René Descartes. In 1637, Descartes presented a study in which he showed how, by applying abstract algebraic concepts, it is possible to formulate geometry's concrete points, lines, surfaces and volumes. He demonstrated a link between our three-dimensional world and a mathematical-logical way of thinking.

In Descartes' work *Discourse on Methods, Optics, Geometry and Meteorology* (Descartes, 1637) in which he presented his revolutionary mathematical theory, the word 'machine' is applied to the human body for the first time in history:

> And this will not seem strange to those, who knowing how many different automata or moving machines can be made by the industry of man without employing in so doing more than a very few parts in comparison with the great multitude of bones, muscles, nerves, arteries, veins, or other parts that are found in the body of each animal. From this aspect the body is regarded as a machine which, having been made by the hands of God, is incomparably better arranged, and possesses in itself movements which are much more admirable, than any of those which can be invented by man.

Descartes continues with an important argument:

> Here I specially stopped to show that if there had been such machines, possessing the organs and outward form of a monkey or some other animal without reason, we should not have had any means of ascertaining that they were not of the same nature as those animals. On the other hand, if there were machines which bore a resemblance to our body and imitated our actions as far as it was morally possible to do so, we should always have two very certain tests by which to recognise that, for all that, they were not real men. The first is, that they could never use speech or other signs as we do when placing our thoughts on record for the benefit of others. For we can easily understand a machine's being constituted so that it can utter words, and even emit some responses to action on it of a corporeal kind, which brings about a change in its organs; for instance if it is touched in a particular part it may ask what we wish to say to it; if in another part it may exclaim that it is being hurt, and so on. But it never happens that it arranges its speech in various ways, in order to reply appropriately to everything that may be said in its presence, as even the lowest type of man can do. And the second difference is, that although machines can perform certain things as well as or perhaps better than any of us can do, they infallibly fall short in others, by the which means we may discover that they did not act from knowledge, but only from the disposition of their organs. For while reason is the universal instrument which can serve for all contingencies, these organs have need of some special adaptation for every particular action.

The notion that '*animals are machines*' lies at the core of the Cartesian view. Descartes coined a phrase to express this opinion: Bete machine. There is a reference to this phrase in one of the earliest documents produced in the French Age of Enlightenment: Man a Machine, published in 1748 by Dr de La Mettrie. To La Mettrie, learning to understand a language, i.e. learning to use symbols, is to become a human being. Culture is what separates man from the animals. La Mettrie means that thinking should turn from general abstractions to consider the concrete, the details. It is the models to be found in the concrete examples we meet that nurture us in a culture. According to La Mettrie, a mind that has received poor guidance is as an actor who has been spoiled by provincial theatres; he goes on to say that the separate states of the soul are in constant interaction with the body. La Mettrie struck a chord that was to characterise the contradictory views of knowledge during the French Age of Enlightenment (Lindborg, 1984).

Denis Diderot, leader of the French Encyclopedia project in the Age of Enlightenment, attempted to track down the paradox inherent in the perception of the way knowledge and competence are developed and maintained. On the one hand there is the belief that everything can be systematised and formalised in a symbolic logical notation. On the other hand there is Minerva's owl which, although it first appears on the periphery of the project, when seen as a link with the current debate on technical change, becomes vitally important to develop further.

Denis Diderot says this: 'If I knew how to speak as I think! But as it is now, I have ideas in my head but I cannot find words for them' (Josephs, 1969).

To be at once within and standing apart from oneself. To observe and be the person who is observed. But thought is like the eye: it cannot see itself. How do we shape the rhythmic gestures of our thoughts? Here we can establish a link with Ludwig Wittgenstein's philosophy of language, which is currently becoming more prominent in the international debate on technical advance.

On Following Rules

Ludwig Wittgenstein's philosophy focusses attention on the particular concrete case or example. He wishes to remind us of the complex and many-faceted logic of the example:

> It is not only a question of the errors in thinking we make when we focus only on the universal. It is also a question of the values that are lost through this intellectual attitude (Kjell S. Johannesen, 1987).

The multiplicity of disparate activities or practices: following a rule in one's activities is what Wittgenstein refers to as a practice; it is the focal point of his interest.

Wittgenstein perceives a concept as a set of activities that follow a rule, in contrast to regarding the concept as a rule, a view that characterises the earlier scientific traditions to which we have referred. In this way, the concept becomes related to its usage. The use of the concept determines its content. It is our usage or practice that shows the way in which we understand something.

The rule is built into the action. The concept of practice brings out this fundamental relationship. To master and coordinate actions implies an ability to be part of a practice. '...But if a person has not yet got the concepts, I should teach him to use the words by means of examples and by practice...' (*Philosophical Investigations*: 201) '...If language is to be a rneans of communication there must be agreement not only in definitions but also (queer as this may sound) in judgements' (*Philosophical Investigations*: 242).

We are taught a practice through examples, through models. The ability to formulate examples is vitally important. There are good examples which lead our thoughts in the 'right' direction and which refresh our minds, and there are examples that make it impossible to understand the sense of a practice. This cannot be made explicit by means of a formal description. It requires the ability to put forward the essence of a practice through examples that are allowed by teaching, by practice. We acquire a deeper understanding of the concept 'tool' by using tools in different activities. Taking part in different practices, when, for example, using computers, can give different opinions about the way computer usage affects the activity, while people sharing in a common practice may have varying opinions about the use of computers in this practice.

What is a Computer?

At an international conference in Sigtuna, Sweden in June 1979 on the theme 'Is the computer a tool?', Allan Janik (Janik, 1980) the philosopher, discussed 'essentially contested concepts' and the part played by these concepts in our attempts to describe reality:

> Basically, the most vexed issues which humans face involve conflicts about how we are to describe the situation we confront...Our evidence may be the wrong sort of evidence and our tradition may lead us to ask the wrong questions. We must be at one and the same time guided by what we take to

be the substance of the issues at hand and also prepared to reconsider precisely what the substance of the issue actually is. It is always necessary to bear in mind that the most serious issues we confront concern 'essentially contested concepts', i.e. disagreement over just what the substantive issues are. To prevail in the conflict is to be prepared to follow the discussion, even when it leads us into unfamiliar terrain.

The content of the concept 'tool' is not self-evident in the same way as understanding what a computer is. There is a profusion of metaphors and parallels about computers in analogies with steam engines, electricity, the motor car, typewriters, etc. In the same way there are numerous analogies of what a human being is in connection with the debate on technological development: man as a clockwork machine, an ant, a piano, etc. A usual starting point in the debate on computers is to compare the memory capacity of the brain to that of a computer. Here, the main function is information processing. A different starting point is the comparison between human language and the 'language of machines'. The point of this comment is to interpret Allan Janik's attention to 'essentially contested concepts', namely that our perception of the man-machine relationship plays a decisive part in controlling our questions on the use of computers.

A Boat Builder on the West Coast of Sweden

The conference on 'is the computer a tool?' was also attended by Thomas Tempte, a carpenter and craftsman who for his part could see no striking similarities between computers and what he in his own 'profession' was used to calling 'tools'.

Thomas Tempte (1981) described Gosta, a boat builder on Sweden's west coast:

> Gosta is a product of the old master-journeyman-apprentice training system in which sophisticated and complex knowledge was passed on without using words. This is not because of any aversion to transferring knowledge by means of the spoken word, but because no such tradition had been developed.
>
> Putting a question to Gosta elicits very precise information, often after a pause for thought. His knowledge is neither unconscious or unrefined, but he is not used to passing it on in words. He demonstrates by doing the job, supplementing his example with a few words of commentary. This often takes the form of a story about a craftsman who did not do the job in a certain way, which caused him to make a mistake. One gets the feeling that he has all the answers, and this allows him to disassociate himself from the

ill-judged behaviour of the offending craftsman. All this is related in the form of an anecdote.

Here, Tempte gives an unusually penetrating description of his professional work. None-the-less, it contains an unacceptable assumption on the nature of knowledge and how it is transferred. Tempte expresses himself from within a tradition which more or less tacitly presupposes that it is possible to express everything in words. At the same time, he describes the master craftsman as 'demonstrating, with a few words of commentary'. This is as far as one can go, providing examples and stimulating practice.

One consequence of the essential operation of following a rule is that special emphasis is placed on practice/learning. Previous experience and problem-solving, so-called sediment, is turned into a process of following rules that form the basis of the practice that we are being taught: 'Is it that rule and empirical proposition merge into one another?' (*On Certainty*: §309) Wittgenstein asks, and goes on to say: 'If experience is the ground of our certainty, then naturally it is past experience and it isn't for example just my experience but other people's, that I get knowledge from.' (*On Certainty*: §275)

There are many ways of following a rule. In Wittgenstein's view, guessing is of central importance to a rule system and to all forms of learning. Applying a rule is a matter of knowing what to do at the next stage. Guessing is done on the basis of examples we have been presented with and continues until we have the talent to do it correctly.

As we grow more sure, i.e., have met a large number of examples through our experience, our competence increases, and we master a practice.

Judging Light in Photography

Peter Gullers (1984), a photographer, has reflected upon his professional work and made a penetrating description of the essential aspects of judging light in photography:

> The text of a recent advertisement for cameras said: 'Instructions for taking good pictures – just push the button'. Thanks to new technology we no longer need to know a lot about the technique of photography before we can take good pictures. The manufacturer had built a program into the camera, a program which made all the important decisions and all the assessments needed to produce a satisfactory result.
>
> New technology has made it easier to take photographs and photography has become very reliable and accurate in most normal conditions. When there

is not enough light, the exposure is blocked or a built-in flash is activated to ensure satisfactory results.

The program cannot be modified and no opinion can be passed on the results until later. The underlying principles are invisible – the process is soundless. Neither does the manufacturer describe how the program makes these assessments. In retrospect, when the picture has been developed, even the uninitiated judge can say that the picture is too dark, too light or blurred. On the other hand the cause of the fault is difficult to establish without a thorough knowledge of technology, or of the conditions under which the photograph was taken.

There are numerous problem areas and the causes of these problems tend to merge with each other.

Physiologists claim that the eye is a poor light-meter because the pupil automatically adapts to the intensity of light. This may be so. When faced with a concrete situation that I have to assess, I observe a number of different factors that affect the quality of the light and thus the results of my photography. Is it summer or winter, is it morning or evening? Is the sun breaking through a screen of cloud or am I in semi-shadow under a leafy tree? Are parts of the subject in deep shadow and the rest in strong sunlight? Then I have to strike a balance between light and darkness. If I am in a smithy or in a rolling mill shop, I note how the light coming through the sloping skylights contrasts with the sooty heat of the air in the brick building. The vibrations from hammers and mills make the floor and the camera tremble, which makes photography more difficult and affects the light-metering. The daylight is enhanced by the red glow of the steel billets.

In the same way I gather impressions from other situations and environments. In a new situation, I recall similar situations and environments that I have encountered earlier. They act as comparisons and as association material, and my previous perceptions, mistakes and experiences provide the basis for my judgement.

It is not only the memories of the actual process of photography that play a part. The hours spent in the darkroom developing the film, my curiosity about the results, the arduous work of re-creating reality and the graphic world of the picture are also among my memories. A faulty assessment of the strength of the light and the contrast of the subject, the vibrations and tremors become important experience to be called upon next time I face a similar situation. All of these earlier memories and experiences that are stored away over the years only partly penetrate my consciousness when I make a judgement on the light conditions. The thumb and index finger of my right hand turn the camera's exposure knob to a setting that 'feels right', while my left hand adjusts the filter ring. This process is almost automatic.

The problem with automatic computer-aided light-metering is that after a long period of use one tends to lose one's ability to judge light conditions.

Few people can manage without mechanical or electronic light-meters today.

But it is not simply the ability to judge the light value that is disappearing. Unless one regularly makes a manual judgement of light, one's sensitivity to shades of light tends to become blunted. Our pictorial memories of past experiences are not activated in the same way unless they have been connected with similar assessments. Unless one regularly performs the actual work of producing pictures, the ability to make the best use of composition and light-modifying techniques when printing will wither too.

The problem with the automatic meter is not only that its program does not consider whether it is day or night, or the nature of the subject, or the inexperience of the user. The most important point is that it denies me access to my memories and blunts my perceptions and my ability to discern shades of light. This intimate knowledge is not linked to what I do when I photograph, i.e. the operations I perform, but to actual memories and experiences when I take photographs and when I develop and print pictures.

Technology and Culture

Gullers' example contains a cultural-critical perspective. The type of change in professional competence that Gullers points to, 'the sensitivity to shades of light tending to become blunted, is a phenomenon that takes a long time to occur. It is one of the reasons for calling attention to links with the past. Without a link with the past through epistemology and the history of ideas, a debate on the future of technological development will lack any contact with reality. It will be devoid of content, and full of clichés and vague rhetoric such as 'placing the human being in the centre'.

The cultural-critical element is constantly present in Wittgenstein's thinking. Describing a practice involves adopting a standpoint on the description of a culture. 'A whole culture belongs to a language-game.' A practice is thus, at one and the same time, both fundamental and relative to the culture and the epoch.

In a study carried out by the International Labour Organization in Geneva comparing 13 industrial countries and their experiences of technical change in the 1970s, a common factor emerged, namely the attention given to changes in professional qualifications. When discussing solutions to the problem of changing professional qualifications, it becomes evident that individual cultural and national characteristics become involved. The problem is a common one, but culture and tradition become decisive factors in the way different solutions are debated. There are culture-specific characteristics that must be observed when making international comparative studies. Why, for example, are 'isolation' and 'lack of identity' emphasised in West German studies of the use of computers? Has the computer any decisive significance in terms of the occurrence of these phenomena or are they culture-specific and can they be discussed separately from the issue of computers?

Routine Practice and Development Practice

We call an activity that can be described exhaustively in stated rules a routine practice. Here, the rules are closed; they can be described in a set of essential and sufficient conditions. There is an obvious relationship to a set of rules adapted for computer technology.

An activity that is characterised by open rules, meaning that their expression admits of a variety of meanings, we shall call a development practice. It is this kind of practice that we are primarily interested in. The rules that form a development practice cannot be entirely expressed in words. As we pointed out earlier, it is essential to have good examples and to learn a practice by training. It is the following of the rules rather than the rules themselves that is the prism in this perspective.

At the same time, it is important to emphasise the intersubjective aspects of following rules in a practice. It is logically impossible to be the only person following a rule. A single practice can therefore not be seen as a logical place for dialogue and shared action.

Error-location in a Computer Program

Per Svensson (1983), who is responsible for developing a computer system for forest valuation, makes the following remarks on error-location in a computer program:

> In the routines at the Agricultural Administration for valuing forests using EDP, error-location and the correction of input data is one of the most important jobs. Programs have been written that search through input data and report any errors, controlled by given rules that are part of the program. It is impossible to make programs to locate and make a perfectly clear report on every kind of error. The input data varies far too much for this to be a practical possibility. Instead, the users must learn this work through experience. After having worked with this application for a long time, the speed with which most experienced users now locate these errors is incomprehensible to new employees. When asked: 'How do you locate this error?', they answer: 'I see that it is an error'. One explanation of why

experienced users recognize errors when inexperienced users do not discover them is that their experience contains memories from earlier, similar cases, even if one cannot with certainty report when they occurred. This is a form of knowledge that is extremely difficult to document, but which none-the-less exists and works in practice.

Attempts have been made to document this particular work operation. The experience gained from these attempts is daunting. The result of the documentation was a very comprehensive catalogue of every imaginable error, how they were reported by the program and what action should be taken on them. For new users, this catalogue was both frightening and of little use, while experienced users worked quicker and more surely if they trusted their own experience and did not use the error-location catalogue. Experience cannot always be documented in a usable way.

This knowledge cannot be taught directly to others, but can be transferred to some people by using analogies and concrete examples. At the same time the individual must strive to win a deeper insight into a practice, and become proficient in its use. There are different practices for error-location, for example the skills mastered by flight mechanics, and in the medical care sector in professional groups such as physicians and nurses in order to make diagnoses. To be skilled in one of these practices does not mean that one can transfer this ability to another practice. Error-location on aeroplanes and error-location in a computer program for forest valuation are not interchangeable skills. At this level analogies and examples are not transferrable between different practices. Today, because these different activities use computer technology, there is growing interest in the possibility of moving from one activity to another if one has mastered the technology. It is this perspective that, for example, André Gorz expresses when he claims that less emphasis need be placed upon professional skills and that computer technology skills must be given pride of place. It is important to emphasise the activity-specific aspect of mastering a practice, and that analogies and examples must be taken from within a practice. Of course, there may be striking examples that can be used to illustrate a number of different activities. A special talent is needed to formulate and present these good examples. There is a continuity in the mastery of error-location in an activity that is accentuated in the conversion from old to new technology.

Three Categories of Knowledge

The exercise of error-location involves the application of what we may call practical knowledge, knowledge which contains experiences obtained from having been active in a practice. At the same time there is a great deal of knowledge within this practice, that we learn by examining the examples we are given by others who have been working within the practice. It is from this aggregate experience that we also build up our competence, and learn from first-hand experience. The interaction between people in the same professional group is of decisive importance here. This latter kind of knowledge, knowledge that we acquire from learning a practice by examining the examples of tradition, we can call the knowledge of familiarity.

That part of a professional tradition that has been expressed in general traditions, theories, methods and regulations and that we can assimilate from a theoretical study of an activity, we can call propositional knowledge. There is a close relationship between propositional knowledge, practical knowledge and the knowledge of familiarity. We interpret theories, methods and regulations through the familiarity and skills we have gained by taking part in a practice. Allan Janik's attention to the inconsistencies in the content of these concepts is of central importance here. The dialogue between the members of a group involved in a practice contains an aspect of friction between different perceptions based on their different experiences: examples in familiarity and practical skills. Being a member of a practice, and at the same time acquiring greater competence, involves participation in an ongoing dialogue. Being professional implies extending one's perspective towards a broader overview of one's own skills. Being aware of anomalies, failure is of particular importance in terms of accepting professional responsibility. The historical perspective is a central factor in the knowledge of familiarity. The paradox in this argument is that, if we remove all practical knowledge and knowledge of familiarity from an activity, we will also empty it of propositional knowledge. These are interpretive actions that are crucial to a pragmatic perspective. What can be stored in a computer, processed in algorithms, propositional logic etc., and reported as a result in the form of a print-out is raw material that has to be interpreted by the actions of a person qualified in a practice. If attention is focussed on the raw material and the action of interpretation disappears, an activity will move towards chaos, disorder, death, according to the second law of thermodynamics.

We get a division of the different kinds of knowledge into three categories:

1. Propositional or theoretical knowledge.
2. Skills, or practical knowledge.
3. Knowledge of familiarity.

There is a clear tendency to overemphasise theoretical knowledge at the expense of practical knowledge and we tend to forget completely the knowledge of familiarity when discussing the nature of knowledge in a philosophical context. One effect of tending to ignore skills and familiarity when discussing knowledge is that one tends to assume that people who lack theoretical knowledge in given areas also lack any knowledge whatsoever of that area.

An Epistemological Error

In a postscript to his book *The Structure of Scientific Revolutions* which is focussed on his rejection of explicit rules and his referral to tacit knowledge for the comprehension of scientific practices, Kuhn (1970) says that, when he talks about intuitions, he is not discussing individual intuitions. Instead, intuitions are the tested and shared possessions of the members of a successful group, and the novice acquires them through training as part of his preparation for group membership.

> When I speak of the knowledge embedded in shared exemplars, I am not referring to a mode of knowledge that is less systematic or less analyzable than knowledge embedded in rules, laws, or criteria of identification. Instead I have in mind a manner of knowing which is misconstrued if reconstructed in terms of rules that are first abstracted from exemplars and thereafter function in their stead.

In the introduction to the Encyclopedia of 1751 J.R. d'Alembert wonders how many questions and problems would be avoided if one finally established a clear and exact definition of words. This conception of an exact definition that removes all ambiguity contains the hope that, in the definition, there would reside a power to make our knowledge clear and explicit.

This perspective on the basis of the theory of knowledge can be used in the construction of designs in computer technology. To adopt a total view to include the use of computers is an epistemological error. The development of the practice of computer usage requires an openness to the paradoxical encounter between different traditions of knowledge during earlier epochs in the history of ideas. This requires a development of interest in the concept of education. Within the framework of the theme of Education-Work-Technology, it is my judgement that this will be a significant factor in the debate on technology, science and culture during the coming ten years.

References

d'Alembert, J.R. (1751) Discours preliminaire des editeurs, in Encyclopedia au Dictionnaire raisonne des sciences, des arts etc. Paris. In: d'Alembert, *Inledning till Encyklopedin*, Carmina klassiker, Uppsala, 1981.

Bergendal, B. (1985) *Bildningsens Villkor*. Studentlitteratur.

Descartes, R. (1637) *Discourse on Method, Meditations and Principles*. J.M. Dent and Sons Ltd, London (1987).

Frangsmyr, T. (1974) *Drommen om det exakta spraket*. Vetenskapens Trad, Stockholm.

Göranzon, B. (1983) *Datorn som Verktyg*. Studentlitteratur.

Göranzon, B. (1984) *Datautvecklingsens Filosofi*. Carlssons Bokdorlag (reference for the example of light metering in photography).

Göranzon, B. (1986) 'Artificial intelligence or the dream of the exact language'. Dialoger magazine, no. 2 (an introduction to the Age of Enlightenment's paradoxical view of knowledge).

Göranzon, B. et al. (1982) 'Job design and automation in Sweden'. The Swedish Working Life Centre (the perspective in the section on technology and culture is from this study. It is a research report produced within the framework of the ILO project and compares the experience of the use of computers in thirteen industrial countries).

Gullers, P. (1984) In: Göranzon, B. (ed.) *Datautvecklingsens Filosofi*. Carlssons Bokforlag, pp. 31–5 Janik, A. (1980) Breaking the ground. [in Sundin, B. (ed.) *Is the computer a tool?* Almqvist and Wiksell, Stockholm.

Josephs, H. (1969) *Diderot's Dialogue of Language and Gesture*. Ohio State University Press, Dayton.

Johannessen, K.S. (1988) Tyst Kunskap: om regel och begrepp. Research Report, Swedish Center for Working Life, Stockholm.

Kuhn, T. (1970) *The Structure of Scientific Revolutions*. University of Chicago Press, Chicago, Illinois.

Lindborg, R. (1984) *Maskinen, Manniskan och doktor La Mettrie*. Doxa.

Lindstrom, L. (1986) Bildningsbegreppets rotter. Det polyteknisks bildingside-alet. Educationwork-technology project at the Swedish Life Center.

Runeby, N. (1978) *Teknikerna, Vetenskapen och Kulturen*. Uppsala University Press, Uppsala, Sweden. (Runeby's study covers the period from 1860 to 1890 and includes a documentation of the restructuring of the educational system in relation to the breakthrough of industrialism. There is a fruitful connection to the current debate on technological change and the demand on the educational system.)

Svenssen, P. (1983) Felsokning i ett datorprogram. In: Goranzon, B. led i *IWtiucv-ecklingens Filosofi*. Carlssons Bokforlag, Stockholm, p. 29.

Tempte, T. (1981) *Arbets Ara*. The Swedish Working Life Centre, Stockholm.

Wittgenstein, L. (1953) *Philosophical Investigations*. Blackwell, Oxford.

Wittgenstein, L. (1969) *On Certainty*. Blackwell, Oxford.

Part 1

DIALOGUE AND SKILL

2 Writing as a Method of Reflection

Maria Hammarén

I have spent many years working with writing groups. At a very early stage I discovered that the work method itself, writing and reading aloud in groups, quickly made communication between people much deeper. It was not simply that the inner dialogue which people carry on with themselves became externalised; there was something more to it, something perhaps more, revolutionary, that writing could be a bewildering encounter with one's own experience. The act of writing provided an opportunity to articulate, structure and remember things to which we had never before given a language. Writing thereby offered the chance to reflect about one's own experience, make it more usable and perhaps, above all, more contentious.

I have written this chapter for everyone who may want to work in a writing group, but also for people who are quite simply interested in the connection language has with experience, and with working consciously with language. This is not a set of instructions. Rather, I try to demonstrate a way of thinking about some concepts that are strongly linked to experiential knowledge. It is my hope that this chapter will inspire people to attempt new ways of working with identity, reflection and organisational development.

What do we do in writing groups that is different from other, more everyday communication? I do not want to attempt to explain here what takes place in these groups, other than to say that a democratic group is more the exception than the rule. I am referring to a fundamentally democratic situation: one in which I speak with absolute sincerity. You listen with absolute sincerity. That changes us. Sincerity can be the eye of the needle in other contexts as well. But I would like to say that the act of a person reading aloud to a room, to a group, something he or she has formulated on paper promotes sincerity: it forces a threshold of communication; the reader is exposed, vulnerable, and has to show courage. In this sincerity, words recapture their luminosity. With the luminosity of words we also create a special kind of joy.

This article is in two parts. In the first part I attempt to lay the foundations of a common use of language related to this kind of writing. In the second part I discuss practical experience of work in writing groups.

Meaning is Something That Happens With Words

I have been keeping a diary since I was seven years old. I have been working as a journalist since the middle of the nineteen-seventies. Recently I have devoted more and more time to working with people writing in groups, all for rather different purposes.

From these years and this experience I have arrived at a conclusion that may seem ridiculously obvious, there are two ways of writing: writing quickly or writing slowly. Both ways of writing have distinctive and fascinating characteristics. The ability to deliberately alternate between these two ways is one of the methods I advocate in this essay.

By and large, the significant difference is about reproducing or creating. If, in my professional role, I use my writing skills to put together an article quickly, apply the rules of writing, such as stating who says what, locating the text in time and referring to sources whenever I say something that is new or in dispute; then, in the best case, I produce an accurate and correct piece of work. If this work is done well, it will undoubtedly have value – as a piece of news reporting.

I use slow writing to create understanding and meaning. In doing so I am at the same time both reader and writer.

I read reality and I weave it into a story. The ability to generate meaning is central to what we call identity, and it lays the foundations of our values, values we then express in our actions.

Earlier generations inherited a structure of meaning from the application of authoritarian patterns, clear-cut traditions, which in my country were the Christian religion, relatively stable social classes and occupational cultures. Most of these visible structures have now disappeared.

To create meaning yourself is something new.

It is a job of work.

I think it is important to be aware that the collapse of these clearly-defined traditions has created a vacuum, particularly in the area of identity. I also believe that the ability of a culture to support the formation of people's identity is decisive in a number of ways, including what we call creativity.

Creativity always involves an encounter, a process in which people's different abilities engage with one another. This may happen in a group, or in the individual. Not least, it may be an encounter between theory and practice, between a new suggestion and existing knowledge of the practical activity in question.

For this reason, one of the most surprising results of my work with other people's writing was the growing insight I gained into the importance of writing, in generating a stronger and deeper identity. The best form for this has proved to be texts that have been written very quickly, that have presented stories of personal experiences, followed by the slow writing phase, i.e. deliberate work with the language.

I shall try to make this a practical chapter. I am aware, however, that without doing active work on original texts I am only able to point to a path forward. Therefore my immediate goal is that this chapter can be used as inspiration, and an introduction to anyone who wants to start and run their own writing group. To me this is ultimately a question of arguing in favour of a path that leads to identity and creativity, which in my view is a matter of making the ability to read and write a part of yourself.

To read the world and to write it.

Learning to Write or Writing to Learn?

This chapter is about writing. But it is not entitled 'How to Write' or 'The Art of Writing'. It is not even called 'The Art of Telling a Story', although it is about stories. All essays about the actual technique of writing assume that you already know what you want to write, that you have a message you want to present as persuasively as possible. These essays simply adapt rhetoric, the art of oratory, and apply it to a presentation in writing. One can learn a great deal from rhetoric, but in my view rhetoric belongs in the areas for which it was originally created, the court of law and the people's assembly.

So if you are looking for a miracle cure, such as a bath of rhetorical purification that will wash your arguments shining clean, you can stop reading here. For this chapter is not about rhetoric. In this chapter I am quite simply not interested in everything you already know and, above all, in all the arguments you have collected to support your standpoints. In fact, I am tired, terribly tired, of all statements about matters large and small and about the way things relate to each other.

Of course, surfeit plays its part in this.

Far too much of what we read and hear today is so tedious, platitudinous and predictable that we do not have the energy to even sigh about it. The rhetorical tricks may change, but the content remains largely the same. How many times in the past few years have I not wished for a description filled with surprise, instead of the know-all statements, the summaries, the ambition to explain, that falls like a woollen army blanket over everything sparkling and problematic, poetic and contradictory, everything that we are and that is a constant accompaniment to our lives.

For my own part, this is also related to a growing realisation that we create identity by working with language. Language governs the way we perceive ourselves and the world – but it can also make us receptive to critical thought. This happens when we grasp the other great possibility that language offers, the chance to observe ourselves from the outside. Only then do we have a genuine meeting with ourselves.

We cannot observe ourselves without distance. Without consciously working with language, words become too familiar and close, formed as they are by our individual experience. Language both carries our experiences and makes them accessible to thought. This dual dimension of language may ultimately be what makes us human beings. To the extent that the Swedish education system makes any effort at all in the field of language and writing, it conforms to the perception that thought comes first and language comes later, that language is the more or less well-trained servant of thought. In fact the aesthetic dimension, which emphasises contemporariness, the work with language as reflection itself, belongs to a completely different educational ideal, that of the classics.

There may be reason to reflect upon how by far the most creative culture in the world, the culture of ancient Athens, educated its citizens. At its peak, which lasted about a hundred and fifty years and was largely limited to its 30 000 citizens, Athens produced most of the world's greatest classic architects, sculptors, dramatists and philosophers. We may summarise its educational ideal as the cultivation of a spirit of criticism, but criticism that went deeper than merely denigrating others. It was a criticism of language that gave birth to creativity.

This chapter, then, is about encouraging you to write what you didn't know you knew.

From the deep basket of unreferenced experiments with which everything can be proved and every speaker should be equipped, I take an apt anecdote about modern western and eastern thinking.

> A group of American students were given twenty minutes to decide on their view of a moral problem. How did they use the time? Well, they spent the first minute deciding what they thought and the remaining nineteen minutes perfecting arguments to support the viewpoint they had adopted. At the same

time a group of Japanese students considered the same moral problem – but the way they allocated the time was the reverse of that of the American students.

True or not, it certainly feels as if we are living in a culture that perfects arguments. It is difficult to find interesting thoughts in the noise of the media, thoughts that are a product of the passionate enthusiasm to really see and really describe, that later I call the ability to really read and write.

Thus we live in a jungle of statements: someone pounds me on the head with new research findings, or with statistics that claim to show this or that. The specialisation that has taken place in working life is monitored by supportive institutes of education that will clip our wings just enough for us to fit into the ready-made machinery, a process which, when we are speaking about adults, we usually call human resources development.

Rhetorical/dramatological templates produce fussy TV series, whose hold on the audience is carefully mapped out down to the smallest sob or terrifying thrill, as long as there is no element of surprise or more profound identification. Sophisticated data processing and information retrieval systems make the world of statements appear almost infinite, and my own task as one long multiple choice school test.

It is therefore with a certain amount of *schadenfreude* that one may note that there are many theories but only one practice. We can, with a touch of smugness, acknowledge the fact that even scientific truths can be read as fiction once enough years have passed. Yet we feel just as vulnerable when a skilfully delivered argument compels us to abandon something we regard as a value. That happens every day, not least at work. Because it is hard to believe that this jungle of statements will be changed in any decisive way in the foreseeable future, it is natural to direct our attention to the place where the world of statements meets the life world, the individual person. It is against this background, among others, that I want to present a method for systematic work with the practice of life.

The Story is the Shape of Experience

Someone once said that in life one must be content with making a sketch; the conditions of life only allow a first draft. This aphoristic statement may have a beguiling charm, but it is not true. We do not make just *one* attempt, but many, and our actions can, in ways that are more or less apparent, be shaped by our experience. This is not to say that we gain control of life; life continues to be an encounter with the constantly new. Experience can be an instinct that guides us.

The research on skill that has evolved in Sweden suggests that experience-based knowledge is the product of both experience and reflection. So working in the same occupation for twenty years is not enough. The ability to cope with the unforeseen, or put in simpler terms, the ability to assess the result of a particular action, is an indication that a high level of skill has been achieved. Therefore, in order to develop skill to a high level, the somewhat high-flown word 'reflection' is also needed.

Writing may be a method for both reflection and for making experience-based knowledge accessible. Making experience visible involves retrieving material from one's personal store, in order to shed light on it. As a method it is the direct opposite of wrapping up the message to make it a convincing package; on the contrary, it is about freeing oneself of all packaging and all preconceived ideas. It is more a question of having the courage to re-establish contact with some of the stories that we carry with us, and to study them. We can also listen to other people's stories.

I deliberately use the word 'story' here, because experience is a special form of knowing that cannot be reduced to quantitative calculations. Experience does not even meet the scientific requirement of being repeatable: its form is unique, and wholly dependent on its particular context. Yet it cannot be denied that it is there, it shapes our actions, actions such as recognition, an understanding of the situation, an ethic. The quality of this recognition, this understanding of the way actions impact upon and re-create the life process, and express our ethic can vary dramatically.

Perhaps the story describes a dilemma. A dilemma draws our attention to a complexity, and presents us with alternative courses of action. Sometimes a dilemma also presents us with the truth that there is no good solution, perhaps not even a half-good solution. When we choose an action to take, we may do so with a clear, or not so clear, understanding of the complexity of the dilemma. We can train that kind of ability to apprehend by focussing our attention on stories. This is not a question of identifying with the text. It is about perceiving oneself as a person who is acting in relation to a clearly-written text.

All knowledge that we put to practical use is this kind of local, context-linked knowledge. It requires us to use our ability to give value to things, not occasionally, but constantly. That is why ethics is not a matter of training to conform to a set of rules. Instead, ethics is about training the kind of attention that grasps the complexity of reality.

That is why ethics is a question of occupational skill.

In this context, stories and examples are the same thing; they are quite simply a reflection of the way we meet and organise reality. As far back in time as we know anything at all about the human race, stories have been our companions. Stories have taught us to find our way through uncharted lands, stories have handed down the knowledge of older generations to the new generations. In the oral tradition of storytelling, the stories are different with each telling. They are the same, but also different, depending on who tells the story to whom. Beginning about 2500 years ago, we also have access to stories that have been written down; they have been given a beauty of form which created the enduring whole through which mankind has been able to see itself: what we call literature.

The literary story addresses me personally, and at the same time it forces me to put to one side the events in my life.

It is only with the help of this distance, this other level, that I see myself.

What, then, of the stories that you carry, stories in forms that do not have the beauty of literature? No, I am not saying that they are in themselves literature; the process that refines a story, that endows it with literary qualities, is an arduous one that requires patience; and is it not also reasonable to say that to achieve permanence it must have aesthetic brilliance? Literary creativity subordinates itself to that special space which separates writing from reading. Literature is expert at replacing the voice in that space, the person who reads for us and makes a connection between the text and a physical body, with a voice in time, a voice that recurs every time a reader confronts the text, that is to say, brings it to life with his creative reading.

I therefore recommend that to begin with we read our stories aloud to each other. Quite simply, we maintain the text's link with the physical voice. It gives our stories an elusive quality. That is not to say that the relationship between writing and reading is a special variant of the relationship between speaking and listening. Reading and writing are distinct actions that open up a separate space, a space inaccessible to us other than by applying the ability to *really* read and write.

The more the writing group's work progresses, the more clearly we see this: that the relationship between reading and writing must evolve as the formula for individual work. I write my own texts, which I then expose to other people's creative reading. I act as a creative reader of other people's texts.

Seeing the Language – and Hearing It

Let us say that your stories are your memory. The memory has the form of a collection of stories. What you were once capable of seeing gave you meaning. (And our ability to create meaning is vast. I shall return to this in the second part of this chapter.) What you were unable to see, you did not store.

Do not be frightened if you think that your store seems meagre. You cannot have an overall view of your entire store, or make an inventory of it in the traditional sense. It is simply not stored according to any external system, but is set in to the biggest system we know of. It is stored in the language itself, and it is in work with words, the 'spheres of association' that the stories reveal themselves. (I shall also return to this.)

To take out one's stories again and read them to a listener allows the twofold function of language to come into play: you are forced to listen to your story through another's ears; what was secret or subconscious is sent out into the space, where it encounters other people's worlds of conceptions. Then you may also reflect on your experience, perhaps deepening it and writing a new story which links new aspects to the old.

Put simply, this method forces your attention to focus. Because language makes all time accessible to us in the present, it allows us to actively process what we call the past. This is, of course, not a question of distorting or improving.

It is about seeing.

It may be that your stories do not have permanence in the literary sense, but articulating them is essential to making a broad and fruitful area of contact with life's practices. For when we take the step of reading our texts to one other, a quantitative transformation of the individual's experience takes place. When you present your story to an audience, project it into a public space, your experience goes with it and becomes the soil in which theories grow and develop, are tested and perhaps rejected.

We do not live entirely in a jungle of statements, but also in an age of suppressed stories. The act of writing is itself a method of bringing these stories forth again. (We may also say that we are exposed to far too few stories, that we live in monologues instead of dialogues, or that the mechanical story dominates our lives.) Through our own and others' stories, we can discover and define aspects of our experience with a precision and discernment that would not have been possible through a discussion, not even the most ambitious of discussions. To read and discuss one another's texts, at a workplace for example, makes possible a new kind of relationship between inner and outer dialogue, a relationship that recognises the value of work and the dilemmas and conflicts related to the orientation of the work.

We can only do justice to the varied nature of experience in a story. Experience cannot be reduced to a list of factors or a generalised model. The shape of this knowledge is personal and, to use a fine word, contextual, i.e. dependent on its specific context.

A theme that may be important to bring up, particularly at workplaces, is, of course, learning, since learning is the driving force in all change and development. The theme may be described more precisely by giving it the heading 'When I *really* learned something'. The word 'really' is important and compels the stories to include a serious examination of the concept of learning. The word 'when' is also important, as it allows the story to be nothing more than a story: a completed course of events with a beginning, a middle and an end.

In his *Poetics* from 350 BC, Aristotle writes that poetry is not an imitation of man but of action, of life. The character of men may be this or that, but it is by their actions they achieve happiness or unhappiness. The task of the poet is not to depict what has happened but what could happen. Even if he composes poems about something that has actually happened, then he is still a poet if what he portrays is also probability. The fact is the poet focusses on the universal, the story writer on the particular.

Therefore to direct one's attention to the action in which people acquire experience, and to give the action the form of a story, is to direct one's attention towards the universal in the practice of life.

At least, that is one interpretation of Aristotle.

Thus, to remember is to recall stories.

To write down one's stories is to focus one's attention on an encounter with oneself.

To read the story to others creates the distance needed to allow us to reflect on our own experience.

We don't have to stop here. You can also create distance for yourself in the awareness of deliberate writing, what I called slow writing at the beginning of this essay. You retrieve material and gain energy through the vividness of realisation and your meeting with yourself. If you then allow the texts to be exposed to the music of the language, and its insistence on clarity, then the dialogical relationship the distance establishes also becomes evident, and with even greater effect. The language becomes the constantly alert teacher, whose ears and eyes nothing escapes. I find it difficult to recommend this as a method for everyone. The work is quite simply so time-intensive that the impelling force must be in the opposite direction: it is the language itself that must be the attraction.

If, despite this, you persist, and go into the form of the text, you will suddenly find yourself in an aesthetic force field which, as you work to develop your ability to be in dialogue with the language, quite simply forces reflection to become even deeper. It is then that you really get your story ready to leave you, and seek an encounter with a reader. In this process, you weigh your choice of every letter and every space between words. Suddenly the music in the language becomes conspicuous; first only as the difference between sound and silence, then with diminuendos and crescendos, with staccato and the integrated contrasts of the ties – the breathing. In written texts it is about the tonal impact of the syllables, short sentences and long, the play of light on the white paper, fragments of sentences and pithy words that are joined together and detonate new meanings, all incorporated into the abstract grammatical skeleton of the language, restlessly pushing thought onwards.

You do not have to be an author to use writing as a process of knowledge. One of the keys is your ability to see your work with the language.

Another key is your ear: your ability to hear the language.

The Link Between Inner and Outer Dialogue

Inner dialogue is a person's conversation with himself. It may include everything from moral considerations to the internal concentrated conversation that accompanies, and constantly evaluates, the work process. That the inner dialogue is about work, and that this inner dialogue is expressed in the outer dialogue, is a fundamental question of democracy: not until the inner dialogue is in a living relationship with the outer dialogue are we in a position to influence developments in the world of work.

Outer dialogue is our public conversation and our dialogue with others. At the workplace, it is characterised by the need to allocate work tasks, sometimes also by discussions about the way the work should be done, and less frequently, about quantitative goals. It is influenced by workplace information and its image of itself. But also by news, the mass-cultural phenomena and political events, in a flow largely determined by the offerings of the mass media. It can be influenced to a greater or lesser extent by people's inner dialogue.

The use of writing as a method for reflection at work aims to strengthen the interaction between inner and outer dialogue. This partly concerns the safeguarding of the quality of the outer dialogue, ensuring it is rich and varied. When the inner dialogue meets the outer dialogue we take knowledge from the work practice and let some daylight into this world of statements with its contextual, situational knowledge. Do I need to say that the light also impacts our own experience, reshaping and developing the inner dialogue when it leaves its own personal base?

This is, of course, also a question of shielding the inner dialogue. For living inner dialogue attempts to improve work and set it in relation to the life world. If one has no influence on one's work, the inner dialogue serves no purpose and becomes impoverished; there is a risk that it will succumb to whatever is dictated by the outer dialogue. From the company's viewpoint, this means that important work on quality and development stops, causing stagnation and paralysis.

The inner dialogue may also cease to deal with work for other reasons. Constant concern about job security will cause the inner dialogue to focus on issues related to finance and security. This is also true of unresolved conflicts at the workplace.

Living conversations about the content and value of work are rare at our workplaces, even if one actually has some influence on one's work. The link between inner and outer dialogue is related to culture. Some groups work in a climate that does not tolerate negative criticism, while other climates frown upon individual success. At certain times, the company climate or the social climate as a whole may make some perspectives untenable, for example, as a result of a narrow and simplified view of knowledge.

Writing is an aid that helps enrich and renew the quality of both inner and outer dialogue. Establishing the writing group is a clear indication that one attaches importance to both reflection on experience, and in its communication. In the work the writing group embarks upon, much that is unexpected may occur. The group may share the discovery of dilemmas that may be dealt with openly. Perhaps a developed pattern of action proves to be fruitless and rigid and in direct contrast to both inner and outer images of the group's goals and activities. Insights into the way people acquire experience may have a direct effect on the way we treat new, or old, co-workers.

Writing may also serve to counter the sketchy nature of actions. We can learn to identify patterns better. We can learn to separate real, quantitative changes from ordinary variations. Put briefly, we work consciously with the practices of life and activities.

I shall take up suggested ways of starting a writing process later. Just remember that the raw material for the groups is stories. It is by avoiding explanations and intellectualised generalisations that we can make experience visible.

My own experience in this particular context is that far too many people have no confidence in their own first person stories. It is 'finer' (and therefore safer) to draw conclusions and have discussions in general terms. To tell a story forces us to take our own position, to maintain that my own perspective is a valid one.

It has surprised me that people are so sensitive, that the use of the 'I' we all carry with us appears to be so threatening. It confuses me even more because it does not match what I can observe from the outside. Most people can tell more or less reality-based tall stories round the coffee table, because they are having a work break and there is room for entertainment. When I ask the same person to write down a story about an important relationship at work, for example, I often get back a few convoluted sentences detailing criteria for good management qualities, and with all the personal experience peeled away.

We live in a culture that separates out the personal side of our lives, places it in a psychological sphere and labels it as a matter for what is disparagingly called the therapy route, or possibly for unguarded moments in the discreet lighting of an office party.

It is unusual for us to take personal matters seriously at work.

I should like to describe the work of a productive organisation as a number of readers' encounter with a good daily newspaper. I would then describe the flow of news itself as being like the effervescent foam that forms when the crest of a wave breaks, but on reaching the beach the full mass of the wave breaks against reflecting knowledge. At this point, the news should twinkle like activated sensory cells, and the splash of the wave on the edge of the beach should carefully weigh up incoming reports, current movements and the existing foundation of experience. The water is then sucked out again, only to return with a new aspect. Every decision taken in this swirling movement would be an example of a genuine human capacity for judgement. Or why not call it the ability to write a new text?

I would also like to describe the earlier age of authoritarian structures of thought as a time of nothing but literacy. To read is obedience, to write is non-obedience. To write in the sense of testing validity and creating new meaning was something that the strongest fought for, but in relative terms they were few in number. Those who wrote new texts met with strong resistance.

The absence of identity that is characteristic of our present times arises from our difficulty in reading a text that falls apart into fragments, and that we, for reasons that are unfathomable to me, do not bother to write.

The Catharsis of Description

Finding the stories can, of course, be an art in itself. It is not too difficult to at least become aware of stories. There are also paths into your own stories, a point to which I shall return later.

As I mentioned before, I usually ask people to write about when they really learned something. There is almost always someone in the group who protests, saying that their memory is an absolute blank. He or she will say with a laugh, 'I've never actually learned anything'. Of course that is not true and no-one believes it either. On the other hand, some people have raised strong intellectual defences; they can give an account of an important period in their lives, or perhaps describe the learning and insights of their children. They themselves experience no dramatic (in the actor's sense of the word) removal to a new situation. Other people may find it very difficult to say anything at all about themselves. Their censorship is strong, and so criticism acts as an effective block of the channel into the private storehouses of our bodies.

A common remark is that learning has continued in an unbroken process; one day has followed another, but no special events stand out. That is certainly the case, at least in part. It may also be true that you need a new perspective in order to recognise your story. The event does not reveal itself as a story before you have come to a complete halt, listened to others, and established close contact with what we refer to here as experience and reflection.

To make writing a routine, by keeping a diary for example, is one way of overcoming the block that may easily occur simply because people are so unused to writing anything other than simple notes related to their work.

More than once my writing groups have given me comments that reveal an academic habit of giving a depersonified and abstract account of results, that is so strongly ingrained that the person who intends to write no longer knows how to begin to make a description. For younger academics in particular, invitations to look at things with their own eyes, for example, or to listen with their own ears, are nothing more than confusing nonsense. On that very point there is the only similarity with miracle cures: in many people the transition from the summary accounting and direct communication typical of scientific research reports to subjective description produces pure cathartic experiences.

I am, of course, horrified. When this happens it becomes clear that much of Swedish university teaching applies with great vigour the simplification of the concept of knowledge we saw in the first half of the twentieth century, namely that all knowledge can be expressed in a single form. In my eyes that is the same as giving people direct training to prepare them for the bureaucratic form of organisation, a completely rigid and, as we know from the history of the twentieth century, highly dangerous, organisational form.

There are, of course, many forms of knowledge and these different forms cannot reduce to each other.

Work interprets theory through practice. The quality of our actions is related to seeing: being enriched by theory and perceiving complexity.

Seeing eyes are eyes that think.

I write this essay in the full conviction that everyone who speaks a language can also put down their thoughts on paper. By contrast, many people find, in purely concrete terms, that they are struck dumb when they are to express themselves in writing. They stutter and stammer. The words just don't come, and what is finally put down on paper sounds dull and flat. For the vast majority of people this relates to the traces and wounds from their schooldays, a period in which many people learned that their own language was inadequate.

But to all of you who have experienced the inferno of torment associated with writing: be of good cheer, the key lies in letting go, and in rejecting the ranks of Swedish teachers from your past who, with raised forefingers, complained about your use of the comma and that you started a sentence with *and* or *but*, instead of entering into the living discourse about the way form and content actually engage one another by asking the apposite question: what is it you want to say?

Let go and write yourself.

Language is yours, and it contains a treasure chest.

Part 2: Out of the Anguish of Writing

When I began my studies at the School of Journalism, I had always been able to write in a constant stream, but when faced with my first assignment I suffered a complete block. I spent long hours staring at a sheet of white paper with an icy feeling in my stomach.

At that time everything was so very concrete, there were no word processors; every letter had to be hammered on to the white paper through a typewriter ribbon. Although now I would never dream of going back to the typewriter, the mechanical process made the responsibility more palpable. It was as if one could not wriggle out of the responsibility imposed by the fact that each letter, each character was the result of a decision I made.

There I sat with my typewriter and my paper. Earlier in the day I had taken a stroll in a new residential area, the writing assignment for that day. The only thing was, no words were forthcoming. I was stuck at the title, which was the very first thing I wrote: 'A High Price for Living' (a title that haunts me even today when I run into friends from that time). The sheet of white paper became irritatingly white. I wrote a word or two and then tore the paper out of the machine. I suffered agonies, and after many hours of work I managed to put together about one-third of a page. The language did not flow, and the fact is I had nothing to say.

I have never experienced such a block since then. Well, I still always have to grapple with the text of course, any text, and the demands and temptations of some texts can make them terrifying. Few people have any idea about the amount of time I spend re-writing, again and again.

The paper has never been so brilliantly white as that first time, and never again have I felt the same despair.

This memory surfaced years later when I was running my courses in writing. For in every course there is almost always someone who has a total block. I explain my own block as being because it was the first time I wrote for a concrete public forum and in a situation in which I did not know which norms applied. What I wrote was supposed to be journalism. My muteness occurred when I tried to understand what external standards my text would be expected to meet.

That was when my courage deserted me.

I lacked the courage to write my own story, about seeing the solitary man sitting on a bench with a violin, not a dog, at his feet. How unwilling the man's back and legs had been when he bent down to grasp the handle of the violin case. Neither did I dare to write that the facades of the houses made them look as though they were made of lego, with their clearly defined joints between the prefabricated blocks, and that the wind blew harder between these long rows of houses than it did in the Castle Park just a stone's throw away.

I wish at that time someone had been able to say with enough conviction: this is *your* story, these are *your* observations, it is *your* thoughts I want! The follow-up session would have begun with the question: well, what do you actually see? Followed by a conversation about how I had harnessed the possibilities of language to work towards a story about what I had seen, i.e. how I immersed a meaning in my perception.

I bring up this episode for two very similar reasons. First, I want to say that most writing blocks are the question of believing that one must meet someone else's standards. Far too often this is a reality in journalism. The approach a writing group should have to writing must never include the standards of others. At all times your work must grow from your own story, even though you may deliberately experiment with yourself.

The second thing I want to say is that the vital concept of the meeting with the reader, the other, plays an important part in the process of writing itself. Writer's block or free flow? For the writing group, which is a forum for personal stories, many of them moral dilemmas and short-comings, the work stands or falls with complete attention and respect. In the writing group there must be unrestricted possibilities to write for a positive reader who accepts and absorbs every text in a creative meeting.

This brings me into the second part of this essay, a part in which I attempt to give practical points of entry to everyone who wants to train apperception and reflection in a writing group. At the same time I want to make a reservation, by its nature the work method dictates that each group must shape its identity and be sensitive to its special needs and conditions. So let my views and advice serve as a starting-point, as strands of thought for you to unravel.

As the episode from the School of Journalism illustrates, I attach considerable importance to the climate in which the group works; in fact, the climate is crucial. The preconditions for the climate are already created in the way the group is set up. Who will join the group, and why? Of course, the most favourable climate is created when all the members of the group clearly understand why they are starting work on writing and that the decision to do so clearly has strong support in the group. The role of leader is equally important; work in a writing group cannot progress without someone taking the considerable responsibility for continuity and preparation, not least, by ensuring that the examples given generate suitable inspiration, and enhance the sensitivity and receptiveness of the group's working method.

Setting Up the Writing Group

This, then, is about working in a writing group. Ideally, it will be composed of about seven people who understand that they must give writing the time it needs. The group meets regularly to read aloud its texts and to discuss. The texts must have a common content or, in time, a common form. Most of these texts are written in the time between the group's meetings. The main purpose of the work of the writing group is to attempt to portray what work looks like from within, but the writing group can, for example, also provide support and guidance in human resources groups that work daily on other people's problems or for the express purpose of developing the organisation.

It is an advantage if the age composition of the group allows at least a couple of people with long work life experience, more than twenty years, to be included. Plan at least five meetings, after which progress can be evaluated and a decision taken about whether the group is to continue. This ensures that groups are formed, in which each member is able to have an overall view of his or her commitment in the group.

The group must be prepared to begin by working through the barriers to writing that are, regrettably, very common. Writing must become routine. This may be achieved by writing every day, for example in a journal or diary. A diary is a good idea because it is a well accepted form, no-one needs to feel unsure about any unspoken demands that may be hidden behind the choice of the form of writing. First of all, I mean that this is something that everyone does for themselves. In addition, its distinct form makes the diary suitable for an early exercise for the whole group. Add to this a quantity requirement, for example one hundred words a day. This quantity requirement emphasises the choice of words, and calls for concentration and compression in the texts: one of the fundamental skills for anyone who writes (no matter whether the text is long or short). Particularly in the beginning, it is also important that the work moves forward in stages: set up well-defined tasks and allow the level of ambition to rise by degrees. It is important to think the home assignments through properly and formulate them with care. Each group member must feel sure that 'this' is really what they are supposed to write about.

The content must invite personal reflection and not an inventory of factual knowledge. This means that writing assignments often consist of personal recall. 'When I really learned something' can be a good introduction. Other possible themes to develop along the same 'when I experienced something' lines are risk-taking and change. Recollecting important work relationships is another theme, questions relating to what one (really) wants to achieve in one's work or how one perceives one's role at work are yet more themes.

Failure is another fruitful theme: how for example, does a leader who has gained insight into earlier failures differ from a leader who has experienced successes following swiftly upon one another?

Then, of course, there are a large number of words that may be important to list. Words that might be classified as essentially contested. These include 'democracy', 'responsibility', 'culture', 'development', 'creativity', 'morals', 'equality'... often quite simply a list of prestigious words that are usually worth making an inventory of from the perspective of storytelling and work. What is usually very interesting to a writing group is to see the similarities and differences in the way we use words, the meanings we give them. It is a good idea to work in combination with another word to create an interface. For example, what does the word 'democracy' mean in relation to the word 'responsibility'?

Try to deflect the external, defined requirements (such as the evolution of Sweden's legislation on co-determination at work, reports taken from essays, inflammatory speeches, etc.). Here, as always, the exercise aims to produce an inventory of your own experiences, through the stories the words carry. Here, as always, associations can be a path into the stories. More about that soon.

The group must fully understand that negative criticism of texts is not allowed. The group's work is about listening and having the inner dialogue occupy a place in the room. That the inner dialogue speaks in the outer world produces substantial intensification and deepens communication. It will also make itself felt, reading aloud to the group requires courage, to break through the barrier of anxiety and dread that wants to keep communication at its existing level. All important communication that captures new knowledge is accompanied by an increase in the level of anxiety.

Writing is not primarily a question of entering into a conversation with another person, it is a question of speaking to oneself. To establish respect for oneself as a source of knowledge is one of the most important tasks facing the members of the writing group. One must of course discuss the issues that the text throws up. I only wish to emphasise here that the quality of the material brought into the discussion is dependent on the absolute respect of the group.

First, Just Words, One by One

When the group meets for the first time, many of its members will be nervous, particularly about reading their texts aloud. It is therefore important to begin to write at once, but in a form that does not make any demands on the art of description. Accordingly, in the first meeting I usually avoid whole sentences completely, and instead begin with single words in the language by doing some association exercises.

I simply ask the group to let go of all thoughts and instead just listen, opening themselves to what the words describe, and writing down associations on a piece of paper. The words we use do not need to have anything at all to do with work, at the moment all that matters is close contact. Choose, for example, the word 'schoolyard'.

When, after a few minutes, the intense scribbling abates, it is time to read. At this point it is important to create the space for reading that will be a part of the group's work whenever they are reading aloud. Everyone in the group should therefore be instructed to read slowly and use their voices to emphasise each word. Of course, the group must listen with full attention to every person's reading.

As a rule, there is a remarkable development: everyone in the group suddenly hears that we have an enormous ability to create meaning. The words, presented separately, and the voice is enough for each member of the group to create an inner context around every presentation. Further, many people are usually surprised that they immediately go back in time, to the time when the concept was established and its main contours chiselled out. Suddenly we are there again: in the schoolyard, in the lunch queue, running along corridors or listening to sounds in the map room.

These association exercises may recur throughout the work of the writing group, or be used separately as a deliberate way of examining individual points of reference. In fact, the method involves concentrated work on something that will, in time, be interwoven into every writing process: the perception that words are insistent and malleable, that the sometimes ruthless wilfulness of language steers us in directions we had not intended to go.

In further use of this exercise one can, of course, make a more systematic examination of work-related concepts. Almost always, memories, stories, related to words will surface. To go directly into our vocabulary is one way of bringing out the stories.

I usually deliberately choose at least some words that develop into concepts early in life; this helps the group to begin to unravel the threads that lead back in time. Even a neutral word like 'lingonberry' has evoked violent feelings, and laughter, when two people in the group found they both had grandmothers from the province of Skåne in the south of Sweden, and particular associations with angel's food, a lingonberry cake traditional in that province.

There are no limits to the variations and developments of association exercises. On the one hand they are a game, on the other the power of these exercises is such that they may become deadly serious if we allow them to touch on concepts that are sometimes far too sensitive. We see both our ability to create meaning and identify words that generate images (words like 'it', 'is', 'to', 'because', 'while' do not normally come up, they belong to the structural requirements of the language or its logical structure). Most of the words that come up are nouns, which evoke still pictures, and some adjectives. When the verbs come, and one may have to steer the group towards verbs, then the movement, the action, comes.

The group can also clearly see the morpheme, the smallest part of a word that can convey meaning, at work. If I say *the* football ground, pictures are conjured up of a particular football ground; if I say football ground, the associations immediately become more general. Association exercises also make it easy to see what is vital in the combination, the joining of words, as I have called it elsewhere. Choose two words from your list and place them next to each other, and meaning is detonated at once. Choose two other words, and you are telling a different story. Or take the isolated word 'mother' and compare it with the joined words 'mother's hands'.

Only from the isolated words taken from someone's paper, we create a story. To make a story more unambiguous we must begin to weave in meaning.

The Concrete Reference

In my view, now that you have read some concrete suggestions for exercises and themes, there will be some change in your picture of what I have written in the first part of this essay. Being concrete is always associated with some risk: what you mean suddenly becomes clear, it may even sound trite, or at least simple and not particularly remarkable. It is important to see this mechanism clearly; how easy it is to create distance or exercise power by refraining from making concrete statements. At the same time, it is in the point of intersection between the concrete and the general that the real conversation can take place, that new meanings can appear.

In the same way, it is generally true that unless it repeatedly refers to the concrete, to words performing in a setting, writing cannot convey meaning. What am I doing when I undergo a dramatic removal to a new situation? What am I doing when I tell a story without becoming intrusive by also explaining it, interpreting it?

To fully understand the power in stories, I believe we must get into the habit of seeing the story we write down at the time as more than a text. To take an example and extend it to become the story or a narrative is to portray an experience. This portrayal of experience speaks in a text that consists of the general perceptions of the group, the company or the culture in question. The story which, with its 'Once upon a time...' almost saga-like form forcefully brings to the fore a person's meeting with life, quite simply works in relation to a text that is not normally visible.

Remember that written text is different from speech in many ways, among them being unable to make free use of words like 'that' (followed by a gesture) or 'over there', or 'under the table' – all these words that in the space of the spoken word work through direct reference to reality. Our language is full of words that require a speaking situation to work. In written texts the concrete reference serves to create a space. When the writer subordinates herself to the story, when she is unswervingly loyal to her inner picture, then brushstroke follows brushstroke, and the picture imperceptibly emerges as a whole.

The creative story produces a gradual recognition in the reader, because each letter actually points to the letters in all other stories; the story seems familiar because it is arranged in a way that reality itself is never arranged. One might say that the text seduces us when it excludes chaos. Recognising something in another person's experience evokes one's own experience, either as an interpretation of what has been recounted, or as a new story.

Why does this matter?

Among other things, because we describe the probable effects of our actions in the form of a story. The form of moral philosophy is literary.

The dimension of the story, its space, can be expanded in many ways. There is an exercise I found helpful which has the writing of a personal portrait as its ultimate goal. The staged progression towards this goal is an exciting journey.

First, a biographical article must be written about a person, written as though it were an entry in a work of reference. The exercise works best if you choose a person with whom your relationship is rich in conflict. In this first part of the exercise, you quite simply make an inventory of your external knowledge of the person in question. In stage two, the task is to write an autobiography, now concentrating on your insights. You must apply all your descriptive power in penetrating the role of the other person, you must transform yourself, and describe him or her in the first person singular. Do not banter or simplify, the person who emerges on paper must be the other person as far as it is humanly possible for you faithfully to portray his or her perspective, and you will certainly discover that you know that person far better than you would ever have thought possible.

These first two stages are actually only a warm-up for the third stage, which is a dialogue between the other person and you. Let this dialogue be a dramatic argument (by dramatic I mean an exchange of words in the present tense, consisting only of rejoinders, with no stage directions or narrators). Here and now, he and you in a conversation that emphasises the other person's perspective with at least as much power as it does your own. This means you alternate between the two roles, and you must be as truthful as you possibly can, with both parties. No intricate explanations are really needed. It is a question of alternating between perspectives, taking the other person completely seriously, as is expressed in your willingness to examine your points of view in the same way as they are questioned.

Because the exercise compels you to face two 'I's' for which you must take equal responsibility, the chances of breaking out of a view of life expressed as a monologue increase; it is, quite simply, a trick.

Insights and knowledge usually grow as this exercise progresses. People with an unresolved relationship with a person have gained painful and liberating experience; suddenly you see the other person, the next moment you see yourself, and perhaps the paralysing game that has prevented constructive action. The exercise is not based on the notion that we are all 'birds of a feather', and it is not about forgiveness, reconciliation or synthesis, it is about the keen discernment that sees through simplification. You strengthen your identity in this process: this is me, these are the values I express in my actions, and this is what my disagreement with X is.

The fourth stage, the portrait itself, may not be necessary to complete. It is not until now, after the exercise in seeing and in openly critical dialogue, that one is actually ready to describe. Not until this stage will I have broken down the clichés that prevented me from seeing, and not until now do I actually have something to relate. When I begin the act of writing, I leave behind me the feeling for distance, for consciousness. Now I have to *see* the language anew, see that I write, create the space in which communication about black letters on white paper is possible, a process in which you choose every letter and every play of light between the letters; well, by this time you know you have heard this before.

Writing to Win Knowledge

The deliberate process of writing can give rise to a bewildering discovery that language does not want to express your thoughts, that language's demand for logic compels you to change your opinion, or at least review old ideas. You discover that the words are alive and speak to each other from the first letter of the text to the last. When you notice that you begin to replace word endings without any logical reason, to change the word order or alternate between synonyms: in other words, begin to work with tone and rhythm, then the language is on its way to being transformed into a living fishing hook. You put on paper things you did not know you knew. Experience that had not been visible becomes organised. When it is organised, it surfaces as examples, as stories, as the text. In that respect it resembles art: unique and unrepeatable, rather than science. For to write is to bind words with words and sentences with sentences in an intricate tree chart that is more like a freehand drawing of the crown of an oak tree than a diagrammatic arrangement. The right conjunctions and propositions throw light on a context far beyond grammatical structure; as the lighthouses of the text, they mark the position of the scarlet thread that runs through the story, which did not exist at the beginning, but was created word by word from the nebulous ideas of the writer.

Therefore writing may be an entering into a knowledge process that disrupts the power the prescriptive structure of language has over one's own experience. The meeting that then takes place between being in the language and outside it; between letting the fishing hook drop into the sea of memory that is experience on the one hand, and then analysing and integrating it with the occupational role on the other, strengthens identity and creativity.

What is meaningful writing for the group is therefore a question of deliberately alternating between two ways of writing: one associative, in which the personal axioms pour out, and the other analytical, which examines the degree of truth in the axioms, and their use. This, then, is about entering into the role of yourself, while at the same time regarding it from a distance. Call it dédoublement, to use Diderot's term, or call it dramatic thinking, in any event, this particular ability appears to be the key to creative occupational skills, and the difference between skill and genuine creativity.

The model of the reality we can create with the written word differs from other models through the basic link between words and experience. I should like to say that we build models from modules of experience that are still moveable. It was in the meeting with life that language was first born.

'My life is in my language', says Ingela Josefson, the language and work life researcher. And she is not speaking about herself and her interest in language, but about everybody. There is a tacit knowledge in every word we say. A person's language is a fingerprint of her meeting with the world; it is loaded with the individual fabric of life that has given concepts meaning. How do we learn language? From the beginning we had no other key than our experience of living. By means of similarities and dissimilarities in our perceptions, the words and usable characters with which to communicate slowly formed. For example, the word 'mother' was linked to smell, taste and the difference in feeling between being hungry and full, desertion and company: rhythm itself in an endless time.

Somewhere in the chain from the multifarious and chaotic sense of the word, to the sufficiently generalised expression, there emerges the ability to make oneself understood. And somewhere in this chain the concept is not yet sufficiently charged with meaning to make it possible to gain insight into another person.

Thus there are no immovable tips of icebergs that we climb around in language. The words are charged with energy, with the potentially excluded reality we call memory. Therefore, one reason to recommend writing is the ability of words to bring back memory; we quite simply go back and unwind the layers of experience that have wrapped words in a strictly human-bound meaning.

The language of man is the basis for his creativity. Aristotle points to the decisive factor: a creature that has a language, characterised by his distance from the contemporary. Or perhaps we can say that language makes everything contemporary.

For what does language enable a person to do?

He can go into the space, the dimension, that allows comparison, valuation and meaning, a space that allows new conceptions to take shape in what we call ideas.

No matter what one thinks of the effectiveness of representative democracy, for example, this is true: without the conception of democracy, of universal suffrage, no free elections would have taken place, either in our own history or in South Africa in the spring of 1994.

Our chance of freedom rests in language.

3 The Dialogue Seminar as a Foundation for Research on Skill

Adrian Ratkic

I

In 1999, an article in the Swedish engineering journal, *Ny Teknik*, caught my attention. The article, 'Can Experience be Gained Faster?', was a brief presentation of Maria Hammarén's doctoral dissertation on Skill and Technology.[1] The article contained phrases like 'philosophy and engineering', 'transfer of experience', 'reflection and dialogue'. I had been interested in philosophy and literature for a long time, but had to put these interests to one side while I trained as an engineer. To my mind, the engineering training was superficial, and when I look back now I believe there were two main reasons for this.[2] Firstly, there was no scope at all in the course for reflection on the kind of knowledge that my colleagues and I were studying. Secondly, the science courses were taught virtually without any historical context. Advances in engineering were presented to us in the form of ready-made mathematical proofs and deductions from formulae. How on earth can one arrive at an idea of reality by deduction? It was not until many years later that I realised that the formulae we were presented with as solutions to engineering problems were only the results of the efforts of generations of engineers to tackle these problems.

---

1 When I discuss the 'research area' or the subject of 'Skill and Technology' later in this chapter, I am referring to the subject that was formally established at The Royal Institute of Technology (KTH) in Stockholm, in 1995 with the creation of Professor Bo Göranzon's chair in the subject. This subject area had been under development from the middle of the 1970s.

2 My comments concern both my studies at the University of Zagreb, 1986–90, and at The Royal Institute of Technology (KTH), Stockholm in 1992.

It is not surprising that I found the article in *Ny Teknik* interesting. Here was someone who could take my curiosity about the nature of engineering knowledge seriously. My interest resulted in an invitation to take part in the course on practice and leadership headed by Professor B. Göranzon, the philosopher Kjell S. Johannessen and the researcher Maria Hammarén. The course was an attempt to apply the dialogue seminar method in the education of doctoral students, and was also a kind of pilot project that introduced a series of courses that came to be called *The KTH Advanced Programme in Reflective Practice*.[3] I had already attended seminars in philosophy and the history of technology, but the dialogue seminars run by Göranzon and Hammarén were quite different. They were a remarkable combination of narratives about the participants' experiences and epistemology and philosophy that illustrated their experiences. Or, to be more precise, philosophy and experience illustrated one another. The philosophy, otherwise so abstract, became tangible and filled with examples.

II

The members of the course met three times in the autumn. Each meeting lasted two full days. We had to prepare for each meeting by reading course literature 'with pen in hand'. We were encouraged to read slowly and make notes of the thoughts and reflections we had as we read. These thoughts were then summarised in a text of not more than two to three pages. Copies were made so that we could all read one another's texts. When the group met, each participant read his or her own text aloud, and the teachers and other group members made comments. One of the teachers was the leader of the seminar. His task was to keep the discussion on the right track, to point to links with the epistemology of the research area and to ensure that all the group members were given time to make comments on the others' texts and have comments made on their own. One member of the group kept so-called 'minutes of ideas'. The main purpose of these minutes was to make a record of the central themes and concepts to which the group could return and develop at the next meeting.

Compared with a conventional course, this working method led to an unusual amount of practice in the application of new concepts and ways of thinking. As a rule, the only time that students in a conventional

---

3 For more extensive descriptions of the dialogue seminar method, see the articles by Niclas Fock and Maria Hammarén in this book.

course, which consists of a series of lectures and an examination, test and demonstrate their understanding of new concepts they have learned, is during the examination. Students in a course that is made up of a series of dialogue seminars put their understanding of the new concepts to the test a number of times in the course of each seminar. Firstly, in their own writing task. Secondly, by using the concept in the conversation after the group has read its written texts aloud. Thirdly, by constantly hearing the way other people in the seminar use the same concepts, both in speech and in writing. Fourthly, by hearing how the seminar leader comments, summarises and relates to a broader context. A dialogue seminar hones both individual and collective understanding of the meaning of concepts.

The meaning in the concept formation that takes place in a dialogue seminar is more than 'honing concepts' or 'creating a common language'. In the *KTH Advanced Programme in Reflective Practice*, we have identified at least two other aspects of the use of this method. One is that, with the help of dialogue seminars, we can support the creative side of the role of researcher. The other is that dialogue seminars can be useful when there is a need to systematise a reality that appears chaotic, or when a detailed description of disagreement in the group is needed.

The interest in creativity is a scarlet thread that runs through the history of this research field. In the very first issue of the journal *Dialoger* in 1986, there is a long article about creativity and environment, written by Anne Buttimer, the geographer.[4] Today, the theme of creativity has a prominent place in the programme's courses, in response to the interest in issues relating to the exercise of leadership in creative environments, or how to lead development projects. The second interest, which is related to creativity, is the interest in analogy and analogical thinking.

Research on skill has shown that reasoning and discussions about experience in professional contexts are based on examples upon which we reflect by means of comparative analysis. This way of reasoning is also used in artistic and aesthetic contexts.[5] This is where the research field relates to art. Here, we use the word 'art' to mean theatre, literature and, more recently, music. In the group of researchers that centres on

---

4 Ann Buttimer, 'Kreativitet och miljö', (*Creativity and Environment*) *Dialoger* 1/1986.

5 So-called constitutive rules may only be established by referring to examples of rule-following. These examples convey tacit knowledge, in contrast to formal instructions that state explicit rules. For a more detailed discussion and examples, see the chapter on Tacit Knowledge in this book.

Bo Göranzon, the art of acting, for example, is used as a metaphor for skill, and theatre direction as a metaphor for leadership.[6] The literature has been used both as an instrument of interpretation in researchers' analysis of skill, and as an impulse to stimulate participants in dialogue seminars to reflect. In the *KTH Advanced Programme in Reflective Practice*, we have attempted, through co-operation with Clas Pehrsson, the recorder player and Professor at the Royal College of Music in Stockholm, to examine the analogy between the problems in the practice of performing music and the creative side of the researchers' 'performing knowledge'.[7] This has allowed us to expand the analogical way of thinking to apply to the researchers' own skill. It is understood that the use of metaphor and analogy requires careful distinction, between when they help create insights, and when they lead to erroneous conclusions.

What we want to achieve in training our doctoral students has similarities to the problems in the practice of performing music. The study of the practice of performing music addresses the question of the performance of music from earlier times, and the related problem of the creativity of the musicians. The earlier composers' music was performed over and over again. A common way of dealing with the need for creative performances in such a situation is to give the musicians a free hand to do what they want. The paradox is that at that point the performances begin to be similar. Someone produces an outstanding interpretation, and in time others begin to imitate that performance. The reproductive aspect of the performances tends to overshadow the creative aspect. This is in conflict with the idea that creativity comes from total freedom.

One of a number of ways for musicians to avoid the problem was to study historical source material such as notes, information about the composer's life, writings left by the composer, contemporary history,

---

6 For a discussion of the role of the metaphor in everyday and scientific contexts, see Allan Janik, *The Use and Abuse of Metaphor*, Stockholm: Dialoger, 2003. The actor's art as a model for skill is discussed in the section entitled Acting as a Model for Skill, in Bo Göranzon (ed.), *Skill, Technology and Enlightenment: on Practical Philosophy*. The book is a record of an international conference that focused on the philosophy of Denis Diderot. The theme of leadership was discussed at the *Dialogues on Performing Knowledge* conference, held in Stockholm in 1998.

7 The role of art has been researched and is still the subject of research by the Dialogue Seminar at the Royal Dramatic Theatre in Stockholm. The Dialogue Seminar was founded in 1985 by Bo Göranzon, the mathematician and work life researcher, Magnus Florin, the author, and Pehr Sällström, the physicist and author, for the purpose of bringing greater depth to the public debate on work, language, culture and knowledge. The seminar may be seen as a laboratory for the humanities, in which research is done on the so-called third culture on the theatre's stage through reflection and dialogue interwoven with artistic events.

etc. The result of these deliberate efforts to carry on a dialogue with the historical source material was that the individual performances became more creative and began to differ from one another, despite the fact that the musicians used the same historical sources.[8]

One may now ask: isn't the training of doctoral students to do with something that is quite the opposite of this? Isn't the scientific method a set of rules that should be applied mechanically in order to always achieve the same result, irrespective of the researcher's personality or temperament? In the book, *Mästarlära: lärande som social praxis* (Master and Apprentice: learning as a social practice), two Danish pedagogics researchers, Klaus Nielsen and Steinar Kvale, give examples that contradict this view.[9] They refer to two studies of the American Nobel prize winners' 'learning paths', in which pioneering research is described more as art and craft than as a mechanical application of methodological rules. The Nobel Prize winners say the acquisition of a researcher's knowledge is a question of learning the mentor's way of thinking, that the critical and independent attitude is transferred more though personal contact than by book learning, that the mentors teach more by example than by instruction, that the masters convey a feeling and taste for what good science is, and so on. The classic studies by Ludwig Fleck, Michael Polanyi and Thomas Kuhn also point in the same direction. In the humanities, Hans Georg Gadamer describes in his autobiographical book, *Philosophische Lehrjahre*, informal and personal teaching in his association with his masters.

III

The next step in the structuring of courses in the *KTH Advanced Programme in Reflective Practice* was to design the course on the philosophy of science and methods for doctoral students who were interested in perspectives that include skill, a course based on reading classical texts from the history of philosophy and science. In the course,

---

8 See Clas Pehrsson, 'Musikalisk uppförandepraxis' (*The Practice of Performing Music*), Dialoger 55/2000, and Adrian Ratkic, 'Analogi och musik' (*Analogy and Music*), Dialoger 60/2001.

9 Klaus Nielsen and Steinar Kvale (eds), *Mästarlära: lärande som social praxis*. (Master and Apprentice: learning as social practice). The two studies of the biographies of Nobel Prize recipients and education are in H. Zuckerman, *Scientific Elite*, New York: Free Press, 1977 and R. Kanigel, *Apprentice to Genius: The Making of Scientific Dynasty*, New York: Macmillan, 1986.

we have read texts by Montaigne, Descartes, Galileo, Leibniz, Diderot, D'Alembert, Wittgenstein and Gadamer. Threads of creativity, the personal expression in 'the performing of scientific knowledge', analogical thinking and reading to obtain impulses for collective reflection weave through this course. The course is also motivated by Gadamer's ideas about the fusion of horizons. The messages in the historical source texts are of relevance for me to the extent that I can apply them to the situation in which I find myself. When it comes to skill, one can, for example, see contemporary attempts to question experts on the kind of knowledge they possess, in the hope of being able to load this knowledge into a computer memory, as analogous to Socrates' attempts to question the prophet Euthyphro about his expert knowledge on the piety of man. One can see Leibniz's idea of *characteristica universalis* as analogous to our contemporary dream of thinking computers, or Diderot's description of the mind, the body and thinking as interwoven in a net-like structure as analogous to contemporary ideas circulating in the forefront of research on consciousness.[10]

This is not a question of summarising and analysing the arguments of the classics to determine whether these authors were right or wrong in the matter. It is a question of using shorter or longer passages from their texts to fuel our own thinking. In some way, in these texts the researchers meet older and successful colleagues to learn something about their ways of thinking and their approaches; the doctoral students' reflections in the dialogue seminars become a dialogue with these colleagues. For example, the dialogue may be about how a prospective researcher approaches the literature. There is rarely time to read everything that has been written on the subject. It is a question of striking a balance: on the one hand, a researcher must be informed about what and how others have thought, and on the other hand, spending too much time on reading about other people's thinking may suffocate one's own thoughts. General 'how to' recommendations are of no help here; a strategy for dealing with the literature is created for each particular situation. What is interesting in our context is that in reading the classics, one may find clues as to their attitude on this matter.

---

10 For a comment on Socrates' interrogation of Euthyphro see Hubert L. Dreyfus, 'Is Socrates to Blame for Cognitivism' in *Artificial Intelligence, Culture and Language: On Education and Work*, Springer-Verlag, 1990, 225–8. For Leibniz and our contemporary dream about thinking computers, see Bo Göranzon, *The Practical Intellect: Computers and Skills*, Springer-Verlag & UNESCO, 1993, 41–51. For comment on Diderot's *D'Alembert's Dream* as a model for present-day research on consciousness, see Gerald M. Edelman, *Bright Air, Brilliant Fire: On the Matter of the Mind*, 1992.

Leibniz: Two things that are otherwise of doubtful value, and harmful to many people proved to be extremely helpful to me: firstly, I was self-taught, and, secondly, I was looking for something new in each discipline when I began to study it, often before I had understood its established content. But this gave me a double reward: firstly, I did not fill my head with empty and tiresome knowledge that was accepted because of the teacher's authority and not because of good arguments. Secondly, I could not rest until I had found the system in each discipline and penetrated its principles. This exercise allowed me to discover by my own efforts everything that interested me.[11]

Montaigne: If I come across difficult passages in my reading I never bite my nails over them: after making a charge or two I let them be. If I settled down to them I would waste myself and my time, for my mind is made for the first jump... If one book wearies me I take up another, applying myself to it only during those hours when I begin to be gripped by boredom at doing nothing.[12]

These thoughts are strikingly similar to the advice the prominent scientists of our times give to young researchers. In *Advice to a Young Scientist*, Peter Brian Medawar argues against excessive reading, because studies are liable to become a substitute for research.[13] In his speech at the Nobel Banquet Anthony Legget, the recipient of the Nobel Prize in Physics in 2003 says to younger colleagues, 'hoping to embark on a career in theoretical physics'.

First, if there's something in the conventional wisdom that you don't understand, worry away at it for as long as it takes and don't be deterred by the assurances of your fellow physicists that these questions are well understood. Secondly, if you find a problem interesting, don't worry too much about whether it has been solved in the existing literature. You will have a lot more fun with it if you don't know, and you will learn a lot, even if what you come up with turns out not to be publishable.[14]

---

11 Gottfried Wilhelm Leibniz, 'Om et universelt tegnsystem' (On a Universal System of Signs), published in the Norwegian philosophical journal AGORA, nr. 3–4 (1990). Original: De numeris characteristicis ad linguam universalem constituendam, in *Sämtliche Schriften und Briefe*, Reihe 6. Bd.4 1677-Juni 1690, Teil A, N.66, Berlin: Akademie Verlag, 1999.

12 Michel de Montaigne, *Essais. Livre second*, translated by M.I.A. Screech, Allan Lane Penguin Press 1991, 459.

13 Peter Brian Medawar, *Advice to a Young Scientist*, New York: Harper, 1979.

14 Anthony Legget, banquet speech at the Nobel Banquet, 10 December 2003. Source: www.nobel.se.

IV

The dialogue seminar method evolved as part of work life researchers' efforts to find an appropriate way of capturing and describing experience-based knowledge. The role of the researcher in skill and technology is strongly related to aspects of so-called action research. In this tradition, research and the application of research findings are not two separate steps. The researcher aims to improve the practice of the subject of the study, but at the same time allows himself to be influenced by what he learns in the interaction with the subject of his research, whether this may involve a readiness to revise his own theoretical assumptions, or to modify the method during an ongoing investigation.

Furthermore, several decades of skills research have shown that it is extremely difficult to arrive, through direct questioning, for example in the form of questionnaires or interviews, at the core of the professional's skills, where – not least – attempts to create so-called expert systems have run into considerable difficulties.[15] Dialogue-inspired methods, in which conversations between researcher and professional continue over a longer period of time, have proved to be more usable.[16] We have called such methods indirect, because both the responses and the researcher's questions gradually emerge in the course of many conversations, conversations that may go on for several years and whose purpose is for the researcher to develop his ability to identify the interaction of the dynamic skill with a changing context. This gradual emergence of appropriate interpretations and composite pictures is something different to responses to direct questions in ready-made questionnaires or pre-planned interviews.

The dialogue seminar method evolved from the confluence of Hammarén's and Göranzon's perspectives. Maria Hammarén's book, *Writing – A Method for Reflection*, gave the impulse for the introduction of self-assessment through writing into both research programmes and doctoral studies. In his doctoral dissertation, Bo Göranzon showed that reflection on experience can be substantially improved by reflecting 'through a mask'. In his case, the mask was composed from four fruitful

---

15 Bo Göranzon and Ingela Josefson (eds), *Knowledge, Skill and Artificial Intelligence*, London: Springer Verlag, 1988.

16 Bo Göranzon, *The Practical Intellect: Computers and Skills*, Springer-Verlag & UNESCO, 1993, and Maja-Lisa Perby, *Konsten att bemästra en process: om att förvalta* (The Art of Mastering a Process : on the management of skill), Gidlunds Förlag, 1995.

sources: texts from the periods of great activity in the history of science and learning, Wittgenstein's philosophy of language, qualitative case studies with concrete examples from an occupational practice, and classic literature and drama. Further, Bo Göranzon's contribution to the Dialogue Seminar has added impulses from the theatre, that are included in the structuring of the seminars; reading texts aloud is like a process of collation, and the role of the seminar leader may be compared with the role of the theatre director. But the method has its roots in an even broader context. As Maria Hammarén points out in *Skriva som metod för reflektion* (*Writing – A Method for Reflection*), reading 'with pen in hand', making notes in the margin and reflecting through writing and conversation, belongs to a classic humanistic tradition. As well as in the seminars of the academic world, preparatory reading and subsequent conversations are also an important part of Sweden's tradition of popular public education. For example, in early case studies in Swedish work life research, the researchers called their meetings with the professional practitioners 'study circles': a term still used in popular public education.[17]

The problems concerning the concept of method in general, a set of rules as against the question of how these rules are to be followed from case to case, also has relevance to the dialogue seminar method. This applies particularly to the question of how the dialogue seminar method can be taught. The most important thing in the transfer of our pedagogical idea to other disciplines is to avoid any superficial use of the method. We require people who will be entrusted with the teaching of the method in other disciplines to have a deep understanding of the areas covered by the method: the philosophy of language, concepts of praxis and tacit knowledge, the philosophy of science and, above all, that they are proficient in the aspects of the method that have to do with preparation, with setting up and leading the dialogue seminars, and with how to write a special form of minutes documenting the important points in dialogue seminar discussions. Education for the leadership of dialogue seminars can be compared with the education of the theatre directors, who have to acquire their skills under the supervision of more

---

17 Bo Göranzon (ed.), *Datautvecklingens filosofi: tyst kunskap och ny teknik,* (The Philosophy of Computer Development: Tacit Knowledge and New Technology) Stockholm: Carlsson & Jönsson, 1983. A characteristic of the study circle is 'the free discussion method'. The study circle is the product of a lengthy process in nineteenth century popular education work in Britain, America and Sweden. (Svenska Nationalencyklopedin). Maja Lisa Perby uses the term 'research circle' in her *Konsten att bemästra en process: om att förvalta yrkeskunnande* (The Art of Mastering a Process: on the management of skill) Gidlunds, 1995.

experienced people.[18] A three-year educational programme in dialogue seminar leadership is presently under construction as part of the *KTH Advanced Programme in Reflective Practice*.[19] The programme will be at PhD level and participants are expected to write a thesis corresponding to at least the Swedish 'licentiate' degree.

Skill and technology research is currently in a phase similar to what Thomas S. Kuhn called the mature phase in a paradigm. When there is a radical paradigm shift, it is important to resolve the remaining problems within the frame of the new paradigm. In our case, the radical paradigm shift was a shift in the view of the nature of skill, from the systems theory view to a pragmatic view in which the core of skill is tacit knowledge. A central assumption in the new paradigm, which has emerged from case studies lasting many years, is that practical knowledge has its primary form of expression in action, and can only in part be expressed verbally. The part of practical knowledge that defies verbal expression, for example, the judgement that shapes every deliberate action, is called tacit knowledge. This does not mean that it is not possible to talk about tacit knowledge. It is possible, but it must be indirect, in the form of examples that provide a context, and by the use of metaphors and analogies. The process of reading 'with pen in hand' of the Dialogue Seminar method, and the subsequent writing exercises, are intended to train the ability to think analogically. To search for and describe examples is an exercise in the ability to speak indirectly about the part of our knowledge that is situation-bound and contradictory, and that evades systematisation and verbalisation.

Given that tacit knowledge is the core of skill, and that it can be spoken of in an indirect way, a legitimate research question is: how

---

18 The analogy of the theatre director enables discussion and problematisation. Does this analogy not produce a picture of the demon director who steers the seminar in the direction that he wants? If not, then what kind of direction do we have in mind? Alf Sjöberg's drama of ideas, or Ingmar Bergman's drama of relationships? What other ingredients come to mind in the director metaphor? Definitely to master the epistemology of the field of research and have a feeling for ways of getting the course members' ideas to expand. Here, there is a link to the Socratic midwife role; the leader must help the course members to use dialogue to formulate what they do not know that they know, and to make their thoughts gradually grow in talking (see Heinrich von Kleist's little publication, 'Om tankarnas gradvisa tillkomst vid talet' (*On the Gradual Genesis of Thoughts in Conversation*), Dialoger 64/02). Another problematic aspect related to role thinking is the selection of people to take part in the seminar. Who is suitable for this role? Unless everyone is instantly suitable, is the method not élitist? We think that 'being suitable for the role' is not a matter of talent; every one of us can, through work, acquire the knowledge that we now require of people who will lead or participate in the seminars.

19 The course on the philosophy and method of science, which is based on readings of the classics in the dialogue seminar form, received financial support in 2003–2004 from the Swedish Council for the Renewal of Higher Education.

can this insight be used to help people effectively convey tacit knowledge?

Tradition's tried and tested answer is master-apprentice teaching, used today in training both élite researchers, cooks, athletes or musicians.

What is to be done in situations where, for various reasons, the traditional master-apprentice teaching situation cannot be applied, yet tacit knowledge still has to be transferred, for example in the industrialised society's work culture, which today is based largely on the written word? The dialogue seminar method was created as an attempt to provide an answer to this question. The encounter between experienced and inexperienced people used to be commonplace, but today meetings of this kind have to be constructed. Further, given that there is a method for reflection that has proved its power in the transfer of experience-based knowledge, the next question relates to research into its potential in other disciplines, here in the education of graduate students.

4 The Methodology of the Dialogue Seminar

Bo Göranzon and Maria Hammarén

Background

Skill and Technology was introduced as a graduate programme at the Royal Institute of Technology, Stockholm, in 1995. The subject, which evolved from long-term case studies on skills from the end of the nineteen-seventies, established its profile through basic research studies on the epistemology of practical knowledge. The tradition of passing on knowledge and skills was a key issue from the outset. Reflection appears to be a vital point. The book, *Writing: A Method for Reflection* (*Skriva – en metod för reflektion*) (Hammarén, Utbildningsförlaget, 1995) was the inspiration for the introduction, both in the research project and the graduate studies programme, of a component of self-assessment that takes place through writing. This writing was steered towards the recollection of decisive events and examples that were a part of a person's experience, and that helped shape the way this experience was expressed: perceptions and values.

The Dialogue Seminar

Today, the perspective on the teaching and the development of ideas seen from an epistemological viewpoint lies at the core of this subject. As a method, the dialogue seminar expands the perspective of the concept of knowledge by extending its field to encompass the nature of practical knowledge. The subject also includes the Dialogue Seminar, a series of seminars arranged in co-operation with The Royal Dramatic Theatre, Stockholm. The Dialogue Seminar places this academic subject in a unique position by introducing co-operation with Sweden's foremost national theatre and all the professions that are represented in the theatre. Here, ideas can be portrayed and tested in simple forms and benefit from the traditions of the theatre. Here, they can meet an audience. And here, people can be invited to prepared conversations, that at times achieve the intensity of drama.

Central to this area of research is the exchange between artistic and scientific forms of knowledge. The Dialogue Seminar and the publication Dialoger are included in this research area, with the aim of stimulating in-depth discussions about work, language, culture and knowledge.

International and National Status

In recent years, the Dialogue Seminar has worked in close co-operation with the European Humanities Research Centre at Oxford University, to revive interest in philosophical dialogue. *Skills and Technology* as a research area has a unique character in both national and international perspectives (see Adrian Ratkic *Dialogseminariets forskningsmiljö* (*The Research Environment of the Dialogue Seminar*), which may be downloaded (in Swedish) from www.dialoger.se). Over the past 15 years, international acceptance has developed through close co-operation with foreign researchers: Malcolm Bowie, Christ College, Cambridge UK; Richard Ennals, Kingston University, London; Allan Janik, Brenner Archive, Innsbruck, and Kjell S. Johannessen, Filosofisk Institutt, the University of Bergen. At the national level, the newly appointed Scientific Council allocated funds for a symposium at which the Dialogue Seminar at the Royal Dramatic Theatre, Stockholm, hosts extended activities relating to the encounter between art and science in co-operation with the Royal College of Music.

The Dialogue Seminar Method

The Dialogue Seminar has influenced the process of methods development for learning in work that has taken place in recent years. In *The Dialogue Seminar Method*, writing has been supplemented with reading and expression. To make our internalised conceptions and interpretations, the results of experience, accessible for reflection is an arduous process that is reminiscent of what takes place in a theatre: it is a creative interplay between the individual and the collective.

The following dissertations are of particular relevance to the development of this method:

Bo Göranzon: *Det praktiska intellektet, (The Practical Intellect)* Carlssons (1990).

Maja-Lisa Perby: *Konsten att bemästra en process. Om att förvalta yrkeskunnande, (The Art of Mastering a Process. On the Management of Skills)* Gidlunds (1995).
Maria Hammarén: *Ledtråd i förvandling. Om att skapa en reflekterande praxis, (Clues in Transformation. On Creating a Reflective Practice)* Dialoger (1999).

Books: Bo Göranzon, *Det praktiska intellektet* (1990), published in English as *The Practical Intellect – Computers and Skills*, Springer Verlag, 1992, which discusses various perspectives on skills research. Bo Göranzon, *Spelregler-om gränsöverskridande* (2001) *(Rules of the Game – On Exceeding Limits)* develops this theme in research and development work that contains the following sections:

(i)   Researching skills
(ii)   Skills and philosophy
(iii) Skills and art
(iv)   Skills and method

An introduction to the method and its epistemological basis is to be found in Maria Hammarén, *Yrkeskunnande, berättelser och språk, (Skills, Stories and Language)* Dialoger 61/2002.

1996 to 1999 was a period of collaboration with Combitech Systems, a Saab Aerospace AB company, which aimed to develop 'faster experience transfer'. This project was carried out by Bo Göranzon and Maria Hammarén. The work was based on a combination of the perspectives of knowledge that evolved in this research area, and insights into the importance of writing for reflection. It was also during this period that an understanding of the importance of reading emerged, and the dialogue seminar method began to be developed. In her dissertation (see above), Maria Hammarén discusses some conditions and conclusions relating to the dialogue seminar model.

–   Dialogue seminars create a meeting place where people work on refining language to achieve more apposite and effective communication.
–   The model requires collective work to continue over time.
–   The language is refined with the help of examples, both one's own and others, in combination with reflection.
–   Reflection requires external inspiration that is taken from both the theory and from artistic portrayals.

The work at Combitech Systems resulted in the company setting up for its learning organisation a 'Learning Lab', with the dialogue seminar method as a cornerstone. Bo Göranzon and Maria Hammarén further developed their experience from Combitech Systems by creating at the Royal College of Technology, Stockholm, the *KTH Advanced Programme in Reflective Practice*, a graduate studies programme for practising graduate engineers, economists, etc. To date, accounts of the research and development work have been published in the following five work reports:

KTH Advanced Programme in Reflective Practice:

(i)   *Managing Reflective Practice* (spring 2000);
(ii) *Creative Environments and Leadership* (autumn 2000);
(iii) *Entrepreneurship and Ideas* (spring 2001);
(iv) *The Philosophy of Science, Skills and Method* (autumn 2001);
(v)   *Knowledge Development in Artistic Practices* (spring 2002).

Epistemological Theory

Awareness of language is often confused with the ability to criticise individual points, while concept formation in understanding is neglected (see also the chapter, 'Praxis och begreppsbildning' (Praxis and Concept Formation) in Kjell S. Johannessen, *Praxis och tyst kunnande*, (*Praxis and Tacit Knowledge*), Dialoger, 2000).

Concept formation in understanding is central to the dialogue seminar method. This method takes as its point of departure the dialogue in the perspective of the structure of knowledge. In Plato's writings on Socrates' dialogue, dialogue is an instrument for understanding. But the understanding is of a special type, and is never a synthesis. It is based on a concept of truth that can never be captured or made permanent.

What is available to us is the variety of perspectives, and the ability to allow them to influence us through dialogue. In that sense, dialogue that creates insight and understanding may also be said to be a concentration of the process of concept formation in general: it takes place between people, it continues over time, and it makes complexity and multiplicity visible.

The dialogue seminar method is based on the participants conducting a dialogue of this kind, a dialogue that, over time, creates insights, with the conversation being broken down into parts, being reinforced and emphasised by means of an exaggerated staging of the process of listening: a 'listening' mode of reading that stimulates (written) responses, reading aloud what has been written down, while the person reading hears how the different parts of the text are received by the group. Each participant is then expected to make a comment on what has been put forward. Speaking becomes a process that involves risk.

Seminar Leaders

The dialogue seminar method requires its leaders to be familiar with the literature that has been developed in the Dialogue Seminar programme since 1985. This literature is documented in the publication Dialoger, and in books that offer perspectives on epistemological theory (see www.dialoger.se). A selection of texts from this reference literature that offers inspiration and provides background has been compiled in the anthology by Peter Tillberg, (ed.): *Dialoger – om yrkeskunnande och teknologi, (Dialogue: On Skills and Technology)*, Dialoger, 2002.

Minutes

The 'minutes of ideas' play an important part in the dialogue seminar method. They are a permanent record of the group's collective reflections. This means that, as far as possible, these minutes should be notes of conversations that reflect the development of the course. The role of minutes-keeper emphasises the act of listening, both to individual formulations and to the sense of what the speaker wants to express. The minutes are circulated in advance of each group meeting, and the session begins with comments on them. They contribute to a continuous evaluation of the seminar, they are a permanent record of what was expressed in the conversations (that might otherwise easily be lost), and they help the seminar leader deal with relevant themes, issues and perspectives in greater depth.

Spelplats

The purpose of the magazine *Spelplats* is to present examples of texts the participants produced during dialogue seminars. So far, these texts have been taken from Combitech Systems (three issues); The College of Arts, Crafts and Design, Stockholm (two issues); The Royal National Defence College (two issues); The Federation of Swedish Industries (SIF) (one issue) and Föreningssparbanken (a co-operative savings bank) (one issue). The texts in this magazine are in themselves thought-provoking, and are also intended to expose the nature of reflection when it is linked in this way to creative collective reading and structured dialogue. The pilot project for what came to develop into the *Spelplats* magazine is the book by Christer Hoberg (ed.): *Precision och improvisation. Om systemutvecklarens yrkeskunnande, (Precision and Improvisation. On the Skills of the Systems Engineer)* Dialoger, 1998, an edited version of the texts produced by the participants in the first application of the Dialogue Seminar method at Combitech Systems AB.

Applications

In the Royal Institute of Technology (KTH), the Advanced Programme in Reflective Practice, which is financed by the Scientific Council's Educational Science Committee, graduate students use the Dialogue Seminar method in their doctoral thesis work. The following organisations have documented applications of the Dialogue Seminar method: SAAB Aerospace/Combitech Systems AB; The Royal National Defence College; The Municipality of Växjö; the KTH Learning Lab; Södra Skogsägarna (an association of forest owners); Nordisk Mediaanalys; SIF; The Royal College of Music; the College of Arts, Crafts and Design, Stockholm.

The Dialogue Seminar Method – A Handbook

The dialogue seminar method is a method of working that aims to:

(i)   create a practice for reflection;
(ii)   formulate problems from the dilemma;
(iii)   work up a common language;
(iv)   train the ability to listen.

From these aspects, participants learn to alter perspectives; the participants become familiar with artistic expressions in order to perceive the paradoxical nature of knowledge. The dialogue seminar method aims to give people an opportunity to practice analogical thinking. This involves discovering connections between the development of knowledge in their own area of activity and in other professional groups, and artistic practice.

Requirements

(a)   The pilot project requires that the people who are to participate in the seminar are 'cast' in roles as a preliminary study that precedes the introduction.
(b)   Size of group: seven–nine people.

(c)   Voluntary participation.
(d)   A binding agreement to attend all five seminars.
(e)   The participants are informed about the work method.

Introduction

Work begins with an introduction to the special characteristics of the epistemology of skill, and its relationship with philosophy, language, art and method. (Literature: Bo Göranzon, *Spelregler – om gränsöverskridande*, (*Rules of the Game: On Exceeding Limits*) Dialoger, 2002).

Further, a creative method of writing is introduced, a method that, instead of imitating, responds to impulses. (Literature: Maria Hammarén, (*Skriva – en metod för reflektion*) (*Writing: A Method for Reflection*).

The participants are informed that for a particular period of time they will form a writing group in which they read; write individually; read aloud to the group; listen; speak; and together make up the collective reflection in which a process of forming new, common concepts takes place.

The introduction is held in the presence of the authors or, if agreed, suitable substitutes for the authors. At the introduction, the first reading and writing tasks are announced. An example is presented of a text produced by a participant.

Reading and writing assignment

Two kinds of texts are used in the course of the seminar. Background texts communicate thoughts and perspectives of a more theoretical character. The 'impulse texts' stimulate the imagination, and contribute to the process of writing. All the texts are taken from the Dialoger publications of books and magazines that for more than fifteen years have published a body of literature that crosses traditional genre boundaries, and is relevant to the skills perspective.

The writing assignment begins with the reading of an 'impulse text', and the participants are asked to write down their thoughts and associations while the text is being read. The text may be read many times, and copious notes taken. The work collected in the notes will form the raw material for a new text, with the participants being asked to expand on one of their thoughts that relates to examples taken from their personal experience.

Seminars

Each seminar follows the same order. For a study of the 'minutes of ideas' from seminar number two, Leadership, see below.

1. Each participant brings the required number of copies of his/her text. For the reading aloud exercise, copies are handed out to the members of the group.
2. A discussion of the minutes. The group leader points out some of the key themes from the previous session, and introduces new impulses for reading that reflect these themes.
3. Writing seminar. Each participant reads his/her text aloud. The text must be read slowly enough for the group to have time to understand the content and make notes on their copy of the text. The participants may then speak in turn, with only brief dialogues being accepted before each participant has been able to communicate their thoughts/reactions from the notes they made. It is important that everyone into the group has his/her allocated time in which to speak, making it easier for them to listen to the others. The participants are told that negative criticism of the texts is forbidden. Instead, it is the personal reactions to the content of the texts that create the framework of the conversation: new connections, participants' own examples, analogies.

Leaders

The leaders have two roles. One task of the seminar leader is to direct the group's working method towards a process of concentrated listening to one another. It is also to create disciplined work routines, with times at which work must be handed in, copying work in advance, completing preparations as agreed, and the way time is allocated during the seminar. In addition, the leader must demonstrate how comments can lift and develop a text. For each text, the leader has the special task of raising the temperature of thought by means of analogies and examples taken from the history of ideas, literature, or the world of work, examples that give the group more profound insights and broaden their horizons in a practical philosophy perspective of knowledge and action.

The minutes-taker follows the conversation throughout the writing seminar, makes detailed notes, and then produces the 'minutes of ideas'. The ability to listen is of central importance here. The minutes of ideas is a permanent record of the participants' dialogue, detailing and examining the conversation, to allow there to be subsequent shifts in focus. These minutes are the results of the group's work, and are an important basis on which new reading and writing assignments are formulated. At each meeting, the minutes must be checked with the group. Each participant is entitled to make changes to his/her statements.

Time required

Five dialogue seminars are a suitable number for a series. A group of eight people needs a five-hour seminar.

5 A Dwelling Place for Past and Living Voices, Passions and Characters

Erland Josephson

This short chapter focuses on the world of the theatre. Actors learn about the theatre's thousand years of experience and carry with them knowledge of the ancient practice of play-acting: how to reach truth by representation, how to communicate with crowds and individuals, with the individual in the crowd, and with a crowd of individuals. The technologist may see the theatre as a framework of learning from old knowledge and experience.

When some students of technology, in the early 1970s, asked to be allowed to study the work of the Royal Dramatic Theatre (Dramaten), in Stockholm, everyone naturally imagined that they were out to demonstrate how irrationally, wastefully and unsystematically the theatre went about things.

This turned out not to be the case at all. In fact, they were curious as to how people could achieve, in such a short time, such an incredibly complicated product as a theatrical production. The technologists, the community planners, experts on rationalisation, programmers, compilers of timetables, directors general of post offices and other confused and imprecise creatures found they had a great deal to learn from Dramaten. An incredible number of human, technical and artistic components could within the space of a few short weeks be brought together in splendid harmony, without the use of squared paper, networks, flip charts and sophisticated discussions of objectives.

The then director of the theatre had no answer as to how these things could be. Perhaps, he thought, it might be due to thousand-year-old experience, to a stored and communicated knowledge; this, also, frequently acquired in a process of agonising pleasure, active doubt, and just as active enthusiasm.

The actors carry with them ancient experiences of the terms of play-acting, and a knowledge, just as ancient, of how to reach truths by representation, how to communicate with crowds and individuals, with the individual in the crowd, and with a crowd of individuals.

Around these miracles of communication, people raise and lower curtains, backdrops and sets, write texts of transient or eternal value, create ingenious lighting, arrange properties, build stages, smear gold on proscenium arches, decorate the public spaces with monumental paintings to underline the glory of the theatre, or serve soup in plastic bowls to emphasise its ties with the common people.

Around the actors, directors weave their interpretations and visions, audiences their dreams. The actors are given their lines and instruction, and they reveal their insight. They serve as midwives to the innermost structures of the spectator, sorting out confusions, or raising important questions. In a few brief months, a complicated internal and external machinery allows us to undergo or renew the experiences of Lear, or Hamlet, or Medea, to take some of the most breath-taking examples. Alternatively, we take to the streets and squares, exulting in the voices all around, and lending the stopped mouths a voice, the tired bodies movement.

In the live theatre, the actor is thus surrounded not by 'viewers' or 'listeners' but by spectators. The theatre audience must never be seen in terms of figures, or as a market. Treacherous and borrowed words like 'marketing' and 'sales department' are now creeping insidiously into the language of the theatre, and can disrupt the ancient and existential agreements that exist between the theatre and its public.

Dramaten is an institution two centuries old, housed in an eighty-year-old building. The building at once contains and expresses the institution. It is a dwelling place of past and living voices, passions and characters. No one can work there without feeling weighed down, challenged, encouraged, threatened, deflated and pumped up by the past. The walls are full of voices. You are forced to open a dialogue with the past, a dialogue that also forces you into a discussion with the future.

An actor or actress engaged for their first year, straight from some academy of drama, will soon find themselves involved in a fruitful dispute with Anders de Wahl (1864–1956), without, perhaps, having even heard of him. An older colleague will try, with no clear awareness of the source, to inject a trace of Hanson into a younger actor. Anders Henrikson (1886–1965) admired Ivan Hedqvist (1880–1935), Mathias Henrikson admires Anders Henrikson, Erland Josephson plays against Mathias Henrikson, and is infected by some remarkable, naked intonations; a common harmony arises, and suddenly it is Ivan Hedqvist who is delivering Lars Noren's text. This is probably true of all theatre, but in a theatre like Dramaten it is clearer than elsewhere.

There are still actors today, vigorously active, who have stood on the same stage as actors who played pages in *Hamlet* with Edvard Swartz in the title role. Swartz was alive between 1826 and 1897, and probably lives on still in some strange phrasing or sudden outburst on the part of a contemporary interpreter. You can see this either as a burdensome tradition, or as a liberating opportunity to test and exploit an intuitive knowledge that was mastered long, long ago. Every age has its intonations, but they will be more human, deeper, if they are played against a wider sounding-board.

There is a danger that the 'national stages', such as Dramaten, will husband the opportunities of tradition so poorly as to become its prisoners. The trouble in that case is often that their perspective has been too short; they seek their way back, but not sufficiently far, and not sufficiently deep.

The rejuvenators of dramatic art, and the avant-garde, have often drawn their inspiration and their starting-points from the truly old and original rites, the masques, the art of telling a story in the market. Basically, no people are more conservative than the avant-gardistes of the theatre.

It thus looks as if the basis of radical drama is an insight into the past. This is why Dramaten is such an important gauge of the health of Swedish theatre as a whole, and why it is more fiercely watched over and criticised than any other theatre in the country. The sign of Dramaten's vitality is the expectations that it excites. Even disappointment is a sort of recognition.

During the greater part of its short life-span, Dramaten has acted in a capital city without a university. This has sometimes contributed to promote a sort of artificial boundary between art and science. There have been times when actors have used the terms 'academic' and 'intellectual' as words of abuse. The academics, for their part, have devoted themselves to an old stout and avid appreciation of actors; if they have felt admiration, then it has been an admiration from above, a reflection of liberal generosity.

Today, even natural scientists speak of art as a source of knowledge. Painters and sculptors, musicians, dancers and actors are necessary to formulate new and astounding insights, to create a language also for the researchers themselves, so that they can move forward. Actors are being assigned a role not just as the providers of an abbreviated chronicle of the times, but also as the keen-eyed explorers of the future. In an age in which people are speaking, as usual, of the crisis in the theatre, its task, its obligations and its opportunities are in fact being broadened.

In Dramaten, then, and in its actors, is stored an ancient knowledge of the future. Perhaps it was this that the young technologists saw, or sensed, when they sought their way to the theatre.

Translated by Keith Bradfield

Part 2

THEATRE AND WORK

Theatre and Knowledge

6

Allan Janik

My theme, the relationship between theatre and epistemology (in the Anglo-Saxon sense as the systematic study of what knowledge is), will doubtlessly strike many people as curious, but it is not so.

Philosophers have been interested in theatre from the earliest days. In the ancient world the Stoics suggested that moral duty should best be understood as an allegory on acting. Just as actors have no control over their roles, but play what is required of them, we do not determine our position in society. Our station in life is assigned to us by fate, over which we have no control. Our duty is to make the best of it, in just the same way that good actors will play any role given to them convincingly, simply because they are good actors.

In the eighteenth century, this interest in acting was revived and expanded in several directions, on the basis of reflection upon the actor's skill in Denis Diderot's brilliant dialogue *The Actor's Paradox*.

Following Diderot's lead (consciously or not) the sociologist Erving Goffman has mapped social life onto theatre, in books like *The Presentation of Self in Everyday Life* and *Interaction Ritual*.

Stanley Cavell and Martha Nussbaum have written eloquently about how plays can illuminate human problems.

In twentieth century French philosophy, Jean-Paul Sartre, Albert Camus and Gabriel Marcel wrote plays, while the eminent historians of philosophy, Henri Gouhier, Lucien Goldmann and Victor Goldschmidt, wrote extensively about theatre and philosophy.

What we do not find in this literature, with the notable exception of the 'irresistible' Diderot, is a consideration of theatre from the epistemological point of view. As long as philosophy remains theory-oriented that is understandable; for, despite all the 'theories' that have been written about theatre, theatre is an eminently practical activity: it is produced in action and must have an impact upon the audience to be successful. It should not seem strange, therefore, that the praxis-orientation that Wittgenstein conferred upon philosophy should also have brought with it a certain interest in theatre. However, apart from the efforts of isolated individuals like Lars Hertzberg in his article 'Acting as Representation', largely inadequate, I fear little has been done in this direction.

So I propose to begin with a reminder of what is epistemologically at stake here, then consider what I take to be central in Wittgenstein's rehabilitation of practice within philosophy, proceed to a consideration of two aspects of theatre that I take to be particularly interesting philosophically, then consider the factors that are involved, and conclude with a consideration of the epistemology of catharsis.

What are my qualifications to discuss theatre you ask? For the most part they are of a practical nature. Apart from having a thorough grounding in classical literature from my undergraduate days, I have been involved in Swedish studies into professional knowledge for over 15 years. This work has, inter alia, focused upon skill in theatre, and has exploited the resources of the Royal Dramatic Theatre in Stockholm fully. For some 15 years I have been dramaturge at Innsbruck's Kellertheater. For five years I have collaborated with Vienna's authority on Stanislavski's approach to acting, Professor Artak Grigorjan, holder of the chair for acting at Vienna's Max Reinhardt Seminar, on an investigation of the concept of catharsis and its meaning for the theatre today. Apart from that I have lectured on my theme extensively at the universities of Vienna, Bergen and Innsbruck. So I can claim some small knowledge of the workings of the theatre, and its relevance to philosophy.

Let us begin by considering what has happened to epistemology in the twentieth century, or what could happen to it now, depending upon where one stands in a number of crucial debates concerning knowledge. The case of Michael Polanyi's struggles to make a place for practical knowledge, and the relationship of cognition to human feelings that it entails, in the philosophy of science should serve as a reminder of how difficult the task of rehabilitating practice was in the second half of the twentieth century. The great wild goose chase in twentieth century philosophy was the effort to measure all of knowledge on the basis of physical theory. Logical positivism's dream of an entirely 'physicalised' neutral observation language went up in smoke as philosophers with a training in physics like Stephen Toulmin, Norwood Russell Hanson, Thomas Kuhn, Patrick Heelan, Ernan McMullin and others protested that the physicalism of the Vienna Circle had precious little to do with the *practice* of physics. It is hardly accidental that most of the philosophers involved in the Kuhnian revolution in the philosophy of science were in one way or another influenced by Wittgenstein and/or Erwin Schrödinger, as was the case with Heelan and McMullin. Not the triumphs of scientific theory, but the structure of scientific reasoning, its practical logic(s), has meanwhile become the focal point of the common efforts of scientists and philosophers to cast light upon conceptual difficulties that arise in scientific practice. Thus the stories that philosophers tell about science went from emphasising the Promethean efforts of heroic individual theorists to explain the great physical riddles of the universe, to the much more modest task of exploring the structure and development of the collective quandaries of a community of mere mortals struggling to grasp what is going on.

In short, science, for all its sophistication, has come to be seen as a human activity no less susceptible to foibles than any other area of human enterprise. However, that was not before logical positivism ushered in a reign of terror with regard to scientific method in the humanities, from which we have not yet entirely ceased to suffer. Despite the change in perspective that thinkers like Polanyi, Fleck, Wittgenstein, and others have wrought within epistemology, in many respects we are still haunted by the ghost of the formalist concept of knowledge, even in our rejection of formalism. Witch-hunting sociologists, for example, ignoring the fact that science is a matter of *producing knowledge* on the basis of public criteria, tell us that science is nothing but a game played by an élite only interested in its own power and status within the community, a game, whose more or less arbitrary character is only fit to be exposed or subjected to 'deconstruction'. Once more the baby has been thrown out with the bathwater in the so-called 'Science Wars', as the distorting formalist perspective on human knowing has been exchanged for an equally distorting sociological reductionism. Practical knowledge, which is at the foundation of all scientific reasoning, has got lost in the shuffle once again. Precisely here is where Wittgenstein enters the story, as a refreshing breath of fresh air.

Wittgenstein's later philosophy succeeded in achieving what pragmatism and phenomenology could not, namely, establishing the *primacy of practice* in philosophy. Whereas pragmatism tended to trivialise practice (think of James's theory of truth), and phenomenology *mystified* it (think of Heidegger's *Being and Time*), Wittgenstein successfully dismantled the basic assumptions of epistemology in the tradition from Descartes to Russell. I find four aspects of his epistemological rehabilitation of practice important for us.

1. The first is the notion that practical knowledge is a matter of *following a rule* in a situation where there are no formal rules but only examples of actions to be imitated (PU, I, §208).

2. The second is the idea that learning in this way is learning to make *practical* judgements about the nature of *situations* and how we should, or should not, react to the demands those situations place upon us.

In fact, what we learn this way turns out to be a 'nest of judgements' (ÜG, §225, cf. §140).

3.   The third is his frequently overlooked *rejection of the idea that experience is the most basic form of knowledge*. Its importance requires a more lengthy discussion than the other points at stake here. Wittgenstein emphasises the primacy of familiarity and learning to follow orders in knowing:

> Now does experience teach us that in such and such circumstances people know this and that? Certainly experience shows us that normally after so-and-so many days a man can find his way about a house he has been living in. Or even: experience teaches us that after such-and-such a period of training a man's judgement is to be trusted. He must, experience tells us, have learned for so long in order to make a correct prediction. But...− (ÜG, §434, trans. Denis Paul and G.E.M Anscombe)

The 'but' at the end of the text is weighty indeed. In fact it poses the question, '*how* does experience teach us?' and in doing so takes Wittgenstein beyond pragmatism. In order to answer it, he must add a third kind of knowledge to the two that we have been accustomed to distinguishing after Ryle, 'knowing that' and 'knowing how', i. e. knowledge by *familiarity* (*Vertrautheit, Wohlvertrautheit, Bekanntheit*). In fact, Wittgenstein is concerned here to establish the *practical* conditions of the possibility of our being able to learn from experience in the first place. Thus he wants to explore how it is possible for us to have experience at all. Experience emerges as we grasp the orders that our parents/guardians give us about, say, avoiding what is 'hot'. Thus we come to have experiences on the basis of their authority, which in fact structures our behaviour as we come to interweave words and actions playing with them. The resulting ensemble of 'language games' forms a nest (ÜG, §225) and introduces a system into our behaviour that in turn becomes the firmly fixed hinge (ÜG, §343) which makes intelligible goal-oriented action possible, as well as developing our ability to learn further from experience on our own.

4.   The fourth aspect of Wittgenstein's rehabilitation of practice that is relevant to our discussion is that *we learn by applying knowledge, which is not our own in a variety of new situations*. We do not subsume facts under definitions, as traditional philosophers have largely assumed, but integrate new experiences and new knowledge into what already stands fast for us (ÜG, §144 *et passim*), which is to say that practical knowing is largely a matter of practical hermeneutics.

However, it might be objected here that all of this has nothing to do with theatre: Wittgenstein was not concerned with it at all. I am not so sure about that. Indirectly his view of meaning focuses our attention away from words, sentences, signs and symbols to situations, which is after all what theatre is all about. Consider paragraph 525 of Part I of the PU:

> 'After he had said this, he left her as he did the day before.' – Do I understand this sentence? Do I understand it just as I should if I heard it in the course of a narrative? If it were set down in isolation I should say, I don't know what it's about. But all the same I should know how this sentence might perhaps be used; I could myself invent a context for it.
>
> (A multitude of familiar paths lead off from these words in every direction.)
> (PU, I, 525, trans. Anscombe.)

The example reads like dialogue from a play; we shall have occasion to return to Wittgenstein's remarks about understanding the sentence in quotation marks later. The important point here is that understanding meaning as use means understanding the situation(s) in which a linguistic expression occurs. This is always more dramatic than we might think. In any case, it is not entirely absurd to think that there is a connection between Wittgenstein's later epistemology and theatre, which can be culled from his texts.

The importance of the *dramatic situation* in knowing can be illustrated trenchantly from Swedish research into skill and professional knowledge. Lotte Alsterdal, who has studied skill formation among nurses, reports upon a typical case (in fact a Norwegian case study) exploring the nature of skill in psychiatric nursing. She describes what is involved in dealing with a violent female patient, whose speciality is creeping up upon her attendants from behind and pulling their hair brutally, so brutally that many nurses have quit rather than go on working with her. Her nurses have to be continually on guard in her presence, and continually on the lookout for tell-tale symptoms in the patient's breathing, gestures and glances that indicate that she is about to assault someone. Working with the patient in question is to a great extent learning to read her signals without directly doing so. However, it turns out equally to be a matter of projecting security to the patient. This turns out to be a matter of such things as how one enters the room in her presence. The meaning of the situation, as Erving Goffman has long insisted, is thus entirely linked to dramatic transactional nuances of a sort that are wholly foreign to traditional epistemology, but by no means incompatible with the later Wittgenstein's view of knowledge. I suggest that considering Wittgenstein and theatre together can enrich both. My efforts here should be taken as a modest contribution to that project.

Two aspects of theatre are relevant to practical knowledge.

1.   The first has already been mentioned: *theatre is first and foremost a practical activity.* It involves a set of skills that have been developed over 2,500 years, skills which can only be learned by doing them, i.e. in performance. The knowledge that first-rate actors have, for example, is developed in endless hours of rehearsal and performance. It is a matter of practical insight that they have gained from experience.

2.   The second is the claim that *theatre can provide us with insight into human problems on the basis of our emotional responses to performed stories*: catharsis.

Moreover, theatre must have pride of place among the arts, as the only human activity that aims at 'concentrating' human life, in the words of Peter Brook, without simplifying it (as any theoretical or even fictional model by its very nature *must*). We shall have more to say about that later. Let us consider these two themes in reverse order.

The question of catharsis is a central point where theatre and praxis-oriented epistemology meet, for catharsis involves knowing through feeling. In classical modern philosophy, emotion and cognition have been opposed to one another for the most part; whereas in the theatre they are two sides of a coin. It was Michael Polanyi's contribution to insist upon the intimate relationship between practical knowing and feeling but Polanyi had great difficulties convincing his epistemological peers. The phenomenon of catharsis attests to that. Catharsis, the kind of insight we gain on the basis of intense emotional experience, is the goal that all theatre aims at (whatever individual theatre people might say to the contrary notwithstanding): catharsis is the *implicit* goal of all theatrical production. To be sure all art aims at reaching the intellect through the feelings, but a case can be made that theatre achieves catharsis most intensively and least abstractly on the basis of showing us what happens to people in certain situations. Theatre reaches the understanding through the emotions, when we *identify* with the plight of a character that we see before us and come to *reflect* upon it by *comparing* the situation playing itself out before our very eyes with our own. In theatre, seeing, feeling and judgement are intimately linked in ways that are readily apparent to anyone who has experienced the concentration of life that goes into first-rate theatre. For that reason theatre can illuminate the relationship between knowing and feeling more profoundly than other art forms. However, to appreciate that point we need to delve deeply into the question of the factors involved in bringing excellent theatre into being.

Aristotle remarks somewhere that the definition of a thing should be a description of what it is at its best. If that is so, then theatre should be defined in terms of catharsis. Our question, then, is how is catharsis at all possible? It is the contribution of Peter Brook to have supplied us with an insider's view of what is involved in a theatre production that is capable of producing catharsis. Brook's assumption is that theatre concentrates life. 'Life in the theatre,' he writes in a book with a good Wittgensteinian title, *There Are No Secrets*, 'is more readable and intense because it is concentrated'. Since the 'pragmatic turn' in epistemology that is my point of departure, Brook must be taken to be telling us that theatre is practical knowledge in a concentrated form. But what does it mean to say that theatre 'concentrates' life/knowledge? In coining the phrase Peter Brook wanted to say something about the way theatrical performance 'concentrates' human action by 'reducing time and compressing space'. However, in doing so, it also 'intensifies' and 'energises' what it depicts. In order to achieve concentration in space and time performing in the theatre demands the utmost 'concentration' in the sense of the undivided attention and effort of a community dedicated to communicating the 'concentrated' or intensified meaning of a text. In this context it is important to call attention to Moritz Geiger's distinction between *inner* and *outer concentration*. The German phenomenologist argues that we can concentrate upon anything we experience in two ways: by focusing upon what it means for us or by focusing upon the structure and form of the phenomenon itself. The latter, outer concentration, makes aesthetic experience possible, the former, inner concentration, prevents it. This will apply to all aspects of theatre. So we must take a look at what people *do* when they communicate to an audience in a theatrical production capable of producing catharsis.

Brook's *The Empty Space* is important to practical epistemologists' crisp and clear account of the division of labour in the theatre between dramatist (and text), actors, director, technicians, audience, and critics that is necessary to 'concentrate' life into theatre. To this list of the 'intrinsic' elements involved in making theatre we could add the all-important 'extrinsic' factor, the management. We must consider each of them briefly.

A theatre text is a unique form of literature that should not be confused with other forms of fiction. Thomas Mann exaggerated the results of the concentration of life that it contains, by insisting that a theatre text cannot be read. This seems to fly in the face of the fact that millions of people throughout the world have read plays (think only of Shakespeare), with delight and profit for centuries. Indeed, that box office flop, Henrik Ibsen, lived on the royalties on the book editions of his works. However, this does not contradict what Mann was getting at. In fact, he did not mean anything very different than Wittgenstein when he remarked that 'I do not know the meaning of the sentence "after he had said this, he left her as he did the day before, without further ado"'. Georg Simmel has said that the text of a play is nothing more than a skeleton, waiting for flesh to be put onto its bones by the actor. The experience of a former novelist colleague, whose works were well received critically without much popular success, is relevant here. Upon writing his first play he showed it to another colleague, who was also a professional actor. Having read the play, the actor said, 'everything is too explicit. You have written the play the way you would write a story, i.e., with a coherent beginning middle and end. In the theatre you can leave things out that can be shown on the stage and contribute to the tension in the piece.' Here it is worth recalling that the Greek word theatre means a place where you take a look at something (it is related to the word *theoria*, which means to take a look at things for yourself rather than accepting opinions on hearsay). A theatre production should show something, whose being said is somehow superfluous. The dramatist's task is to entice us into participating in the story. The plot of a play has to be dramatic. The mere reading of such a text taxes our imaginations, as anyone who has read a Shakespeare play before seeing it knows: the small roles seem superfluous in the reading; and the tone with which they can be spoken is difficult for a normal reader to supply. However, it is always a challenge for actors to play what is written, as Brook emphasises. The point is that there is a lot to learn about meaning and communication here.

The actors must bring the dramatist's story (or non-story) to life by speaking his words, but as Brook insists, 'Shakespeare's words are records of the words that he wanted to be spoken, words issuing as sounds from people's mouths, with pitch, pause, rhythm and gesture as part of their meaning. A word does not start as a word – it is an end product which begins as an impulse, stimulated by an attitude and behavior which dictate the need for expression. This process occurs inside the dramatist; it is repeated inside the actor'. And 'the only way to find the true path to the speaking of a word is through a process that parallels the original creative one. This can neither be by-passed nor simplified'. Rehearsal, what Wittgenstein terms training (*Abrichtung*), then, is an essential part of the natural history of meaning. Only when the actors have established the kind of gesture (both internal and external, i.e. physically and psychologically) that 'fits' the words can they begin to 'interpret' the text, but they never reach 'bedrock'. For the actor, this means possessing sufficient outer concentration on the dramatist's work to catch its drift, not concentrating upon himself in the role. What actors must say is always *ambiguous* (cf. PU, I, 525), and even self-critical, brilliant actors cannot exhaust the works of the greatest dramatists (Shakespeare, Chekhov, Strindberg, etc.). They require the context of intense rehearsing (usually four to twelve weeks full time) under the watchful eye of a knowledgeable director. Moreover, the crucial element that is unsaid in a dramatic text is something that the actors *share*. If they do not act *together*, the sense of the author's text cannot be conveyed. This was the crucial element in Stanislavski's 'method': that the actors experience their roles in all their emotional intensity *together*. In acting, the ensemble is everything. In many ways, acting out a dramatist's text can be compared with applying knowledge. In fact, performance of a dramatic text is an excellent paradigm for understanding what it means to 'apply' knowledge. Here the relation between giving shape to knowledge, and the hard work of rehearsal, comes clearly to the fore.

The director is there to supply discipline to the actors, and to be their eyes and ears. His role is that of a coach. He must tell the actors what is too much, and what is too little, in matters of tone and gesture. He must guide them in realising the dramatist's intentions. He provides the authority for interpreting the text. His authority is only legitimate as long as he serves the text. That too is a matter of outer concentration. The roles of giving orders and drilling, that Wittgenstein emphasises in connection with following a rule where there are no formal rules, could hardly find a better illustration. The director's job is to assist the actors in finding the right tone for what they must say.

The dramaturge is there to assist him with textual matters, while the assistant director keeps a detailed record of the rehearsals in which the performance takes shape. Light and sound technicians, set and costume designers, music and dance coaches all assist the director in realising his concept of the dramatist's work. However, their contributions are hardly negligible. After all, Adolf Appia's concept of the employment of light to accentuate the drama in Wagner's operas was a major innovation in twentieth century theatre. It should serve to remind us that realising a play is a matter of teamwork in which every role can be crucial; this was, after all, Wagner's original sense of *Gesamtkunstwerk*. The circumstances in which we learn to follow rules are entirely relevant to the practice of doing so.

One of the main differences between an internal and an external view of theatre bears upon understanding the role of the audience in theatrical productions. It comes as a surprise, even a shock, to laymen that the audience has a part in the performance of a play, but only the most casual acquaintance with actors will show that nothing is more crucial to them than the reactions of the audience. 'Were they lively?

Were they following the action? Did they notice when x made that mistake?' are the words that are in actors' mouths in the dressing room and after. If actors cannot succeed without concentrating upon their roles as opposed to their egos, they cannot do so unless the audience is concentrating upon them. One of the reasons that today's theatre is so superficial is that audiences seem to be unaware that they have an important active role to play in the theatre. Shakespeare reminds us of what that is in his Prologue to *Henry V*:

> On your imaginary forces work.
> Suppose within the girdle of these walls
> Are now confined two mighty monarchies,
> Whose high upreared and abutting fronts
> The perilous narrow ocean parts asunder:
> Piece out our imperfections with your thoughts;
> Into a thousand parts divide one man,
> And make imaginary puissance;
> Think when we talk of horses, that you see them
> Printing their proud hoofs i' the receiving earth;
> For 'tis your thoughts that now must deck our kings,
> Carry them here and there; jumping o'er times,
> Turning the accomplishment of many years
> Into an hour-glass: for the which supply,
> Admit me Chorus to this history;
> Who prologue-like your humble patience pray,
> Gently to hear, kindly to judge, our play.

In short, there is no play if the public's imagination is not engaged. When it is, there is a continual non-verbal communication taking place between actors and audience, that is perhaps the most important element in the success or failure of a well-rehearsed play. The role of the audience in the theatre can usefully be compared to the reinforcement and encouragement that we need to master any practical skill.

Another surprise to the layman is that theatre is an eminently *critical* activity. Theatre is suffused with criticism internal and external. Peter Brook emphasises that, however annoying critics may be, they are absolutely indispensable to excellent theatre. The critic keeps the theatre honest, as it were, by demanding competence from the people who make theatre. In order to fulfill this function properly, the critic must have a clear view of what theatre is and what a particular play can become on the stage. Oscar Wilde, who was not exactly a stranger to the stage himself, insisted that criticism was the consummate creative activity, for it fell to the critic, rather than the artist, to explain how something novel and unexpected can be seen as worthwhile in terms of commonly acknowledged standards, in effect an exercise in cultural hermeneutics. However, criticism is also characteristic of every aspect of theatre, from the first moment of rehearsal, till the curtain goes down on closing night and even after. Brook suggests that the criticism that theatre people make of one another is frequently devastating but always precise. This bears not only upon, say, one actor's critique of another; it pertains to everyone involved in a production. The technicians or the dancing master are as likely to come up with constructive suggestions for improving a production as the director or dramaturge. The point is that everybody involved in producing plays knows all the time that it is crucial to keep their eyes open for weakness. Those philosophers who consider criticism the very essence of philosophical activity could learn a great deal by observing a theatre company at work.

In addition to these intrinsic factors involved in producing plays there is also the extrinsic factor of *management*, which is not mentioned by Peter Brook but obviously crucial to the undertaking. The management is responsible for organising and financing the whole enterprise. It has to be mentioned here because, as far as excellent theatre is concerned, outer concentration, i.e. concern with artistic excellence and not mere profit, is also required. It is every bit as much part of the heritage of Stanislavski and Nemirovitch-Danchenko as their views about acting and costumes. For the skeptical, who would ask what in the world this might have to do with practical epistemology, I would call attention to the American philosopher, Robert Crease's book *The Play of Nature*, which is about theatre as a model for understanding scientific experimentation. He emphasises that we would do well to compare the financing and organisation of scientific research with the role of management in the theatre.

Let me close with a brief epistemological reflection upon catharsis. That *insight* which is catharsis is an entirely personal form of knowledge, emerging from an emotional experience with a cognitive dimension. Catharsis comes for *reflection* upon the meaning of concrete situations: think of what it is to be deeply moved by a performance of Othello. Our reflection takes the form of the comparison making between our own experience, and what we see and hear and, therefore, of forming judgements on the basis of examples. The emotional force that drives the insight depends upon our ability to *identify* actively with the action or one of the characters. This assumes that the 'story' acted out before us is sufficiently enticing (the element that the Greeks called *peitho* must be present) to motivate us to identify ourselves with the action. In effect, we come to understand the plot as an *allegory*, upon whose facets we come to concentrate intensively. Thus attaining catharsis is an *active* process that is the full antithesis to being passively entertained. Its moments, which can only be distinguished for the purposes of analysis, are identification, comparison and reflection.

At the close of *The Empty Space* Peter Brook writes:

> In everyday life 'if' is a fiction, in the theatre 'if' is an experiment.
> In everyday life 'if' is an evasion, in the theatre, 'if' is the truth.
> When we are persuaded to believe in this truth, then the theatre
>   and life are one.
> This is a high aim. It sounds like hard work.
> To play needs much work. But when we experience the work
>   as play, then it is not work any more.
> A play is play.

The sheer number of epistemological concepts involved in theatre, as Brook understands it, seems to have gone unobserved by philosophers. I hope that I have been able to suggest that all this is highly relevant to anybody that takes, say, the idea of 'language games' seriously.

7 Dialogue Seminar as a Tool: Experience from Combitech Systems

Niclas Fock

Introduction

The Dialogue Seminar, a concept created and introduced by Bo Göranzon and Maria Hammarén of the Royal Institute of Technology (KTH), Stockholm, is a method for reflection and the transfer of experience that Combitech Systems, a subsidiary of Saab AB, Linköping has applied in its work and further developed in co-operation with Bo Göranzon and Maria Hammarén. This work began as part of a joint research project that started in 1997. In 1998, this project produced the first publication in a series of books on the theme of Philosophy and Engineering. The second book in this series, *Ledtråd i Förvandling*[1] (*Clues in Transformation*) (1999), a dissertation by Maria Hammarén, concluded the first joint research project. The process of developing the methodology of the Dialogue Seminar has continued since that time.

A dialogue seminar is an environment for thought. Such an environment must foster the elements of surprise and the unexpected, and allow diversity and disparate perspectives to fuel reflection and the generation of new, common, knowledge.

Skill does not develop through methods and rules, says Diderot. Skills are developed and deepened by a great deal of practice. Reflection is a

---

1 Maria Hammarén's doctoral dissertation, published as *Ledtråd I förvandling* (*Clues in Transformation*) (Dialoger, Stockholm 1999), brought to a conclusion the research project that began in 1966 as a joint project between Combitech Software AB (now Combitech Systems AB) and the Department of Skill and Technology at the Royal Institute of Technology (KTH) Stockholm. The seminar project itself, which started in January 1997, ran for 18 months and was attended by nine engineers and managers from Combitech Software.

crucial factor: 'There are days when I have to reflect. It is a sickness that must be left to run its course.'[2]

Together with Bo Göranzon and Maria Hammarén we have created a method in which dialogue is brought to the fore as an instrument for generating a creative environment. Four components form the whole that characterises the method, i.e. what we call group writing exercises, a way of applying a form of the dialogue seminar in Combitech Systems. These four components are as follows.

Reading. Reading has produced new perspectives and the opportunity to see one's own experience through the experience of others.

Writing. Writing has been a method for reflection.[3] Concentration and training has shaped the inner dialogue.

Dialogue. In the collective dialogue, diversity emerges as a whole. Experiences interlock, disagreement creates energy. The form of the dialogue was initially strongly directed towards concentrated listening to one another's written texts.

Minutes. These 'minutes' are notes of the ideas that emerged in the dialogue, a permanent record of what can only occur in a dynamic, and they are a link to the next stages in the process.

The dialogue seminars give us an opportunity to identify parts of the skills of the system engineer that are so complex or unforeseeable that they evade the control of formal rules. Knowledge of how this work is

---

2 From Denis Diderot, *Rameau's Nephew*. We may differ between inner and outer reflection. Inner (individual) reflection: listening, through one's own reflections, to one's experience, one's inner voice. People do not receive (obtain) knowledge passively. It is acquired through reflection, reflection-in-action or reflection-on-action, according to Donald Schön. In the dialogue seminar method, writing is done slowly and the formulation of sentences is central to the method. Writing begins in reading. Thought and reflection need to be awakened, they do not come about by themselves. Through (individual) reflection, we gain access to our own experience, and can articulate/formulate conclusions and knowledge we did not know we possessed.

Outer (collective) reflection: is spontaneous or controlled (refined through preparation), and through interaction with the surroundings, in particular, through dialogue among people. By its very nature, dialogue is unforeseeable (knowledge is born in dialogue), and involves knowledge transfer (what is said addresses the recipient's fund of experience and references). Dialogue is forced to formulate/articulate tacit knowledge. As it is always unfinished, there is always an opening for the dialogue to continue.

3 From the beginning, the writing in the method has been based on Maria Hammarén's book *Skriva – en metod för reflektion* (*Writing – a Method for Reflection*), Utbildningsförlaget Brevskolan, Stockholm 1995.

performed cannot be expressed in exact terms; yet we can still discuss it by highlighting different examples and dealing with them in depth.

Heading a dialogue seminar therefore requires not only the ability to lead meetings, but also a more in-depth knowledge of epistemology (knowledge about knowledge), and practical skill. The leader must be able to move the collective dialogue forward, and gradually build up a more profound understanding in the group of the issues that relate to the connection between formal and practical knowledge, one must constantly be one step ahead of the group. In the course of collective reflection, a process of collective concept formation takes place that must be captured. This is done partly by focusing on important core concepts by bringing forward examples and providing references to literature, which requires that the seminar leader is familiar with both the subject in question and the literature relating to the dialogue seminars and practical philosophy, and partly through subsequently producing, from notes and memory, 'minutes' that contain information about the concept formation, a record of ideas that reinforces this process, and circulating them to the seminar group members.

On the Aim of Dialogue Seminars

A dialogue seminar achieves an aim and deals with a subject or a theme. It may be a one-off event, or it may be part of a series of meetings, or of a more comprehensive idea or plan for a group, either in-house or outside the company. Holding a series of dialogue seminars for a customer requires special arrangements in which the seller's judgement is final on whether or not the client is ready, and has understood the epistemological arguments, and is prepared for both the long-term management commitment required for success, and also to allocate the time for thorough preparation in advance of our seminar. One-off seminars may sometimes work, but they need to be given a different focus than concept formation if they are to succeed, and if the group members are to perceive some benefit that is different from the result of a more traditional type of workshop or group exercise.

It is important to clarify here that a dialogue seminar may be used for very different purposes.

The Dialogue Seminar – What are the Objectives?

We identify five separate and parallel objectives, or effects, of the dialogue seminars we are currently running at Combitech Systems.

1. To create a language with which to handle epistemology and access the areas of the history of ideas that relate to the philosophy we may find applicable. This objective involves creating, with the help of the research and literature on, for example, epistemology, practical philosophy and knowledge-oriented leadership, an understanding of experience and tacit knowledge and of the function of dialogue and the value of reflecting on one's skill.

2. To build up over time a common practice by means of collective reflection, dialogue and concept formation, i.e. establishing a professional practice for a group in their common professional roles and professional collective. This is a part of the development of judgement in the professional role.

3. To train the ability of analogical thinking, the ability to see similarities and differences between different examples, analogies, and in the situations people encounter in their working lives. To create greater awareness of the value of personal and collective reflection.

4. At one or more meetings, treat in depth a particular topical set of issues, a dilemma or the like, i.e. contribute to knowledge building in an occupational area related to something that for this group is unexplored or burdened with anomalies.

5. To identify through individual and collective reflection individual elements of skill in which experiential knowledge is expressed and transferred, i.e. elements that are not described in traditional sets of rules and process descriptions, and therefore have to some extent been invisible or regarded as irrelevant or quite simply self-evident, despite, or perhaps because of, their complexity.

All these five objectives are encouraged and fulfilled in varying degrees through work in the dialogue seminar form. They are interrelated and cannot be separated out to allow a seminar to focus on only one objective, obtain only one or some of the effects and thus results for only one objective. It may, however, be possible to place different focuses on different objectives, but results are obtained for all of them. Objectives two, four and five may involve the formation of completely new knowledge, while objectives one and three have more to do with improving the ability to do just that.

It is worth noting that the first three are all long-term objectives. They cannot be fully achieved in one-off dialogue seminars. The knowledge acquired here is largely tacit knowledge, although of course reflection and writing also reveal implicit knowledge.[4] On the third point, analogical thinking ability, one may perhaps say that it is partly a question of a kind of skill one develops through practice, even though it is in no way of the 'physical' type normally associated with the knowledge of familiarity. But the point here too is to encourage the other members of the group to reflect and further develop individual insight, experience and convictions.

However, the important factor to see is that the effects of these three first objectives are long term, but not all three require people to be members of the same group. The third objective, for example, training and greater awareness, is achieved over time, among other things by attending several seminars, without necessarily taking part in one and the same group.

The fourth objective is more short term in nature. In one or two meetings, topical problems are illustrated for the group, and new perspectives are highlighted that have the effect of drawing on the group's aggregate experience to clarify something the group wants to examine. This creates a common understanding of something. Here too, the result is mainly tacit or implicit knowledge. A common understanding of something is created. Here is an opportunity to illustrate something closely related to a profession that is not essentially to do with acquiring an epistemological perspective or creating a common practice, although it is, of course, very close to the latter. Concept formation takes place, of course, but as part of the process and not as the main point (at least not consciously) of this objective.

The fifth objective is also short term and perhaps the least important. It could almost be regarded as a side effect of using that particular work form, yet it is important enough to be given priority here too. An examination of the results of the seminars produced in written form, the course members' written reflections and the minutes of the seminars, can often identify elements in the practical work that are examples of the way in which informal decisions are made, for example, or how a common picture of what is to be achieved in the project is conveyed to others, work forms that have proved to be successful or otherwise. These are examples of areas of the work that are not normally described in the work processes, complexes of rules and instructions that govern the way work is to be done in the project, and they are rarely mentioned as being of particular importance. They are not described in the rules partly because of their nature, which requires them to be

---

4 Kjell S. Johannessen describes the concept of implicit as against tacit knowledge in *Praxis och tyst kunnande* (*Practice and Tacit Knowledge*) (Dialoger 1999).

illustrated, and they may often be made visible only by means of examples. The multitude of ways in which dialogue seminars have been applied at Combitech Systems have given us the insight that it is in these very elements that most of the knowledge-building work in a system development project takes place. We want to be able to make use of these examples in understanding the ways in which experience-based knowledge can express itself in order to create a transfer of experience in other groups in the company. Accordingly, we are currently looking for forms for processing the written material produced by the seminars. It is, above all, the group members' written reflections that, after some processing, may be valuable experience or simply inspiring reading for colleagues, even colleagues outside the group of seminar participants. Thus, we now want to open up various kinds of possibility for the internal publication of these reflections, including the publication 'Spelplats', not least to stimulate individuals in the organisation to learn to see and understand work elements of this kind, and reflect on their importance in projects. Not infrequently these reflections also create the basis for simple case studies that can be used as work material in future seminars, both internally and in clients' organisations, in which case perhaps foremost as stimulation and in working towards the second of the five objectives listed above.[5]

When dialogue seminars are run in which at least two successive meetings cannot be arranged, it is important to be aware that this only meets some of the requirements of the dialogue seminar method. In our internal training, in the Combitech Training Institute,[6] for example, the main objective is to establish a common company practice, provide basic training in epistemological concepts and styles of thought, and train analogical thinking and the methodology of the dialogue seminar. For practical reasons, the composition of groups may change from one meeting to the next, so concept formation and the establishment of practices in the group cannot be done in the same way as if the same group had completed a series of seminars. Thus, this is an important departure from one of the fundamental ideas of the method, but in this case it is a deliberately-chosen path. If the different effects or objectives of the seminar can be co-ordinated, then the long-term benefits will, of course, be significantly greater.

---

5 One example is a company conference, planned in 2003, on the theme of 'Managing Our Own Projects', with the latest issue of 'Spelplats' (which contained texts produced by employees) as reading material for other company employees, to stimulate writing assignments in preparation for the conference.

6 The Combitech Training Institute is the internal training department of the Combitech Learning Lab.

The following are some examples of ways that dialogue seminars have been used in Combitech Systems.

(i) At the inception of a development project. Before a development project is begun, a phase is necessary in which the outline of what the activity or project is to deliver takes shape. Many different interests, represented by people with different backgrounds and conceptual worlds, need to be brought together to shape the requirements and wishes relating to a new system, for example (customers, marketing people, product management, etc.). The dialogue seminar method can create perspectives and enable those involved to achieve a greater understanding of one another's different interests and their ways of expressing their needs in the new system. At the same time, the dialogue seminar is a way of ensuring that the participants have understood one another.[7]

(ii) As a method for transferring knowledge and experience from one group of people to another, for example when gathering the most important experiences from a concluded project and transferring them to a new project,[8] or transferring core skills from one organisation to another, when a company relocates, for example.[9]

(iii) As a way of preparing for an impending intensive and important phase in a project or an organisation when the group has no shared experience of this new phase, in advance of a phase of a project that introduces a new work method, for example, or before a major process of change, etc.[10]

---

7 This method was first tested in preparing a major project for a client in the medical technology sector, which was to develop a new handheld terminal for nursing centre staff (2001). The result exceeded expectations and the client expressed very positive reactions after the seminar.

8 The first time this was applied was in an exercise called 'Lessons Learned' for a client in the automobile industry. Experience from a project that failed completely was presented in a dialogue seminar and became the point of departure for a project that was about to start.

9 When closing down a business operation at a Linköping-based client in the multimedia sector where a Germany-based part of the business was to take over, several parallel dialogue seminars were run on a number of prioritised knowledge domains (key areas) identified by the company management. In the exercise, which was carried out in English, the students were given preparatory texts, then wrote and read aloud – all in English, i.e. not in either party's mother tongue. This is considered to have been an important factor in the success of this seminar.

10 In a major project, a client in Karlskoga faced a phase of integration in which all the system components were to be linked together and tested for the first time. This was a particularly critical phase in the project, as staff that were not involved in developing the components were to take over and attempt to put the system together, guided by the overall description set out in the original specifications from the orderer.

(iv) A series of seminars for the purpose of developing and establishing a new practice in an organisation that needs to prepare for some kind of comprehensive and lasting change or paradigm shift.[11]

(v) A one-off seminar aimed at resolving and examining in depth a single dilemma, a complex set of issues, such as a group that wants to know more about system configuration.[12]

(vi) As part of a training course for a larger number of people in an area of strategic importance for the business operation; for example, the course entitled 'The Architecture Council' that Combitech Systems ran in 1999.[13]

(vii) As a leadership course for a management group or project management. Here, it is useful to work in two phases. One phase that opens up the area of concepts and brings together the group members, with their respective points of departure and diverse perspectives (the dialogue seminar), and then a focusing phase that results in the production of a concrete plan of action (in line with traditional methods for structured brainstorming, risk analysis, etc.).[14]

---

11 From 1995 to 1997, Saab in Linköping carried out one of Sweden's biggest programmes of change in the field of system development, known as the EMPIRE project, in which, with the assistance of Bo Göranzon, we carried out two dialogue seminars aimed at capturing the complex of problems relating to the introduction of new technology and work method changes in a large organisation. Another example is a telecommunications company in Lund that wanted a method, but it turned out that what was needed was a process of change.

12 The configurations management example had been tested internally in the company on a number of occasions, and is now a practice as a method used in preparing for complex problems in our own projects. Another example is a client in the medical technology sector who, having come to a standstill in a project, observed that after 'completing' the work according to the original project plan, more than half of the project lead time still remained. We brought together all the staff for one week and carried out an intensive series of seminars. An important goal for this exercise was to transfer a number of concepts we saw as essential for the project members and company management if they were to understand the situation they found themselves in, and how they could loosen the logjam and move forward.

13 This application may be seen as a more in-depth application of the above, where an area of strategic importance for the company had been identified and efforts made to create a common practice or raise the knowledge level in a larger group of people. It was at the company conference in Nice that this was put to a serious test, a test in which 200 people took part. Just a couple of years after this company conference we had gained an international reputation in the sector as a leader in the field of system architecture.

14 This was applied to management groups, including those in parts of Saab in Linköping (2001–2002), and in a client company that develops marine engines and ship systems (2003). The first step was to carry out a dialogue seminar with texts, reading aloud, etc. The second phase involved a structured brainstorming session and detailed planning, run along the usual lines. Unlike normal brainstorming and activity planning, these sessions generated enormous focus and shared understanding in the group about what is important. It is interesting that the concepts that emerged as the most important, concepts that had been created and discussed in detail in the dialogue seminar, recur like mortar that binds the bricks of understanding in the collective dialogue and planning at this stage.

(viii)   As a meeting place for reflection where the participants have different jobs but come together on a common theme, to exchange experience and establish a common practice: one example is our internal 'Organisational Change Management' course for our management consultants. We prefer to call these meeting places and groups of people that gather round a created theme 'Communities of Practice'.[15]

On Preparing for a Dialogue Seminar

The reading and writing assignments given in advance must be carefully prepared to ensure that they illustrate the theme in question. It is vital that the text be written in a way that invites reflection.[16] Texts that relate to the theme should be supplemented with texts that are a source of analogies on the theme from an epistemological or philosophical perspective.

When choosing material, it may be helpful to ask someone who has experience of arranging seminars for tips on text reading that can relate to the theme in an appropriate way. It is crucial that the texts are seen as inspirational and generate a desire to read in the great majority of course participants, because this is, of course, to some extent an individual matter. If it is not clear whether the text will work, a number of texts may be included to increase the chance of all course members finding at least one text that captures their interest. It is interesting to see that some texts that work in one context do not work at all in another. This means that there are connections between the group and its individual members, the text and what the seminar is to address.

The following three types of text may be identified, each with a slightly different role in the preparatory work.

---

15 In our own operation this is now a natural part of business development. That is to say, the input from our most experienced colleagues in a particular knowledge area is used to create a deeper understanding of the problems in customer situations where we have consultant assignments, and from this common concept formation a new concept of service is developed, based on this deeper insight into our customer's requirements.

16 To be able to motivate the course members to share their experience is a central aspect of the dialogue seminar. The method invites the students to reflect on their experience and want to share it. This is a question of unlocking the door to the individual's experience and, as Peter Tillberg writes in the introduction to his book, *Dialoger – om yrkeskunnande och teknologi* (*Dialogues – On Skills and Technology*) (Peter Tillberg [ed.] Dialoger 2002), selecting texts '[that] awaken the desire to write . . .'. Put simply, the texts to be read must be stimulating, and therefore preferably written by quality authors. Experience of selecting texts and how well different texts were received in the groups shows that literary texts were consistently those that worked best. Tillberg also supports this observation, and emphasises that a text must be a 'good story'.

1. Thematic texts: texts that relate directly to the subject in question and depict the set of problems or the complexity the seminar is to deal with in depth.

2. Analogous texts: texts that are about something else, but with evident similarities with the subject in question, for example in the form of identical terms that are used in a different context (for example, system architects versus building architecture) or other professional areas with similar complexes of issues. Analogous texts are texts that aim to fuel reflection and create perspectives.

3. Epistemological texts: texts that convey an essential fundamental understanding of the epistemological argument as the theme, situation or subject to be addressed in the seminar. Epistemological texts deepen and add concepts that give better opportunities to create understanding of the complex contexts, and to formulate questions and groups of problems.[17]

Different texts also have different functions in another respect.[18]

1. Background texts: texts that explain fundamentals, provide a holistic perspective, give a deeper understanding of causes, etc.

2. Impulse texts: texts that inspire thoughts, associations and personal reflection. Impulse texts are well written, capture the reader's interest, and are often examples of descriptive writing or fiction. Impulse texts should bring issues to the fore; they may often be caustic, pointed and subjective, preferably taken from literature, and sometimes in the form of dialogue or prose.

---

17 Bo Göranzon expresses this in his Research Programme for Educational Science (KTH, 2002), and writes, 'For our purpose we turned to texts that can be counted as part of the philosophy and tradition of ideas of practice, authors such as Montaigne, Shakespeare and Diderot.'

18 Peter Tillberg groups reading texts into impulse texts and background texts, with these groups being used for somewhat different purposes. Tillberg writes that 'the texts also differ in form and language. An equitable division into categories is not easy. But a direction may be suggested by saying that some of the articles have proved to work better than others in stimulating the reader's reflection and writing, with the focus on the reader's own experience'. Tillberg also writes about the selection of impulse texts. 'This has been mainly a question of choosing the articles that, as a reader, for one reason or another have a particular appeal for me, texts I have wanted to return to and that do not leave me unmoved. They almost always bring up aspects in which one recognises oneself, but also leave room for the imagination . . . The texts leave me as the reader scope for interpretation that opens up alternative possibilities.'

The reflections that are generated are, of course, individual. At the same time, many texts both use a language and convey an idea that we can all receive. All the selected texts must be well written and, as Per Tillberg puts it, written so that they 'give me, as the reader, a space for interpretation in which alternative opportunities open up'.

Texts must be found that speak directly to the reader's experiences, i.e. that invite the reader to look into his/her own experience. This is the interface in which the inner dialogue takes place and new knowledge is born. 'Put briefly, the best literature speaks to us in the very words that we ourselves do not have'.[19] This is what reflection is about, and what is central in the dialogue seminar.

The assignment must be structured in a way that gives no opportunities for group members to 'cheat' or be unprepared when they come to the seminars, and should emphasise the importance of each group member spending enough time on the preparatory work. Anyone who fails to do the preparatory work must be prepared to be excluded from taking part in the seminar, and the seminar leader may judge from case to case how strictly the standards must be applied in practice.

1. The Reading Assignment

The reading assignment should be structured to encourage a process of reading 'with pen in hand'.[20] The term 'reading with pen in

---

19 From Allan Janik, *The Concept of Knowledge in Practical Philosophy* (Stehag).

20 The following is a real-life example of the way a reading assignment can be formulated. 'For the purpose of demonstrating the effect of the dialogue seminar method, and to extract valuable experience from the work in your project that can be applied in the next project, we are now planning a dialogue seminar for February 1. The people selected to attend this seminar have a number of tasks to complete.

All these preparations must be completed before the seminar can take place. They will also be of real benefit to you! So you must give them priority as additional reading at home in the evenings, etc. and plan time for your writing. We may have to exclude people who have not completed their writing assignment before the seminar begins.

Reading assignment: Begin by reading Maria Hammarén's book *Writing – A Method for Reflection*. Then read 'with pen in hand' (i.e. continuously noting your reflections while reading – see Maria's book) the articles in the compendium we have distributed. Write down your inner dialogue while you are reading, putting your thoughts, impulses, reflections and associations down on paper. Try to listen to your inner thoughts while you are reading! The following articles must be read:

A. On skills and the concept of knowledge: 'Models for Studies of Skills' (Bo Göranzon).
B. On tacit knowledge: 'Method Issues in the Human Use of Technology' (Stephen Toulmin).
C. On two different views in engineering: 'The Two Cultures in Engineering' (Peter Brödner).
D. On the dream of the exact language: from 'The Practical Intellect' (Bo Göranzon).

hand'[21] refers to a measured pace of reading that allows the reader to attempt to listen to his inner dialogue, his thoughts, associations, queries and the inner search for similarities between what he reads in the text and his own experience, while continuously making notes to which he may return later. Maria Hammarén makes the following comment on reading.

> The method is based on a variety of ways of achieving concentration. Both individually and in groups. Individual reading first: to be aware of the flow of thought during the process of reading is to train 'dédoublement' – being in the text and at the same time outside it. The pen, the need to make notes, focuses concentration on my role as the reader and interpreter of what I read, a role for the critical assignment.[22]

This reading may be compared with reading aloud, but to oneself, so that one also listens to the intonation, or cadence, of one's own reading.

Questions on the reading material.

   (i)   Describe the connection between tacit knowledge and Dreyfus's five stages of development.
  (ii)   What analogies do you find in Toulmin's text compared with your own organisation?
 (iii)   Where, in Brödner's view, did the rational tradition go wrong?
 (iv)   What is the nature of the complex of problems relating to developing the exact language?

At the end of the compendium there is further reading on, among other things, Bo Göranzon's research on skills (from the New Scientist) and an article on dialogues 'On Dialogue, Culture and Organisational Learning' by Edgar Schein, which is strongly recommended and should be read if time allows.

Writing assignment: When you have finished the reading assignment, write 2–3 A4 pages of text on one of the following themes.

- 'Improving efficiency in system development work.'
- 'Introducing improvements in the project.'

Base your writing of the reflections you noted down during the reading assignment, and develop these notes, or some of them, into texts that describe your own experience – factory from the project. This should be a short story that contains concrete examples from your own work in system development, and reflects on the connections with something you have read in the articles.'

21 In the work with 'The Gang of Nine' in 1997, the very first book we were asked to read was Maria Hammarén's *Writing – A Method for Reflection* (Utbildningsförlaget Brevskolan, Stockholm 1995). It was from the reflections on this book and the related discussions in the group that the term 'reading with pen in hand' came up and was adopted, to become a recurring term that we use to describe the method of noting down brief reflections while reading texts or listening to others reading aloud. As Peter Tillberg puts it in *Dialogues – on Skills and Technology* (Dialoger, 2002), 'We all carry experience and stories about what we have experienced in real life. One way of examining these is to reflect them in the light of someone else's story'.

22 Most of the quotes from Maria in this chapter are from a comment on a text she wrote to the 'Gang of Nine' in response to the group's questions and thoughts on writing and as a personal reflection on the dialogue seminar method and its various components.

One's own cadence and rhythm is, of course, different from the voice of the author at the moment the text was written. This difference is the dialogue between the reader and the author; the different interpretations, the differences in experience and in tacit knowledge are all to be found here. The cadence is in itself an expression that is very close to the musical expression in musical performances. Voice or song: there is no clear boundary separating the two.

2.   The Writing Assignment

In the same way, writing may be difficult for anyone who has not done any writing before. 'What should I write about: is this what you mean?' is a common reaction, after which the person produces a more clear and controlled piece. In these cases, giving the course members an example of such a text may be a way of breaking through this writer's block. It may be useful to attach an example to the reading assignment, preferably with a note about the purpose of the text (particularly if the example does not contribute to the theme of the seminar in any other respect). Maria Hammarén again:

> Writing is, of course, a way of processing one's material, one's thoughts and experiences, and giving them a deliberate order. The difficulty is the order; the importance each individual gives to the critical voice determines how far thought is allowed to wander (and time, of course). But concentration is also an ongoing process that may intensify after a number of meetings.

A date some days before the seminar should be set as a deadline for submitting the written assignments, to allow time to copy and distribute these texts before the seminar. If time is short during the seminar, the leader may include in the assignment a request for all the participants to read through one another's texts ('with pen in hand' of course!), thus allowing the group to miss out the 'reading aloud' stage during the meeting. However, this is not recommended if it can be avoided, because reading aloud has a very important impact on the course members' perceptions of one another's texts.

About the Seminar Itself

1.   Introduction

It goes without saying that a dialogue seminar must have an introduction given by the leader of the seminar, to both convey the purpose of the exercise and remind the course members of it, and this introduction should also include a brief description of the way the seminar will be run and why.[23]

2. Reading Aloud

Reading aloud is a way of giving each person a chance to speak without interruption, as is the case when, at the end of this stage, course members speak in turn, which is an essentially democratic process. Maria Hammarén:

> Having each group member reading his or her text aloud in the room is an important aspect of the process. Not only do we hear immediately anything that sounds simplified when it is made public, but also the need for clarity in what is written down works better when one is, so to speak, notified of the reactions of those present. Much of what was thought to be conveyed by implication may be revealed as not actually implicit but incomplete. And what actually was implicit should have been written out, because it immediately becomes apparent that the implicit is not shared by everyone in the group. Reading aloud is quite simply a way of bringing this requirement into focus: for some, the process involves a great deal of anguish; they want to 'excuse themselves from' what they have written, but this is inappropriate: discussions take place later. Here, it is a matter of presenting a piece of work in this particular form.

The origins of the dialogue seminar are, in part, in the theatre. Rhythm, pausing and intonation[24] are important, as is actually reading what is written, so that the listener has the opportunity to follow in the text. Further, the presence of the author allows in-depth discussions and clarifications of the text, but also direct corrections of any errors in the text. It is best to leave questions to the author until the reading is completed.

---

23 For the very first compulsory seminar in the Combitech Training Institute, a lecture has been produced that addresses the content of fundamental epistemological concepts such as 'tacit knowledge', etc. together with the dialogue seminar method itself. This lecture lasts about two hours.

24 It is interesting to note that the term 'cadence' provides a connection to music (song). When I read, the cadence is my own.

Reading aloud also focuses the group; it creates collective concentration on something common to the group.[25] To have access to the texts while they are read aloud, and being able to 'listen with pen in hand' and make notes is also of benefit in preparing for common reflection.

3. Collective Reflection

Concept formation takes place in the group inasmuch as a dialogue is carried on around the reflections that evolve from reading aloud and from the written texts. As Bo Göranzon writes in his books and articles, this concept formation, which is one of the most vital parts of the dialogue seminar method, is the basis for creating, for the group, the practice relating to the subject. Maria Hammarén writes:

> The importance of the group has already been mentioned. It is important that individual work is made public. Nothing must be left to chance; as much of individual reflection as possible must be presented to the group. This is done both through reading aloud and, of course, in the discussions that follow the reading of each text. Discipline, for which the 'group leader' is responsible, is important. The conversation must constantly refer back to the material the meeting is dealing with, i.e. the theme of the seminar, either by developing or problematising an idea contained in the current writing assignment, or by means of a way of making connections with the 'original documentation', i.e. the material to be read before the seminar. Elementary rules of discipline apply here too, such as each group member being given a reasonable amount of time in which to present his/her material: it is here that thoughts are to meet, this is the time we have at our disposal and the rest is, in theory, a matter of keeping things in order – without degenerating into rigidity. The first texts usually take longer because at that time a great deal is still unsaid.

---

25 In an interview in *Computer Sweden*, no. 2–2002, on storytelling as part of a self-sustaining ecology, Dave Snowden (head of the IBM Institute of Knowledge Management) says, 'what you learn from storytelling is at a higher level than what can be put in print in rules and regulations'. For IBM, Snowden has introduced three simple rules for storytelling: 1) it must be voluntary. No-one tells stories under orders. 2) I know more than I can tell, and I can tell more than I can put down on paper. 3) I only know what I know when I need to know it. Snowden also points out, with some irony, 'The mechanical metaphor for knowledge breaks down in this perspective. One cannot order up knowledge. Organic structures are robust and can mend themselves, mechanical structures cannot. So, back to square one. We must learn to manage without computers. – One of my most important tasks is to teach managers to give lectures without PowerPoint.'

The form is intended to support collective reflection: that what is said matters. *What* is said must be supported by reflection on some set material. First, the recommended literature and then the written work the course members present when reading aloud.

The Role of the Seminar Leader

The most difficult aspect of the dialogue seminar method is undoubtedly that of leading the seminar itself. Leading a dialogue seminar is to be immersed in it. It requires a basic knowledge of how to lead a meeting, and also a comprehensive understanding of the dialogue seminar method. Some knowledge of the subject is also required but, more importantly, an ability to identify where in the dialogue between the students communication fails, and which concepts the students interpret in different ways. One must be sensitive to, and observant of, the times when the conversation suddenly brings clarity to the students, and then be able to lead the session onwards, towards greater depth, clarity and elucidation. A dialogue seminar leader must be able to introduce new concepts that unravel the knots in a dialogue, with the right timing, while also grasping the points individual students put forward, and moving both the group as a whole and the individual group members forwards.[26]

In practice, this is a question of making one's own contributions to the dialogue, well-considered contributions that do not interfere with or disrupt a dialogue when it is at its most intense and vigorous in generating new knowledge and understanding. The nature of these contributions may vary.

- Personal examples, which by their wealth of detail and concrete approach can bring more precision to a dialogue that revolves around something but fails to get to grips with the exact point.[27]
- Analogies that have a bearing on what the dialogue concerns, that may facilitate understanding of complex contexts by demonstrating similarities or differences in a way that enables access to tacit knowledge and experience. An analogy must be carefully considered and perhaps even 'tried-and-tested' in the sense that one knows where it

---

26 In his article 'The Practice of Musical Performance', (Dialoger, 55/2000), Claes Pehrsson describes how a composer (leader) can deliberately create a space for interpretation, allowing the person who performs in a dialogue to express their skill in the performance. Thus, a dialogue can generate quality in performance, creativity and new knowledge for both the person who performs and the person who listens! The analogy to reading texts aloud is clear; this is precisely what theatre is all about.

27 Examples must be presented in an illustrative way if we are to accept them, and we often need to illustrate what we want to show with numerous and varying examples. In the transfer of experience, it is important that the examples are not altered in any way.

will lead and that it will have the intended effect. The analogy must be able to be understood by the course members and also be introduced at exactly the right moment, so that it fits into the dialogue and steers it in the right direction.[28]

- The introduction of understandable metaphors that can build bridges in understanding where complex contexts cannot be developed explicitly in words. As with analogies, metaphors must be well thought-out and tested, and be introduced at the right time and in the appropriate context in the conversation. A metaphor can create recognition and fuel further collective reflection, but it may also, in itself, be a part of the process of creating new knowledge, and be an innovation in the way it is used and connects to the content of the dialogue.[29]

- The introduction of new concepts that the group can adopt and that may unravel complications in a dialogue that is tending to lead into a debate. Concepts that may cover the different viewpoints, perspectives and experience that are represented in the group.

---

28 Analogies are metaphors intended to demonstrate similarities and/or differences. They may be seen as examples to explain the meaning of a metaphor. The role of the analogy: 1) to see similarities between examples/situations, and 2) to see and analyse the differences between examples/situations. Analogies serve to sharpen and focus by illustrating the similarities that are important in an argument, and by observing and understanding the unique through analysing the differences that give precision by showing what is not being addressed. (Cf. Shooting, precision and accuracy – note the analogy.) If we did not recognise the outer extremities, we would not be able to hit the bull's eye – after all, the 'centre' is defined by what surrounds it. This is not an interesting synthesis because it means learning where the centre is without seeing anything around it, i.e. without a comprehensive picture. The synthesis then becomes something that attempts to detach itself from the overall picture. Rather, it is by researching the extremities that we create a better overall picture, and thus know where to aim to score a hit. The analogy supports the narrative of approximation. The analogies that work best are those that are imprecise but hit the mark!

29 Through metaphors we shape new patterns for our knowledge, and are able to express things we had known but could not express. '. . . metaphors create novel interpretation of experience by asking the listener to see one thing in terms of something else . . . and create new ways of experiencing reality' (Donellon, Gray and Bougon, 1986). Richards, described the metaphor as two thoughts about different things supported by a single word or phrase, whose meaning is a result of the interaction between them. 'A needle in a haystack' and 'mushroom woods' are a couple of examples of metaphors that have proved to work well in accurately describing different situations encountered in troubleshooting. One can approach metaphors through reflection. Together, they are the actual carriers of knowledge and constitute the basis for the transfer of tacit knowledge, they allow one to speak indirectly (but not explicitly) about tacit knowledge by addressing it from different perspectives, for example by demonstrating the implications of an action. By giving meaning to articulated tacit knowledge (which is, of course, not in itself tacit) in a specific situation, from which general conclusions can be drawn in a practice. 'Through metaphors, people put together what they know in new ways and begin to express what they know but cannot yet say' (Richards, 1936). Or, to take Richards' definition, '. . . two thoughts of different things . . . supported by a single word, or phrase whose meaning is a result of their interaction.'

– Corrections of misunderstandings by clarifying the message in the reading material or in the texts produced by the participants. This requires the leader to have some knowledge of both the reading material and the authors so that, by referring to other texts, he can provide a more varied picture of an author's aim, the meaning of the concepts used in the period, culture or environment in which the author lived, etc., or perhaps comment on the role of the text in the intellectual debate and the context in which it was written, against which other texts and authors are placed in order to be fully understood, etc.

In other words, the seminar leader must be able to direct the group in its formation of a common inner picture,[30] both in the discussions and in the longer perspective, in the formation of a practice. At the same time, the leader should also be able to give individual group members further guidance based on their various levels of experience and the orientation of their perceptions and experience, by providing the students with carefully selected individual references, advice and steps in the continued process of building knowledge both in the particular subject area and in epistemology. This is done both in real time during the meeting, but also, of course, in the 'minutes' or in personal feedback after the meeting.

As we can see, the full role of the leader is an impossible task. Yet one must have great respect for the importance of this role and also be able to make both essential and reasonable demands of the person who leads the seminar. This in its turn is strongly linked to the purpose and expectations of the exercise, and the students' own progression of knowledge and experience of the method are also important factors.

Writing the Minutes

The minutes from the dialogue seminar have a decisive effect on the way work using the texts, and reflections from the dialogue during the meeting, are processed and can be put to practical use. The minutes, the

---

30 To me, the inner picture is two things. First, there is a kind of plan or idea from the very beginning. As Stephen Coby says: 'You do the work twice'. But second, one may not have solved everything with a plan – but one must know what needs to be solved.

'record of ideas',[31] are the link with further progress in the seminar, as they are the only concrete record (apart from the students' own notes) available for reference and as material that may be processed after the seminar is over. It is often not until the minutes have been written that one suddenly sees the pattern in the subject the seminar revolved around but may not have been able to penetrate. For the student, the minutes are the starting-point for further explorations of knowledge. For the seminar leader, the minutes are a guide to the issues and concepts a subsequent seminar may examine in depth. The minutes do not aim to be an authentic reproduction of the conversation as it actually took place, but strive rather to convey the point of what was said, what each one of the participants wants to express through what he/she said. This requires an attention to the conversation that may be difficult to combine with writing it down. Thus, the minutes try to convey the message, the conclusions and the most important questions and reflections that took place in the course of the dialogue.

Neither can the minutes-taker be the person who leads the seminar: the minutes-taker must be appointed in advance. He/she must be someone with the ability to formulate well-written minutes that everyone understands and in which what everyone said is recorded in the way they said it, i.e. minutes-taking requires respect for the group members even if one does not sympathise with their opinions and statements, or even feel one understands the person in question. Note that the demands made on the minutes-taker limit that person's ability to take an active part in the meeting. Also, make sure that the minutes-taker is appointed well before the seminar, and that he/she is someone who does not need to do the writing assignment (but who should have read the reading material).

---

31 In his Research Programme for Educational Science (KTH, 2000), Bo Göranzon writes, 'When reading and writing are interwoven in this way the students are compelled to reflect. Reflection acts on individual experience and is then shared with the group through reading aloud. Important parts of the conversations that then take place have been processed, and a record is then made of these more distilled conversations in the "minutes of ideas". Different language games are separated out, nuances and differences emerge with a precision that is not possible in an ordinary conversation. In the best case, the students manage to return to a story that is about how a concept is established. When that story becomes visible and accessible for reflection, work takes place in the most vulnerable point in the process of concept formation. The question of how one learned the meaning of a word, through which examples and in which use, has a strong link to certainty in action. If the way to use the word is influenced by the group's dialogue, the language game is changed, and therefore the concept and the deliberate action as well. The "minutes of ideas" are a permanent record of a preliminary course of concept formation.' Note in particular that Göranzon speaks of making the story 'accessible' to reflection.

Maria Hammarén writes that the minutes should perform the following functions:

- to adhere to what we, in Kleist's[32] sense, 'know in a condition'

- initially, to generate a sense of trust in clients/co-workers by presenting the actual meeting place (to go to considerable lengths to give an account of people's views and descriptions so that they recognise what they mean, which is most difficult when one does not feel confident oneself on that point)

- to identify, when reading through the minutes, what one did not catch at the time (Bo and I developed new writing assignments while reading the minutes).

As in all texts, it is important to highlight the drama and maintain the pace (avoiding repetition). An important part of the conversation may need to be emphasised or clarified by developing it, i.e. bringing forward the thoughts that might only be alluded to in what was said – but this must be kept within limits defined by the speaker's horizon, that is to say, when something is not clear, the quotes should be 'evocative'.

In a brief instruction on writing minutes, Maria Hammarén says:

Essentially, I think that at this point you should keep in mind that minutes are written in two stages. First, you make notes, to the extent that time allows, and write them out. The next stage is to go through your minutes 'with pen in hand' and mark important sections. Then write out the minutes again, putting in lines such as, 'The conversation then shifted to . . .'. Here, use your second reading of your minutes to express more clearly WHAT you are talking about, that is to say, try to structure more clearly the thoughts that actually came up. If you look at the minutes I have written, you will see that I also use them to clarify input from Bo and others, i.e. I reinforce what I identify as giving energy (or being provocative in some way). This latter is the difficult part. How does one raise the discussions to an epistemological instead of a socio-psychological level, a turn the discussions may easily take?

---

32 In her book *Ledtråd i förvandling* (*Clues in Reflection*) (Dialoger, Stockholm 1999, note 113) Maria Hammarén refers to an essay by Magnus Florin, 'Samtal pågår hos Wislawa Szymborska' (*Current Conversations at Wislawa Szymborska's*) from *Artes* no. 1, Stockholm 1997, in which Florin reproduces some of Heinrich von Kleist's thoughts, taken in their turn from 'Världens bästa essäer i urval' (selected essays by Magnus von Platen, *Natur och Kultur*, Stockholm, 1961).

Another point in my minutes is that I do not simply reproduce what is said in the form of direct quotes. I vary what is said by sometimes summarising, and sometimes using reported speech: 'Tomas explained that was something they were not normally involved in at . . .'. I do this to make the minutes easier to read, quite simply by varying the presentation. The point is that the minutes should be easy to assimilate. This is also why I often used phrases such as 'Some pauses in the discussion here' or the like. Otherwise, the word 'minutes' may easily make people expect either a comprehensive record or a decision-oriented report – it is important to make it clear that the minutes are an attempt to HOLD ON TO what is said, in the form of notes.[33]

Concluding Remarks

It should be clear from the above that leading a dialogue seminar is no trivial matter. The leader must have completed several seminars before he/she has acquired the necessary insight into the method, and the leader should have carried out a course, preferably some form of graduate studies in the subject area in question under the supervision of someone who is very familiar with matters relating to the skill of system engineers and epistemology. In Combitech Systems we have developed for this purpose a series of courses that train, in stages, staff members in the roles required to lead and carry out dialogues. This has proved to be essential to prevent the method from becoming eroded by applying it in a simplified way, without the necessary insights and understanding of its more profound purposes and strengths. It is when one believes that one has understood what the dialogue seminar is about that one has the greatest reason to ask what one has not understood.

Maria Hammarén again:

Work in the group may be described as language work that transfers interest from the lexical meaning of words to their actual use. In this work, it is essential to emphasise examples and stories, i.e. to connect language use to concrete situations that are capable of working analogically. Not all stories or examples do so, but some stories/examples are paradigmatic, that is to say they have considerable power to act as reminders of our own experience of *similar* situations.

To emphasise the importance of concentration is to affirm the work method of analogy. Analogy is dependent on being able to generate a shift: from one

---

33 Maria Hammarén's little 'instruction' on writing minutes was produced at the request of 'The Gang of Nine', 1997.

example to another. It addresses differences and creates understanding, some kind of similarity. It is dependent on its aesthetical form: it must, just as with the metaphor, be to the point, appropriate or striking. The concentration in a group of seminar participants can capture an example that would have fallen flat if it were 'just text'. The reading, the silence, the pitch and emphasis of the voice can endow an example with considerable power, even if the author is not – an author.

It is important that the material the group must have in its work, introduced through lectures and texts, ensures that tried-and-tested paradigmatic examples are included. The Skill and Technology researchers have worked for a long time on developing 'paradigmatic' examples from the perspective of their research interest. These examples have been taken from the history of ideas, literature, and case studies.

The analogy is in essence a phenomenon that is parallel to the generalisation, in the sense that it has the form of a result. But while the generalisation 'completes' the circle around what must, at least in the field of the humanities, be uncompleted, the analogy lives on in the uncompleted. Ideally, it should act as a working example, an aid in arranging reality in the encounter with the new.

The work in the group is a stage in improving the possibilities for communication between people who do not meet on a daily basis, and where words are therefore not tested in close contact with action.

A dialogue seminar requires preparation, but to carry out a dialogue seminar hosted by an external client also requires that the thinking on the meaning and purpose of the seminar be integrated, otherwise it may easily be regarded as rather muddled and poorly-prepared. Carrying out a dialogue seminar at a client's requires the client to have a certain maturity that by no means everyone has. Whether or not to run a seminar or integrate the idea is a decision that must be given serious consideration, and it may sometimes be better to withdraw until the client has developed a more mature attitude and a more humble desire to learn something new.

And finally, a reflection on the method, which I once wrote at an early stage in my own process of maturing (April 1997).

Reading with pen in hand is actually a matter of finding a tempo in one's reading, but by far the most important factor is learning to listen to one's inner voice. To take the time to write down what it is saying. For me, this particular factor has been an insight into myself, that I have begun to listen to my own reactions to the text. Sometimes because I have arrived at a standpoint, and sometimes because a question has been raised, 'exactly what does this mean?', or perhaps 'but if it was like this instead, what would that mean?'. Sometimes because you have suddenly understood something you immediately wanted to put into your own words. And sometimes by being reminded about something you have experienced yourself and may see in a new perspective, in the light of what you are reading. Putting all that straight down on paper is an experience. There may be a lot of unconnected thoughts, yet they may still help me reinforce the feeling of what I have read or learned. But just as often there may be more extensive insights or, indeed, ideas that I can apply directly in my work. Sometimes I have arrived at an understanding of something I took part in and experienced many years ago, and of which only now I have understood the benefit, the point, or equally often, the reason why something failed. The thoughts that were written down I used later to help me write my own texts or stories in the texts produced for a dialogue seminar but, equally, they have had an impact on what I have done in my role as consultant, and what I have written in my work on system engineers' handbooks and process descriptions, for example. Thus, these descriptions have been complemented with more explanatory sections; for example, to place the complex of rules in a larger perspective. The stories I create from my notes are used in dialogue seminars for reading aloud, and for collective reflection in the group. But the notes themselves are of little or no value to others – not until they have been developed into stories. For myself, however, when I re-read them they become a way to re-create the feeling I had when I read the original text for the first time. It goes without saying that the texts we read in this project – which were, of course, carefully chosen for their relevance to the concepts and themes we addressed in our dialogues – made a contribution as well. They are the prelude to one's reflections; they provide the inspiration and trigger the entire internal thought process. Now I still read these texts from the kind of literature to which the door was opened, and that would appear to be enough for a lifetime if one so wished, with the whole of classical philosophy as a foundation, together with debate articles and newly-written research articles relevant to my professional field of system engineering, or essays on the subjects of professional knowledge, experience, dialogue and reflection.

Part 3

CASE STUDIES

8 Maximum Complexity

Christer Hoberg

1. On Work Methods in Systems Development

As computers and built-in 'intelligence' become increasingly widespread and complex parts of product development, methods and technologies have been developed over time to support the work of systems development.

The complex of problems associated with developing software in major projects was identified many years ago. As functionality requirements for products increased, methods and instruments were developed to create understanding and order in these ever-bigger systems.

Systems Developer – a New Profession

The profession of systems developer is a relatively new one, and it has no established work practice. It is largely true that a new work method has been developed for each new project. There are some types of problem that systems developers intensify: a lot of people have to work at the same time on a large and complex problem. At the initial stage, many possible solutions present themselves, but the end result of the work must be a logical, coherent, consistent and correct solution. This has meant that systems developers cannot directly apply methods used in other professions.

In the process of developing standards for descriptive language and models, we have created an interface with our own challenge, to describe the complex problem step by step, and can begin to look beyond our own professional group to see how we can handle the overall issue, how to create a holistic view and how to find the path forward to a good solution. We may be unique in our application, but when it comes to working on problem-solving, others have gone before us.

A Holistic View Cannot be Delegated

If we consider the issue of how to generate understanding of the way a system is to be built, we find there have been many different approaches over the years. Should we begin from the top or the bottom? Examples of methods include top-down programming, extreme programming, iterative development, etc., but none have proved to be the one true faith. However the problem is tackled, no path automatically leads to a good system. One has to create one's own understanding of the problem.

A holistic view cannot be delegated to an instrument.

Let us move away from the world of systems development and look at work methods for problem-solving in other contexts.

The philosopher Hans Larsson (1862–1944) offers perspectives on work methods in scientific research, where, on the one hand, clarity can be achieved (a synthesis created) by collecting and having a good command of scientific material, but . . .

> This is, however, only one side of the development we have in the current discussion on the progression from material that has already been studied, and its details clarified, to a synthesis. Just as often the point of departure may be a predetermined synthesis, the content of which must be analysed. In one case, the approach may be compared to travelling through a country and, little by little, forming an overall picture of it; in the other case, from some vantage point we already have the general configurations of the country, the particulars of which we must then adjust by examining them point by point. Analysis and synthesis are two currents that are constantly meeting, like one thread in a fabric meeting another.

Descartes' Four Precepts

Efficiency is often considered a function of working methodically and according to plan. Of course, we have a problem in facing a task when we do not really know whether or not (and how) it may be technically possible to solve. René Descartes' (1596–1650) '*Discourse on the Method of Rightly Conducting the Reason . . .*' gives us a good approach to a general work method that may also be applied in systems development:

> The first precept was never to accept anything for true . . . – that is to say, carefully to avoid precipitancy and prejudice, and to comprise nothing more in my judgement than what was presented to my mind so clearly and distinctly as to exclude all ground of doubt.

The second, to divide each of the difficulties under examination into as many parts as possible, and as might be necessary for its adequate solution.

The third, to conduct my thoughts in such order that, by commencing with objects the simplest and easiest to know, I might ascend by little and little, and, as it were, step by step, to the knowledge of the more complex; assigning in thought a certain order even to those objects which in their own nature do not stand in a relation of antecedence and sequence.

And the last, in every case to make enumerations so complete, and reviews so general, that I might be assured that nothing was omitted.

Both Hans Larsson and René Descartes describe parts of work methods that to a great extent capture individual work. In systems development we must also weave in a process of interplay by creating a common picture, understanding, in a group.

The sections below describe how we at Combitech Systems worked on the question of the skill of systems developers, and on an approach to problem-solving methods that are applicable to systems development but that can certainly provide inspiration in other areas.

A Walk Through the Landscape of Skill

How we progressed!

When we, nine course members from Combitech Systems, Bo Göranzon and Maria Hammarén, met on 7 January 1997 to start a development project for learning organisations, our point of departure was that we wanted to test the dialogue seminar method with a view to improving our professional skills. We had identified a clear need to find new approaches to skill improvement for systems developers. In engineering, a knowledge of mathematics and logic is important for creating models, but more is needed.

The Dialogue Seminar method has a clearly-stated structure that includes reading, writing and dialogue. We had the rather brutal practical experience that there was essential knowledge that we could neither transfer nor describe. This was the knowledge we wanted to capture.

We began by testing a method, but we moved more towards attempting to understand what skill consisted of. Every time we thought we were getting close to the core of skill, it seemed to slip through our fingers.

In the course of the first year we made an in-depth examination of the central issue in development work, how to solve a task or problem.

Intuition, rhythm, complexity, the inner picture and creativity were terms that, after reading Harry Martinson and Montaigne, were filled with examples from our own experience and that of others.

We were quick to link the question of problem-solving to existing software development work methods. Not until then did we really understand that the question of skill would have numerous aspects: it would not converge to produce a single answer, but diverge to produce more questions. *The question of method* divided itself into the understanding of the type of formal support we need to formulate our own results, the dialogue with ourselves and the models we create in the individual task, and the support we need to describe these ideas and pass them on to others.

When new aspects came into the picture, we also saw another difference. Quite soon we were able to express ourselves and describe examples, dilemmas and experiences relating to individual problem-solving. When we addressed the issue of conveying ideas, visions and principles to others, it became clear that we had far fewer concepts, structures and analogies to use, we had left the area of traditional engineering.

We needed a different language and a different way of thinking; perhaps an author could help us move forwards?

2. Experiencing New Connections

In May 1998 the course members from Combitech Software made a trip to Iceland to meet an author who reflected on his writing. Einar Màr Gudmundsson had already taken part in a Dialogue Seminar in Stockholm in 1997, for which he prepared by writing an essay, 'Who Are Healthy and Who Are Not' for the Dialoger journal number 39/96, *Metaphors and Analogies*. Gudmundsson was given the Nordic Literature Award for his novel, *Angels of the Universe*, on which the essay in Dialoger is based.

As preparation for our meeting with Einar Màr Gudmundsson, all 120 course members read the article in Dialoger and the manuscript of a work in progress by Einar Màr on writing, entitled 'Mindship of Words'.

Although a great deal separates the artistic professions from engineering, in our view the creative parts of the work, building up the inner picture that is supported by details and experience, share the same assumptions in many respects. Our ability to see solutions beyond what can be arrived at by calculation is a skill we can train by stimulating the ability to take analogies from our own and others' experience.

To enable us, who work in a relatively 'young' profession, to build up a professional culture with the support of experience from other occupations, we must understand what it is that separates and what it is that unites. In many respects, the circumstances that apply to an author are completely different to those that apply to us in systems design. Further, the work of an author requires different work methods. When we examine in depth how thought and reflection requires support and how knowledge and creativity are created, we can see this as more clear and unencumbered in a different occupational group.

It is important that we create understanding for the creative part of the profession. This is an aspect often overshadowed by mathematics and rationality, but on the other hand, it is the most important factor in the creation of new solutions. The possibilities of finding similarities between authors and computer engineers aside, there is a conviction that it is possible to achieve something more when 100 computer engineers travel from Sweden to Iceland to meet Einar Màr. It may lie in finding the difference, placing oneself in the middle of the different way of looking at things, and moving beyond the logic that is our security but also that keeps us captive; the logic that requires each step to follow from the previous step. Instead, we are invited to study the logic to be found in the art of writing, to master the multiplicity of sources of inspiration and analogies, to 'strike' when the time is right, to be confident in one's command of analogical thinking. By looking at the difference when it is placed in a system, in a whole, one sees it as more than an anomaly in one's own way of seeing things: suddenly, a new area comes into focus in one's own experience, as when we change the distance setting on a camera.

Storytelling is a subject that creates energy, perhaps precisely because we are active in the profession where all rationalisations attempt to create precise, uniform and correct documents that will contain the whole truth, attempts that do not meet with success. Everyone knows that the projection of thoughts and ideas requires something else, but, captured in the demand for 'good engineering practice', it evades description. By taking authorship as a starting point, we can make our thinking more unfettered, and deepen the possibilities of storytelling.

When we discuss the way systems architecture is designed in a system, we have seen that stories about the background to the project, the sequence of events and its problems, have provided knowledge that was necessary for us to understand why a systems architecture had that particular structure. There is no single correct answer, but rather a large number of different ways of designing the system that could find successful defenders. It is therefore not interesting to examine quantified comparisons between different alternative solutions with the benefit of hindsight. Rather, what adds knowledge is the storytelling about the situations in which the decisions were taken. From which earlier experiences were analogies taken? What elements in the situation attracted attention? What did one feel confident about, and where was there doubt? Design decisions are taken by people with their own specific backgrounds of experience and their own personal views of the situation.

The strong connection between personal experience and decisions renders all efforts to describe decisions from a general perspective redundant. On the other hand, by making experience visible, the descriptions of the decision-making situations help us make our eyes see the same things.

Einar Màr points out the importance of reading in the process of improving the ability to make one's own experience visible: 'Through other authors, you find yourself. You cannot teach yourself to be an author by means of academic speculation. The stories come from people, authors take the stories from life from themselves, but it is through the power of literature that they can formulate them'.

The modelling language and tools we have to build systems models in our profession are like a lantern that shines a beam from one direction only. They are formal, and cannot express what cannot be given a formal description. How does this affect the process of thinking?

Precisely that language would restrict the way we think directs us into a complex of questions about methods in systems development. The methods and language of modelling we use is often described as universal in the sense that they can be used to describe all types of system. In this view is a risk that is difficult to describe. Can we be thought up by a method? Does a modelling language do our thinking? We can find the answers to these questions by examining the way we work. We do not begin by thinking through the way a system is to be built, and then describing it. What we think is sharpened in the description, which in its turn creates new thoughts. We get a dialogue between the thought and its formulation. A dialogue that is, of course, governed by what is possible to formulate. This opens up the method question at a different level. Not methods that have been developed to (methodically) solve a problem under given conditions, but work methods that attempt to describe how the work of creative thinking is done.

'Do you use a method when you write?' was the simple, but difficult, question put to Einar Màr.

'You can only see the method as time goes by', answers Einar Màr. 'If you apply a method when you write, it will, I think, be mechanical. But you can certainly find a structure afterwards. A good novel is structured, but no-one can explain the way the imaginative work is done. You create links between two different phenomena that had no logical connection. For me, the narrative is a journey into uncertainty. The concept changes while the work is in progress'.

This work method, having the concept open for a longer period of time, we recognise from our own work when new systems must be designed, but also from descriptions of the systems architect's work, which constantly explores suggestions and has ideas tested in the process of concretisation and design that in its turn provides new knowledge and new ideas.

This is, then, a method in itself for the work of thinking that requires a particular outlook on its own result, a process of working and observing at the same time. A process of building up understanding.

Gudmundir Gudmundsson, Einar Már's brother, a cancer researcher at Sweden's Karolinska Institute, sees experimentation from this viewpoint:

> I always argue in favour of the experiment. There are no mistakes, only results that we may not understand. You often meet the attitude that, 'we don't need to test, we already know the answer'. The truth is we know very little.

This attitude to mistakes is taken a step further by Einar Màr, who says:

> You ask about negative results. I allow myself a certain amount of fatalism, but not to the extent that I wait on inspiration. One must work towards inspiration. In this work process there is no difference between good days and bad days. The negative is essential if the positive is to be achieved. You have to begin to work: if you aren't making any progress, then read a book. And suddenly the carousel will start. It is like a funfair.

But how, then, should one look at the work process: the way ideas, reality and experience are woven together to become a thought, the building-up of an inner picture? Is it built up in some sequence in which there is a progression from one element to another?

> I would not describe the work process in preparation for 'The Angels of the Universe' by saying that I began by doing research and then read fiction to stimulate my imagination, and then even later I began to write. The book was a long time coming. I knew the circumstances from my brother, I had written short stories on the subject. But suddenly – you have a presentiment within yourself – you know you are going to write. It takes time for the voice to emerge. And then comes the tone in what you're going to write, and then you go to medical conferences etc. If I have to study psychology and medical science, then that, quite simply, is what I do,

says Einar Màr.

This interplay between reality and fantasy, between detailed knowledge and the feeling for the whole is also described in 'The Mindship of Words', which contains the following section:

> Where does art come from? From desolate lands, from the rain, fog, from the grey, from the ordinariness of every day. The closer the artist comes to the core of reality, the higher the spirit soars. Fish and bird, fin and wing, and somewhere in between is man. His imagination is linked to reality with ties that cannot be loosened. And vice versa; in art, there is no reality without the power of imagination.
>
> The foundation of creativity is knowledge of reality – it is not floating in the air. This brings into focus the insight that the computer systems architect must have detailed knowledge of conditions and solutions; they become the basic elements in what his thinking builds up.

When Einar Màr commented on the question of how he knows that he is writing the 'right book', he says, 'When I have found the tone, I become a slave to the story', and, 'It is never the "right" book – a bubble of air or works that crystallise out as classics, you don't know which until afterwards. Laxness' notes on *The Light of the World* tell us that his intentions and the first draft of his book are completely from the end result. One writes, over and over again, but something is missing. After two years, a completely new element comes in. That is how you work, layer after layer'.

From confidence comes uncertainty, from uncertainty comes confidence. When is it time to 'strike' and make a start? To find your rhythm and be able to act with confidence and to know when you can no longer wait, never faltering in the conviction that you are doing the right thing, and at the same time convinced that on reflection you will see that there were other opportunities.

In the course of this dialogue between the engineers at Combitech Systems and the author there emerged an understanding of storytelling and the role of portrayal in building knowledge that gave us new ways to approach the question of how we should deepen that part of skill which deals with passing on visions and ideas.

Taking storytelling as the point of departure, we met at a company conference the following year to go deeper into the issue of understanding the skill of a systems architect. At that time the degree to which the sequence of events and results were controlled by other aspects than the technical became clear.

This was underscored when some of us attended a seminar on the science fiction author H.G. Wells. All at once we were struck by the idea that it was not predictions or forecasts but stories, shaped by visions, that had a strong influence on many people's thinking, and thereby also on the advance of technology.

The understanding that came from this 'long shot' was that we must have the courage to venture into new areas, to examine them in depth and to be receptive to alternative viewpoints. Having acquired this knowledge, we are then able to see connections with our own skill. We gain understanding of our own skills through an understanding of other skills. We have now made advances in creating long-term perspectives in this work, and have set up the Combitech Learning Lab, in which we place all internal knowledge development. This includes both formal knowledge in traditional education, and also the transfer of experience in all areas by using dialogue seminars, for example.

We also link to the Combitech Learning Lab the transfer of experience from consultant assignments, where we have found ways of dealing with situations for which we used to have no tools. We move forward step by step, and have learned to use the Dialogue Seminar method to deal with, for example, the following.

- A medical company developing a new product, and where everyone learns that 'easy to use' has a completely different meaning for different people. The act of creating a deeper dialogue avoids the trap of agreeing on the word 'easy' and stopping there. Instead, progress is made in creating understanding of other people's aspects and experiences.
- A telecommunications company that is to transfer knowledge between two teams, and that develops metaphors in its dialogue. These metaphors become a tool for the creation of understanding outside the technical models.
- A motor manufacturer that is to gain experience from a completed project begins to give examples from the project, instead of formulating generalities. As the result, the course members acquire knowledge that makes them act differently in their next project.

While we are building up a structure in the enterprise to pass on knowledge using the methods and concepts we have learned, the journey through the landscape of skill continues. We are constantly finding new places where the light falls on our experience from a different direction, but a good guide is essential.

3. In-depth Discussions of Work Methods – the Path to Understanding Maximum Complexity

Following the meeting with Einar Már Gudmundsson, one of the questions that produced energy was about work methods and their relationship to building up understanding. One of the dialogue seminars that began to tackle this question was held by a group from our Stockholm office. The following is taken from the minutes of that seminar.

It is eight o'clock in the evening of February 12th, and we have gathered in the conference room at the hotel in Åre. Mikael and I have attended the first Combitech Software dialogue seminar project for 15 months now, and it is time to test the concept on a new group. The day has been full of activities and now we are to hold a dialogue seminar on the use of methods. After a long journey and a full day of conference and skiing, I do not think the discussions will be very energetic. Tomas is ill. He was not well when we left Stockholm, but hoped to get better on the way up. Although he has spent the day in bed, he is no better. But suddenly he arrives. He has taken some aspirin and wants to be as active as he can. All eight participants are well prepared and have read Peter Brödner's 'The Two Cultures of Engineering', Stephen Toulmin's 'Method Issues in the Human Use of Technology'. Everyone has completed the written assignment, 'My Experience of the Use of Methods in Systems Development' and some tension begins to be felt in the air. It is time to play our cards – will they be good enough?

'We must have a secretary', I say. 'Yes, yes' says Micke, confirming that he has agreed to take the minutes. He attended the first series of seminars and knows what is involved – that he must be constantly alert and interpret, take notes, summarise, avoid being drawn into the debate but keep an objective stance.

Johan begins by reading his text, and everyone follows his written paper. He points out the different factors that make the method good, is critical of far too much work on analysing demands, wants more prototypes and mentions the danger of a software architect who does not have enough knowledge about details. Tomas, who has worked in a research department for formal methods, adds that prototypes can be used to test performance at an early stage. The others agree. The group goes on to discuss the architect. 'The architect must be strong, and know what he is doing', says Tomas. Then Johan says, 'It is easy for the architect to stop acting as a mentor and begin to overrule people.' Now here comes the energy. Two statements that are almost complete opposites, and that are certainly based on concrete experiences that each member of the group is thinking of. Some examples are put forward, there are more contributions, and then Tomas says: 'The role of the architect is often too strong in the organisation, and he may be difficult to put in his place'. No-one reacts to the fact that this is almost a complete contradiction of his earlier statement, and neither does he. He did not change his viewpoint, he simply broadened his view to include other aspects from the dialogue, a dialogue that did not turn into a debate. 'This is where it is good to take minutes', I think. 'In dialogue the participants inspire one another, but they do not remember these rejoinders, neither their own, nor others.'

We move on to the texts from Anders, Tomas and Odd, and the dialogue begins to take up the same questions, that the methods are not fully comprehensive, nor do they give opportunities for communication, that they must provide opportunities for creativity, etc. It feels as if the participants' experiences begin to find one another, and the participants refer to one another's examples. They are circling round, but I feel there is something they are failing to get to. I look at the clock – ten-thirty pm – 'We should bring this to a close soon because we won't get any further today'. Then Kjell reads his text. He has fifteen years' experience from Erikssons and has used both function-oriented methods from AXE and object-oriented methods such as Objectory. He points to the problems associated with the different viewpoints, and as he has many years' experience everyone listens attentively to what he says. In an attempt to get to the core of the matter, Odd says: 'It is interesting that with your experience, you are critical of methods'.

Then Kjell answers, 'It depends how they are used. I want a method that structures what I have arrived at. Object-orientation describes how to carry out analyses and produce examples of applications, but when one reaches the difficult areas, producing objects and creating systems, they are supposed to be simply pulled out of a hat in some magical way. That is where the difficulty lies, it is here that experience comes into play and you get no help from the method here'.

There is a moment's silence. Somehow there was nothing more to say, that is just the way it is. We were standing on a new platform. The evening's dialogue had created something that made Kjell's answer a message for everyone.

Suddenly a new discussion begins, at a different level and with greater concentration and purposefulness, on the software architect and his role in the project. What does he have to know? In the discussion earlier in the day, Johan had said that he was critical of the method developed for the Swedish Power Board where they had begun with an empty hole that was filled with details. Now the discussion is circling around *the way to reach a level at which the whole can be seen*. This work must be completed before the work on the component parts of the assignment can be controlled. 'How does the systems architect build up an overall view?' – and it was here that Kjell gave the answer. By first making a detailed study of the conditions, and then by drawing on experience, seeing a way forward. 'I believe that is how an architect works when designing a house', says Key, 'You know that what you draw is possible to build: many of our projects start with an overall picture that we do not know will be practicable. *Other methods have to be found.*' We continued to discuss a working model in which the project was not allowed to progress to the design stage until it was known that the architecture meets the requirements. Suddenly it is midnight. Everyone had become so involved in this formulation of a new way of working that they had forgotten the time. Now there is a common view that is recorded in the minutes, but most importantly, that resides with the participants in the discussion.

As we gather our papers together I feel we are on the right track, that we are beginning to create a way of working to develop skills. At the same time I understand why it took ten years to come up with it: the hard work needed to gain new perspectives by reading, writing, listening and reflecting makes people prefer to look elsewhere.

Seeing the Overall Picture

At the seminar reported above, the question of an overall picture came up. That experience and knowledge are needed to see the overall picture is evident if one notes the way designers with different experience react to the task of creating an overall picture. Those who have no experience they can relate to often want a method that gives rules on the basis of which one can, without making a decision oneself, arrive at the 'right' solution. It is often difficult to understand that an overall picture cannot be forced into being by using a method.

To ask an experienced designer how he has arrived at the solution he proposes is like asking someone how they know a strawberry is red. You simply see it! What is unimportant in the conditions and demands retreats into the background and the important aspects come to the fore. The situation is obvious. It seems that an experienced person possesses a wealth of comparative material.

But when one sees a picture of a solution, a different aspect of the lack of experience may emerge: one becomes convinced of the excellence of one's solution, and one is eager to test it. Then there is a real risk that the analysis of the solution will be faulty. Important aspects are forgotten. Experienced designers speak of a 'calm' in the work. A calm that one has to struggle to achieve in order to allow insights to occur. To achieve this calm people must rely on their ability and be sure they are on the right track: their experience gives them a good 'view ahead'.

An experienced person also knows that he must have his solution tested by others who have different experience that will give different perspectives. He also knows that this will take time. And since the solution was produced without using any method, other people cannot be taken through the stages of this process. It can be described, and it can be explained in a methodical way. However, others must gain an understanding of it in the same way as understanding occurs in oneself, intuitively. This too takes time. As Lars Lundqvist put it in a dialogue seminar on intuition we ran at the Malmö office, 'One must learn to keep a check on oneself'.

Methods as Support

At this same seminar we went deeper into the view of methods and the help they give in producing models of the system. Key Hyckenberg said, 'A model in a method must be created, not generated'. This statement contains two important points.

Firstly, it is only models that are produced at each stage. Reality always consists of more. It is the intellectual process that must be kept consistent throughout the process: models do not make up the whole, although they may reflect large parts of the whole.

Secondly, the models are created at each stage by means of decisions, by the designer seeing models that were developed at earlier stages, and weaving these together with reality and experience.

This is not a question of data transformation or generation.

The models are a way of bringing order and structure to what the designer creates: they are a way of creating mental control.

Taking this as a starting point, we had a number of lively discussions in seminars on different aspects of the introduction and use of models.

This question is a central one, because it is virtually impossible to carry through large and complex projects without models that give the kind of support that allows control of the logic. But this does not mean that it is the models that were developed that are the main carriers of knowledge throughout the project. Continuity between the various stages of the work process must reside in the knowledge of the designers. The picture of what is to be designed: support for the design decisions to be taken, is far more complex.

More than models are needed to enable this to be conveyed to others.

In this perspective the most important questions in the introduction and use of methods are both whether the method assists the designer in a particular assignment in a way that allows him to gain mental control of his *problems*, and also whether the method will create a model that will help him communicate the knowledge he has created.

People with little experience have a resistance to the use of methods because they fail to see what they are supposed to describe. The methods give no help in doing what one cannot do: seeing the solution.

4.   A Method – Disorder, Order, Complexity

Taking as a starting point the dialogue in Combitech Systems and with Descartes, Hans Larsson and Einar Már Gudmundsson, we can begin to formulate an approach to a method for problem-solving.

Building a new computer system requires extensive intellectual and creative work. Methods and tools offer support in this work, but this does not mean that they create any knowledge.

In order to use methods and tools we must have an understanding of the process of thinking required in a project, and how methods and tools can support it. To build up skill relating to the use of methods, we have to begin by understanding the process of thinking: what takes place in a project?

We need a model to which we can relate when we are carrying on a dialogue about the reality; that is to say, what stage a project has reached, what the problem is, what we will do. We also need this model to be able to describe what we want to achieve at different stages and with the methods used and action taken in a project.

We frequently use general development models as a basis for planning and for establishing what kind of work result is to be achieved at different stages of the project. To create understanding of the development model's relationship to the way the picture of the system is built up and transferred, and also to explain deviations from the general development model, a model is needed for the thinking process.

We have begun to discern a preliminary outline of such a model from the dialogue seminars we have had. At Combitech Software's first in-house dialogue seminars with staff from our Stockholm office we agreed to adopt a common view on how we should work: 'Beginning with a detailed examination of the conditions and then, by drawing on our experience, identifying a path forwards...– many of our projects start with a picture of the whole that we don't know will last – one has to find different models [for the process of thinking]'.

Intuition, Methodical Work and Discursive Thinking

Intuition and complexity are among the points of departure in the model we are trying to develop.

From its beginnings, a development project is made up of a complex collection of components: customer requirements, experience, new technical possibilities and information about competitors. From these components, successful projects create a common and coherent picture of the way the work should proceed.

How, then, does this complete picture come into being? Sometimes the answer is, 'through intuition'. Then what is intuition? Is it something we can rely on? Can we practice and perfect it?

We thought we were on an interesting track when we read the philosopher Hans Larsson's book, *Intuition*, from 1892. Hans Larsson calls a thought process that examines an object or argument step by step and gains insight into its component parts before the whole picture discursive – a methodical work process. He calls the opposite thought process intuitive – when one sees a solution without any deliberate thinking.

> ... intuition; ... the act is the same, whether it is a poet who, in the moment of inspiration sees life suddenly lit up as if by a bolt of lightning, or a researcher to whom the depths of life are exposed for an equally brief instant, only to be hidden again just as suddenly ... (Hans Larsson, *Intuition*).

It is important to establish that there is an intuitive component in the work of systems development. Otherwise, we could not understand how to use methods that appear to be incomplete. This was what Kjell expressed at our seminar in Åre when he said:

> Object orientation describes how to carry out analyses and produce examples of applications, but when one faces the difficult areas, to produce objects and create systems, then they are supposed to be simply pulled out of a hat in some magical way. This is where the difficulty lies, it is here that experience comes into play, and we get no help from the method here.

But methodical work provides a different kind of support. It retains the knowledge that emerges through intuition.

We use both these work approaches, intuitive and methodical, in successful systems development, and the skill lies in the ability to alternate between the two, in being able to use the intuitive process to create new knowledge, and the discursive process for critical comparative evaluations. They become interwoven so that the discursive process in its turn opens the door for the intuitive process.

Two processes are to be followed to gain clarity about the role and position of intuition in thinking...In the one case we proceed as though we were wandering through a country, gradually forming a complete picture of it, while in the other case we already have, from some vantage point, the general configurations of the country, to which we must suit the individual components, point by point (Hans Larsson, *Intuition*).

New knowledge is created through intuitive work. Methodical work can do no more than make clear the truth implicit in the method. The choice of method is made with an understanding of what truth has to be clarified.

It may be noted that in the process of thinking there is no equivalent to what in systems development is called the waterfall method, i.e. that one begins by creating an [empty] hole which is gradually refined or filled until the knowledge of the component parts is reached.

The picture of the whole in systems development is created by an intuitive process, which has been preceded by a work process in which sufficient knowledge of the component parts is created in various ways. But there is also a process of selection in the information here. Due weight is given, with the benefit of experience, to what one feels is important. The connection to the level of 'skilled' and 'expert' in Dreyfus's model of the way skill develops over time is clear.

Intuition is a part of skill. When we examine this concept in greater depth, we will certainly see that it divides into new concepts that describe the ability to see problems in projects, to gather essential information to make cost estimates, to be able to produce a good systems architecture, etc.

On Complexity

We use complexity as a criterion for how much meaning a statement contains, but this is more than a question of the volume of information. Rather, meaning is derived from the information that has been filtered out.

This filtering takes place because one cannot connect or relate the information to the complex whole. Complexity needs time to develop, time in which order is created and information is filtered out.

Great complexity has great depth, but less surface.

This kind of complexity is not the same as information complexity or algorithmic complexity.

The Principle of the Work Method

As a starting point for a dialogue on how the inner picture of the project emerges, is passed on and becomes a reality, we have taken a model inspired by B. Huberman, T. Hogg and C. Bennet.

At the beginning of work on the development project there is information and knowledge taken from a number of different sources. There is experience from development work on similar applications, experience from users, knowledge of the components and subsystems one may use, and knowledge of the market and competitors.

All this disorganised knowledge and information must be compiled to give a picture of a system that may then be designed and put into operation.

We progress from disorder to order. On the way, we reach a point between order and disorder where the inner picture is at maximum complexity.

Development Work – the Upwards Path

Descartes' description of his work method is one starting-point.

> The first precept was never to accept anything for true ... – that is to say, carefully to avoid precipitance and prejudice, and to comprise nothing more in my judgement than what was presented to my mind so clearly and distinctly as to exclude all ground of doubt.
>
> The second, to divide each of the difficulties under examination into as many parts as possible, and as might be necessary for its adequate solution.

In the first work we have two important questions: what does one want to develop, and what can one develop? To get a comprehensive picture of how to carry on this work, one must let it come into being.

We have used intuition as a term that describes when a comprehensive picture forms. We cannot force this picture to develop, but we can create the conditions in which it can form. Important cornerstones in creating these conditions are demands, prototypes, performance tests and familiarising oneself with the background material, even if only a small part has been formulated. The dialogue between different experiences must be given its place and its time.

The comprehensive picture cannot be produced by decisions, but dialogue creates the conditions in which it can come into being.

Tomas Sandén examines this in depth in a text for a dialogue seminar: 'On Demand Specifications':

> If we are faced with building a system we have not built before, it is difficult to acquire a feeling [use one's intuition/instinct] for an abstract functional demand level: we have no prior experience of this functionality.
>
> If, on the other hand, we can go into the system through design, it is likely that, as experienced systems designers, by means of a general feeling for the way systems should be structured, begin to identify design elements/system components similar to those we have designed before, and thus have a feeling for. We then begin to relate to a 'fuzzy' picture of what the system must do, and in this process we also find design elements that are new to us. The point is that we can then apply old knowledge to narrow down to what is actually new, at the same time gaining a feeling for the way the new elements fit into a whole: the design picture is the bridge we use to be able to apply our knowledge to the new problem.
>
> We have to build landscapes in which to wander, in which we feel reasonably at home, and where we can see the topology as something more than a great maze or a tangle of yarn.

The diagram in Figure 1 shows that by moving to the right one can create greater order. This is done by producing better basic materials, for example, by describing experience in detail, carrying on a dialogue with groups of people with different experience of models of proposed solutions, by testing solutions, failing, and then trying again.

Figure 1—Creating order

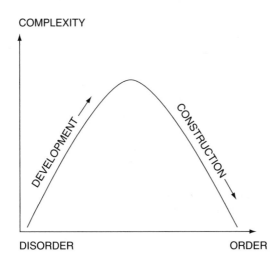

Much of this work has routines and is done methodically, which creates a basis for moving higher, to the next platform, that emerges though intuition.

By going deeper into the [right] details, one creates the conditions for solving the problem of the task. The work moves in stages towards greater and greater complexity, a more profound view of what one is to do in a process that filters out non-essential information. At the same time, one makes connections between different parts of the information and the assessment of it: for example, links between experience and suggestions, between demands on the system and knowledge of technical solutions, between demands for a completion time and the experience the group has.

The view becomes deeper as one makes syntheses and summaries of pieces of information, through intuition, that are then linked to one another. One brings together experience, information and syntheses to form a system of judgement, or as René Descartes expressed it in his Discourse on the Method:

> The third (precept), to conduct my thoughts in such order that, by commencing with objects the simplest and easiest to know, I might ascend by little and little, and, as it were, step by step, to the knowledge of the more complex; assigning in thought a certain order even to those objects which in their own nature do not stand in a relation of antecedence and sequence.

Because up to the point of maximum complexity the work is focused so intensely on the fusion of different aspects and different experience, dialogue becomes a central factor. Even though the development of models and descriptions is part of the work, it does not constitute a platform in the work. For that reason, the leadership of the dialogue is important.

If we are to create a dialogue that moves forward and converges towards a picture in an effective way, it has to be systematic and have control of the rhythm between the intuitive, which creates knowledge, and the methodical, which captures knowledge, the rhythm between dialogue and the individual work. The form and content of the dialogue must be controlled so that preparations, personal reflections and the diversity of experiences meet and fuse together to produce a result.

There must be form and roles in the dialogue to give it the stability the model and the descriptions will provide in the later stages of the work. By having the preparations for the dialogue in the form of reading material that both gives a background and also the opportunity to become familiar with others' experience, one is compelled to reflect and broaden one's perspectives. This is followed up in what one writes and what one can bring to the dialogue.

The participants in the dialogue represent different experiences, and this in itself gives an allocation of roles, but *an experienced and committed leadership is essential to create energy* and to make the dialogue converge. Here, respect for the dialogue is important – and this is created by the minutes, which capture and retain what is known. Participants make their contribution both to the minutes and to the other members of the group.

Writing the minutes requires distance; this is an important part of the seminar form, the minutes-taker does not take an active part in the dialogue.

The need for this phase in the work, the path upwards, is often underestimated because in most situations the kind of experience we have lets us carry out this work without reflection, we are experts in this field and our actions are immediate. It may seem that we make the general and fundamental decisions first.

To take a simple example, if we make a weekend trip with the family to visit relatives, it may seem that we decide on how to get there, by car, train or plane, at the general level, and then go into the details of planning the trip. Closer analysis of the decision-making process shows that it is far more complicated than that. We weigh up the factors large and small, like 'what does the flight cost with the weekend discount?', 'do we have to fit the car with snow tires?', 'is there a bus from the railway station?', etc. We can do this if we have detailed knowledge and experience of the various means of transport. If we have no knowledge of something, we also have to examine the details that can create serious problems or obstacles. We speak to people who have experience, and we consider both positive and negative examples: 'we couldn't get a taxi to the airport', 'the roads are narrow and the traffic is slow', etc.

But decisions cannot be forced by adding detailing information; the final decision must only be made once the details have been combined with overall pictures, such as risks of delays, weather problems, do you like flying, is it worth the money, etc., to finally feel confident about making a choice.

At Maximum Complexity

One arrives at a point that Einar Már Gudmundsson describes thus: 'But suddenly – you sense it within yourself – you know that you will write'.

Once you have reached this point, where you have a comprehensive picture of the way the work is to be done, you have weighed what is technically possible against what the client or the market needs to make a complete picture.

This picture is made up of in-depth knowledge that confers judgement and the opportunity to make decisions in the work to come. All aspects have been linked together, the different risks have been 'played through' in your imagination, and you feel confident.

In this there is also the view of which tools and methods should be used to arrive at solutions and to provide support for the elements that are critical. This defies formal description. It is too complex.

To transfer the inner picture to other people requires a dialogue that does not shy away from analogies and metaphors, that the recipient interprets on the basis of his experience. The decision that one has reached this point must be rooted in one's conviction that the participants have built up this kind of inner picture. There are no formal criteria to show that this has happened: courage is needed here.

Fritjof Nansen summarises his thoughts on such a decision on an action based on his experience from his adventurous travels.

> Try to keep Mr. Irresponsible in check, and consider well before you take any action. Make your preparations with care; they can never be too thorough, for the road is long. No conjecture, no approximations.
>
> But once you set off, then throw yourself wholeheartedly into the enterprise. Set all the sails; no vacillation, for the main secret of self-confidence is 'the all'; – put the helm hard over when you go about.
>
> We pass many crossroads on this passage through life, and the test of a man is how he acts at each crossroads. Some people can't make up their minds, they waver, they want to keep all paths open, and because they are always looking back, they never get anywhere. – The right kind of traveller is good at making considered judgements; but then he chooses a path and keeps to it and he always wants to get somewhere.

Further, Fritjof Nansen reflects on his experience of even cutting off the path of retreat to create decisiveness.

> The method proved to be a good one, the absence of a line of retreat simplified the matter and acted as an incentive, it made up for any shortcomings in our preparations. The same method was used on the next voyage as well. Of course, once we had embarked on the Arctic adventure, and had heard the call of the wild and unknown, we could no longer turn back to the microscope and the histology of the nervous system, however much I might have longed to do so.

Design Work – the Downward Path

If the work is to be broadened, new people must be brought into the design process. To transfer the inner picture to these people is a difficult job for those who had built it up during the development work. As this cannot be formalised, a dialogue, a presence, is needed to create this inner picture in the people who are to further refine it. The more complex the whole, the more difficult it is to find ways of conveying it.

In his book, *Intuition*, Hans Larsson points to characteristics in the poet that the leader of the development project must also have.

> The poet can – and from the technical viewpoint this is the secret of his art – in a single word, a completed picture, a fortunate composition, capture a wealth of ideas that we would otherwise certainly take one by one, but when we grasp one, the other slips away, and therefore it is a connection between a lot of ideas that we notice evades us...

The leader must also 'feel' the way the picture develops among the people who are working on development. An actor gives the following description of a good director.

> He is phenomenal at listening to the actors – not to find out what they want, but to know where the play is.

To be able to read 'where the project is', it is essential that you can carry on a dialogue and understand what inner picture the participants have built up. By constantly being active, and by doing this as early as possible, one creates room for action. If one waits until the result of the work is produced, then it is too late. If something has gone wrong, you have to start all over again.

When, having reached maximum complexity, you move downwards towards the right of the diagram in Figure 1, you transfer parts of the inner picture to other designers, parts of the picture that are less complex than the whole, and from there you create further order through the design work. Experience from design work is always fed back. This feedback must always be a proactive process and be set in its context by the people who built up the complex picture of the whole.

One must constantly add to and modify one's picture. We can see here terminology with the meteorologist's inner picture of the weather and its trends. Maja-Lisa Perby writes in *The Inner Weather Picture*:

> A well-founded inner weather picture does not mean simply that the meteorologist is very familiar with the weather, but just as much that the

meteorologist has focused his attention on the way the weather is developing. The inner weather picture gives the meteorologist a basis on which to modify and change his opinion.... Here, a firm inner weather picture is ultimately a question of a well-founded search of the information that is available,.... No matter how much information is available, the meteorologist builds up his inner weather picture in an interaction between information and know-how about the weather; irrespective of the quantity of information, the meteorologist must maintain an active approach to the information.

This analogy shows how a leader in a development project has to build a well-founded picture of the condition of the project, and constantly be active in monitoring developments. Knowledge from this feedback will be absorbed into the picture, a picture that is the point of departure for the management of the project.

The interim results that are prepared become a concrete platform for what is passed on. As the design work proceeds, an inner picture may be used that has a greater surface and less depth; it becomes less complex.

In the work of creating the design, models and descriptive language are used to create order, describe structures and detailed solutions that are stored in an information structure that may be compared to a cupboard with a large number of drawers in which everyone knows what should be where. The structure makes it possible for everyone to go and look at what has developed. One gets an increasingly concrete platform from which to work. This is what is shown by the downward sloping curve – the transfer can take other forms when it is possible to relate to more concrete parts.

It would, of course, have been preferable to have been able to formalise all the knowledge that is expressed in judgements during the design work, but the objective must be set at the right level. Fewer changes can be made taking the documentation as a starting point, while extensive changes in design can only be made by the people who built up the picture of the whole.

How Do We Use the Model?

To deepen the dialogue on skill and processes of thinking, we may use the model to go deeper into arguments such as: how do we link a development model with its documentation requirements to this model?

One may say that there are three different needs for descriptions and models: to allow a dialogue and the building of an inner picture during the development work; to pass on this comprehensive view to the people who come in to the design work; and to enable the people who come in to the maintenance work to build up a picture of the completed design.

Different descriptions are not needed for these requirements, but it is important to analyse what needs a description must fulfil and then link this to a development model.

Other points are also important to address in more depth. For example, when a completely new systems concept is built, the path upward to a higher point of maximum complexity, with more aspects to consider and fewer concrete platforms to stand on, is less steep. What impact does this have on the way of working, work forms, leadership, follow-up and planning?

The model for the process of thinking will constitute a system of concepts that we can use to further develop our view of skill, how it is trained and improved, further refined and passed on. To give the concepts meaning, we must pursue and deepen arguments on specific situations and projects.

Summary

A model for the work of thinking in a project is described here. We progress from disorder to order. We use intuition to create new knowledge, and methods with which to capture it. On the way to order, a point is reached when the inner picture reaches a maximum of complexity.

The decision that this point has been reached must be based on the leader's conviction that the members of the project have built up a common inner picture of what must be designed. This conviction occurs, *inter alia*, at meeting places for common dialogue.

In design work, parts of the complete picture are transferred to other designers. As the design work progresses, one can use a less complex picture that is broader and more shallow. The inner picture must have continuity throughout the entire project so that it is directed towards an order that has a good structure, and for which understanding can be created.

A concluding comment from an experienced designer.

I can make comparisons with other projects I have been involved in, where there have been a lot of inexperienced designers and a weak project leadership. Even if the 'picture' may have existed, it was overshadowed by too much interference in the form of poor solutions and an imperfect understanding of contexts.

One then attempted to deal with the problem by introducing standardised coding rules and interfaces etc., without gaining anything. Instead, the situation gradually deteriorated, to end with everyone heroically sitting and doing 'more of the same' in order to save the situation.

I have experienced that several times, and seen the heroes thrive (and then become burnt out). The argument about complexity explains it all. One has tried to achieve order without crossing the threshold of maximum complexity by means of a thorough analysis of the problem. Maximum complexity then appears to take on a hydra's ability to be able to push its way up through every point in the final system.

9 Better Systems Engineering with Dialogue

Göran Backlund and Jan Sjunnesson

Introduction

Managing knowledge involves having the ability to establish intersubjectivity between a group of individuals. This chapter describes two case studies where an advanced and highly structured dialogue is used as the key instrument for generating new ideas, and for establishing a common understanding of a new subject. Together with Professor Bo Göranzon at the Department of Skill and Technology at Sweden's Royal Institute of Technology (KTH), Combitech Systems AB spent four years developing Dialogue Seminar method. After a period of thorough testing at Combitech Systems, the method has been in use at a number of other development organisations. The method is based on a view of knowledge developed by philosophers such as Aristotle, Descartes, Diderot and Wittgenstein, where tacit knowledge, or experience-based knowledge, is central. The purpose of the concept is to give a wider understanding of knowledge, and the basic procedure involves training people to change perspective in order to stimulate new thinking. The three different cases clearly demonstrate that the Dialogue Seminar method can be successful in different situations, for example, gathering experience from a completed project, establishing a common language in a newly formed team, or helping to specify a new product.

The Dialogue Seminar Method

The Dialogue Seminar method is a result of research conducted by Professor Bo Göranzon at the Royal Institute of Technology in Sweden and Combitech Systems, a consulting company where for the last few years management has realised that knowledge, in the minds and bodies of the employees, represents the 'tangible' resources of the company. Therefore it is essential to nurture knowledge, sharing it with individuals and keeping it within the company. The Dialogue Seminar has become a practical method for dealing with tacit knowledge and developing leadership. This chapter is divided into the following sections:

- Knowledge (knowledge in engineering, tacit knowledge, a knowledge model)
- The Dialogue Seminar (the method, the desired results)
- Three cases

Knowledge

What human knowledge really is, what we can know, what we cannot know, how we learn, what an expert is: these questions have been discussed by philosophers throughout history. The ancient Greeks were preoccupied with the question of what knowledge really is, so the subject is hardly new. For an interesting elaboration on the subject of what makes an expert, see a summary of the works of Socrates and Plato by Dreyfus and Dreyfus (1984).

Knowledge in Engineering

What constitutes an engineer's knowledge? What constitutes a development team's knowledge? You can roughly divide knowledge of systems development into formal knowledge and experience-based knowledge. Formal knowledge is expressed through descriptions, methods like UML, SDL and VHDL, operating system primitives, programming languages, reviewing rules, etc. Experience-based knowledge is manifested when you build a system from a complex set of requirements, or manage a project with constantly changing requirements, or conduct process improvement, or perform cost-effective system testing with sufficient quality. The expert uses his experience-based knowledge and judgement to make the right decisions and choices without the support of a manual, which would nevertheless be useless in giving direction in difficult system development situations. But we often tend to consider tangible artifacts, such as documents, models, software, etc. as representing all the knowledge about a product that has been developed, see Figure 1.

Figure 1—A Product Development Process and some artifacts it has produced

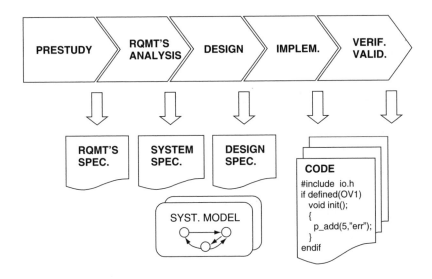

However, much knowledge is communicated, or ought to be, between the individuals participating in the product development process. For a development project to succeed and a good product to emerge, it is necessary that a common inner picture of the product be created and shared between the people involved. All the information that builds such a picture cannot be put in documents. Consequently, we must acknowledge that much of each individual's knowledge must somehow be articulated and understood by other individuals, so that handovers between different phases will be successful and new members of a team can become effective team members, see Figure 2.

Experience-based knowledge will be in focus when new technologies, methods and tools applied to development work are spread to a large group of individuals. Improvement work often focuses on the formal descriptions and blanket solutions, such as object orientation, CMM, design patterns, XP (extreme programming), or the like, but the developers may still have trouble finding the core knowledge, which involves establishing and communicating the intuitive practical knowledge (professional knowledge) required to build a good system. You cannot write a requirements specification that *guarantees* that you will develop a good system, no matter how good the specification may be. There is almost an infinite solution space of possible systems (given any requirements specification), so how can you possibly build the best one?

Figure 2—How is knowledge exhibited interpersonally?

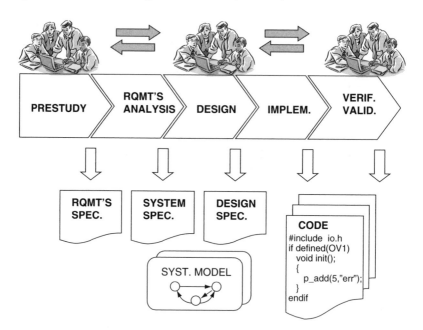

Tacit Knowledge

Considering traditional systems of education, it is easy to get the notion that real knowledge is theoretical, that it is formalised, and what cannot be formalised is not real knowledge or science (the 'Something Else' part in Figure 3). According to the Austrian engineer and philosopher Wittgenstein, a rule can only have a meaning if it is based on practice; in other words, formal knowledge rests on the foundation of empirical practice, Figure 3.

Figure 3—Formal vs. experience-based knowledge, two views

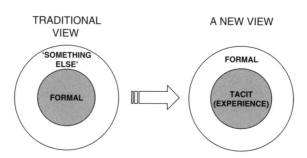

One can also argue that practical experience is not only original, but also easier to comprehend. The eighteenth century French philosopher Diderot, expressed the insight that general abstractions don't generate understanding 'An abstraction is merely a symbol emptied of its idea'. Where abstractions fail, examples can bring understanding of an idea.

The theory of tacit knowledge as such is presented by Polanyi (1967). Many writers acknowledge the concept of tacit knowledge, including Nonaka and Takeuchi (1995). They express the importance of tacit knowledge as 'knowledge that can be expressed in words and numbers represents only the tip of the iceberg of the entire body of knowledge'. However, they seem to be of the opinion that tacit knowledge can and should be made explicit through different mechanisms for exchanging knowledge; by using metaphors, analogies, models, etc. Metaphors and analogies are very important to the creation of concepts; however, we must be aware of the fact that not all tacit knowledge can ever be made explicit. Johannessen (1992) gives a better presentation of the nature of tacit knowledge, based on Wittgenstein's work. It is not the rule (explicit) that expresses what we know, it is really in how we *follow* a rule, in practice, that we exercise all our knowledge (explicit and tacit).

What is tacit knowledge really? When does it come into play? The following quotations from everyday engineering work give a hint about the experience-based knowledge that underlies engineering judgement:

- 'How did you manage to define this architecture from a 400-page requirements specification?'
- 'Why do you think this design is better than mine?'
- 'That guy is incredible – he found the error almost immediately. And we've been trying to find it for a week now...'
- 'Define user friendliness? Well, I know it when I see it.'

Often tacit knowledge is simply called intuition. Now, how do we deal with the tacit component? The knowledge that, by definition, cannot be expressed explicitly in text, formulas, graphs, etc.? According to ancient philosophers such as Plato (Dreyfus and Dreyfus, 1984), as well as more modern philosophers such as the seventeenth century French mathematician Descartes, it is the specific example that can convey knowledge that might otherwise be impossible to articulate. Descartes also stated that practical experience becomes more important as you grow wiser. The specific example told by the person who experienced it reveals how that person exercises his/her professional judgement in a specific situation. A well narrated example can create a 'feeling' for the judgement based on specific experience and can serve as the key to a transfer of experience between individuals, see Figure 4.

Figure 4—Transfer of knowledge and experience

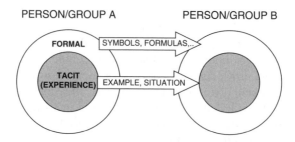

Janik (1988) argues that understanding and grasping the context in stories told by people who have lived them is essential to understanding experience; 'armchair speculation is futile'. The sixteenth century French philosopher Montaigne points out that the accumulation of experience is only useful if it leads to better professional judgement – using experience to grow wiser. Göranzon (1988) states that '...we are taught a practice through examples...' and where formal descriptions fail, it is possible '....to put forward the essence of a practice through examples that are followed by teaching, by practice'.

A knowledge model

Dreyfus and Dreyfus suggest a knowledge model illustrating the different levels of skill from novice to expert, see Figure 5.

Figure 5—Dreyfus' Knowledge Model

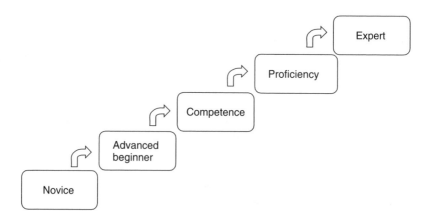

At the novice level, a person follows explicit rules. An advanced beginner begins to notice 'examples of meaningful additional aspects of the situation'. The competent performer seeks new rules to cope with new situations. A proficient person gradually replaces rules, principles and reasoned responses with intuitive behaviour but still needs to make judgements. Finally, the expert no longer needs to decide, but automatically discriminates between a vast repertoire of examples, in other words, he sees how to reach a goal. A person can only reach the proficient and expert levels by developing professional judgement based on experience, i.e. tacit knowledge.

As shown in Figure 4, experience-based knowledge is expressed indirectly through examples of specific situations. The basic means for sharing this knowledge between individuals and groups of individuals, is dialogue. Senge (1994) discriminates between discussion as a means of solving a problem, and dialogue, whose purpose is not to solve a specific problem, but to deepen and increase understanding of a complex subject. As Bohm (1996) points out, the prerequisite for a good dialogue is that each participant must 'suspend' his/her assumptions and regard the other participants as colleagues.

These views are all necessary prerequisites for a successful dialogue, but still the dialogue itself does not guarantee that everything can be agreed upon between the participants. The main purpose of the dialogue is to *understand*, not to agree. The dialogue might end in a conflict about essentially contested concepts but still be successful in the quest for knowledge. This is well illustrated by the dialogue between Turing and Wittgenstein (Göranzon and Karlquist, 1995).

The Dialogue Seminar

Using some of the above as a foundation, the Dialogue Seminar has been developed by KTH as a method for creating knowledge and transferring experience. The specific example is the tool for training, judgement is the form in which the knowledge is expressed, reflection is the method for examining the knowledge, and dialogue is the form for collective reflection. The Dialogue Seminar method is outlined in Figure 6 below.

The Method

We start by identifying a group of people with a difficult and urgent issue: a project team, a department, or any other group that feels the

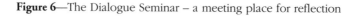

Figure 6—The Dialogue Seminar – a meeting place for reflection

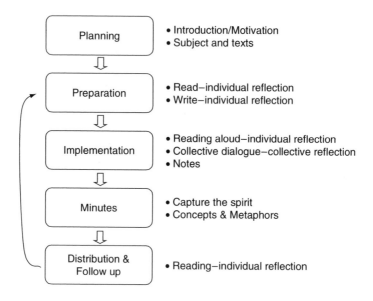

need to understand a subject better. Experience has shown that a group of six–eight persons is optimal for a good dialogue.

At a start-up meeting, the group is introduced to the Dialogue Seminar. We also present three–four texts as homework for the group. The texts are deliberately chosen from professional areas other than those of the team members. The texts must be of good quality from an epistemological point of view and must relate well, by analogy, to the chosen subject.

During the next couple of weeks, each team member reads the texts, 'with a pencil in hand', writing down personal reflections and associations that occur while they read. Good texts inspire a lot of associations related to the subject, and each person is urged to capture examples from his/her own personal experience. After having read the homework texts, each person writes a text (a maximum of two pages), based on the notes taken during reading. The text can be written in everyday language and in a story-telling form, in which the writer presents his/her own experiences/events as they relate to the subject. Reading and writing are the methods for individual reflection.

The next step is a one-day seminar where the members of the group meet for a dialogue. Two persons lead the seminar: one, the facilitator, leads the dialogue and keeps it 'on track', while the other takes extensive notes. Everyone reads his/her own text aloud to the others bringing the text to life by using a tone of voice that includes emphasis, pauses, etc. The others listen and make notes of their personal reflections. After each reading, the members each comment on the text, one at a time. No personal criticism is allowed (the experience described in the text cannot be 'wrong', just different). Thoughts that add to the experience, or present new perspectives, are encouraged.

After the seminar, minutes are written, but the minutes of a Dialogue Seminar are not like the usual minutes of any meeting. The idea is to capture the spirit of the meeting, the energy; in particular the concepts that were presented or developed, and the metaphors used. The group often develops new meanings from old words, and the minutes must reflect this. The author has the right to add his/her own reflections and associations to the written dialogue, thus adding to the group's knowledge.

Finally, a follow-up meeting is held with the group after they have read the minutes. At this meeting, they read their reflections on the minutes. The minutes can be one of a number of new texts used as input to the next seminar, which could have a different subject.

Desired Results

The purpose of the Dialogue Seminar is to:

- Create a common language – intersubjectivity
- Build a common practice
- Train analogical thinking
- Explore a subject
- Share professional experience

The first three objectives are really long-term objectives; it takes time to shape a language or a practice, or to train one's thinking. Consequently, the Dialogue Seminar must be established as a forum where knowledge can grow, in other words, a meeting-place for reflection.

Three Cases

The objective of presenting these three cases is to demonstrate the effectiveness of the Dialogue Seminar, and to show that this method is generally applicable in different areas: expanding knowledge within a certain area, helping teams function better and supporting the evolution of a common inner picture of a new product. In every case the seminars were led by the authors.

The 'Lessons Learned' Case

Old and New Projects

Projects are often concluded by collecting experiences and putting them in a final report, but those reports are seldom used and the experiences remain individual knowledge. At a company that develops embedded, real-time systems that are critical to safety, a new project was started in the reverse order. The members' first task was to collect experience from previous projects, thereby learning their lessons right from the start. The Dialogue Seminar was used as an important part of this exercise.

History

The 'Alfa' project's progress had almost stopped, still activity was more intense than ever. It was like a 'stockmarket in free fall'. Everyone had more to do than the available time allowed, but very little progress was made. The developed product did not function properly; the frequency of faults was far above acceptable. The projected lead-time had been exhausted months before, causing the anxious customer a 'big head-ache'. A task force of experts was brought in to diagnose the problems and find solutions to them. After a couple of weeks they came up with an answer. The main problems were seen in project management, system architecture and software quality.

Mistakes as an Investment in Knowledge

The management of the company decided: 'Don't search for people to blame. Instead let's use the experience as an investment in knowledge'.

Who is going to get experience? Who should learn from the mistakes of others? If the result of the transfer of experiences is to be visible, it has to be demonstrated by improved project perform-ance. It is not enough to have members of the Alfa project learn from their mistakes. They will all soon be working on other projects with new members. Therefore, a new project in an early phase of starting up, 'Beta', was singled out as an example. The idea was for the members of Beta to learn from the mistakes of Alfa thus allowing for a real transfer of experiences from one group of people to another.

Story-telling

The first step was to visualise the history of Alfa. A number of project members with different roles were assigned to each write his/her own story telling his/her view of the project and his/her own version of what went wrong. These were people with unique knowledge of the project. A time-line was drawn from the start of the project until the current time. The most memorable events mentioned in the stories were listed on the time-line using direct quotations. In this way the history of Alfa was described from several perspectives.

Stimuli for New Ideas

Now, how could we get the members of Beta to learn from these stories? How could we get them to utilise the experiences of Alfa in their new project? We knew it would not be sufficient to just let them read the Alfa story. That is the kind of thing one does in school, and forgets straightaway as soon as the exam is over. We needed something else, something that would remain as a true experience in the minds and bodies of the group itself; in other words, group knowledge that could be used daily without thinking.

So we turned our attention to the bookshelves, calling on the observations of philosophers and the experience of experts in different fields to broaden our perspective, to give us some distance from the challenges of the present, and to stimulate our minds to further reflection.

At a seminar with Beta's members, the story-tellers each related their own history of Alfa. What went on was not just storytelling; it was more like a dialogue between all the participants. For each event on the Alfa time-line, the author of the particular quotation explained what had happened and why. A dialogue followed in which more explanations, questions and new ideas were examined. At the end of the seminar each of the participants shared a clear view of how Alfa's problems had arisen. Intersubjectivity of the project and its history had been achieved.

Now, the exercise could have stopped there, but it did not. It is not sufficient merely to understand the mistakes of others if you want to find alternative ways of solving problems. Therefore three new seminars were arranged for the members of Alfa and Beta. The seminars focused on examples of system development from other parts of the industry, addressing architecture, project management and software quality. These were not the ultimate perfect examples to follow, just other examples from outside the company, showing how each project encountered advantages and drawbacks in their specific way of working. The purpose again was to stimulate the conception of new ideas.

Reflection

For a couple of weeks the groups were exposed to this approach, and finally the time seemed right for reflection. The Dialogue Seminar form was used and the texts chosen dealt with knowledge and management. Some of the texts were practical, others more philosophical. The philosophical texts were introduced in order to provide insight into tacit knowledge.

The members of Beta received their texts and spent a couple of weeks reading them, and came back with their own written reflections for the Dialogue Seminar. Having explored the texts, they felt they had experienced an inner dialogue when writing their essays. They were now prepared for the real dialogue.

The one-day seminar developed a number of concepts, with specific meanings such as:

- *Management by walking around* – the project manager walked around among the project members measuring 'the project temperature'.
- *20% left to do* – an example of useless progress reporting.
- *A shared picture of the system* – the members need to share the same concept of what is to be developed. They were all aware of what happens when this is not the case.
- *A shared picture of progress* – otherwise the project management will be fooled.
- *Warning signals* – listen to your intuition. Early on, everyone knew something was wrong with Alfa but...
- *Risk management* – risk analysis is not enough, you have to take action to reduce risks.
- *Prepare for the unexpected.*

The End

We had a final meeting that concluded the transfer of experiences. The Beta project was discussed in terms of the new knowledge its members had acquired and how it should be utilised. Now, a year later we can see the following effects on performance as compared with the Alfa project:

- The project members now share a common picture of the system.
- The company has kept the same project members from start to finish.

- They all work under the same roof.
- They cooperate closely.
- They have well-defined roles.
- The architecture has been developed and maintained in workshops.
- The design is much less complex.
- A new process is being followed.

Like all other projects, Beta has its problems, but in terms of the aspects listed above, there has been significant improvement. We see this improvement as an effect of the method applied.

The Multimedia Case

The New Team

At a European company that develops multimedia terminals, a new software development team,'Rookie', was organised consisting of seven people from several different European countries. Most of them were young and recently hired, and communication between the Rookie members was sparse. Rookie was the receiving part in the handover of software development from 'Expert', a team in another European country.

Motivation and Preparation

The Rookie team was chosen to participate in a Dialogue Seminar. The subject chosen for the seminar involved pin-pointing the most crucial skill of the Expert team. The Expert team was very skilled, and one person from Expert participated in the seminar.

The texts for reading were 1) on knowledge theory, 2) on the development of the inner picture among meteorologists, 3) on Diderot and building architecture, and 4) a final report from an earlier project at the company in question.

The Seminar

On the day the seminar was held, six out of seven people had produced their own written reflections, initiated by the texts. The seminar was alive with energy. Numerous stories were told and examples given, and several interesting concepts and metaphors were developed to directly address the situation Rookie found itself in. Among the examples were:

- *The specification does not cover it all* – the product has properties that we want to describe, but never will be able to do (formally).
- *Play ping-pong* – do something unrelated for a while, when you run into difficult problems and get stuck (there was a long story behind the metaphor).
- *The five 'whys'* – a metaphor for going to the root of the problem (from the Toyota Production System). Do not correct *the symptoms*.
- *Some people boil without water too* – never be afraid of asking stupid questions when there is something you do not know because sometimes other people seem to be more knowledgeable than they really are.
- *Describe the problem to others* – in the process of formulating the problem, you may really learn something yourself.

Some of the metaphors and analogies above may sound strange, but the Rookie team developed their own specific, but perfectly sensible, glossary in the course of the seminar (there is a story behind each example above). An outsider would not understand the meaning of the concept/metaphor, without an extensive explanation (the space here is too limited). The point is that the Rookie team members understood these concepts perfectly well after the seminar.

The Results

A few weeks after the seminar, we held a follow-up meeting where we evaluated the seminar and reflected on the minutes. Some results were obvious:

- The Rookie team now used the metaphors they arrived at to guide them in their daily work (with the specific meanings agreed on during the seminar).
- The seminar had been an 'ice-breaker'. They now dared to ask each other questions and communicate more.
- The Rookie team had started communicating extensively with other teams in the project.
- A number of suggested improvements surfaced during the seminar.

The line manager who ordered the Dialogue Seminar was very pleased with the results. He had noted new insights and a new team spirit in Rookie.

The Product Development Case

Measure-oriented, Not rustic and *Porsche feeling* were among the concepts formulated in the Dialogue Seminar in the initial phase of one product development project.

A European company that develops and manufactures equipment for performing chemical analysis asked us to write a requirements specification for their new product. They presented their current products, and described the scope of the new product. We returned to our office and defined a plan for realisation of the specification. We sent it to the company, but after a week we got a negative response. They explained that they came to their decision after discussing the idea with their own marketing department. In the course of the discussion, different opinions about the future product had surfaced. The marketing department needed more time to evaluate different alternatives, and the company promised to contact us when they were ready to define the scope of the product.

Three months after that, the company contacted us again. We paid them a visit and the staff of their development department presented the new scope of the future product.

In their product portfolio a similar product already existed, but it was too complicated. Besides, the marketing department had specified new requirements regarding connectivity; they needed something more easy to handle. We received a one-page list of suggestions prepared by the development department, and it was filled with high-tech functionality.

At the office again we considered the situation:

- The Company had a strong marketing department.
- Different departments held different opinions about the new product.
- The most important property of the new product was *use-friendliness*.
- Communication between the marketing and development departments could have been better.
- The list of requirements we got from development was full of high-tech functionality. Did marketing also support this list?

As usual in product development, the future product was perceived from several different perspectives. It was important that these perspectives become visible in the early phases of the development. Explicit knowledge can easily be shared in documents, but tacit knowledge presents a more difficult problem. We suggested that the work of defining requirements begin with a Dialogue Seminar in which representatives from different parts of the company would participate. A Dialogue Seminar is not only a method for sharing experience, it is also a creative environment where new ideas are born and can grow.

The persons selected for the Dialogue Seminar had to prepare themselves by reading pre-selected texts and writing a personal reflection. At the seminar the participants read their written texts aloud, one at a time. Sometimes the dialogue was very intense, and sometimes people disagreed. Different meanings of common words were explored: 'Is *this* what you mean when you say *that?*', which gave rise to a common understanding of new concepts. The dialogue was captured in the minutes, and the new concepts were written on a whiteboard. At the end of the seminar we had three columns on the whiteboard: one for concepts that were fully understood and agreed on ('These are the necessary features of the new product'); the second for concepts agreed on but not fully understood (more information was needed) and a third column for concepts that the group disagreed on, but agreed to exclude from the new product ('The new product is *not . . .*').

Proceeding from the seminar minutes, we drew up the product's requirements specification. As always when requirements are defined, the work sometimes came to a full stop, and we could not find a way forward. If we then returned to the seminar minutes, we found the rationale and the background for the product design: the 'inner picture' we had all agreed on.

Finally the requirements specification was approved and a project was initiated to develop the product. A group of designers was called in, and as might have been expected, they started by reading the requirements specification. That done, they raised a number of questions. In response, we urged the designers to read the minutes. When they had read them; their reaction was: 'This gives the specification a colour, a soul.' In the minutes, they had found the condensation of experiences from people working in the marketing, quality, development and sales departments.

A product requirements specification is like the musical notation (score) of a musical composition (a symphony, say). Even if you follow it exactly you can perform the composition in many different ways.

Summary and Discussion

The Dialogue Seminar has been shown to produce good results in the three cases described. This shows that it can be used as a generic method for developing knowledge and understanding, especially in terms of project experience, team learning and product development.

Combitech Systems has internalized the method in the corporate training programme, and uses it extensively as a means by which to broaden employees' knowledge of systems engineering practice. The method is continuously developed and refined in collaboration with KTH, as well as by practicing the method together with clients in different system development environments.

References

Bohm, D. (1996) *On Dialogue*, Routledge, London.
Descartes, R. (1998) *Discourse on Method*, Translated by D. Cress, Hackett Publishing Company.
Diderot, D. (1976) *Rameau's Nephew & D'Alembert's Dream*, Translated by L.W. Tancock, Viking Penguin.
Dreyfus, H.L., and Dreyfus, S.E., 'From Socrates to Expert Systems: The Limits of Calculative Rationality,' (1984) 6(3) *Technology in Society* 217–33.
Göranzon, B. (1988) 'The Practice of the Use of Computers. A Paradoxical Encounter between Different Traditions of Knowledge', *Knowledge, Skill and Artificial Intelligence*, Editors Bo Göranzon and Ingela Josefsson, Springer-Verlag, 9–18.
Göranzon, B. and Karlquist, A. (1995) 'Beyond All Certainty', *Skill Technology and Enlightenment. On Practical Philosophy*, Editor Bo Göranzon, Springer-Verlag.
Janik, A. (1988) 'Tacit Knowledge, Working Life and Scientific Method', *Knowledge, Skill and Artificial Intelligence*, eds B. Göranzon and I. Josefsson, Springer-Verlag, 53–63.
Johannessen, K.S. (1992) 'Rule Following, Intransitive Understanding and Tacit Knowledge. An Investigation of the Wittgenstein Concept of Practice as Regards Tacit Knowing', *Skill and Education: Reflection and Experience*, eds B. Göranzon and M. Florin, Springer-Verlag.
Montaigne, M., Seigneur de (1993) *The Complete Essays*, Penguin Books.
Nonaka, I., Takeuchi, H. (1995) *The Knowledge-Creating Company*, Oxford University Press.
Polanyi, M. (1967) *The Tacit Dimension*, Routledge and Kegan Paul, London.
Senge, P.M. (1990) *The Fifth Discipline: The Art and Practice of the Learning Organization*, 1st ed.
Wittgenstein, L. (1986) *On Certainty/Uber Gewissheit*, ed. by G.E.M. Anscombe and G.H. Von Wright, Harpercollins.

10 Some Aspects of Military Practices and Officers' Professional Skills

Peter Tillberg

Introduction

A defence organisation based on compulsory military service began to take form in Sweden at the end of the 1800s. The culmination was reached through a parliamentary decision entailing the abolition of the allotment system in 1901. One of the chief promoters of a conscript army was the general staff officer Knut Bildt. He was an innovator in many ways. Bildt argued strongly for both theoretical studies and practical experienced-based knowledge as two necessary ingredients for all military training. He believed that knowledge should not primarily be conceived as a personal property but rather as something that is developed in a military practice. That development of officers' professional skills entails not just following established rules and instructions was thus something that was understood as early as the turn of the century. The following was written by Bildt in a book that he frequently cited during his lectures at the national military academy, Karlberg.

> The art of war area is now so broad that what an individual experiences in the field can no longer be called war experience, but rather this is only gained through the summarisation of several persons' collected experiences into war history...Where can a so-called practice lead that does not strive with its knowledge for more than the ability to enforce the current drill book? With this, one holds ground but does not move forward.[1]

---

1 Ed. G. Artéus, (1996) *Svenska officersprofiler under 1900-talet*, Karlskrona: Militärhögskolan & Axel Abrahamsons Förlag, 29.

Bildt was hence a person who believed firmly in the importance of professional officers. It was primarily through qualified training, where one constantly reflected upon military examples and experiences, that the officer would achieve skill and expertise. He maintained that it was absolutely necessary that Swedish units be led by what he referred to as 'experts' and not by novices and advanced beginners.

In 1942, the commander of the army corps gave Colonel Axel Gyllenkrok the assignment of implementing a troop-training course for all officers in the army. The primary reason for initiating this project was constituted by the observed conflicts that arose in encounters between conscripts and officers during the Second World War. Conflicts that were mainly a result of the officer corps having developed their own culture and traditions that were in disharmony with the conscripts' expectations and conceptions. For the military command, it was therefore important to quickly initiate a massive training effort for the purpose of changing the practices that over the course of several years had been developed in respect to leadership, organising and training. Gyllenkrok, who probably is the officer who most strongly influenced military leadership during the 1900s, wrote in his book *Synpunkter rörande utbildning* (1943) about that which characterises the officer's professional skills and military practices. He wrote in a temperamental language containing many exclamation marks, drastic formulations, examples, metaphors and analogies. The officer's professional skills, he maintained, are primarily characterised by proficiency in being able to make scrupulous preparations at the same time as one must be able to improvise and use one's judgement based on the current situation.

> Training work is primarily organisation. But the organising may not be driven to absurdity, not to rigidity, because the ability to improvise is thus obliterated. . . . He who can improvise can also organise – if he desires or is forced to do so – but he who has the ability to 'organise', often does not possess the ability to improvise. For improvisation is nothing more than organisation in a very short period and often under troublesome or difficult circumstances. . . . goals and basic concepts, principles and guidelines are the same. This must be clear to the cadre – especially to the officers. Because if this is not the case, volumes must be centrally written and details regulated for each training period or school. . . . commanders by reason of this become indifferent and complacent in thought. Its members glide down from their positions as military commanders to civil servants and functionaries.

A person who can hardly be described as a civil servant or functionary is Colonel Ulf Henricsson. Fifty years after Gyllenkrok finished writing his book, Henricsson is in the heart of Bosnia. He is the commander of the first Swedish UN battalion to be deployed in the former Yugoslavia. The tasks to be resolved are as many as they are ambiguous and it is no exaggeration to say that professional skills, military practices, leadership, and the ability to organise and improvise are put to the test. The order the unit received before departing was worded as follows:

> Transport to and assembly in Tuzla. Assembly of the entire battalion at temporary assembly point in Tuzla and at Tuzla aerodrome. Seize control of Tuzla and secure the aerodrome. Expand the assembly area and establish a protective zone around Tuzla. Operate by: showing UN presence, deliberations. Establish negotiating commissions. Monitor ceasefire and escort humanitarian aid. . . . The mission includes: create preconditions for evacuation of injured, protect and care for people, improve living conditions for the people and terminate hostilities.[2]

All who read this order can probably easily agree that it places considerable demands on those who will carry it out. How the information is interpreted and understood differs considerably, however, between persons who lack experience of similar missions and those who have trained for many years to be able to handle closely related missions. It is not just about the person who is more experienced having learned more techniques, models and rules for his conduct than that which the novice has achieved. What primarily differentiates them is how one fundamentally perceives the information in relation to his own professional skills and the practices in which one participates. One has succeeded in developing a type of judgement that, for example, many times goes beyond the rules formulated for how one shall perform certain tasks. In the remainder of this chapter, certain epistemological and linguistic philosophical aspects will be presented to provide a picture of how one can understand the development of military practices and officers' professional skills.

Practice – A Weave of Language and Action

Ludwig Wittgenstein says that 'practice gives words their meaning'.[3] This statement argues that it is in the exercising of a practice that our comprehension of a phenomenon or concept makes itself evident. To be well-versed in a language entails according to Wittgenstein learning to master a large number of situations in which linguistic conduct is

---

2 SWEDINT document, 1993.
3 Wittgenstein, L. (1978) *Remarks on Colour*, Berkeley: University of California Press, §317.

included as an important element. He also maintains that it is in a practice that concepts and language are formed and receive their significations. A summary of this epistemological perspective is that there is a very complicated net of mutually constituted relations between (i) how concepts in a language are formed, (ii) human conduct and that which in everyday language is referred to as (iii) our reality.

This approach to language and conduct can serve as a basis for describing some aspects of officers' professional skills and military practice. Let us take an example that illustrates this approach. A concept that often recurs when members of the armed forces speak of what characterises their profession is the word 'leadership'. With the above approach as a basis, understanding of the leadership concept is manifested by an officer both through the way in which it is practised but also in the way one uses the word in various situations. By exercising leadership, with time the officer can develop skills, adeptness and judgement in this area. This occurs by one involving oneself in concrete situations in which the officer is given the opportunity to learn to recognise how the language is used, and thus become adept at identifying similarities and differences between different situations in which the concept of leadership is used. This learning occurs both when one performs various leadership actions, and often in a dialogue between members of the armed forces in which both those who listen and those who speak develop a type of situation comprehension. It is this situation comprehension that constitutes the basis, or even the prerequisite, for the establishment of a military practice. According to this epistemological approach, it is not primarily a matter of creating an intellectual, in fact theoretical, comprehension of how the language is utilised, but rather a very practical one. Practice refers here to investigating and involving oneself in the context in which the concept is de facto applied, formed, developed, and with time, even forgotten. It is in conjunction with this interest for the concrete context in which the language is used, interwoven with how actions are performed that Wittgenstein introduces the concept language game.[4]

Practice Consists of a Large Number of Language Games

The language game concept is introduced to make us observant of language's situational dependence and its utilisation dimension. Referring to

---

4 In *Philosophical Investigations* (1953) and *The Blue and Brown Books* (1958) Wittgenstein commonly uses the language game concept in his investigations.

a phrase or stated view is equivalent to referring to the role or function that it has in very specific situations, i.e. various language games. This entails that one and the same concept can be used in a number of different language games in which it is given different meanings by its user. To understand language in this manner differs strongly from focusing on and attempting to find out what a word or statement means. Wittgenstein writes that placing questions of the type 'What does a word mean?' produces a state of intellectual cramp.[5] One is enticed by the question's form into searching for something, an object or property, which corresponds to a specific word. To bring the question down to earth, and thus make it manageable, he suggests instead that one rephrase the question to 'How is this word used?', 'In which way did we learn the word?'.

The differences that arise between different language games do not thus concern just the logical or grammatical placement the word has in a statement, but also to the highest degree the question of the context in which it is expressed. When the concept of leadership, for example, is used by officers it occurs in a number of different contexts with almost as many meanings. In one language game, leadership is used and comprehended as characteristics, in another as abilities, in a third as organisational structures, etc. There are considerable differences between how the officer uses and comprehends the concept of leadership when he is engaged in combat with a military unit and when in an academic conversation. When the officer practises and speaks of leadership with friends on a football team, it is different than when he talks about leadership in conjunction with bringing up children, etc. Depending on which language game one participates in and what is practice, concepts and actions receive varying meanings. The language becomes a bearer of various meanings and functions depending on the context and user. This is why each practice must be investigated and understood separately.

There are Both Similarities and Differences Between Various Language Games

The various language games are not identical but are often related to one another. The similarities, those things that are common and unify, provide meaning through the concept of *family resemblances*.[6] If one examines various language games, for example, where the word leadership

---

5 Wittgenstein, L. (1958) *The Blue and Brown Books*, Oxford: Blackwell Publishers Ltd.

6 Wittgenstein, L. (1953) *Philosophical Investigations*. Oxford: Basil Blackwell, i.e. §66.

is used in a military practice, one will discover a certain amount of family resemblances between them. They demonstrate similar characteristics or relationships between one another in much the same way as, for example, characteristics in a family: height, features, eye colour, hair colour, temperament, etc. Just as important as it is for an officer to learn to see similarities between various language games is being able to identify differences. What at first glance can appear very similar can often upon closer examination also prove to hold many differences. Imagine, for example, the experience (and statement) *to be led.*[7] There are nearly an unlimited number of cases of being led where many of these situations resemble one another but where there are also large dissimilarities. Imagine the following cases:

- You are led by someone holding a superior rank giving orders and instructions.
- You are led through violence towards a location that you do not want to reach.
- You permit yourself to be led in a dance where you are attentive to your partner's intentions and dance steps, and the rhythm of the music.
- You and a friend are out for a walk. During your walk, you let yourself be led by him, i.e. where he goes, you follow.
- You are hiking alone in the woods and find a path that you let lead you on the rest of your hike.

In one way, one can say that the above situations are similar, but one can ask oneself if there is anything that is in common to them all.

When members of the armed forces talk with one another about their profession in regards to leadership, there are a number of differences in respect to the meanings included in the concept. That leadership is spoken of in different ways is because comprehension is closely interwoven with each individual's experiences and knowledge of how the word is used. What can be said to be practice at one military unit when it comes to leadership can differ considerably from what is practice at another. Although aware that this is the case at a rational level, officers still often speak of leadership as if there were *one* prevailing practice and *one* military leadership. A well-developed military practice is therefore characterised as having developed a skill in being able to see both similarities and differences between various actions, and how the language is used in the practice. Discussion of leadership in a similar manner, despite all the dissimilarities, can be explained in terms of deficiencies

---

7 Ibid., §172.

in the usage of a language. This is an ongoing process where the joint search is for a deepened understanding of a certain phenomenon, for example, leadership. According to this approach, it deals not at all with reaching total agreement on a concept but rather with building up a type of intersubjectivity[8] surrounding the phenomenon under discussion.

Essentially Contested Concepts

There are differences between executing a certain action, and putting words to and describing actions, in terms of why and how.[9] Many times it can even be easier to make something complicated, than to be able to interpret an action for other people in a language. When beginning to speak with others of what leadership is or is not, it easily becomes problematic; it is obvious that there are varying perceptions and opinions. Many times it can end in conflict, with a choice of references in order to convince the opponent of a correct answer. A person who believes strongly in training and formal methods might now say that this disagreement arises because of (i) insufficient theoretical knowledge to agree, or (ii) a lack of personal experience in the area discussed, and with these, no problem would arise. It can also be (iii) because of the absence of learning of the correct usage or meaning of the concept spoken of; there is a lack of a language for what needs to be expressed. Learning this language is the solution. Perhaps there is something in the manner of reflecting on the concept of unity, but according to the English philosopher W.B. Gallie, this can then make things a bit too simple. In the article 'Essentially Contested Concepts' (1955) he repeatedly writes that it is often not possible, regardless of how much time, effort and argument is used, to assign a complicated phenomenon or concept an unambiguous and absolute meaning. Considerable differences of opinion will remain after the conversation, despite great efforts being made by all parties. Gallie's conclusion is naturally not to avoid trying to reach agreements that have points of departure in difficult questions at issue. What he is saying is that, with an excessively large, yes, perhaps even naïve, belief in it being possible to reach indisputable agreement, we should be aware of the problem in making and relying on concept

---

8 'When the insight-creating dialogue really comes about it is a constriction of the concept-forming sequence in general: it occurs between people, continues over time and lays bare complexity and manifoldness. The group develops a new intersubjectivity.' (Tillberg, P. (ed.) (2002) *Dialoger – om yrkeskunnande och teknologi*. Stockholm: Dialoger.)

9 See, for example: Ryle, G. (1949) *The Concept of Mind*. London: Hutchinson.

definitions. Many times, it concerns learning to live with, and accept that, certain dissension remains after a conversation. Perhaps what is paradoxical is that the very thing that is most important to agree upon is dissension on a concept's meaning.

What then characterises the concepts that Gallie calls essentially contested? First of all, an essentially contested concept has always a value dimension. It will express something one strives for as valuable to achieve. When the concept of leadership, for example, is used by members of the military, it nearly always occurs as interwoven with evaluations. One speaks of leadership in terms of good and bad, right and wrong. Secondly, these concepts are complex in that they always include other concepts. Leadership can, for example, be said to include a nearly unlimited amount of concepts, such as: resolute, judicious, fair, confidence-inspiring, imaginative, wise, active, etc. The third characteristic for an essentially contested concept is that which one wants to achieve, i.e. desirable leadership, is always comprised of a very complicated relationship between the concepts that were previously presented as a type of sub-concept. According to Gallie, one can comprehend leadership as a combination of resolute, judicious, fair, confidence-inspiring, etc. The combination differs considerably depending on by whom and in which situations the concepts are used and how they are evaluated. Fourthly, that which is sought after must always be able to be modified based on conditions changing. These modifications, he maintains, are not possible to predict. As to what, for example, shall be comprehended as leadership or not, he refers to the circumstances that are currently accepted as given in a practice. Different practices are in variance and therefore the concept of leadership is described, used and comprehended in many different ways. Gallie therefore calls these concepts open in character.

Knowledge of Different Methods for Investigating Practices

The primary indicator that one understands the meaning of, i.e. is well familiar with, a certain concept, is that one is considered by those around as a competent practitioner of the established line of conduct that embraces the concept (Johannessen, 1999). It is therefore important to learn more of how one performs a conceptual investigation. Developing various methods for investigating practice constitutes important knowledge for officers serving in a military environment. One reason for this is that the practice that is subsequently created makes no distinction between what is right and wrong, good and bad. An organisation in which one does not continually reflect upon and test patterns of conduct and language usage can therefore easily become rigid. Where this occurs, actions are uncertain and seemingly arbitrary. Maria Hammarén, researcher at the section for professional skills and technology, Royal Institute of Technology, writes in the essay 'Yrkeskunnande, berättelser och språk' (editor Tillberg, 2002): 'Experience in itself is no guarantee for good judgment – clichés and rigid perspectives arise when old experiences lie in the way of new.' Hammarén's observation shows that a prevailing practice must be continually examined and subjected to testing. It is primarily through investigating with others how the concepts are used in various language games that one can approach a common understanding of their different areas of use. Such an investigation initially consists of describing, and thereby also refreshing one's memory of, the usage of language used in a specific practice. This is done by placing questions, presenting examples and making comparisons between different language games. It concerns investigation of how language works in our daily environment rather than intellectualising over the meaning of words. Presentations of problems that from the beginning are often considered as meaningful can later, as the investigation progresses, prove to be meaningless and the questions that were initially asked with regard to a phenomenon may even need to be reformulated. For example, trying to answer the question 'What is leadership?' in a universal sense is hardly possible. Instead one can rephrase the question to focus on as 'In which situations do officers practise leadership?' and 'In which contexts do officers use and encounter the leadership concept?' In this way, the investigation can be put in concrete form and one reduces the risk of nearly unending dispute on definitions and references.

Normative and Constitutive Rules

Neither officers nor anyone else would in practice assign arbitrary meanings in a concept such as leadership. To the contrary, one should understand a language game in which concepts are used as rule-guided usage of a language. The philosopher Allan Janik writes in *Kunskapsbegreppet i praktisk filosofi* (1996) that 'Through repetition a pattern is introduced, a regularity in my behaviour, while I at the same time learn the signification in an entire word constellation. What I have actually learned is to follow a rule, despite no formal rules being mentioned.' A professional group that is well familiar with various types of rules is that of officers. Some of these rules are formal in the respect that they are formulated as statements, while others are learned as customs and habits. The former are called normative and the latter constitutive.

The normative rules are formulated to specify which actions are permitted and not permitted, what is considered true and false. Examples of these types of rules are laws, regulations, directives and user manuals. We are all familiar with them and it is difficult to imagine that it would be possible to live without them. It is important to observe, however, that the normative rules are arbitrary in more than one sense. First of all, they should always be able to be formulated in a different way than what is the case for a particular occasion. The laws and rules that, for example, apply in war in respect to the right to use violence could very well be different than what they are today. Secondly, it is often shown that these types of rules are arbitrary because they can be interpreted in different ways. This entails that two different persons could very well be said to follow one and the same rule but that their actions would differ significantly for an observer and the results would seem different. Thirdly, a normative rule cannot either be formulated in such a way that itself specifies how it will ultimately be complied with. The philosopher Kjell S. Johannessen writes in his book *Praxis och tyst kunnande* (1999) 'The point is simple but profound. Because a definition or rule cannot itself specify how it will be used, it is not worthwhile to produce a new rule to establish how the first shall be used. For then one would just shift the problem to the new rule. It can, of course, also be perceived and followed in different ways. And so one can continue for eternity if one tries to resolve the problem by formulating even more rules for the usage of the first rule. This thus proves to be a dead-end.'

The normative rules are formed in such a way that they are universal. It must be so because they are not conceived to serve in a unique situation but rather in a number of different situations that nonetheless are reminiscent of one another. For this reason, one can say that there is often 'play' between the concrete in the situation or action and the general in the rule. Based on this, a normative rule is always more or less abstract in that it very seldom can capture all the aspects that the individual case embraces. Therefore the application always demands of a rule a personally acquired experience.[10] Therefore experienced officers, in contrast to advanced beginners, perceive the normative rules as a tip of sorts or rule of thumb, i.e. the rule indicates a direction for how one should act in various situations rather than marking off the action. This does not entail in any way that the normative rules lack importance. On the contrary, they are entirely necessary for a military practice to be able to develop. For an

---

10 Ramírez, J. L. (1995) *Skapande mening – En begreppsgenealogisk undersökning om rationalitet, vetenskap och planering.* (Avhandling 13:2) Stockholm: Nordplan.

advanced beginner, this type of rule plays a particularly decisive role in being able to develop a professional skill, which entails that with time, one becomes a proficient and experienced officer.

The constitutive rules differ from the normative in many ways. The constitutive rules often exist unreflected in a practice in the sense that we are not always aware of them. Not because one has neglected to learn of them, but rather because they are not formulated in written statements as are the normative rules. They are rules that exist in our natural manner of behaving in specific situations, i.e. customs and habits. The constitutive rules are implicit in an action and make themselves apparent through the ways in which the action is carried out (Göranzon 2001). In each practice there are constitutive rules and customs that are not formulated in expressed rules. In the Swedish armed forces, for example, it is practice that soldiers name their combat vehicles. Officers of higher ranks begin personal letters to colleagues with 'Dear brother!' and army officers who meet for the first time normally begin the conversation with ascertaining when and where the other underwent officer's training at Karlsberg Castle. The officer who has the highest rank or is oldest sits in front in the passenger seat in general purpose vehicles; the idea that he would sit in back is nearly inconceivable.

The constitutive rules do not just exist in the action; it is also where they are created.[11] It is the actions that bear up the rule, not the opposite, as one often might be led to believe. The constitutive rules arise by us becoming accustomed to acting in a certain way in concrete situations and they do not differentiate between good or bad actions. They are a form of agreement that is not described in words but rather instead makes itself known through the way in which people normally behave in situations that resemble one another. A perceptive observer can often differentiate patterns in how people act and it is in these patterns that the rule reveals itself. Learning to see these patterns is an important part of military professional skills. Not the least it is advantageous to be able to detect pattern-forming actions that run the risk of leading to negative consequences or destructive behaviour.

Rule-following Forms a Practice

The knowledge of how one follows or obeys a rule is not primarily in a person's mind or in a set of rules and regulations. The know-

---

11 Molander, B. (1996) *Kunskap i handling*. Götebor: Daidalos, 225.

ledge of various rules is in the action, i.e. implicit in the activity in which one is involved.[12] The practical know-how that the experienced officer possesses requires a type of sensitivity and attentiveness that is primarily based on the following of a rule. Wittgenstein writes in *Philosophical Investigations* (1953, §199): '...To obey a rule...(involves) customs (uses, institutions).' A few paragraphs later (§202) he writes 'obeying a rule is a practice.' If one is well versed in the normative rules and follows the constitutive, together a practice is formed.

The obeying of rules that characterises an officer's actions shall not be perceived as one always making conscious interpretations and assessment before one acts. When one follows a rule, one often does so entirely unconsciously. Wittgenstein writes in *Philosophical Investigations* (1953, §219): 'When I obey a rule, I do not choose. I obey the rule blindly.' It is so, however, that to be able to speak of obeying or following of a rule, it is necessary that afterwards one is able to determine that which is a correctly or faultily performed action or use of a concept. By together with others reflecting on which criteria that a practice consists of, one can investigate if someone acts in accordance with a rule or if one follows a rule. There is a significant difference here. One can, for example, through luck, chance or coincidence act in agreement with a rule without for that sake following the rule. The rule can only be said to be followed by someone who has experience and knowledge in the area. It concerns above all one having developed sureness in what is considered as like and that which is unlike. By making these comparisons, one can reach a number of fixed points that can be utilised to determine if one follows a rule or not. These fixed points are not always conscious but can become so through the performance of a practice being questioned and by beginning to reflect on the exercising of various rules. These must be able to be commented upon and revised in an inter-subjective space. A single person would never be able to ascertain if he is obeying a rule or if he only believes that he is following it (Johannessen, 1999). Because a rule cannot ultimately rest upon a definitive rule, it is in an institutionalised mode of action that one must seek answers to whether a rule is used in a correct manner or not. This is the only way that exists for a definitive determination of whether an action is performed correctly or whether a concept is used correctly or not (Johannessen, 1999; Winch, 1994).

---

12 Tsoukas, H. (1996) 'The Firm as a Distributed Knowledge System: A Constructivist Approach.' *Strategic Management Journal*, Vol. 17, 11–25.

Differences Between Novices and Experts

An important aspect of military professional skills is being able to differentiate between different types of rules and observe in which way action patterns develop a practice. Dreyfus and Dreyfus (1986) have developed a model that describes the difference between how a novice and a more experienced person follow rules and how these persons develop practical skills in relation to various types of rules. According to them, development occurs in five different stages: novice, advanced beginner, competent, skilled and expert. It shall be pointed out now that there is no natural relationship between which rank or position an officer holds and the various knowledge levels. An officer who, for example, holds the rank of colonel and works high up in the military hierarchy can very well be perceived as a novice or advanced beginner in his position, while a captain who serves as a platoon leader is perceived as an expert by those around him. It is also so that the person who is a novice in one situation can very well be an expert in another context.

According to Dreyfus and Dreyfus, the *novice* learns and develops skills by someone more knowledgeable than himself giving orders on how an action shall be carried out. It is not considered important to explain to the novice why he should act in a certain way, since he lacks the experience that is required for the explanation to be of any great help. The novice's learning can be compared to the newly recruited soldier's first encounter with a military practice. An experienced officer gives him orders to do different things based on established rules. The learning can be compared to a drill of sorts where corrections are continually made in conjunction with the novice's actions.

The *advanced beginner* also learns primarily through normative rules. He imitates how other, more experienced soldiers act in different situations. As he becomes more knowledgeable and learns the fundamental techniques for correct execution, he begins to apply these techniques in other, similar cases as well (Göranzon, 2002). An officer who, for example, in the beginning learned to use a firearm has learned about more than just the weapon. He has also learned a technique that applies to other weapons, i.e. that there are safety directives, firing rules, instructions for how the weapon shall be loaded, etc. At the same time as the advanced beginner utilises normative rules, he also learns the constitutive rules in parallel. Knowledge and understanding is now successively assimilated for how one shall act in different situations. The rule, one can say, is internalised as the advanced beginner trains (Janik, 1996). Besides the novice and advanced beginner having in common that they rely on normative sets of rules and regulations, they also blame the rules if something should go wrong or a mistake be made. Dreyfus and Dreyfus write that '*Novices and advanced beginners feel little responsibility for what they do because they are not applying learned rules: if they foul up, they blame the rules instead of themselves.*'

The *competent* officer begins to be able to see differences between situations that he previously believed to be alike. He also more often draws analogies between the areas that were previously perceived as very different. The competent officer links newly gained experiences with previous experiences and prefers to use reason to progress towards new action patterns that he considers desirable. Despite the normative rules later having dwindling importance, the competent officer still most often acts based on various plans, instructions and templates. He shares the novice's and advanced beginner's lack of experience in such a way that he many times cannot resolve unanticipated problems that occur.

He who has reached *skilled* status also follows rules but not primarily the rules that are in regulations and instructions. He follows the rules that he has learned in practice and that are often implied and taken for granted. These rules are primarily formulated not in a direct language but instead are demonstrated by more experienced officers in actions. A capacity that differentiates the skilled from the earlier stages is that he has learned through assessments of when one or the other is appropriate to execute. He is sufficiently experienced that he can determine what falls under a rule and what is an exception. The skilled also understand when one should act instinctively and when it is appropriate to consider different alternatives for action (Göranzon, 2001). He has with time developed judgement that entails that he seldom panics in unanticipated situations but rather can improvise a solution to the problem.

The *expert* often acts without planning or making assessments. When he encounters various tasks, he does not solve problems or make decisions. One shall instead perceive it that the expert performs what he would refer to as normal duty (Göranzon, 2001). The expert has learned this mode of action in regards to his duties by participating in a large number of different situations. He has learned to see similarities and differences through long training, and is sufficiently familiar with the context in which the expert is involved, that actions are performed without reflection. The expert is the person who has the trust of those around him to question prevailing practices because of his extensive experience and knowledge. He is also the one whom others consult when they face a difficult problem. Not problems that one can find answers to in a formulated set of rules and regulations, but rather in the experience gained through long training and reflection.

Differences Between Breaking Rules and Growing Beyond Them

The persons whom Dreyfus and Dreyfus refer to as skilled and experts do not break rules other than in exceptional cases, even if it can appear so to the less experienced. One should instead perceive their behaviour as having grown beyond the rules. Thomas Tempte writes in the book *Arbetets ära* (1982): 'Transgressing given rules is not foremost the opposition of the old authorities but rather a growing beyond. It requires not defiance but reflection...and in a certain situation one must perceive and sum up in one's mind: there is now a cut-off point, one cannot go back but only forward. If one has then worked sufficiently long, one has learned to rely on intuition, professional affiliation...a stability and continuity. The changes are material but task execution is the same.' The growing beyond that Tempte writes of is strongly connected to one reflecting on the situations that one is a part of or that one has heard about. It is through these reflections that one finds out which rules exist in the practice that one is active in and their possible relations to the following of rules that can be observed by studying action patterns. The development of a practice occurs when rules and the following of rules are changed. Writing a new leadership book, for example, containing a number of premises under the delusion that this alone would change officers' leadership and military practice is naïve. Deficient knowledge of rules and the following of rules can, however, entail that one only focuses on trying to make changes by introducing new normative rules. One attempts to remove a statement from the rule book and replace it with a new one and then expects that people will behave differently. This line of action is insufficient if one wants to change a practice. It is primarily the encounter between constitutive and normative rules that one must focus on.

With the Help of Examples a Practice can be Developed and Established

In the borderlands between different types of rules, officers often use examples and accounts to describe their professional skills. Wittgenstein writes in *Philosophical Investigations* (1953, §208) that 'if a person has not yet got the concepts, I shall teach him to use the words by means of examples and by practice.' This is well in agreement with how members of the armed forces learn practices. The examples used are taken both from concrete events in one's own activities but also many times through analogies, accounts and metaphors from related areas. They serve as objects for comparison, i.e. one often uses images in a broad sense to deepen understanding of the practice that one is a part of and the establishment of a new practice. The examples acquire, in this way, a meaning-constitutive role.

The reasons for using examples to develop both professional skills and practices are many. First of all, usage of examples means that one reduces the risk of conversations ending up in abstract generalisations and opinions. It is also so that they are of service when opinions, perceptions, rules and logical explanations no longer suffice for understanding the phenomenon to which one directs one's interest. Another motive is that one always takes a personal standpoint when one chooses an example to clarify something that one wishes to explain. It is often a risk of significant measure that requires personally acquired experiences on the part of the relater. Without these experiences, it often happens that the example falls flat and is perceived by a more experienced audience only as opinions, platitudes or clichés. Only he who has experience in the area is able to be concrete. It is also so that recognition of others' examples is the core in the inter-subjectivity that can later be developed around a concept or phenomenon.

In addition to being able to recognise oneself in examples, it is also important that they capture something that the group as a whole does not itself have words or a language for (Janik, 1996). With support of a good example, one can receive help in examining one's own experiences in the light of someone else's accounts. To listen to other's stories is thus not just a way to ensure that one is in agreement on the content of a certain concept or phenomenon, it is also a way to progress in a common knowledge process. Examples differ above all from definitions and claims in such a way that they are always open in character. With this, it is meant that they are diversified. Just as everyone can recognise themselves in a good example, examples can also be given different interpretations. This entails that a good example does not simplify complicated arguments and issues that one is trying to come to grips with. It is rather so that a good account contributes to one seeking further towards underlying lines of thought, i.e. towards a deeper understanding. To use an example is often the same as to learn something through something else. They open the way for new interpretations and discussions that one could not previously anticipate. José Luis Ramírez writes in the dissertation *Skapande mening* that 'An example is nothing more than a concrete episode, actual or fictive that, just as is the case with an illustration, permits us to understand something other than what it directly relates.'

It is in this encounter between example and reality that various types of comparisons of rules and professional skills are made and learning can occur. It is here that different types of knowledge are developed and practices created. If one listens to officers discussing military professional skills and leadership, one often hears that they interweave the concept of practice in the various language games. This is well in agreement with Wittgenstein, who argues that a practice is a type of helping or fundamental concept that is primarily used to interpret and analyse how other concepts in the language are formed, used and spread. It is primarily when one studies how language works between people and when the concept of practice is linked to other words that it can be given a meaningful function.[13]

Various Forms of Knowledge

The first person to establish a typology of the various forms of knowledge was Aristotle in the third century BC.[14] He made a distinction between practical knowledge/wisdom (*phronesis*) and two other forms of knowledge, scientific knowledge (*episteme*) and craftsmanship (*techne*). Scientific knowledge, Aristotle maintained, embraced that which is eternal and unchanging, i.e. that which cannot be different than what is the case. Craftsmanship (*techne*), on the other hand, is knowledge that one learns through gaining various abilities through practice. Here it concerns learning various techniques for achieving skills within an area that is intended to be productive, i.e. an activity that has a goal. Officers learn various techniques, for example, to be able to disassemble and assemble a weapon, drive a tank or salute. The practical knowledge (*phronesis*) in turn embraces changeable conditions, i.e. such knowledge that can be changed from one point in time to another. To have practical skills in an area primarily entails being well familiar with a given situation and its possible rules of behaviour. He who has practical knowledge in an area has developed a type of wisdom, judgement or habit. Officers primarily develop this ability through training and reflection on a large number of different situations that are embraced in military professional skills.

At the beginning of the 1900s, the logical positivists tore down the knowledge typology that Aristotle had so laboriously built up. What remained after logical analysis was a coarse simplification of the knowledge concept. Knowledge was now just that which could be formulated in a language and empirically supported or proven with logical and

---

13 Wittgenstein's philosophy can in many ways be described as a practice philosophy (see, for example, Johannessen, *Praxis och tyst kunnande*, 1999).

14 Aristotle (1967) *Den nikomachiska etiken*. Göteborg: Daidalos AB.

mathematical methods. The moral and ethical dimensions, for example, had vanished and what was left was a depleted knowledge-theoretical legacy. One of those who during later years invested considerable effort in shading understanding surrounding the concept of knowledge was the philosopher Kjell S. Johannessen. In the articles 'Tankar om tyst kunskap' and 'Det analogiska tänkandet' (Tillberg, ed., 2002) he writes of four different forms of knowledge that are both close to Aristotle's ideas on the nature of knowledge and Wittgenstein's discussion on rules and the following of rules.

Propositional or theoretical knowledge encompasses what one would commonly refer to as facts. It is the knowledge that is formulated in a language and that one can learn in books, accounts, instructions, etc. Declarative knowledge shall be perceived as a product or the result of investigations and deliberations. Officers often encounter this type of knowledge in regulations and training descriptions. *Skill, or practical knowledge* cannot be gained by studies. It is the knowledge that is created in conjunction with one doing something. It is in the actual performance that one gains proficiency knowledge. Afterwards, as one becomes more skilful in an area, one begins to master a trained technique. This technique can be described in various texts that one can have use of, but one learns the technique primarily through actions. Being able to shoot, drive a general purpose vehicle or perform first aid are examples of proficiency knowledge that most members of the military have acquired. *Knowledge of familiarity* is also a form of knowledge that cannot be captured in a language or normative rules. To be familiar with something is often about learning to handle that which is unique and deviating. Knowledge of familiarity resembles what Aristotle called practical knowledge. It is primarily created when a person trains in a practice by finding out about its traditions and examples.[15] Officers can, for example, develop familiarity in making assessments in critical situations where the use of violence is one of many possible alternatives for action. In conclusion, *judgement*, entails, according to Johannessen, having developed a moral sense for what is right or good to do both in the individual and general case. Having developed judgement based on moral and ethical principles constitutes perhaps one of the most important parts of a soldier's professional skills. This is done primarily by reflecting on different rules' applicability in critical and difficult contexts in which the officer makes decisions, gives orders and uses violence.

Johannessen's description of various forms of knowledge does not entail the same as stating that different knowledge is used on different occasions.

---

15 Göranzon, B. (1990) *Det praktiska intellektet.* Stockholm: Carlssons, 138.

Instead, one should perceive it that the various forms of knowledge in action complement and overlap one another.

Establishment of Practice Requires more than Declarative Knowledge and Normative Rules

As we can see, propositional or theoretical knowledge is formulated in a similar manner as normative rules. Because a normative rule in itself cannot guarantee that the rule is followed in the same way from case to case, it is not possible to establish a practice with the support of these types of rules alone. The answer to how a practice is created is found primarily if the focus is directed towards the performance, i.e. people's actions and the use of the language (Johannessen, 1999). It concerns learning to observe pattern-forming actions, trying to understand how these arise, are performed, and perhaps eventually, even disappear. Instead of focusing on the rules, interest is attention to the *following of rules*. Consequently, the knowledge that is needed to be able to follow a rule in practice concerns something more than just knowing of the formulated rule. An understanding and knowledge of sorts is required on the part of the user of the rule, and what it attempts to relate.

Let us now use a little example from military practice that does not concern leadership but rather cooking. We are at a field kitchen where we meet the cook. Because he knows that the soldiers like pancakes, he had planned to make pancakes for lunch. To be able to make pancakes, he uses a recipe in his cookbook. There he reads 'First beat 30 eggs to a smooth and porous batter.' At first glance, it is a declarative piece of knowledge that seems clear and distinct, impossible to misunderstand. Upon a closer examination, however, one sees that the person who reads the recipe, the cook, must know more than the rule expresses. The recipe assumes, among other things, that one knows what a pancake is, what it entails to beat, the meaning of the word 'first', the number 30, the difference between smooth and coarse, the concepts of porous and batter, etc. It is thus insufficient to be able to read the statement (recipe/rule) verbatim; one must also put it in a context where the user's understanding of the situation is central. It is also so that if one investigates what is meant by beat, for example, the cook needs to know what a whisk is, etc. This seemingly uncomplicated example is intended to show that theoretical knowledge, expressed as normative rules, does not constitute the basis for human action.

Cooking here serves as an example of a practice that entails usage of a language closely associated with the performance that the cook demonstrates in actions, i.e. beating, counting, etc. In the performance of his duties, the cook learns, through training, more than just the rules formulated in writing. He learns something more. He sharpens his skills, familiarity and judgement through training. At the beginning when he is a novice and advanced beginner, he learns many normative rules expressed as declarative knowledge. Afterwards, as he becomes more experienced, he learns by seeing how others act when they cook. He tries out what is possible to accomplish with various ingredients and utensils, sometimes failing and subsequently, he may act differently the next time. When he has become truly proficient, other less experienced cooks ask for his help. He has now learned not only how to cook various types of food, but also a large number of language games that are encompassed in the cooking practice. Despite the cook having learned a new language, this does not at all mean that his professional skills can be captured in this language. On the contrary, a large portion of the professional skills is embraced by what is referred to as tacit knowledge (Göranzon, 1990; Janik, 1996; Johannessen, 1999).

Tacit Knowledge

We all have tacit knowledge in various areas. One can, for example, very well have knowledge of walking without this entailing that one would be able to explain or capture everything that happens in the body during a walk in a language. Most can also speak, dance, think, love, hate, read, wash, sleep, etc. without being able to give an all-encompassing description of what and how one does to someone who lacks knowledge in these areas. That much of our knowledge is tacit is not the same as language not being used when we acquire this knowledge or that it cannot be used to provide a more general description of an action. On the contrary, language plays an important role in all knowledge acquisition. When it comes to tacit knowledge, however, it is not possible to describe for someone how one learns to perform a practical action with the help of statements, normative rules or logical propositions alone (Janik, 1996). If an officer, for example, is to learn leadership, he does not accomplish this just through the acquisition of knowledge through various books; it is something that must be learned through actions and training.

Tacit knowledge is experience-based knowledge. It is not supported, as is declarative knowledge, by models, theories and formalised methods. It is instead anchored in a type of rules of thumb these shall be perceived as approximated summaries of previous experiences. It is often expressed in an illustrative language (analogies, examples, metaphors, similes, etc.).

The cook in the example above might, for example, be able to describe how he holds the whisk by saying 'You should not hold it too tightly, but not too loosely either. Imagine how carefully you hold, for example, a small bird. Not too tightly because it would then be injured, but not too loosely because it would then fly away. This is approximately how it is when you hold the whisk in the right way.' When this is not enough, he demonstrates how one beats by getting a whisk and a bowl. He could also let the person who asks to hold the whisk try it, rebuking and correcting as needed. Once can also encourage and give praise. Experience-based knowledge proves to be a combination of actions and words.

The origin of rules of thumb is in human behaviour in concrete situations. It is not something that one primarily has studied to obtain but rather such that one learns with the passing of time as one is involved in various situations. Tacit knowledge is a combination of developed judgement and ability in analogical thought. Knowledge is acquired primarily though practical tasks, training and examples. In various examples, it is possible to see family likenesses between various problem situations. Here it deals with analogical likenesses that one learns something from; one has through these opportunities to become familiar with the specific problem area that is the subject of one's interest. The purpose of the examples is to contribute that which rules and descriptions cannot attain.

Conclusion

The chapter began with reference to a few brief examples from influential Swedish officers of the 1900s. An extract was also presented of the order given to the first Swedish UN battalion just prior to being sent to Bosnia. The purpose of these short passages from military practice is primarily to show the complexity that officers can encounter when faced with the performance of their profession. Regardless of whether this applies to military training or command of a unit, there are certain aspects that recur in their descriptions. It is also clear that the approach to what characterises military practice and the officers' professional skills is well in agreement with the epistemological perspective that has been presented. What is distinctive is primarily the emphasis on how one learns in the military profession by involving oneself in a large number of situations where one's knowledge and experiences are heavily taxed. The next step in knowledge development primarily occurs when one together with others in various contexts is given the opportunity to reflect upon one's experiences. Development of both military practice and the knowledge that the individual officer possesses also have a close relation to understanding of how language functions between people. Language must thereby attain a meaning beyond what is implicitly expressed in many of the sets of rules and regulations used in military practices. It concerns both a knowledge-related shift as well as a mental shift of sorts from reliance on concept definitions and rules, towards a contextual understanding of how the language functions in varying contexts. The proficient officer has both learned to see differences between various practices and situations, and at the same time, must be open to seeing likenesses and analogies between widely varying knowledge areas and cultures. Let us now conclude the article with a brief quote from the Swedish Armed Forces' 'Militärstrategisk doktrin' (2002) that demonstrates the need for a qualified dialogue and reflection on the experience-based knowledge that exists in various areas:

> Culture is based on individuals not learning everything from their own experiences. Similarly, professional skills within the armed forces are based to a high degree on utilising the knowledge and experience of others, and on drawing relevant conclusions for the future.

References

Aristotle (1967) *Den nikomachiska etiken.* Göteborg: Daidalos AB.

Artéus, G. (ed.) (1996) *Svenska officersprofiler under 1900-talet.* Karlskrona: Militärhögskolan & Axel Abrahamsons Förlag.

Dreyfus, H. and Dreyfus, S. (1986) 'Why Computers May Never Think Like People.' *Technology Review,* Vol. 89, January.

Florin, M. and Göranzon, B. (eds) (1996) *Den Inre Teatern.* Stockholm: Carlssons.

Försvarsmakten (2002) *Militärstrategisk doktrin.* Stockholm: Försvarsmakten.

Gallie, W.B. (1955–56) *Essentially Contested Concepts.* London: *Proceedings from the Aristotelian Society,* Vol. 56.

Göranzon, B. (1990) *Det praktiska intellektet.* Stockholm: Carlssons.

Göranzon, B. (2000) *Spelregler – om gränsöverskridande.* Stockholm: Dialoger

Gyllenkrok, A. (1943) *Synpunkter rörande utbildning.* Malmö unspecified publisher.

Hammarén, M. (1999) *Ledtråd i förvandling.* Stockholm: Dialoger.

Janik, A. (1996) *Kunskapsbegreppet i praktisk filosofi.* Stockholm: Brutus Östling Bokförlag Symposium.

Johannessen, K.S. (1999) *Praxis och tyst kunnande.* Stockholm: Dialoger.

Molander, B. (1996) *Kunskap i handling.* Göteborg: Daidalos.

Ramírez, J.L. (1995) *Skapande mening – En begreppsgenealogisk undersökning om rationalitet, vetenskap och planering.* (Avhandling 13:2) Stockholm: Nordplan.

Ryle, G. (1949) *The Concept of Mind.* London: Hutchinson.

Tillberg, P. (ed.) (2002) *Dialoger – om yrkeskunnande och teknologi.* Stockholm: Dialoger.

Tsoukas, H. (1996) 'The Firm as a Distributed Knowledge System: A Constructivist Approach.' *Strategic Management Journal*, Vol. 17, 11–25.

Winch, P. (1994) *Samhällsvetenskapens idé och dess relation till filosofin.* Stockholm: Thales.

Wittgenstein, L. (1953) *Philosophical Investigations.* Oxford: Basil Blackwell.

Wittgenstein, L. (1958) *The Blue and Brown Books.* Oxford: Blackwell Publishers Ltd.

Wittgenstein, L. (1969) *On Certainty.* Oxford: Basil Blackwell.

Wittgenstein, L. (1978) *Remarks on Colour.* Berkeley: University of California Press.

11 Science and Art

Karl Dunér, Lucas Ekeroth and Mats Hanson

MATS HANSON:

Science and Art – University and Theatre – a common environment for knowledge formation

The process of learning and education at the tertiary level is, even today, often considered to consist of the transfer of information from teacher to student. This is particularly true of the engineering graduates of today. This chapter takes as its starting-point the notion that education must be based more on the individual student's own concepts and framework of reference. From these, the student can build up new knowledge and gain broader understanding and experience.

It is misleading, inaccurate and unfair to attribute failures in education simply to the idea that the students are intellectually feeble and unmotivated. Interest, focus and commitment are generated by an intimate interplay between the student and the environment (teachers, fellow-students and their milieu) in which he operates. The student's development of knowledge and maturity is linked to a rich and complex body of influences that may also be indirect, unintentional and unconscious. When we set the scene for learning, we must make planned and considered use of the range of influences at our disposal. To structure a course of education around the theory that knowledge is best 'learnt' by transferral from the teacher to the student in lectures, exercises and laboratory experiments is narrow-minded, inadequate and wrong.

This chapter attempts to show how interaction across traditional cultural and disciplinary boundaries may enrich the people involved, in this case in the Master of Science programme, and the development of a multidisciplinary work of art, Company I-VII.

The Course as a Stage for Learning

We ask, from an educational perspective, if an ordinary course that is part of the regular Master of Science programme can be transformed into a stage for learning: a stage in the figurative sense, a platform for new types of teaching and a meeting-place for largely student-controlled learning in a dialogue with people from a different culture and tradition, in this case with people from the arts and the theatre.

The course discussed in this chapter is the Advanced Mechatronics course at KTH (The Institute of Technology, Stockholm), a course which has run since 1984. The development of mechatronics as a subject is linked to the evolution of microelectronics and programming, and also to that well-worn term, IT (Information Technology). Already in the 1970s, the then professor of Machine Elements, Jan Schnittger, put forward the idea that '*the microprocessor is a machine element*'. The idea was that we would treat electronic components in the same way as we had always treated cog wheels, ball bearings, etc. At the time, this statement was new and epoch-making. It introduced an entirely new approach to the subject of mechanical design, namely mechatronics. It was evident to some, but not all, that mechanical machines would change radically as a result of microelectronics and computer technology. Facit, the Swedish electromechanical company, is only one of many examples of the way a shift in technology drastically changed the conditions in which a company operates.

Since 1984 the Advanced Mechatronics course has been deliberately used as an 'experimental workshop' for introducing and developing new pedagogical forms and theoretical content. Although the content of the course changes from year to year, it has a clear philosophy and a defined framework based on the following three 'balances'.

- Feedback, reward and assessment of the students' performance.
- The interplay between knowledge and skills, the balance between theory and practice.
- The balance between assuming individual responsibility and the ability to co-operate in large groups.

The amount of feedback has a strong influence on the learning process. Sophisticated and appropriate feedback on student performance gives better results in the form of lasting understanding, knowledge and competence: so-called in-depth learning. Feedback is linked to the way we assess performance. Students usually expect a course to end with a written examination. The results of this examination are often the only feedback they receive.

In this course we attempt to balance feedback by identifying hard and soft stimuli. Examples of hard stimuli are still the written or verbal examination of the individual's knowledge. Examples of soft stimuli are feedback and the external assessment of group performance.

The interaction between knowledge and skill relates to the way the individual performs, structures, builds up new knowledge. Most of the teaching at an institute of technology is based on behaviourism. In this view knowledge is a correct in-out relationship, there is a correct answer and knowledge can be learnt by transferring it in verbal or written form. Our approach relates more to the perspective of constructivism, in which knowledge is constructed from the individual's earlier knowledge and experience. The new knowledge must be given a context for each individual.

Further, knowledge must be operational in some sense; it must be possible to use it in new, complex situations, and it must work in different socio-technical environments. Here, the balance comes in between being able to work individually, to take responsibility and to operate in a social context in which many people are involved. The interplay between different people in a learning process is an important point to illustrate as an integrated part of the course.

On these three foundation stones we have built a stage for learning: the Advanced Mechatronics course, see Figure 1.

I have chosen to organise the course as a project that aims to develop an actual product, an artefact, in co-operation with an external partner. The project and the product are a motivation factor in the learning process. The choice of external partner is important. A new partner is

Figure 1—A stage for learning

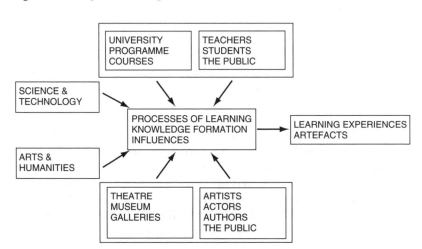

chosen for each year, for each new course. In most cases it has been an industrial partner, often from Sweden's engineering sector. However, we shall focus here on the Company I-VII project, which combines in a joint project art and the humanities with the natural sciences and technology.

KARL DUNÉR:
Company I-VII

How can an unexpected event appear to give a more powerful emotion than an expected event? This is a simple question to which I have failed to find an answer. The symphony orchestra rarely gives me the same strong feeling of the essence of the piece that the street musician evokes by simply playing its theme! Even more rarely do I experience any emotion in a theatre. When I read a book, the experience is coloured by my expectations, with the very title or cover of the book channelling my thoughts along a particular path.

The unexpected picture, thought or piece of music enters the consciousness in a different way. This may be one reason why I have long had the idea of a performance that runs itself entirely, that is controlled neither by the actors, nor the reaction of the audience or myself, the director. This performance should not begin when I have taken my seat in the theatre and the curtain has risen, but should be going on round the clock, year in, year out, whether anyone is watching or not.

In contrast to the nature of theatre, this production must have absolute integrity. Neither can it repeat itself. Each moment must be unique, as in an eternal improvisation on a given theme.

I imagined seven box-like forms hanging on the wall. I call them Company. Each has a human-like figure. These figures move forward slowly, very slowly, in all directions and across the whole floor area of Company. Their movements are only limited by the dimensions of the room. Sometimes they stand still, perhaps for five seconds, a minute or a whole day or more, then they turn, stop, and move in a different direction. The figures may also be in constant motion for hours or days. Sometimes they position themselves behind a couple of shapes in the room and are invisible to the observer for minutes, hours or days. Their movements are determined by a kind of randomness, an arranged chance.

When, after an undetermined period of slow, wandering movement the figures arrive at certain unmarked places in the room, they stop and listen to a thought, a monologue. In other places they hear a piece of music or some other sound. This may happen every fifteen minutes, once an hour or week, at night, or not for a month and then three times in succession, etc.

The random algorithms that control the movements of the figures determine when they will pass these different unmarked places. This aimless wandering is also punctuated from time to time by the figures walking along a little path of their own. Each figure has its own path, usually in the form of a geometrical figure, sometimes a more complicated pattern. The slowness of their movements means that it takes the observer many months to see the paths the figures take. Over the years, their paths may form tracks in the floor. These paths are controlled in the same way as the places where there are texts and sounds.

It is important that each Company is unique. They must be in equal parts sculpture, painting and theatre. Each of them has its own character, both in appearance and content. Each has its own texts, its own specially-written music, etc. down to the last detail. The main texts are from Beckett, Queneau, Perec, de Chirico and Rousell. All the texts are read by the actor, Sven Lindberg. The main piece of music was written and played by Richard Pilat, the composer. It is made up of a large number of short pieces, lasting from ten seconds to many tens of minutes. It may be a mathematical possibility that all the pieces are played in a particular order, one after the other, moving from Company to Company. If this happened, the piece of music, which is many hours long, would appear to have been composed as a single whole. It is, however, more likely that after many years one would still be surprised by pieces one had not heard before.

Now let us give you an idea of how much sound there is in the work. If we sit in front of a Company for a whole year we will probably hear most of the music, provided we have sat there twenty-four hours a day. That is how much music there is recorded or, if you will, this is how rarely do we and the figures hear anything! (Normally between three and fifteen times a day.) Some sounds occur more often than others. The probability of hearing some pieces is so remote that they may not be heard until four o'clock in the morning in three years' time, or just now and then not until next summer. Some rare sounds have a completely different character from the others, which will disturb our impression of the whole when, suddenly, one day, they reach us.

Essentially, I have no control of this. It may happen that the texts that are central to me are only heard at night. (This was something that amused us, particularly the actor; certainly seventy per cent of my work (programming, recording and almost all the input of the actor), can hardly be imagined from the finished work.)

These wall sculptures are intended to be Company. They can be hung at home or at the office, in your dentist's or doctor's waiting-room, at the airport and so on. If two or more are displayed together, brief and unexpected dialogues will take place from time to time. A sentence from

Beckett will get a response from Perec or Queneau, or the reverse. A piece of music will accompany someone else's monologue, or play a duet with a third Company. Two figures move together, apart, parallel, alternating. New pictures are constantly occurring which can never be repeated.

To return to what I began by saying, about the unexpected, it sometimes happens that the Company I have hanging at home at the moment suddenly breaks in when I am idly watching a TV programme. All I can say is that it puts special thoughts into my mind!

I am also amused by the effect produced by the Company that the Principal of the KTH has. In the middle of an important meeting the voice of Sven Lindberg may suddenly intone, '*You are on your back at the foot of an aspen. In its trembling shade.*' I assume that the meeting may take an unexpected direction.

The expressions of the Company were created through close co-operation between myself and Peder Freiij, the artist and scenographer. If I sought a kind of hesitation in the figure's movements, or an unceasing, resolute roving, we wanted to find in the shape of the figure an equivalence, as if it is at once about to emerge and vanish.

One day a visitor made an agreeable comment, that the figure looked like a man from the front and a woman from the rear. We also wanted to instil into the Company's room some kind of hesitation, as if it was about to be developed or crumble away.

I recall how surprised many of the students were when they saw the result of the work. They had delivered a box, filled to overflowing with sophisticated and exclusive electronics. It reeked of 'high tech'. Every angle had been calculated exactly, every wiring and programming detail was logical and essential. What they now saw had no association whatsoever with technology and good order. Rather, as many thought, it looked half-finished. Filler, artist's canvas, glue and wood. Doubt, chance and persistent randomness.

Perhaps it may be described as a paradox. That the expressions of the Company are opposed to every aspect of their prerequisites – the computer and mechatronics.

LUCAS EKEROTH:
From the Perspective of the Students

Once Karl had given us his basic ideas for Company I-VII they had to be translated into definable, measurable requirements which were brought together in a demand specification. From this demand specification a number of essential functions crystallised out that the finished work must have. These functions are grouped into sub-systems, or modules. Which functions are needed and which are suitable has evolved from the *knowledge and experience* that the *28 students, including teachers and the partner in the project* can contribute. The functions and interfaces of the sub-systems are set out in a systems specification. At the next stage they are implemented and tested.

The step from specification to implementation often involves a modification of existing design ideas. The ability to recycle design ideas and place them in a new context is invaluable. Why re-invent the wheel when someone else has already done it? Or, '*not invented here, just stolen with pride...*' Thus it is a good idea to study the way other product developers, programmers or designers have achieved a function that is included in our system specification. A new and quite unique design is not created until the different sub-designs or solutions are put together to form a functioning whole.

MATS HANSON:

At the Royal Dramatic Theatre all the costumes are saved, to be brought out, re-worked and used in new plays. A look at the wardrobe tells us that a single costume or pair of shoes has been used by many actors and in many plays over the years. And at the design office all mechanical drawings are saved, as are computer program lists and other design material, to be brought out later, modified and used in other contexts. The capability to re-use things is part of the knowledge of creativity.

LUCAS EKEROTH:

Have we thought of everything? Will two different modules with common interfaces match? When 28 students are working in parallel, a great deal happens almost simultaneously. There is always the risk that a detail is overlooked, that it falls between two stools, so to speak. How long does it take to order, manufacture, assemble and test a function? What does it cost? Who is responsible for making sure this is done? Avoiding bottlenecks is a difficult task. Manufacture cannot easily be begun before there is a drawing. The mechanical design cannot be fully tested unless there is a computer program that allows the mechanics to be tested.

When the sub-functions have been implemented, they are brought together to form whole functions. These sub-systems are then integrated to make a single unit, a complete system. At last, all that remains is the last step in our product development cycle: the final inspection. Have Karl's demands been met?

MATS HANSON:

A designer must have many strings to his bow. Sophisticated mechatronics products consist of more than technology. Creating a product is the result of an interplay which requires many role figures. The people who work on the design of the main functions and master the most advanced technology are considered to have the main role here. It is easy to overlook the ancillary functions, functions that no-one sees or considers, that are vague or hard to express. It is the small details that make up the whole – the supporting roles may be more important than the main role.

KARL DUNÉR:

In working with the students I took roughly the same role that I normally have, that of director. They were 'actors', each with a specific task, with small and large roles. In the theatre if one neglects the supporting roles, the effect of the whole is lost. Without a believable servant, there is no king, so to speak. This is also true of Company I-VII and the students. If the design of the supporting bracket is neglected, there is no point in the actor having learnt huge amounts of text, while others have produced a programming solution. Company will fall off the wall.

LUCAS EKEROTH:

In the work of meeting the demands, technical solutions are put forward that are already known or that one has learned about to meet the demands generated by Karl's ideas. It is important that progress is checked with Karl at regular intervals. If part of a result is not satisfactory, we have to iterate one or more stages backwards in our product development cycle and then attempt to improve on the solution. There is, of course, quite a lot of give and take here.

Karl's ideas cannot always be carried out by using reasonable means. In these cases, one must draw upon one's full engineering expertise, and attempt to present an alternative solution that gives a different end result, but is still close to the original idea. Sometimes the reverse occurs as well, i.e., the technology opens up possibilities for better solutions than were originally envisaged. An ability to be able, *at the development stage* to both *see the work in an overall perspective* and *at the next moment focus on a detail* which may be *vital to the whole* is very important.

Using sketches and models, and after much discussion, we approach a solution that both parties believe will work. Of course one has to leave scope for changes in the technical solution as a hedge against a result not being fully satisfactory. Further, the part-solutions that require Karl's fine adjustment must be user-friendly and functional. A computer program for setting parameters is there to make things easier, and not to complicate and obstruct. Once this requirement is met, Karl can concentrate on what is important; for example, what does it look like when figures move over time, and how does it feel? If Karl is satisfied with a setting, it is of no interest at all if the figure is finally set at a speed of 1.395 mm/sec.

KARL DUNÉR:

The students built up an entire program which I, even with my minimal knowledge, could fully control. I can give each separate sound its volume and its probability of occurring, each figure has its own pace and carries itself in its own unique way. The programs allow me to simulate the events of several weeks in a few short minutes, or follow up retroactively the events of a few days. I was given very precise and organised tools with which to build chance.

MATS HANSON:

What is right and what is wrong? There is not always an unambiguous answer to this question. How do we deal with the ambiguous, the unclear and the unknown? What is negotiable? The ability to interpret visions, emotions and unstated demands requires knowledge that cannot be learned from a schoolbook. One must get into the situation and create an inner picture by modelling and simulations, etc., but also by studying and living with people one learns from the masters. We usually call this process apprenticeship.

Will Company I-VII work faultlessly for many years to come? From one viewpoint, this is an uninteresting question. Has the co-operation between the theatre and the university enriched the education of, in this case, the Masters of Science of the future? To return to the beginning of this chapter, I note that the co-operation between art and theatre brought forward our 'three balances': feedback and reward, knowledge and skill and co-operation across cultural boundaries.

LUCAS EKEROTH:

'*The ability to think differently today than yesterday is what separates the wise from the obstinate*', is a quotation we were often reminded of during the development work. *An example*: a cable for a vital sensor that constantly followed the figure's movements failed after a while. We tried different types of cable, attachments, routing, etc., but sooner or later it failed again. It is in situations like this that *creativity and unconventional solutions* come into their own. In hindsight, the solution may seem ridiculously simple, as is often the case with ingenious solutions.

When those of us who were responsible for this function sat down and pondered the problem, we began to joke about it, and one of us said, '*What shall we do with a cable that simply fails? Let's just take it away*'. And as if by magic, we began to think along different lines. It proved possible to read the electrical signal which would indicate if a motor stopped on the circuit board that controls the motors that drive this work of art. This signal changes its value from low to high when the motor stops because it does not reach its intended goal. By simply adding a few lines of program code we managed to reinstate the sensor function in a way that was also durable.

The basis for finding the solution to the above problem lies in the fact that the knowledge of individual students is drawn into the group's dialogue. A student shared a wild and 'impossible' idea. Another student had detailed knowledge of a circuit board...Together, we were able to solve the problem we had been struggling with for weeks.

Some of Karl's ideas are hard to express as concrete demands with measurable values. These demands therefore become diffuse, but they are sometimes even more important than the simple measurable demands. They may be based on an overall impression or an emotion.

'*Karl, at what speed should this figure move?*'
'*Very slowly*'
'*Can't you show us how slowly? Take this tin. Move it along this ruler at the speed you think the figures should move...*'

By measuring the time of this movement over a given distance we could calculate what was a very vague 'slow speed' as about 10 mm/sec. We were satisfied. We now believed we had managed to get a measurement of the speed at which the figures should move. Later in the process, we had to revise this several times. When the first prototype was to be built, we felt that Karl would not keep to an exact 10 mm/sec. when he had a chance to change the speed in discrete steps of 1mm a second. It was when he had gone from the 'original' 10 mm/sec down to 2 mm/sec. that he began to be satisfied, but not fully satisfied. Karl then felt that 2 mm/sec. was too fast and 1 mm/sec. was too slow. Something had to be done... By simply increasing the speed setting by a factor of 1,000 we gave Karl new opportunities he had not dreamed of when we first asked him to move a tin to give us an idea of the speed of the figure's movements. Today, all seven figures seem at first glance to be moving at the same slow speed. But if one watches them for a while one notices that they all move at slightly different speeds, at different degrees of slowness. It may seem quite unnecessary to be able to change the speed by 0.001 mm/sec., but Karl found this to be an important principle, one of the tools that would give each figure its particular character, its pace.

KARL DUNÉR:

This is undeniably a good example of how the work surged forwards. On several points my ideas were developed. I had imagined that the seven figures would all move at the same speed. Now I can give each of them a stronger personality by introducing individual paces of movement. Then I was also given access to a whole palette of random algorithms which gave me broader possibilities to give the seven figures their own relationships to space and time. Equally important was the number of sound points. At first I had thought there would be five points/places; that is, only five possible sounds. Soon I was offered a virtually unlimited number of sounds!

LUCAS EKEROTH:

As we all know, the advanced technology had to be built into the box in some way. At first we had no idea at all of how to do this. After a while we heard a rumour that we had been 'allocated' a wall with a 10 cm. cavity. Still no easy task to squeeze everything in, but at least something to start from. At an important design meeting the different groups presented their results. One group had been given the job of building a mock-up (a 1:1 scale model). Karl was obviously satisfied with the result. Now everyone knew the spatial limitation of the box. Various technical solutions were then developed. Several weeks later, however, the people working most intensively on building-in the technology got a slight shock... Karl had changed his mind... He writhed a little as he told us that he thought the wall was not satisfactory. It was far too thick!

It had to be removed...(gulp!). Had weeks of work been in vain? Many of us began to wonder if Karl really knew what he wanted. Would the project ever be completed if he was always changing what we thought was a set demand specification? After that, we took great pains to check with Karl that he was sure he wanted something to be in this way or that...Of course he changed his mind several times as the work proceeded. Looking back, we can agree that the thick cavity wall would not have been a satisfactory solution.

KARL DUNÉR:

An essential feature of the whole idea was the invisibility of the technology. The observer must have no idea where it is located or how it works. A 5 cm. thick floor would immediately reveal where the muscles were, and the lightness we were striving for in the sculpture would be compromised.

One day at the exhibition at the gallery I was pleased to hear a group of youths suggest that the figures had to be battery-powered. That is how simple it looked. I was just as pleased when an elderly lady wondered if the figures actually moved towards the observer if one actually stood and watched for long enough. That was the impression she had, as if the figure responded in some way, establishing contact with the observer. Illusory life is nothing more than just that – illusory.

LUCAS EKEROTH:

Many of us thought at first that it would be easy to develop the technical design for Company I-VII. To move an object in different directions in a single plane did not appear to be difficult. Some of Karl's demands were more difficult to meet than we had originally thought. The mechanical design that allows the figures to move must be so thin that it would not be conspicuous. The solution would also have to be silent, i.e., it should emit no sound that an observer could associate with technology. The final solution would have to run constantly, 24 hours a day, week in, week out. How can one determine that it will do that? Will the figure ever cross the front edge of the box or go in to the wall? Will the computer programs that consist of thousands of executable lines of program code work perfectly? All we can say today is that we only have left all the program bugs that, after many months of testing, we have not uncovered and put right.

Tacit Knowledge and Risks

12

Bo Göranzon

Confronting the Unforeseen

How are risks and disasters prevented in high-technology environments? This is a question that has many facets. In this chapter I shall discuss the aspects related to the history of knowledge, and to tacit knowledge in particular.

My first example is a description of action taken by a railway employee, Chief Conductor Sterner, from the Swedish town of Linköping. The report is from 1915, which gives a distance in time to the complex question at the beginning of this essay.

It is not only the theatres of war that see heroic actions. From time to time, everyday civilian life provides opportunities for exploits that are far more praiseworthy than the exploits on the 'field of honour', in as much as they save lives and property instead of wreaking destruction. Such a feat was performed at Kimstad last Tuesday evening, when Chief Conductor G J Sterner, with great presence of mind and no thought for his own life, averted an imminent rail disaster that could have cost many lives. . . . One of my colleagues in Östgöten called on Mr. Sterner to obtain some more details about this sensational incident.

'I was only doing my duty,' he explained, when we congratulated him on his creditable action. 'But for heaven's sake don't make any fuss about it.' . . .

As mentioned above, as the train was entering Kimstad station a fault was discovered in the train's vacuum system: it was passenger train number 411, and the train was stopped. The driver got down to locate the fault and opened some valves on the side of the carriage chassis, releasing air from the vacuum system. After the brake shoes had been freed on a couple of carriages, the driver climbed back up into his cab, but found he could still not move the train – other than lurching a couple of centimetres backwards – so he got down from the train again to take another look at the vacuum system. It is likely that he had moved the control lever to the forward position to set the train in motion, and the regulator was set to full speed, that is, 70 to 80 km an hour. The driver continued to check the train all the way back to the last carriage. As soon as he opened a valve on the last carriage, the brakes released and the train suddenly began to move.

'Don't let it move!' I shouted to the driver, who evidently thought the stoker was still on board. 'And that is what I thought too,' explained Mr. Sterner. 'I expected he would bring the train into the station, where we had orders to meet the goods train number 1352 (foodstuffs). The driver rushed forwards along the train in an attempt to catch up with the locomotive, but the train picked up speed alarmingly. I jumped up on to the second to last carriage, and saw the stoker climb up on the other side. I was both surprised and alarmed, and asked him, "Who is in the locomotive?" "The engine-driver" he answered. "No, he was out here" I replied.

I immediately understood the situation: no one was at the controls of the locomotive. I rushed forward through the carriages. I opened an emergency brake valve, but because there was a fault in the vacuum system it did not work. If the system had been in working order I could have stopped the train. But it picked up speed instead, and there was nothing else to do but to try to reach the locomotive and help the engine-driver bring the train to a halt. I thought that the engine-driver had managed to get on board one of the front carriages, but I went through carriage after carriage without finding him. I later found out that he had tripped over the points on the line and hurt himself. I had to open several locked doors and put down gangways between the carriages, which caused delay. Finally I reached the tender. There is no proper gangway between the tender and the locomotive, just a couple of small footplates. Fortunately I had the signal lamp with me so I could find my way forward by its light. I managed to find a foothold, reached for the door of the driver's cabin and pulled myself in. It only took a moment to shut off the steam and apply the brakes, although the vacuum brakes were still not working. At the same time Engmark, the conductor, who was at the back of the train, applied the brakes there.

This saved the situation. The entire episode had lasted about three minutes, during which time the train had covered about the same number of kilometres. We had been accelerating all this time, and reached a speed of between 70 and 80 kilometres an hour. I could feel the locomotive lurching and swaying as it does at top speed. We had hurtled through Kimstad station at about 60 kilometres an hour, and then negotiated some s-bends. At each bend I had looked anxiously ahead to see if the goods train was approaching. When we finally came to a stretch of straight line and the other train was not in sight, I felt immense relief. And I felt even greater relief when I heard the stop signals in Norsholm. It was the most beautiful music I had ever heard, as it told me that the goods train had been stopped there.

When the train had come to a halt, the stoker ran forward and I told him to back the train up to Kimstad. Shortly afterwards the engine-driver arrived, with blood on his face.

There were about 30 people on board the passenger train. None of them had the slightest idea of the danger they had been in. And that was just as well, for they would certainly have panicked, and who can tell what that might have led to?'

This story of Chief Conductor Sterner, which was reported in 1915 in 'Östgöten', the local newspaper, contains some elements of the way leadership applies sound and reliable judgement in an encounter with the unforeseen: the way the struggle, together with a familiarity with the practice, pervades the way responsibility is assumed for action.

Here we see a quartet working together to prevent panic spreading among the passengers: they were the Chief Conductor, the stoker, the engine-driver and the conductor. This incident in Kimstad attracted a great deal of attention, and Chief Conductor Sterner had honours heaped upon him, among them the Carnegie medal, for his 'resolution and disregard of the risk to his own life'.

Art as a Source of Knowledge

The story of Chief Conductor Sterner could have been taken from one of Joseph Conrad's novels. Conrad, who was a ship's captain at the end of the nineteenth century, wrote artistic accounts of his personal experiences, with leadership on board a vessel as a recurring theme. Conrad wrote that there is no room for 'bluffers' on board a ship. Navigating a ship through a storm required a high level of skill.

In the Preface to 'The Nigger of the Narcissus' Conrad writes about the purpose of art:

My task which I am trying to achieve is, by the power of the written word, to make you hear, to make you feel – it is, before all, to make you see. That – and no more, and it is everything.

The artist creates a more intense image of the reality he describes. He takes hold of reality and recreates it so that everyone who reads what he has written says to himself, 'That's the way it is. I recognise what I have always known but have had neither the peace nor the gravity to dwell upon'. Or perhaps the opposite: 'For me, this is a new experience which I will take with me. It gives me the chance to cast new light on well-worn clichés, and to develop my imagination'.

Reflection is not always a process that is in harmony and balance. It may occur after 'touching bottom' as Joseph Conrad describes:

Imagine a blindfolded man set to drive a van over a bad road. I sweated and shivered over that business considerably, I can tell you. After all, for a seaman, to scrape the bottom of the thing that's supposed to float all the time under his care is the unpardonable sin. No one may know of it, but you never forget the thump – eh? A blow on the very heart. You remember it, you dream of it, you wake up at night and think of it – years after – and go hot and cold all over.

This is an excellent description of the way the struggle with the practical builds up skill. See also Notes [1] and [2].

Three kinds of knowledge in a practice

Our knowledge, in an occupation for example, is in three parts: the knowledge we acquire by practising the occupation (knowledge expressed in skill), the knowledge we gain by exchanging experience with colleagues and fellow-workers (the knowledge of familiarity) and finally the knowledge we can learn by studying the subject (propositional knowledge).

There is a clear tendency to give too much emphasis to theoretical knowledge (propositional knowledge) at the expense of practical knowledge (experiential knowledge and the knowledge of familiarity); the last two kinds of knowledge are often overlooked in discussions of the nature of knowledge.

But these three kinds of knowledge are, in fact, interrelated. The relationship between the three kinds of knowledge in a practice may be expressed like this: we interpret theories, methods and rules by means of the familiarity and experience we have acquired through our participation in a practice. The dialogue between people who take part in a practice contains an element of friction between different perceptions, friction that arises from differences in experiences and in examples of familiarity and experience. The more in-depth development of occupational skills requires the introduction of a constant dialogue. To be professional means expanding one's perspective to achieve a broader overall view than one's own familiarity with the practice in question permits. We may conclude from this argument on the relationship between the different kinds of knowledge that if we remove from an activity the experiential knowledge and the knowledge of familiarity, we are also emptying it of its propositional knowledge.

Practical knowledge is not susceptible to systematisation in the same way as theoretical knowledge. But it plays an equally important part, and it is best maintained and applied by means of reflection on examples taken from places of work and from art. See also Note [3].

Philosophy and Engineering

In the period of the French Enlightenment there was a lively debate about the relationships between different aspects of knowledge. To give an example, in *Émile* (1760), his book about education and apprenticeship, Rousseau maintains that the concepts of theoretical knowledge must be reconciled with a reality that the senses can experience.

> It is only by walking, feeling, counting, measuring the dimensions of things that we learn to judge them rightly. But, also, if we were always measuring, our senses would trust to the instrument and would never gain confidence.

To Rousseau it was not only true that theoretical knowledge was enriched by experience. Without experience, it creates chaos. To borrow a term from cybertechnology, the entropy in the system increases. In his dissertation 'Experience as Tacit Knowledge' Terje Sörensen, chief engineer at Statoil quotes a slurry engineer of many years' experience:

> We have lost skill in the oil industry of today. Young people come straight from university with no experience. And there is something about their attitude; they do not want to learn from older employees, and they become aggressive. They seem to be more interested in computers than in getting a feeling for the job. Instead of using their 'feelings' to gain experience, they sit at the computer. They should walk around the platform, be there all the time, look at the work, feel and smell the drilling slurry and learn what goes on.

In his dissertation, Terje Sörensen quotes the same slurry engineer again:

> People have no real grasp of what they are doing when they just key raw data into the computer. And later, when they read out the result, it is nothing more than new figures. They have no feeling for them.

The discussions of skills development in engineers on Norwegian oil platforms are like an echo from the discussions of epistemology during the French Age of Enlightenment.

'The Tacit Knowledge of the Hands'

There is an epistemological dimension in the work of the Swedish author Harry Martinson. He used the expression 'approximation' for what he called the 'fresh grass' of the human spirit. He thought he could see how our culture had become a seedbed for what he called 'the skilled commonplace'.

In his novel, *Vägen till Klockrike* (*The Path*) Martinson writes of Bolle, a lifelong tramp:

> But sometimes the woodfolk came out of the forests and crafted long channels on frames and trestles, which rose above the streams, sometimes to the height of a man and more, and then lower, depending on the slope.
>
> Bolle never learned the half of all that. No, the more he travelled the roads the greater the respect he had for artless, ingenuous work; for occupations that were rarely spoken of, but that were, in fact, complex disciplines. The tacit knowledge of the working hands.

When Harry Martinson discusses the way concept formation develops to reinforce confidence in actions; he expresses this philosophy of language through his character, Sandemar:

> Sandemar loved the unlikely, that is to say reality as it is for the most part, and outside the world of the entrepreneurs of probability. He would rather accept fragmentation in the truth than the dishonest, sensible attraction to symbols that were supposed to express everything...but that in reality expressed nothing other than lies about themselves, the false trustworthiness.

And he has Sandemar expand on the nature of all certainty and uncertainty:

> The truth is that we do not know anything, and so we are tired of one thing and another. This comes from uncertainty. We visit with our senses and thought all kinds of things, but we are never certain what they are, or what they really signify.
>
> I write here on the blackboard a lot of thoughts that come and go. But why do they come and go so much? Well, because we have found nothing.
>
> We only find that almost everything can be expressed in words. But as time goes by we cross out everything that can be expressed. At least, that is what I do here on the blackboard. I crossed it out because other things that can be said want to have a place on the board for a few minutes. Before the sponge arrives.

In his work, Martinson takes the sponge on the blackboard as a metaphor for work in progress. In a dialogue with himself and others, there is always something to add. There are no absolute syntheses. The tip of the iceberg in his work is the language that comes to be expressed in words. To develop certainty in action and judgement means developing a process of concept formation that contains a tacit dimension. See also Note [4].

Personal Responsibility

In his last play, *The New Trial*, Peter Weiss depicts personal responsibility in the encounter with the clients in an insurance company. The play had its premiere at the Royal Dramatic Theatre, Stockholm, in the autumn of 1981. K, the lead in Weiss's play, has been promoted from his earlier position as a clerk in an insurance company, where he had had direct contact with the customers:

> K: I stopped by Kaminer's office. Wanted to explain a few cases to him. He said he knew about everything.
>
> Rabensteiner: Dealt with everything yesterday. He had been in on everything for a long time anyway.
>
> K: How is he to understand things that have cost me years of work?
>
> Rabensteiner: But you know that we've introduced the new system. The simplified procedures mean that what used to require a sizeable team can now be accomplished by just a few workers. You yourself had become superfluous. You with your card files –
>
> K: It's those card files that matter to me. They bring their human beings behind the particular case close to me –
>
> Rabensteiner: Everything can be accessed by the new system. My dear fellow, you were our museum piece!
>
> K: One must listen to everyone, Mr. Rabensteiner, one must talk with everyone –

K wants to take personal responsibility in the eyes of the company's customers. He feels that the personal responsibility is gradually becoming thinned out.

The Transfer of Experience of Driving a Car

Without a foundation in the knowledge of experience and familiarity, theoretical knowledge cannot work. The example of driving a car may illustrate the point of experience transfer between master and apprentice. This example is taken from a 1986 conference on road safety.

> Beginners run an 8–10 times greater risk than experienced drivers of being involved in accidents. There is not much we can do about their age or the psychological and social factors that affect the way they drive. But we can

help them get more experience.... The way inexperienced drivers observe the road is passive; they have a narrow field of vision, and this means that they are late in noticing obstacles, and they have an unsystematic way of watching the road ahead. This means there are gaps in their observation or they miss things completely.... New drivers believe that they have very fast reactions, although in reality their reactions are slower than those of more experienced drivers.... Novices behind the wheel spend more time looking at the edge of the road. They concentrate on the position of the vehicle on the road. Experienced drivers focus their gaze farther ahead. They manage to watch the road and look out for risks at the same time.

Young drivers' accidents curve peaks two years after they pass the driving test. This is because their ability to handle the car improves, while their ability to keep an eye on the road does not improve at the same pace. The method for transferring experience to young drivers is that they must drive with an experienced teacher by their side and constantly describe what they see and what they are looking at while they are driving. The teacher assesses the new driver, and after the session goes through the important things the driver missed and the unimportant things he allowed to distract him. The result is a real improvement in both attention and observation.

See Note [5] for additional remarks on the transfer of experience in driving.

Reflection: When Different Instruments Play Together

In his book *Kunskapsbegreppet i praktisk filosofi* (*The Concept of Knowledge In Practical Philosophy*) the philosopher Allan Janik writes that reflection is a process of restoring balance. The unexpressed knowledge of an occupational group is articulated by reflecting on situations in which one's judgement is very severely tested. Stories must be brought out, made visible, stories that are the group's collective interpretation of their practice. This collective aspect is important, since all knowledge originates in experience, but not only in my own experience. See Note [6].

Reflection requires peace of mind: 'It is a sickness that must run its course', writes Denis Diderot, the French encyclopaedia author. It begins with a surprise, which may be pleasant, but is most often not pleasant. It is the unexpected that is the decisive factor. Tried and tested routines no longer work. Put briefly, we no longer have instinctive knowledge of what to do. Where there used to be order, the opposite now prevails. In such a situation reflection offers us an opportunity to restore the balance, which creates the conditions we need to get our bearings in a situation where incomprehensibility dominates. It is in the error that we find the greatest need for reflection. Among other things, leadership involves creating meeting places for collective reflection on 'scraping the bottom', to refer to Joseph Conrad's example – to benefit from mistakes. Joseph Conrad made an ironic comment on the tradition of knowledge that perceives words as identical with the reality they are intended to portray:

> Words, as is well known, are the great foes of reality. I have been for many years a teacher of languages. It is an occupation which at length becomes fatal to whatever share of imagination, observation, and insight an ordinary person may be heir to. To a teacher of languages there comes a time when the world is but a place of many words and man appears a mere talking animal not much more wonderful than a parrot.

A quotation from Michel de Montaigne that Allan Janik refers to in his book may illustrate this perspective on reflection. Montaigne – who lived in the latter part of the sixteenth century – is the philosopher of experience-based knowledge:

> I should willingly tell them, that the fruit of a surgeon's experience, is not the history of his practice and his remembering that he has cured four people of the plague and three of the gout, unless he knows how thence to extract something whereon to form his judgement, and to make us sensible that he has thence become more skillful in his art. As in a concert of instruments, we do not hear a lute, a harpsichord, or a flute alone, but one entire harmony, the result of all together. If travel and offices have improved them, 'tis a product of their understanding to make it appear. 'Tis not enough to reckon experiences, they must weigh, sort and distil them, to extract the reasons and conclusions they carry along with them.

Dealing with the Unexpected

We are used to regarding disasters as critical events that take place in a brief period of time. The course of a disaster describes, event for event, the swift development of that critical happening, precisely as in the report from the runaway train in Kimstad and the confident action of Chief Conductor Sterner.

The example from Kimstad draws attention to the phrase culture of security. To focus on the culture of safety we must first develop a perspective that also accepts that disasters may be cumulative trends: a tidy, well-ordered deterioration over a long period of time whose results would be described as disastrous if this deterioration took place at a specific time.

We must not expect to avoid crises. The fact is that some crises are to be regarded as beneficial: they test the strength and flexibility of the organisation. A learning organisation learns from its mistakes by coping with the crises they generate. The essential point in this essay is the question of how we can prevent crises developing into disasters.

With the examples I presented here I have attempted to give a picture of the tacit dimension that exists in all practical work. To nurture and develop what I have called here the knowledge of familiarity and knowledge expressed in skill are vital if we are to prevent disasters in the long-term. The professional people who, by accepting responsibility in their actions, develop their tacit knowledge are well prepared to deal with the unexpected, and thereby bring down the level of risk. Creating the conditions this requires is a central task of leadership.

References

For ten years the publication 'Dialoger' has been discussing skills and technology in the perspective of tacit knowledge. Two examples are to be found in number 36/96, 'Work and Skills' and number 44/97 'The World of Work Knowledge'. The Dialogue Seminar at Stockholm's Royal Dramatic Theatre, a programme run in co-operation with the Royal Institute of Technology, also produces books that relate to the theme of this essay. Some examples of the books used are: *The Honour of Work* by Thomas Tempte (1997), *The Epistemology of Work* by Bengt Molander (1997), *The Nigger of the Narcissus* by Joseph Conrad (1997) and a new edition of Hans Larsson's *Intuition* from 1892. Mention should also be made of the new edition of Harry Martinson's, *Vägen till Klockrike*, (*The Path*) Bonniers 1998.

Doctoral dissertations that have influenced the contents of this chapter are Bo Göranzon, 'The Practical Intellect', Springer-Verlag (1992); Maja-Lisa Perby, 'Konsten att bemästra en process. Om att förvalta yrkeskunnande' (The Art of Mastering the Process. On managing skills) Gidlunds förlag 1995; Terje Sörensen, 'Erfaring som tyst kunskap' (Experience As Tacit Knowledge), NTNU, Trondheim, 1996.

The following texts on the theory of knowledge and the history of ideas have provided inspiration for this essay: Herbert Joseph's, *Diderot's Dialogue*, Carlssons, 1993; Allan Janik, *Cordelia's Silence*, Carlssons 1991; Michel de Montaigne, *Essays, books 1–3*, Atlantis, 1986.

This new version of 'Risks in Technical Systems' also includes examples of extracts from texts inspired by the earlier version of the essay, 'Tacit Knowledge and Risks', see below.

Notes and comments

An earlier version of this chapter was used as part of the Dialogue Seminar Method, where one of the first common actions is to take a text that is chosen to stimulate the members of the group to put forward examples from their own experience or from the company culture with which they are familiar.

The Dialogue Seminar Method was developed in the research field of skill and technology at the Royal Institute of Technology (KTH) in close co-operation with Combitech Systems. See www.dialoger.se under 'Böcker', the 'Filosofi och ingenjörsarbete' category, and 'Spelplats', which documents the method as it is applied at the Swedish National Defence College and the Stockholm College of Arts, Crafts and Design.

The extracts from texts that took 'Tacit Knowledge and Risks' as their inspiration are reproduced below as Notes. Those who have read 'Risks in Technical Systems' may also find impulses in this new version of the chapter.

[1] Note by Göran Backlund (CS) on 'Art As a Source of Knowledge':

As the rule, we are only willing to learn from others when our own failure is so painful that we have no desire to go through it again – once burned, twice shy. However, it seems that there has to be constant pain – very few people and organisations have the inner drive to work on constant improvement without having the experience of a disaster as motivation. One changes one's view from being driven by pain to dispelling pain by working actively on constant improvement. Pain is motivating, but we forget all too soon!

A bad example is more powerful than a good one. This is clear, even to engineers. It seems that it is the bad examples – failed projects – that are the most powerful motive to review one's work method, more than any example of the benefits of using a new method, for example, or a new tool. It is easy to dismiss the excellence in a new method, unless there is some painful failure in the background, which this new method could have avoided. It is the bad example that generates pain – and pain in its turn generates humility and sensitivity.

[2] Note by Jonas Höglund (CS) on 'Art As a Source of Knowledge':

'There can be no bluffers on board a ship. Good seamanship is the only thing that will take a ship through a storm', wrote Joseph Conrad. Neither can there be any bluffers at the helm of a project. We sometimes tend to appoint young, promising, forward-looking but inexperienced people to lead challenging projects 'in order to put them to the test'. This is not the right approach. The ship must be run by an experienced skipper. He should have an apprentice by his side instead. When the storm dies down he can hand over the helm to the apprentice, and take over again when the wind rises. The apprentice can stand beside the skipper on the bridge and watch him steer the ship through crises without going aground. He has already experienced the feeling of the ship touching the bottom, and to expose the ship to more of this treatment purely to give the apprentice more experience, a better frame of reference, is unnecessarily harsh. The apprentice has to build his frame of reference in some other way.

We sometimes give the apprentice project manager a mentor instead of a master, with the task of talking the apprentice through the archipelago of the project with all its hidden shallows.

It is often not enough for a beginner to have nothing more than a mentor. The mentor is a sounding board, but if he is to benefit from what the mentor has to say the apprentice must have enough experience of his own, his own frame of reference, in which to set the mentor's advice. Neither has the mentor the same commitment to the project in question, not because he does not want to or he cannot, but because he is not compelled to. And the mentor is often not there when he is needed. When we are dealing with a novice project leader, an apprentice, we should work on appointing a master, an experienced project leader.

[3] Note by Fredrik Jernquist (CS) on 'Three Kinds of Knowledge in a Practice':

For the first five years after I graduated I worked on electronics and software engineering. In smaller companies, in the thermal 'printer' sector. Although the companies were small and in time were either bought up or merged, we were world leaders. The technology and the products were interesting from the technical viewpoint – there were microprocessor-controlled electronics, mechanics, sensors and software. And inbuilt technical real-time systems on a small scale. . . . I remember that I saw these as extremely creative – but not without elements of frustration. We solved problems as they arose, and in some ways we had to be inventors. Our practical experience grew as the project progressed. It is true that we placed a high value on practical experience, but for us, skills development was something you did by attending a course. We equated knowledge improvement with theoretical training, but as we were in the front line in our technical niche, there were no courses to give us a broader view, to make us reflect on our activities or encourage us to go forward. With the benefit of hindsight, I now think that this could have been one of the reasons why I moved on to a different company and a different sector. . . . I have now been working for nine months as the head of a business section at Combitech Systems, with responsibility for hardware developments in the Gothenburg/Trollhättan region. During this time, my view of knowledge has developed. . . . Seeing knowledge as being made up of three parts seems entirely right to me, although I am already asking myself when the next stage is coming. What will the fourth component be?

[4] Note by Lars Lundquist (CS) on 'The Tacit Knowledge in Our Hands':

To put the outcome to one side at the right time, to let it rest, and focus on the next step – in that, I think, lies much of the secret of skilled practitioners, at least in the development of software, the area in which I an experienced. To be able to say 'that's enough now' as well as 'that's not good enough yet' and to have support for that. To have integrity, if you will. The ability to ignore what outsiders think when your own professional identity is at stake. In particular, to stand by your insight that 'that's not good enough yet' needs nerves of steel.

When faced with external pressures and demands for immediate results, one must be able to continue, to put on blinkers and trudge stubbornly onwards towards the goal, with an inner conviction that once on the last lap, you will be in a far better position.

To bring new people into a project is sometimes like spending a long time rehearsing a play, only to bring the real actors on to the stage at the dress rehearsal. That may work for 'soap operas' and the like. But if we are aiming at the really advanced assignments, we have to have a different approach.

The dilettante always has something to add, improve, or remove. And he won't be ready until the work is brought – abruptly – to a close. Do not confuse this kind of fixation with attention to detail. Nothing important actually happens, except that the surface becomes more and more highly polished. The novice never tires of seeing his reflection in his own work, while the master leaves something of himself in his work for others to discover.

[5] Note by Jonas Höglund (CS) on 'The Transfer of Experience of Driving a Car':

This is a very good metaphor. Compare it with project management. An inexperienced project leader concentrates on the theories of project management. He is preoccupied with writing a project plan, and although he spends a lot of time on it, he has little understanding of the impact the plan will have on the project and which parts of its are more important than others. He cannot relate the content of what he writes to actual experience, he does not have an inner picture of the goal and a feeling for the way to reach it. On the other hand, the experienced project leader can focus his gaze farther ahead. He can let the project run, while avoiding risks by concentrating on what is happening ahead. Neither does he become unnecessarily agitated about the crises that unavoidably occur along the way. He has a feeling for the way the situation can be put right, for how the obstacles can be avoided.

[6] Note by Gunnar Berg (CS) on 'Reflection: When Different Instruments Play Together':

> I was head of a group of eight people that was responsible for the development of hardware and software, CPU cards and operative systems. Because we were successful, we had plenty of support from higher up in the company....
>
> The way we communicated can, by and large, be compared with a dialogue....The freedom to carry on a dialogue without knowing from the beginning where we were going created a learning climate. As a result, the group could deliver a great deal of knowledge and experience....If we focus for a moment on the idea of collective knowledge as against individual knowledge, I should like to say that the body of common knowledge in the group was greater than the sum of the knowledge of the individuals in the group. By this I mean that there was 'tacit knowledge' in the group that could not be expressed....
>
> In a project, the project group builds up knowledge of how things are supposed to work. It is impossible for everyone to know everything; the group has a 'whole' that is dispersed when the project ends. How can we preserve the collective experience that exists in a project group?

Part 4

DIALOGUE SEMINAR AS REFLECTIVE PRACTICE

13 Skill, Storytelling and Language: on Reflection as a Method

Maria Hammarén

In *Paris, Capital of the Nineteenth Century*[1] Walter Benjamin discusses various aspects of the phenomenon of information. He observes a world in transformation. The factory whistle and the soot go hand in hand with modern demands for freedom: fashion, the flow of news, and sensation to ward off tedium. Long before anyone came upon the idea of the information society, he identifies information as the form of communication for the industrial work process. He relates it to sensation and sets it against the narrative:

> Just as the industrial labour process separates off from handicraft, so the form of communication corresponding to this labour process: information, separates off from the form of communication corresponding to the artisanal process of labour, which is storytelling. . . . This connection must be kept in mind if one is to form an idea of the explosive force contained within information. This force is liberated in sensation. With the sensation, whatever still resembles wisdom, oral tradition or the epic side of truth is razed to the ground.

In this chapter on skill I take as my starting point Walter Benjamin's association of information with the industrial work process. I suggest that the industrial work process is incapable of creating skill without conscious efforts to revert to cultivating the form of communication of (handi)craft: the story. I shall try to give the word 'story' a content that relates it to two central activities that originate in the memory: imagination and

---

1 Walter Benjamin, *Paris, Capital of the Nineteenth Century*, in *The Arcades Project*.

thought. Imagination and thought are at the core of a living and versatile skill. The memory is the melting pot of skill.

Walter Benjamin traces the *connections* the memory makes with the imagination while also tracing the *stories* the memory creates for thinking: 'It is imagination that presents correspondences to the memory, it is thinking that consecrates allegory to it. Memory brings about the convergence of imagination and thinking.'

Baudelaire, whose intensive presence informed much of Benjamin's work, compares the mind to a palimpsest. (From the National Encyclopaedia: **Palimpsest:** (Latin. palimpsestus, Greek. palimpsestos, from pali(n) 'once again' and psestos 'scraped') **1 A** manuscript with a hand-written text superimposed on an erased, or partly erased, apparent additional text. The underlying text is said to be 'in palimpsest'....A better, but less common, term is *codex rescriptus* ('rewritten text'), because the underlying text was usually washed, not scraped, away. The older, underlying text may often be recovered by using ultraviolet light....).

Baudelaire writes:

> What is the human brain if not an immense and natural palimpsest? My brain is a palimpsest, as is yours, reader. Innumerable layers of ideas, images and feelings have successively built up in your brain, as softly as light. It may seem that each new layer buries the one beneath it. But in reality none of them are lost.... However incoherent existence may be, human unity is not disrupted. All the echoes of memory, if awakened at the same time, would make a concert, pleasant or painful, but logical and without dissonances.[2]

But not all the echoes of memory are awakened at the same time. On the contrary, we are normally at the mercy of our memories: they give us random reminders of a past, and the metaphor of the library as an encyclopaedia ready to give us information is true of only part of our memory. After Marcel Proust's novel, *Remembrance of Things Past*, we recognise that sensations: a taste, a smell, can suddenly take us back to a random place in time, beyond space. And this place in time appears as a story. We remember only what we were once capable of seeing, and we give that meaning. Meaning has the form of a story. And that is exactly what Baudelaire points out when he speaks of recalled memories as a 'concert...pleasant or painful, but logical and without dissonances'.

Can Proust be challenged? Are there other ways of wakening the echoes of memories? How else can we approach the task of systematically processing our experience, if most of our experience is

---

2 Baudelaire, *Visions d'Oxford* in *Un Mangeur d'Opium*, Oeuvres complètes, 451.

stored in a system that governs us and is not accessible for conscious reflection?

Skills research rightfully belongs in the humanities, or even better, in knowledge of the human condition. That is why it is natural to seek points of departure and positions outside the traditional branches of knowledge, to find one's way instead through the writings that broke new ground in learning about man as a creature of ideas. Fiction, fiction of quality, is the unique space where people develop their understanding of self.

Research on skills addresses something that is crucial to the development of man and society: how/when do we learn from the experience of others, how/when do we re-examine our own established perspectives? If we believe in the possibility of learning from others, and in some sense, in development, then investigating the underlying mechanisms is to be regarded as basic research on how man changes his world. This perspective differs from pedagogics, for example, by centring on concept formation. But the processes of concept formation are not visible to us, and we have no easy way of winding the film back to examine how we formed our concepts. We face the creation of meaning and memory; inaccessible courses of events that have placed on our noses spectacles with a particular kind of lens. We view the world through the lenses of our concepts. Furthermore, and this is important, we did not create our concepts on our own. They are dialogical and evolved in interaction with the finely-meshed system of rules and gestures that make up the practice of which we are part.

All this is important if we want to approach the difficult area of constructing, and for this purpose also reconstructing, a concentrated process of concept formation. And that is what we are doing if we are serious about addressing the transfer of experience in the new knowledge paradigms of which skills research is a part. For if we fail to recognise that experience may be transformed, and if we do not know the conditions that apply to this qualitative transformation, then it would appear that developing methods for the transformation of experience is a difficult process.

On page 313 of Göran Printz-Påhlson's influential collection of essays, *The Sun in the Mirror*, he writes, in the chapter entitled 'The Gardener, the Pirate etc.':

The divorce of aesthetics from criticism that first took place in the nineteenth century must surely be regarded as an expression of the twofold liberation of science and of the personality that is so typical of that period. Science saw to facts, the personality saw to values: the belief in progress of the times paid no heed to any no-man's land between the two.

We are given a heading here: no-man's land. It is in this no-man's land that we settle when we speak of concept formation and set it in relation to memory and experience. To develop skill is to allow one's concept formation to be influenced within the framework of an occupation, and in a dialogue with all the powerful examples of practical judgement that link words to actions. This process recognises no boundaries between a constructed world of facts and personality and values. And in this passive phrase, 'to allow one's concept formation to be influenced', lies something that is particularly active. What must be added is reflection.

The development of methods for what is popularly known as experience transfer is a matter of shedding light on the meaning we give to the language we speak, and thereby to our actions. It also involves creating a meeting-place in the organisation, in which the experiences of others have the opportunity to expand one's own horizons and make them more complex. It should be recognised that the term meeting-place has a twofold meaning. A physical meeting-place, certainly, a location where conversations can take place. But it is more a question of creating the conditions in which experience can meet experience: bringing to life the vital examples that set tacit knowledge in motion. We should also be aware of the twofold meaning of the term experience transfer. It means learning from the experience of others, but also qualifying one's own experience as knowledge. In both cases, reflection has an impact on experience. Although the Swedish school system encourages critical thinking, most young people appear to have very little practice in actually reflecting, it may be that the school system has as little understanding of the nature of reflection as the world of work has a grasp of insights into the special expressions and paths of learning related to experience-based knowledge.

When we speak of skills, we are not speaking only of experience and its conversion to knowledge that takes place through reflection. We are speaking of a whole, in which different aspects of knowledge interact. Skills can only be assessed in relation to the way we act. It is in our way of acting that our aggregate knowledge is fully expressed. It is a matter of judicious/responsible action. Skill is dynamic: when we speak of developing skills we are speaking of refining behaviour that is generated in response to situations we have not encountered before, we have only encountered situations that are comparable. And in this situation we only have recourse to comparison: comparing one situation with another, one course of events with another. The greatest source of mistakes that leads to misdirected actions is probably not that we have lost our bearings. It is rather that we are overeager to bundle one thing together with another. 'Exactly', we say about a description we hear. 'I've had exactly that experience'. The word 'exactly' announces the existence of clichés that express a simplified, and thus fairly prosaic, reality.

No-man's land: *a* no-man's land or *the* no-man's land? The answer is clearly not skill. But skill is a prism through which we can observe this land, a prism that makes certain aspects of it visible. Skill is linked to people's language; at a deep, a fundamental level it is about meaning and the ability to see. Learning to see is linked to our imagination and insight: insight into other people's stories and into the outside world. Imagination, the connections the mind makes, has an effect on us as we create meaning.

Reflective Practice

We have many words for the changes that take place in people as they journey through life. We call it maturing, learning from experience, growing. The term 'learning organisation' is an expression of a desire for the individuals in an organisation to be flexible and willing to learn new approaches to their work and new work methods, within the limits of the organisation's business concept. The popular term 'experience transfer' roughly expresses the hope that people will not repeat their earlier mistakes. In the context of skill, experience transfer stands for something more, namely the creation of a reflective practice.

To create a reflective practice, one works systematically with imagination and thought, through the crucible of memory. The word 'practice' emphasises that this work takes place in a collective context. And the word 'reflective' denotes that this practice is the subject of constant examination, the space for imagination and thought is institutionalised.

A practice may be poorly developed or it may work well, and it may also be rigid. At places where practice is poorly developed, actions are erratic and appear to be arbitrary. In many cases, this is attributable to high employee turnover. In addition, many older employees disappeared from workplaces during the 1990s in a series of cutbacks which, although planned, showed a lack of understanding in their implementation. One may suspect that many older employees were marginalised because their experience had not been refined into knowledge. Experience in itself is no guarantee of sound judgement, clichés and rigid perspectives appear when old experience gets in the way of new experience. Experience is a raw material, and its supply can be choked off.

A practice may also be poorly developed because constant efficiency-improvement has reduced communication to the level of information processing. The whole dimension of use, the way information is digested and becomes responsible action, is left to the individual. Individual actions, anything from a speech act to making a choice, become difficult to improve because there are no reactions to them. The reaction does not occur until the final results and the entire finely tuned, or halting, chain of different events has gone into oblivion. Communication may also be restricted for other reasons: in a culture that devotes itself exclusively to either negative or positive criticism, the discourse about the content of work will, in time, become inhibited. If we are to refine our actions, someone else must offer us a horizon against which the action can be contrasted, and we must have the ability to refer back to the action and all the possible alternatives available at that time. In sum, we must learn to reflect.

The question to ask about a well-functioning practice, be it a hospital department, a spin-off company in a small industrial community, Facit, the office machine company before the microprocessor revolutionised the market, is: when does a well-functioning practice become rigid? All practices are rigid in some way. It is this rigidity that gives us confidence in our judgements and the ability to deal with unexpected situations. It creates discernment and the trained eye, but it does not protect us from changes in the world around us.

Fast and relevant communication is typical of a well-functioning practice. The words used are loaded with meanings that are understood by everyone involved. As Maja-Lisa Perby writes in her book, *The Art of Mastering a Process*,[3] one 'points to' experience. With the help of words, one points to something that has been built up over time: a world of knowledge.

Pointing to something that has been built up over time is radically different from referring to information. It is to abandon once and for all the dictionary with its definitions, and feel the way words are used in a range of contexts. How, then, do we learn to 'feel' the way words are used? The answer is surprisingly simple: words must be made to perform in a setting, to make their way into a living example. All that remains for a person who wants to communicate clearly at a given point in time is, strictly speaking, the word woven into the fabric of action. It is a question of becoming acquainted with many language games: the term Ludwig Wittgenstein invented to show, by the use of analogy, how a single word does not have a precise meaning but is a part of different games, different contexts of meaning, in which meaning works. If this does not happen in real time, where action connects language and reality to make a meaningful whole, then we are reduced to what Walter Benjamin calls the communication form of handicrafts: the story. But a single

---

3 Perby, Maja-Lisa, *The Art of Mastering a Process. On the management of skill*, Gidlunds (1995).

story, a single example, is not enough. Words take part in different games, and it is the games that we must become familiar with.

The Norwegian philosopher Kjell S Johannessen has attempted to convey a pedagogical formulation of the epistemology of skill by breaking down the knowledge a practice contains into propositional knowledge, knowledge requiring familiarity with the particular phenomenon, and knowledge expressed in skilled behaviour. The cross-section he uses, which is a constructed section, considers the way the different components of knowledge are formed. Skill and familiarity can only be formed through direct participation in a practice. And that is where concept formation takes place, i.e. knowledge becomes interwoven with language events in a fabric of meaning that frames the opportunities for action present in each individual situation. There is an analogical transfer of understanding through examples. His conclusion is that propositional knowledge is unusable unless it rests on a foundation of familiarity and skill: we interpret theories, methods and instructions by means of the familiarity and skill we have acquired by participating in a practice.

It is clear that a local practice, such as the practice developed at a workplace, is not independent of the superior practice that is the whole in a language community. We grow in to a form of life, and in doing so we acquire the outer limits of a culture's perception of reality. But the more specialised an occupational culture, and the more occupation-specific language and specialised work tasks there are, the more clearly we can see the distinctive characteristics of the local practice.

Johannessen has extended his three-part model to include judgement. In doing so he adds an aspect of quality. At the core of the epistemology of skill lies the way that the ability to make judgements is built up and developed. Judgement is, quite simply, visible in the ability to interact, in a particular area and in an intelligent way, with the diversity of reality and its constant change. When the actions of the genuine expert, whether a Master of Engineering, a teacher or a craftsman, are in concord with the innermost qualities of her knowledge, then her senses occupy a world with a history, a world open to new experience.

I use the word 'expert' deliberately, to relate to the American philosopher Hubert Dreyfus's division of skill into stages from novice to expertise. This division is to be found in *Mind over Machine. The Power of Human Intuition and Expertise in the Era of the Computer.*[4]

Dreyfus refers to an analytical approach to solving work tasks as 'calculating rationality'. According to Dreyfus, calculating rationality can never take a person beyond the competence stage, the level of

---

4 Dreyfus, Hubert L. and Dreyfus, Stuart E., *Mind over Machine. The Power of Human Intuition and Expertise in the Era of the Computer*, Blackwell (1986).

mediocrity. What is needed to go further Dreyfus calls intuition, which he identifies as being the result of deep, situational involvement with similar situations. The product of intuition is an understanding that 'performs effortlessly in seeing similarities to earlier experiences'.

The risk of stagnation in a practice springs from the very soil it grows in and is nourished by. We are far too likely to see what we meet as 'more of the same'. When we deal with a task that cannot be solved by calculation, and that is true of most qualified work tasks, we are dependent on our judgement. Judgement operates in real time and is obliged to think in analogies. Diderot, the French philosopher of the Enlightenment, uses the term *instinct* to mean an expression of forgotten experiences,[5] the background that has become absorbed into us and has become a way of seeing. Our judgement rests on instinct, and a billiards cannon shot is needed every time our judgement is altered, every time we want to read new patterns from the old.

A point of departure for work on a reflective practice therefore includes an examination of our analogies. All analogies are false in certain contexts, and our stories are analogies. To create a reflective practice is to have the courage to pause in a paradox: to create room for the stories, re-examine them and make connections with the new. And not least, to try to bring to life the examples that were once so important in the way we established our concepts.

Methods Development

In his essay, 'Semiotiken och historievetenskaperna' (*Semiotics and the Historical Sciences*) Jurij Lotman criticises the retrospective perspective of traditional history.[6] He speaks of an inevitable double distortion: on the one hand the tendency of the text to reshape events by placing them in a narrative structure, and on the other the historical determinism that occurs when the gaze is turned on the time axis and only registers what actually happens. The retrospective view arranges a chain of events that seem to follow one out of the other.

---

5 Marian Hobson and others have developed this aspect of Diderot. In her article 'Diderot, Implicit Knowledge and Architecture. The Experience of Analogy', published in Göranzon, (ed.), *Skill, Technology and Enlightenment. On Practical Philosophy*, she finds that Diderot's 'digressive practice', 303, has a profound connection with his perception of analogy as instinct – an expression of experiences that we no longer remember, but that, as 'unexpressed relations', i.e., analogies, 309, still have an impact on us.

6 Lotman, Jurij, O.M. 'Semiotiken och historievetenskapen', in Florin, Magnus and Göranzon, B. (eds): *Den inre teatern. Filosofiska dialoger 1986–1996*, Carlsson (1996).

Is it the case that the distortion that Lotman speaks of does not apply exclusively to the sphere of history, but also to the very way we spontaneously manage our memories? Do we have a tendency to transform our experience of the power game between potential possibilities to a journey from one point to another?

There is reason to take Lotman's warning seriously when it comes to work related to experience and experience transfer, particularly as stories and examples play such a large part here. Conscious work on experience transfer is done in a different dimension than out in the field, where words and actions are tied together to give meaning. It takes place after the event; it carries the signs of re-examination and must be qualified and separated from general urgings to 'put your story on paper'. We are not primarily interested in recognition, not the standardising word 'exactly'. We want experiences to clash with one another, to create a resistance to one another. It is in the dialogue between different meanings, the different ways of seeing and describing, that experience can influence us, refine our vision and extend our language. When we are involved in experience transfer, the conversation must be taken past the stories already in circulation.

It must reach deeper.

In recent years the development of methods for experience transfer has been a priority task for skills research. A preliminary result was presented in my dissertation *Ledtråd i förvandling – om att skapa en reflekterande praxis*[7] *(On Creating a Reflecting Practice)*, which largely dealt with an experience transfer development project in Combitech Systems. This work was carried out from 1996 to 1999 by Bo Göranzon and myself. Put very briefly, the aim of the project can be captured in the meaning we placed in the word 'expertise'. 'The expert has mastered a very large number of language games, the beginner only a very few.' The development project was tasked with producing a systematised path to the expert's familiarity with a large number of language games.

But the project at Combitech Systems was also pioneering work with the basic aim of producing a different view of knowledge. It was our ambition to make visible a background that had been assimilated and therefore was not directly accessible for introspection, and thus could not be influenced by any direct means. This was a question of bringing to life those examples that could be set in relation to the way the concepts were first established. An assimilated background may be compared with an opinion. An opinion is a condition. The questions we

---

7 Maria Hammarén, *Ledtråd i förvandling – om att skapa en reflekterande praxis*, (Doctoral Dissertation) Dialoger (1999).

wanted to ask, without being able to put them directly, were 'When did you form that opinion? With the help of what examples and in which language games?'. Developing external impulses that brought the stories to life became an important factor. The source of external impulses is classical literature in a broad and qualitative sense. But if an external impulse is to have an effect, the method of reading cannot be left to chance.

The method that was developed is founded on humanistic traditions and traditional humanist reflection: reading slowly, while constantly making notes in the margin, and recommending that the notes be used as a permanent record of the connections to the examples the text generates. For our purposes we looked to texts related to the philosophy and philosophical traditions of the practice: to Montaigne, Shakespeare, Diderot, and Wittgenstein.[8] But the participants' preparations do not end here. Slow writing,[9] which involves examination and reappraisal, is just as important as reading. Taking their notes as a point of departure, and by concentrated thinking, each participant pieced together a new story, a written reflection.

When reading and writing are interwoven in this way, the people in the group are impelled to reflect. The reflection, which works on the group members' individual experiences, is then shared with the group by reading aloud. The preparatory work can be taken to this point. From here, progress is made through conversation, but a conversation that is broken down into its component parts and reinforced and emphasised by exaggerating the process of listening: one person reads aloud and the group listens in silence. Reading aloud is important, it is as if the text only becomes complete through the acoustic dimension; when written words are spoken, the voice gives reality to them. Some significant qualifications have been made to the conversation that is produced in this process, and this qualified conversation is then set out in the minutes, capturing in permanent form what has been said. Different language games are brought into play, and nuances and contrasts stand out in a detail that is not possible in an ordinary conversation. In the best case, we manage to return to a story about the way a concept is established. Once the story becomes visible and accessible for reflection,

---

8 Since its beginnings in 1985, the Dialogue Seminar held at Stockholm's Royal Dramatic Theatre has used this philosophical tradition in an attempt to arrive at a more profound understanding of work, culture and language. In the autumn of 2001, Bo Göranzon, who is responsible for developing the discipline of Skill and Technology and the activities of the Dialogue Seminar, published his book, *Spelregler – om gränsöverskridande*, (*Rules of the Game – on exceeding the limits*), which has its starting point in this philosophical tradition.

9 More about writing as a method for reflection is to be found in Maria Hammarén, *Skriva – en metod för reflektion*, (*Writing – a method for reflection*), Utbildningsförlaget (1996).

we find ourselves working at the most vulnerable point in concept formation. The question of how one learned the meaning of a word, through which examples and in what context of use, has a strong link with confidence (and even absolute confidence) in action. If the way the word is used is affected by the dialogue in the group, the language game changes, and concept and conscious action also change. The meaning of a word can be displaced; spectacles' lenses can be altered. The minutes keep a permanent record of a concept formation process.

The minutes also act as a starting point for new written assignments. A theme insists on a deeper treatment, literature is used that brings in new, unfamiliar, impulses, starting the hermeneutic spiral in which meanings can be displaced and new interpretations of experience created under the influence of imagination and thinking.

When a dialogue that creates insights actually takes place, it is a compression of the concept-forming process in general: it takes place between people, continues over time and brings complexity and diversity into play. The group develops a new kind of intersubjectivity.

Notes in the Margin

We must apply indirect methods to establish communication with an underlying familiarity. The Swiss physician and literary scientist Jean Starobinski has devoted much of his perceptiveness and diligence to variations on the theme of 'notes in the margin', through Diderot, among others. In his essay, 'Diderot and the Speech of Others'[10] he describes Diderot's method of reading and writing by quoting from one of his letters:

> I do not compose, I am not an author: I read or I converse, I ask or I answer.

Starobinski's main point of departure is the text that Diderot, in his last year as an author, was asked to write on Seneca. The above quote is from the time at which the first draft of the essay was completed. To answer his rhetorical question, 'Why take this view about writings in the margin?' Starobinski writes that it was a method that attempted to favour the critical interventions, the constant rejoinders:

> A method that gives Diderot the right to freely address all the discontinuous aspects in his ideas which follow one after the other, while continuity is assured by the book to which he is responding.

---

10 In Göranzon and Florin (eds), *Den inre teatern. Filosofiska dialoger 1986–1996 (The Inner Theatre. Philosophical Dialogues 1986–1996).* Carlssons (1996).

New tools and new knowledge can supplement established concepts such as the dialogue that broadens existing language games in various ways. To ask that notes are made in the margin is a way of opening a space for the imagination. This is not a question of underlining or making a brief summary, but rather of capturing oneself while reading. These are my own replies, fancies of my own, the imagination's processing of the text. This flow of connections contains material on which thought can work.

Reading is a mysterious activity. Marcel Proust calls reading 'that miracle of a communication in the midst of solitude'. The miracle is that a meeting with the text can take us to vantage points: places from which we may briefly glimpse the time and the perspectives in which we are immersed. The vantage point is not immovable. Different readers are taken to different places. A new reading may take the same reader to a different place. The responsibility for the miracle of communication is not in the text alone. The text must have literary qualities, the words must project images, albeit fragmented images, into the reader's imagination, the tone and composition of the text all charge the words with meaning. Our purpose, to bring about a radical shift in perspective, also requires all-important analogies that will change the way the light falls on the very landscape of concepts we inhabit. And of the reader? A contract: to alternate between subordination and creative reading, between receiving and responding.

From the perspective of methods development, the purpose of the research is to bring about a communication that penetrates more deeply than the conversations we are used to having, to initiate in the members of a group a reflection in which imagination and thought interact. It is the importance and the nature of this reflection that enables a new relation to experience which this chapter addresses.

References

The methods development mentioned in this chapter has been documented on a regular basis in the series 'Philosophy and the Work of Engineers':

Göranzon, B. (2001) *Spelregler. Om gränsöverskridande*, Dialoger, Stockholm.

Hammarén, M. (1999) *Ledtråd i förvandling. Om att skapa en reflekterande praxis*, Dialoger, Stockholm.

Hoberg, C. (ed.) (1998) *Precision och improvisation. Om systemutvecklarens yrkeskunnande*, Dialoger, Stockholm.

Kjell, J.S. (1999) *Praxis och tyst kunnande*, Dialoger, Stockholm.

References

Benjamin, W. (1990) *Paris, 1800-talets huvudstad. Passagearbetet*, Band 1–2, översättning Ulf Peter Hallberg, Symposion, Det oavslutade Passagearbetet tillkom mellan åren 1927 och 1940.

Hammarén, M. (1995) *Skriva – en metod för reflektion*, Utbildningsförlaget, Stockholm.

Lotman, M.J. (1996) 'Semiotiken och historievetenskapen', in Florin, Magnus & Göranzon, Bo (eds): *Den inre teatern. Filosofiska dialoger 1986–1996*, Carlsson, Stockholm.

Printz-Påhlson, G. (1996) *Solen i spegeln*, andra upplagan, Bonniers, Stockholm.

Starobinski, J. (1996) 'Diderot och de andras tal', ingår i Florin, Magnus and Göranzon, Bo (eds): *Den inre teatern. Filosofiska dialoger 1986–1996*, Carlsson, Stockholm.

14 Reading and Writing as Performing Arts: at Work

Øyvind Pålshaugen

Introduction

This chapter is based on a lecture given at the conference 'Dialogues on Performing Knowledge', which was arranged in close connection with the conference 'Philosophical Dialogues' in Stockholm, October 1998. For the reader to understand the way I performed this lecture, and thereby also the way in which this chapter is written, I have to note that the task of my lecture was a double one. Firstly, my lecture was expected to critically highlight what I considered some essential points of the recently issued book *Precision and Improvisation – on the skill of System Developers* (Hoberg, 1998). Secondly, my lecture was to serve the function of making explicit the relationship between the two conferences.

The point of that second task was somehow to show that the logical relationship between the two conferences was not to be regarded as sequential or hierarchical, in the sense that the first and thematically more philosophical one was of mostly theoretical interest, and the second one, related to working life issues, was of mostly practical interest. Metaphorically speaking, their relationship was to be regarded rather as one of intertextuality: the one was, so to speak, grafted into the other. The challenge of my lecture, then, was to show this kind of relationship by means of specific examples, instead of trying to explain the relationship in general terms.

In this written version I have retained a flavour of the oral presentation form. As remarked by Adorno years ago, the oral and written scientific presentation forms have turned into two different genres. In an oral presentation, you have to do injustice to the subject under consideration, in order to do justice to your listeners. Only the ephemeral character of the spoken word can justify the oral presentation form with regard to the matters presented (Adorno, 1986: 360). When writing a text, your obligation is to do justice to the complexity of the matter of which you write. To pose the question, whether matters of any kind can be justifiably treated linguistically, may, after the linguistic turn, be regarded as a precondition for any scientific presentation. However, there is no other way to answer this question, than by the way you perform your writing. So here goes...

Listening to Words

Dialogues, if they work, always imply making personal experience and reflections public, in one way or another. Thus, it might perhaps be an appropriate way to present the connection between the two conferences simply by giving a couple of examples of reflections which arose from my experiences with the 'Philosophical Dialogues' conference. As will be shown, these reflections have a specific relevance for the 'Performing Knowledge' conference, even though the topics at stake seem to be of quite a different nature.

'Philosophical Dialogues' lasted from a Sunday evening to Wednesday. Monday evening we attended a wonderful lecture on *Alice in Wonderland*, given by Gillian Beer. She reminded us of the passage where Alice is wondering about the fact that it is impossible to remember how it was, not being able to read. That reminded me of one obvious, almost too obvious fact: when you can read, you cannot not read. Certainly, this is a kind of peculiarity not only at the individual level; it is even more peculiar at the level of culture. On Tuesday evening Bernard Williams gave a lecture on Plato's dialogues, in which he touched upon Plato's negative attitude (or ambiguity) towards writing. Williams reminded us, among other things, that Plato was worried that the art of writing would weaken our capacity for personal memory. This is a very interesting though speculative thesis, impossible to judge. Even more interesting was another, no less speculative thesis, which Williams' lecture evoked. It might be that the art of writing makes us 'forget' that every use of language is a kind of performance; that it is an activity which takes place in the course of time. It is easier to be aware of this fact by the oral use of language. When you speak, there is a sound for a while; when you stop speaking there is no more sound, the performance is ended, the speech is, so to speak, 'left behind' you.

In contrast to this oral use of language, let us consider the experience of reading a book. An example close at hand would be the reading of some scientific study. When we read such a kind of book, we are inclined to think that in the end, when the reading is finished, we are, in principle, in a position to 'see' the whole content of the book, more or less 'in one glance' (to quote God, from Lars Gårding's dialogue *Von Neumann and God*). Probably, this inclination to think that we can see it all in one glance is due to the fact that the written words are seen, and the words therefore remain as virtually visible to us in the book. In contrast, spoken words simply dissolve when there is no more sound. The act of seeing is in our culture mostly considered as an experience of simultaneity (Jay, 1996), while the act of hearing is considered an experience of time flow (as in listening to music). Havelock, in his book *A Preface to Plato*, mentions that one of the words that we still use to signify memorising, may be regarded as a reminiscence of an oral culture: 'We use the word recall for remembering' (Havelock, 1963). Memorising in this sense is not an act of 'looking' into your memoir, instead you repeat the soundings of words, of tellings.

My reflections are, of course, almost pure speculations. Among the audience attending the lecture on which this text is based, there were a number of people who were well acquainted with, and in sympathy with, Wittgenstein's claim for specific examples, if you want to join the business of speculation. Therefore, instead of continuing my speculations on a general level, I decided to elaborate my line of thinking by making a new start, with a new exemplar in the beloved genre of examples.

Looking at Words

If it is true that we cannot not read, it is also true that we cannot not think. As just promised I will give an example, or rather, I will show you one:

TH!NK

When you see the five symbols above, you immediately make yourself read 'think'. Letters are very authoritarian. If you can read, you have to read; the letters make us read, almost by dictate. Thus, when I show you the five symbols above, it would be wrong to say that these symbols make you think of the word 'think'. What happens, is simply that you – immediately – read 'think'. However, in the very same moment as you read those signs as 'think' you already also have started to think. I cannot tell what thoughts those symbols will evoke in each one of my readers. But I can make some guesses, or general assumptions: Some of you will wonder: What does this really mean? Is this way of writing only for fun, or is it something to think about? Is it meant as a way of expressing an imperative: You shall think! Or, is the exclamation mark simply meant to mark a surprise, to attract attention: look at me!?

The power of letters is strange. They can make us see a colour by just lining up, in black on white, the three letters: red. Once we are captured in the magic circle of letters, we are subjected to their dictatorship; we simply have to read the letters as words with certain meanings when they parade in front of us. However, the power of letters is strange in more than one way. Even though they can make us read by dictate, they cannot dictate our reading. Neither can I, as a writer, dictate what meaning my text will have to the reader. Letters can create meaning, but there is no meaning apart from the (temporal) act of reading the letters. The meaning of the letters is literally hermetic apart from the hermeneutic act of reading. The spirit of the letter is no property of the letter itself, a part of the act of an agent between them, the *interpretis* (= between the parties), which is the performing act of interpretation. Thus, instead of trying to confirm what is the 'real meaning' of the symbols TH!NK, I will just sum up what thoughts I make around the experience of reading those five symbols, in the form of three statements:

–   When you can read, you cannot not read.
–   Any reading is an interpretation, and any interpretation is a creation of meaning.
–   The dominant model, or the paradigm, for meaning is linguistic meaning, that is, the kind of meaning which is produced in various kinds of language games.

Words at Work: Language Games

When in the next section I will present some of my reflections on the Combitech Systems case, I will make use of the concept of language game. As will be known, this concept stems from Wittgenstein. It may be understood and used in many ways. Most interpretations of this concept claim to be in accordance with Wittgenstein's own, which can hardly be the case, considering the number of diverging, not to say contradicting interpretations. Rather than joining the game of trying to give an interpretation, more elaborated and understandable but nevertheless just as elucidative as Wittgenstein's own attempts, I will recall two general aspects of the concept of language game:

(1)   The concept of language game is used to focus on the use of language, when the task is to come to grips with the meaning of words, to obtain an adequate understanding. The meanings of words are thus not considered inherent in the words; the meanings are dependent on the use of words.

(2)   The term 'game' is introduced to remind us that any use of language has to take place according to a certain kind of rules, which, among other things, implies that the play of words is never a totally free play. However, there are different kinds of rules, and thus different kinds of language games, whose interrelationship is not regulated by some kind of superior rules, or a superior kind of language game. In that sense, there is no *a priori* limitation on what kinds of language games we may have, and those we have co-exist in a non-hierarchical order.

The meaning, or the consequences, of these two general remarks, is of course dependent on the specific use of these perspectives in particular examples. Instead of following the conventional rules in the discourse on Wittgenstein interpretations, which is to underpin one's own interpretation with some carefully selected quotations, I will just quote a couple of the remarks Wittgenstein made, when he was confronted (by himself) with the problem of giving some definite explanation of the terms that make up his concept 'language game'. These two remarks are quite instructive as regards the question of what it should mean to come to a full or (de)finite understanding of what are language games:

> But when the concept of 'game' in this way is unlimited, what do you mean with game? – When I give this description: 'The ground was fully covered with different plants', would you then say I didn't know what I was talking about, until I had given you a definition of the word plant? (Wittgenstein, 1953: § 70).

> You make it easy for yourself! You talk about all kinds of language games, but you have said nothing about what is the essence of language games, and thus the essence of language. Nothing about what is common to all these examples, and of what makes it up to be language, or parts of language.... And that is true. Instead of saying what is common to all that we call language, I am saying that these phenomena have no one thing in common which makes us use the same word for them all.... – but these different language games are related to one another in many different ways. And it is because of this relationship, or these relationships, that we call them 'language' (Wittgenstein, 1953: § 65).

Commenting upon his book *Tractatus Logico-Philosophicus*, Wittgenstein remarked in a letter to his publisher, Ficker, that this book consisted of two parts: what was in the book, and what was not in it. And he added that 'precisely this second part is the important one' (Wittgenstein, 1980). There have been arguments for regarding Wittgenstein's views on what is to be written (or said) or not as an important aspect of his ethical attitude. Departing from his own practice, considered as an example of his own moral code, the two quotations above tell us, without saying it, that in the matter of language games it is better to try to play the game, than to try to define it.

Before exploring more thoroughly some of the details on how they performed their language games at Combitech Systems, and investigating some of the experiences they made, I have to remind you that my knowledge of all this mainly stems from only reading, from my reading of the book *Precision and Improvisation*. Even though my knowledge of their particular activities is limited only to this reading, I would not necessarily subscribe to the phrase I just myself made use of: 'only reading'. Because, among the kind of language games which in our culture are developed into an almost plastic flexibility, is the kind we could call 'the simulation game'. That is, the language game in which language simulates reality. Our ability to simulate reality by means of words has been cultivated to the extent that language seems to be able to present pictures of reality. Such concepts of language as a kind of simulation game by which we can create pictures of reality, are conceptions which have been subject to severe criticism, not least by Wittgenstein, or perhaps more correctly, his followers.

However, no word is able to create any meaning apart from the human interpretation, and the criticism of the so-called 'picture theory' of language is thus not a criticism of this kind of language game in itself. Rather it is a criticism of a certain generalised interpretation of these kinds of games, their logical status. What in particular is criticised is the conception that the simulation game is the only kind of language game in which reality is presented 'as it really is', like in pictures. A very effective subversion of this misconception is performed by Nina Burton, in this short story: 'Pablo Picasso was once accosted by a man who wanted to know why he did not paint people "as they really are", and produced as an example a photograph of his wife. Picasso answered, "Isn't she rather small and flat?"'. This story also very nicely reminds us that what you see depends on your way of seeing – like what you read depends on your way of reading. Let us now, with this in mind, turn to the firm Combitech Systems, to the book *Precision and Improvisation*, in which some of the people working at Combitech Systems have made some impressive efforts to come to a better understanding of their own work on system development.

From Local Theory to Local Meaning

After the introductory chapter of the book, the next one which is entitled 'The creative process', opens by stating: 'The basis of all system development is individual thinking' (Hoberg, 1998: 29). Thus, to understand the character of system development work, we have to understand: What does it mean to think? According to the preceding discussion in this chapter, it is legitimate to reformulate this question into: What kind of language game is thinking? As we have been told, there are many kinds of language games, and in other words many ways of thinking. Or perhaps better expressed: Language games may be performed in many ways, and new thoughts may be created in very many ways, for instance by means of philosophy, by means of art. The experiences from art, philosophy and the humanities may widen your repertoire of language games. As we know, new thoughts may also be created by the kind of language games called dialogues, not only philosophical ones, but dialogues within working life as well. The acknowledgement of this is the rationale behind the Combitech Systems people's choice of trying to make use of dialogue seminars as the work form by which they should come to a better understanding of their own work, and thereby also be in a better position to develop an improved practice.

The 'dialogue seminars' contain a number of devices, all of which are performed mainly by means of language: reading; writing; talking; listening. To put it in very simple terms, the purpose of these dialogue seminars is to come to a better understanding of what the Combitech Systems people themselves are actually doing when they perform their work, that is, how they perform knowledge, especially those parts of it where their performance in some respects has to be innovative. To put it in their own words: 'The dialogue seminars have initiated work on identifying those elements in the professional knowledge of the system developer which are too complex or too unpredictable to be governed by formal rules. The knowledge of how this work is performed, is not to be expressed in exact terms. By generating different examples, however, we became able to talk about it' (Hoberg, 1998: 21).

We see that at Combitech Systems they are far from searching for any general theory to cover their experience of the ways in which they are working with system development. Instead, we might call their efforts at the dialogue seminars an effort to develop a 'local theory' which has also come to be a rather well-known concept within working life and working life research (Elden, 1983; Gustavsen, 1992). However, to designate the outcome of their efforts a 'local theory' would be to overburden the claims of a strict logic in their narratives, their dialogues and their discourse as a whole. The reason for this is that when you listen carefully to what they say, that is, read what they have written, you will find that the main criterion that the narratives they tell each other is telling the truth, is not that these narratives strictly correspond to the experiences they have made during their work. The main criterion is that their narratives give sense, are meaningful, considered as some kind of (meta)perspective on their own experience. If so, their narratives are not to be labelled a local theory. It would be better to say that these narratives express a local meaning, as their own interpretation of how they perform their own system development work.

This 'local meaning' is created by the combination of different kinds of language games, consisting mainly of written narratives, which are read aloud in meetings, and the dialogues which thereafter emerge. An example of the creation of this kind of local meaning, is presented in the following excerpt from a note written by Hoberg:

> An experienced system developer, named Kjell, reads his text, in which he gives a critical account of the use of formalised methods. Another guy, Odd, says: 'It is interesting that you, with your experience, are that critical to methods'. Kjell answers: 'It depends, of course, on how they are used. They may be very useful for analyses, until you reach the critical point where the new system is to be really created. This is the crucial point, where you have to rely on your experience, not on any method.'...For a while, silence occurred. In a certain sense, there was nothing to be said.... The dialogue that afternoon had created something which made Kjell's answer have a meaning for each one of us (Hoberg, 1998: 23).

If the narratives in this book tell the truth, these narratives also are an example of another concept of truth, which differs somewhat both from the conventional scientific one and the one we know from daily life. This concept of truth neither has the form of some banal fact (like: The Stockholm School of Economics is located in Saltmätergatan), nor does it have the form of a logically constructed truth, as (ideally) in science. Rather, these narratives bear on a concept of truth in the sense of a true meaning, a meaning which is created by those who share it. This illustrates that the true meaning of any social praxis has to be created, it can never be 'found' in the sense of discovered, which literally means to dis-cover, that is, to remove what covers something which is already there. Whether this concept of truth may also have some implications with relevance for social science, I will return to at the end of this chapter. Firstly, we have to investigate some more specific problems of reading and writing, as they occurred to the people at Combitech Systems.

The Art of Reading and Writing at Work

An important aspect of the problems pertaining to writing may be evoked by a question which perhaps ought to be asked more often: What is worth writing? This question is easily asked, but not that easily answered. In principle, there seems to be no part of a problem, no aspect of a situation, no detail which could not be part of the kind of description which we make in order to give a full account of, and thus a full understanding of, a problem or a situation or a system. However, if we try to write everything down, it ends in a breakdown, literally. The result would be just like the one we are told about in the book on Combitech Systems, namely the experiences they had while trying to give a full description of some system by making use of a particular method of analysis and description, labelled 'Structured Analysis' method (SA).

The SA-method was applied to describe a data system which consisted of a network of twenty nodes (data-machines) working in real-time (Hoberg, 1998: 33). By means of this SA-method it was possible to produce very detailed specifications (also by using graphics), which gave a very exact picture of each particular detail of the system. However, this gigantic description, which comprehended everything, was not comprehensible, especially not to the users of the system, the customer. As they themselves tell, they had reached the phase, or state, known as 'Analysis Paralysis'.

To produce an image of such a complex system as a whole, one should remember the dictum that: *'The whole is more than its parts, but it is certainly also less'* (I. Wallerstein). In other words, you cannot make a meaningful presentation of the whole by simply adding its parts. This means, in turn, that a meaningful presentation of the whole has to be created, whereby there is invoked the need for linguistic creativity.

This example shows that to write in a way where you only follow the rules of the game, in this case the rules of the language game of simulation (or exact empirical description), is not to master the art of writing. In such a case you are not at all the master, you rather have become the slave of writing. This reminds us that to write, like all kinds of use of language, is to master a technique, and as we know it is generally easy to become the slave of a forceful technique. Now, in the Combitech Systems book we will also find more successful stories of practising the art of writing. As a matter of fact, we are presented some examples which show very clearly two quite different, though both very important effects (or functions) of writing. Let us have a look at these.

In a chapter devoted to what they call 'the creative part of the process' (of system development), we are presented with some narratives of how this creative process takes place. The reason for focusing particularly on this part of the process, is that even when, as we have been told, the basis of the system development work is individual thinking, very little attention is devoted to this individual 'thinking work', according to the authors themselves. In the first part of this narrative, Tomas Sandén tells about how he works in a process when the task is one of solving some particular given problem.

Sandén tells us that he starts by interrogating two or three selected people among his colleagues, using them, one by one, as sparring partners for his own thinking; back and forth, rather intensively in the course of some days. Lots of ideas arise. The bad ones are sorted out, he goes deeper into the problem, and after some more days the contours of a possible solution gradually appear on his whiteboard. At this point, he starts writing down the solution. And what happens then? I quote from his own presentation (p. 30):

> The first time I started this, I thought that the solution was more or less already there, and that what was left was only to write it down. I became really disappointed to discover that when I started writing, my insight in the system solution was considerably deepened, and lots of new problems emerged.

This part of Tomas Sandén's narrative informs us very instructively on one important function of writing, one so obvious that it is easily forgotten: Writing makes it possible to read our own thoughts. You get an expression of your own impression, so to speak, and you may then very well, as Thomas did, have the experience that your initial thinking was not that impressive. In this example, Tomas Sandén is confronted with the fact that the language game of description (which I, above, also termed the 'language game of simulation'), which is only one kind of language game among others, has to be taken very seriously, when this game is the right one to be played.

The other function of writing which I would like to draw attention to is not really presented in Sandén's narrative. He only touches upon it *en passant*. At this time he is coping not with finding a solution to a given problem. What is at stake is to find out what the problem is. Something is wrong with the data system, but he does not know what the problem is. Thus, the task is to be able to conceptualise the problem, to formulate it. Once he has been able to formulate the problem, the solution of the problem usually will be quite close at hand. His way of coping with this kind of problem, which he himself terms as one of problem formulation, is very different from the way he works to find the solution to a given problem. Instead of interrogating some of his colleagues, he listens to the radio while driving, he now and then also discusses the matter, but mostly he is thinking, or as we shall see: it thinks within him.

This process takes some time, sometimes several months. What is of particular interest to us, is his description of his experience of one way progress is made in the course of this process (p. 32):

> What never stops fascinating me and surprises me during this kind of process, are the sudden 'jumps' forwards which may occur while you discuss the problem with somebody else. Initially, I only intend to tell the other what I'm thinking of, but suddenly I hear myself formulate the problem much more clearly than I have been able to until then. I wonder if one could obtain the same kind of effect by trying to write instead?

The answer to his question is yes. Even though new thoughts, a new way of thinking, and new formulations may be experienced as being suddenly there, there is no such thing as immediate thinking, in the literal sense which means thinking without (or beyond) any kind of medium. The main medium is of course language, which is not external to thought. Thus, thoughts may take shape as you shape your linguistic expressions/formulations (oral as well as written). And just as you do not always know beforehand what you exactly are going to express, you do not always know beforehand what you think, even in the very moment you are thinking, that is, in the very moment you are speaking (or writing). We noticed Thomas used the expression: 'I hear myself formulate'. While writing, you can read yourself formulating.

Let us now investigate what these two examples tell us about the different functions of writing, by contrasting them. The first example shows that you may obtain both a more comprehensive and more exact understanding by reading what you think (from what you write down). In this case the function of writing is, so to speak, one of disciplining one's ability of logical thinking. If so, in the second example, the function of writing is, so to speak, to discipline one's ability to think creatively. While writing, you are forced to express yourself, that is, words have to materialise. The materiality of language is, literally spoken, the stuff that thoughts are made of. In the process of writing, of creating this materiality, you may very well have the experience that the language you write creates thoughts you never knew you had in mind.

How to Judge the Meaning of Divergent Language Games at Work

To sum up: The dialogue seminars, which give the participants experiences of art, philosophy and new experiences, both with performing dialogues as well as with reading and writing, obviously can have as an effect that the participants increase their competence, by mastering a larger repertoire of different kinds of language games. To be able to master a larger 'set' of language games will surely increase both their creative and reflexive capacity. Of great importance, of course, is that these participants have experienced a kind of linguistic liberation: if you master a broader scope of language games, you also posit a broader scope both of thinking and, not the least important, of communicating (whether in oral or written form).

This kind of linguistic liberation then, means that you are no longer such a slave of the language game of simulation (or the 'social-realist' kind of language game) as you may very well have been. My appreciation of this liberation is by no means meant to reduce the importance of the language game of simulation, rather the opposite. The point is to be aware that this 'social-realist' language game is not a superior one, it is only one among others. An even more precarious point is to be aware what kind of language game you at any time are participating in, and to follow the rules if it is an appropriate game, and perhaps to break them if it is not. What is the right thing to do, the right words to use, is dependent on each particular language game, and is not a topic to be judged in general.

This way of 'concluding' may seem to contradict the arguments for practising dialogues as they are performed within working life development projects in Scandinavia. Both in the use of 'dialogue seminars' and by other kinds of use of dialogues within development projects in working life, emphasis is put on the very form of use of language, that is, the way discussions and conversation are organised, and the rules to be followed by the participants (Engelstad, 1996; Gustavsen, 1992; Pålshaugen, 1998). However, if we cannot rely entirely on just following the rules of the game, the question may arise: how do we know that we are performing our language games in the right way, so that we create a true meaning?

The answer is as simple as it is complex. We have to use our power of judgement. We read and write, speak and listen, we perform different kinds of language games, and there is no separate language game serving us with unequivocal criteria for how to judge in each one of them. We have to make use of our power of judgement within each particular language game, in which the relevant criteria are also to be found. The necessity of having to rely on our power of judgement does not mean that the question of how language games ought to be organised is of no importance. Rather the opposite: With all the knowledge we have from language games at work which do not work, we should clearly acknowledge the need to organise language games. To stage them and to guide or direct them in appropriate ways, may be of crucial importance to the quality of the performance and the outcome of language games like, say, dialogues of different kinds.

The point I underlined above is that no way of organising will guarantee the quality of the actual performance and the outcome of such dialogues. In the very performance of any kind of dialogues we will always have to rely on our power of judgement, which therefore constantly needs to be refined and empowered. In this process of refining and empowering, the efforts of arranging common reflections upon work experiences, as well as experiences of art and philosophy, as they have done at the 'dialogue seminars' at Combitech Systems, is appreciated, to judge from the results they have presented in their book. We should not be surprised then, when they themselves say that the kind of skill required for system developers, '...in spite of the strong importance of mathematics, logic and formalism,...the most important part is power of judgement' (Hoberg, 1998: 62). My guess is that their conclusion would also be valid in occupations and working places where technical knowledge plays a far more modest role. That is, at work places where the language games are less technical, but where the importance of how the games are played, is no less.

References

Adorno, T.W. (1986) Zur Bekämpfung Antisemitismus heute. In: *Gesammelte Werke* Bd. 20.1 Frankfurt am Main: Suhrkamp Verlag.

Elden, M. (1983) Democratization and participative research in developing local theory. *Journal of Occupational Behavior.* Vol. 4(1), 21–34.

Engelstad, P.H. (1996) The development organization as communicative instrumentation: Experiences from the Karlstad Program. In: Toulmin, S., Gustavsen, B. (eds): *Beyond Theory. Changing Organizations Through Participation.* Amsterdam/Philadelphia: John Benjamins Publishing.

Gustavsen, B. (1992) *Dialogue and Development: Theory of Communication, Action Research and Restructuring of Working Life.* Assen: Van Gorcum.

Havelock, E.A. (1963) *A Preface to Plato.* Oxford: Belknap Press.

Hoberg, C. (ed.) (1998) *Precision och Improvisation. Om systemutvecklarens yrkeskunnande.* Stockholm: Dialoger.

Jay, M. (1996) *Downcast Eyes. The Denigration of Vision in Twentieth-Century French Thought.* Berkeley & Los Angeles: University of California.

Pålshaugen, Ø. (1998) *The End of Organization Theory?* Amsterdam/Philadelphia: John Benjamins Publishing.

Wittgenstein, L. (1953) *Philosophical Investigations.* Oxford: Blackwell.

Wittgenstein, L. (1980) *Briefwechsel mit B. Russell, G.E. Moore, L.M. Keynes, F.P. Ramsay, W. Eccles, P. Engelmann und L. Von Ficker.* (edited by McGuiness, B., von Wright, G.H.) Frankfurt am Main: Suhrkamp.

15 Knowledge and Reflective Practice

Kjell S. Johannessen

Intelligent practice is not a step-child of theory.

Gilbert Ryle[1]

Introductory Remarks

Professional knowledge is a genuine subclass of experience based on practical knowledge. In epistemology there is next to no analysis of this kind of knowledge. And the reason is not hard to find. Professional knowledge is essentially characterised by two basic traits: (a) It is acquired over a relatively long period of time by individuals; and (b) attempts at articulating it in some reasonably satisfactory way all fall short of even elementary standards of plain speech.[2] Both of these traits stand out as inherently provocative to the adherent of the received and positivistically tinged view of knowledge which is predominant in our time. The first trait threatens to make knowledge dependent on individuals; and the second more than indicates that some kinds of genuine knowledge may in basic respects be resistant to verbal or notational articulation and thus be beyond the reach of language.

In my 'Rule Following, Intransitive Understanding, and Tacit Knowledge' included in this volume, I have looked into some of the central questions pertaining to various forms of knowledge which are expressed by other

---

1 The quotation is taken from Ryle's most renowned work (1949) *The Concept of Mind*, London: Hutchinson & Co, 26.

2 This comes close to how the well-known philosopher of science, Thomas S. Kuhn, sees the matter. He refers, with approval, to Michael Polanyi's conception of tacit knowing in *Personal Knowledge* (1958) and renders it in the following way: 'knowledge that is acquired through practice and that cannot be articulated explicitly'. See Kuhn's book (1962) *The Structure of Scientific Revolutions*, Chicago: University of Chicago Press, 44, footnote.

means than the verbal or notational ones. Three main components of tacit knowledge were identified: knowledge acquired by perceptual and behavioural familiarity and expressed by metaphors, analogies and similes; knowledge acquired by guided learning in the mastery of skills and expressed by the successful exercise of them; and knowledge expressed by the exercise of judgmental power while extending the application of concepts.

In the present chapter I intend to take a further look into matters concerning professional knowledge and the use of discretionary powers in a more general perspective. In particular I shall review what two of today's leading philosophers (Gilbert Ryle and Paul K. Feyerabend) have to say about experience based knowledge and then address the history of philosophy to let Kant and Aristotle speak on the matter. It will turn out that exercise of discretionary powers is intimately wedded to reasoning based on examples and reflecting on particulars in general. This way of thinking could in fact quite legitimately be called *analogical thinking*. The point of the following text is to make you see this. It will probably facilitate matters if I introduce an example from an actual work life situation and reflect upon it. Christer Hoberg, the director of Saab Combitech Systems, the electronic division of one of the largest companies in Sweden, has just published a book describing a project focused primarily on the transmission of professional knowledge in the company and the conditions for speeding it up.[3] An example of this kind is quite suitable for my purpose.

The Combitech Systems Case and Epistemology

The case study from Saab Combitech Systems displays a remarkable complexity. It is a sustained effort to delve into the dark corners of professional knowledge in order to reveal some of its secrets. It addresses three main issues. The first has to do with the problem of *articulating* various aspects of the experience one acquires over the years as a systems designer in companies like Combitech Systems. The second is connected to the question of how to establish a working inter-subjectivity among the individual systems designers in such a way that it both contributes to the development of the company and prepares them for meeting the challenges involved in making use of new technology. The third is related to the question of seeing more clearly the role that

---

3 See Hoberg, C. (1998) *Precision och improvisation. Om systemutvecklarens yrkeskunnande*, Dialoger, Stockholm.

the experience based knowledge plays when *new* systems are to be designed.

Confronting such a task, no immediate help is to be expected from the theoretical knowledge acquired through education and later reading. There are no laws or principles to rely on when one is bound to find *new* ways of combining and applying the established theoretical knowledge to produce the solution in demand. What is needed is some sort of *creative* response from the designers involved.

What is at stake when such an inventive response is needed? To get an inkling of an answer we have to look at the resources accessible to the designers who are put to work to produce the expected result. Their formal training involving a lot of mathematics and formal logic is of course necessary, but in no way sufficient as no solution is *derivable* from the available theoretical knowledge alone. In addition they need to rely on their experience with similar cases in the past to be able to handle the task in a satisfactory way. This experience, however, does not permit the designers to formulate *inductively* some general strategy for attacking the problem at hand. It operates more like a kind of guiding horizon during the search for the desired design. The main challenge does in fact consist in precisely this lack of theoretical and experience based tools for handling the task. Something new has to be brought into existence. Thus we realise that there is a certain *particularity* connected to the creative response expected from the designers. And that is an aspect of the situation which tends to be overlooked by epistemologists when they happen to look at cases like the one sketched here. In the following I intend to reflect a little on what is at work when we are said to bring our experience to bear on tasks like those confronting the systems designers at Saab Combitech Systems.

The declared aim of the Combitech Systems project was to produce an improved understanding of the professional or experience based knowledge of systems developers in order to speed up the transmission of professional knowledge. Newcomers in the field cannot, for obvious reasons, be trusted to handle complicated and demanding tasks in systems development. They will have to learn the trade by being members of project groups conducted by one of the more experienced systems designers, as gaining experience here generally is a matter of taking part in whole series of particular projects. The character of learning in contexts like this has scarcely been the object of serious scrutiny in work life research or in any other relevant social sciences. Accordingly the management at Saab Combitech Systems decided that an extensive investigation of the learning situation would probably contribute to improving matters. Not only might a better grasp of the knowledge in question be conducive to developing the working abilities of the individual systems designers in general; it might even contribute to reducing the time it takes to pass from novice to expert.

Any transference of experience based knowledge will, however, be a matter of handing over ways of going about the task to people who are facing different though in many ways related challenges in other projects. Generally such projects are characterised by the fact that the conditions for finding suitable and reliable solutions are constantly changing. There is thus no common factor that permits the formulation of a principle or a rule for treating the ever new cases in a uniform way. There are only rules of thumb based upon some sort of *family resemblance* between the particular cases. In each new case a moment will come where the individual designer has to decide for himself which comparisons are likely to be the more fruitful in attacking the task in hand. Often it is not even a matter of consciously *making* the comparisons. One just has a hunch that a certain approach may work. This is one of the ways in which experience based knowledge expresses itself.

If someone should complain that this amounts to no more than an intuition, he is, of course, in one sense quite right. But it has to be added that it is an *informed* kind of intuition, the character and history of which it is possible to trace. And that transforms it into something intellectually accessible with a logic of its own. It is my contention that experience based knowledge can, at least in part, be regarded as some kind of *analogical* thinking. In the following I shall try to substantiate this way of approaching the seemingly intractable matter of professional knowledge.

As a start we may note that our preceding reflection revealed it as being something necessarily dependent on individuals and in that sense radically *subjective*. An obvious consequence of this is that it becomes extraordinarily difficult even to talk sensibly about the kind of professional knowledge acquired in the systems development which takes place at Combitech Systems. This is, of course, a rather unhappy circumstance and quite contrary to what should be expected if looked upon from the point of view of the received conception of knowledge. According to this view a piece of knowledge should of necessity be something intersubjectively accessible, true of some aspect of the world, expressed in some form of language, supported by empirical or formal evidence and open to further checking and scrutiny. Thus it is assumed that knowledge is exclusively of a *propositional* nature and to be regarded as a reliable representation of how the world is. In sum: knowledge only makes sense as some sort of *product*. The ways in which it came to be, the judgement displayed in applying it, the inventiveness needed to develop it, the formation of the concepts used to express it, the contexts in which the concepts where formed and the conditions under which it took place, are all elements systematically excluded from the mainstream way of conceiving knowledge. There is a total lack of understanding of the basic fact that knowledge is also part of an ever ongoing *process* anchored in particular kinds of human activities aiming at certain goals, for instance improving the control over nature in order to utilise it more efficiently, furthering the understanding of ourselves as human beings and thereby freeing the human race from superstitions of all kinds, etc., etc. Human beings do not act aimlessly. The possibility of *applying* what gets established as knowledge is thus to be understood as a constitutive part of it.

Conceptions of knowledge incorporating the process-perspective are normally called *pragmatic*: derived from the Greek word *pragma*, which among other things means *action*. The following comments on the discretional and analogical aspects of the tacit component of professional knowledge are made within the horizon of a pragmatic view of knowledge inspired by Ludwig Wittgenstein's later philosophy. The concept of practice as sketched in my following chapter 'Rule Following, Intransitive Understanding, and Tacit Knowledge' contains the gist of my position in this respect. The present study is an attempt to decide if, and in what sense, the language-involving practices found in various types of work life situations are to be characterised as *reflective* practices. The sense of 'reflective' in this context will be unfolded step by step in the following text.

So much for the epistemological complexity of the task that Combitech Systems set for itself in the co-operation project established with the researchers from KTH, Bo Göranzon and Maria Hammarén. In an earlier draft of the report, written by Christer Hoberg, it was remarked that it came as a shock to the Combitech Systems people that tacit knowing should be considered a central component of professional knowledge. Equally strange appeared the claim that one had to work out and reflect on *particular cases* drawn from one's own experience to put oneself in a position to improve the transmission of this kind of knowledge.

This initial reaction is of some significance. It indicates that at the start of the project the management at Combitech Systems was held captive by the received and prevailing conception of knowledge, a conception which in fact boils down to a certain widespread *picture* of knowledge. Regrettably it is still quite common to think about knowledge in this way. And it has rather grave implications for the understanding of professional knowledge. It reduces it to a matter of *applying* propositional knowledge with varying degrees of efficiency. And *how* one becomes more efficient is, as already noted, not even part of this picture.

Professional Knowledge and Truth

This is the dismal story of the mainstream conception of knowledge. It makes a mockery of experienced practitioners of all kinds from the most advanced and inventive engineering work done in companies like Combitech Software in Sweden and Statoil in Norway, to the modest carpenter involved in a one-man enterprise. Experience based knowledge gained in various sorts of work life situations is simply left out of consideration not only in this popular picture of knowledge but also in most epistemological studies of an academic nature. One may wonder why. It cannot be an utterly arbitrary decision. Looking into the matter it turns out that there is, at least, something to be said in its favour. Truth is considered essential to knowledge and the concept of *truth* seems to be inapplicable to professional or experience based knowledge. Instead the possession of this kind of knowledge expresses itself in a series of non-propositional ways in work life situations, as for instance through sureness in action, through reliable judgements, and through intuitive acting, in short through task-related *achievements*.

In its formal aspect the situation may be likened to the practical syllogism where the premises are propositions (what has been gathered from the formal education in the case of the engineers) and the conclusion is an *action*. Under such circumstances the concept of truth does not find a foothold. The achievement in a work life situation is itself just an additional fact *in* the world, not a proposition *about* it. It must therefore be described and talked about accordingly. We say such things as 'This was the only sensible thing to do in our situation', as a comment upon, for instance, selling out one of the minor divisions and investing all the money in the mother company. Speaking like this we are implicitly applying a criterion which could be called *situational appropriateness*. But how do we decide this kind of appropriateness? What is the basis of applying it? How do we learn it?

The last question is fairly easily answered: from being attentively engaged in related business activities for quite a while, from listening to more experienced people in the trade and trying out their hints; from discussing and reflecting upon more or less similar cases in relation to the particular situations confronting the companies in question, etc., etc. This is then the basis of applying the criterion. But the actual recognition of appropriateness in a particular case in no way follows from this basis. Something like a *creative* response to a contextually determined challenge is needed here.

In other cases, referring to some organisational reform or a major change in production equipment, we may say things like 'It functions very well in our company'. Here we apply a criterion that could be termed *workability in context*. Once more it is a matter of intervening in a situation which might have developed in a unwanted direction if nothing had been done. And again it is a question of being able to size up the situation and 'see' what has to be done. It is a knowledge of a seemingly intractable nature that displays itself in these cases.

It is the use of complex criteria like these that replaces the concept of truth in matters of professional knowledge. That is, I think, the main reason why it is overlooked in epistemological studies. It is beyond the reach of the concept of truth. Its primary mode of expression is the intelligent *performance of actions* of various sorts, including task-related problem solving. It is not primarily our talk but our skilled and insightful ways of *acting* which bear witness to our professional knowledge.

Is it reasonable to talk about knowledge in these matters? That is the question Thomas S. Kuhn poses to himself in the *Postscript* added to the second edition of *The Structure of Scientific Revolutions* (1970). He answers it in the affirmative, to be sure on a basis of some sort of neural programming. His reasons are the following: (a) the neural programming has been transmitted through training and education; (b) it has, by trial, been found more effective than its historical competitors in a group's current environment; and (c) it is subject to change both through further education and through the discovery of misfits with the environment (p. 196). So much for the 'nose' that, according to Kuhn, is essential to researchers when they are more or less forced to respond creatively to unsuspected circumstances in their discipline.

The Nature of Professional Knowledge

The English philosopher Gilbert Ryle is one of the few philosophers who has bothered to reflect a little on the matter of practical or professional knowledge.[4] In his book *The Concept of Mind* (1949) he made a distinction between knowing *that* (propositional knowledge) and knowing *how* (practical knowledge) in order to refute what he calls 'the intellectualist legend'. This legend looks upon intelligent practice as a

---

4 The one philosopher who has in fact written quite substantially on various aspects of professional knowledge is the Hungarian chemist who later in life became a philosopher of science as well as a British citizen, Michael Polanyi. His main contribution to the latter field is his rather monumental work, *Personal Knowledge*, Routledge & Kegan Paul, London (1958). At the bottom of his writings there is, however, an adherence to a unity of science perspective, and this produces a lot of trouble for him in handling questions of basic importance for understanding professional knowledge.

function of having consulted the appropriate theory. Ryle describes it in this way:

> To do something thinking what one is doing is, according to this legend, always to do two things; namely, to consider certain appropriate propositions, or prescriptions, and to put into practice what these propositions or prescriptions enjoin. It is to do a bit of theory and then to do a bit of practice (p. 29).

Ryle launches several rather devastating objections against this view of intelligent practice, the most striking of which is his pointing out that to consider a theory or proposition is itself an operation which can be executed more or less intelligently. If it were the case that any intelligently executed operation presupposes a prior theoretical operation which in its turn has to be intelligently performed, it would become logically impossible to act intelligently. Accordingly, there must be some kind of practical knowledge which cannot be reduced to propositional knowledge.

Ryle's execution of this criticism is ingenious and well worth studying in its own right. But even if his distinction between knowing *that* and knowing *how* no doubt points in the right direction it is too limited to cope with the complex weave of problems that the tacit component of professional knowledge presents us with.

One simple example, borrowed from Michael Polanyi, should be enough to make us realise that. Without the slightest hesitation I would say that I know the face of my friend Allan. I know it in the sense that I would be able to pick him out from among a great multitude of people passing me by at the Bergen airport where I am waiting for his arrival. This is definitely not a matter of knowing *how*, as I need not do anything but look attentively at the people passing by. In the traditional picture of knowledge it would have to be treated as a kind of observation. But observations of the familiar sort are supposed to be expressible by means of language. That is, however, exactly what I am unable to do in this case. I may of course produce some sort of *general* description of the main characteristics of his face. Such a description, though, cannot be of any use to another person as an instrument for identifying my friend Allan at the airport. It would lack the specificity needed for such a task. The particularities of the physiognomy of the human face seem in fact to be beyond the grasp of verbal language. That is one of the reasons why a single picture tells more than a thousand words, as the saying goes.

However, this does not only apply to a small class of perceptual achievements. It goes for *all* our informed perceptual dealings with the world. Thus there are definite limits of a general kind to what we are able to transform into propositional knowledge concerning perceptual knowledge. It is not a 'shortcoming' pertaining only to the field of perceiving physiognomies. This is, accordingly, not a kind of knowledge which *in toto* can be transmitted by means of propositional language or become part of text books. Quite the opposite, it is a kind of first hand knowledge that always goes with particular *individuals*. And it is far beyond the reach of Ryle's rather simple distinction. I touched upon this issue in connection with aesthetic understanding in an article published quite a long time ago, and I decided there to call it *knowledge by familiarity*,[5] a term which is far from ideal but it has to do for want of a better.

Another philosopher who has touched upon the tacit component of our knowledgeable hold on the world is Paul K. Feyerabend. In a fairly recent article he argues rather inventively and convincingly to make us realise how little backing our thrust in scientific theories in fact has.[6] He attempts to draw a picture of human knowledge quite different from the received one. Concerning nature he emphasises that an

> enormous amount of knowledge resides in the ability to notice and to interpret phenomena such as clouds, the appearance of the horizon on an ocean voyage, the sound patterns in a wood, the behaviour of a person believed to be sick, and so on (p. 158).

And concerning human beings he expresses himself even more strongly: 'Our lives would fall apart', he says, 'if we could not read people's faces, understand their gestures, react correctly to their moods. Only a fraction of this knowledge can be articulated in speech and if it is, then knowledge of the same kind is needed to connect the words with the corresponding actions' (pp. 158–9).

Feyerabend indicates here that even the use of language has a tacit dimension. And I shall have more to say about that in a while. His main idea at this point is not, however, connected to the use of language. He is, on the contrary, anxious to make us understand that various forms of knowledge have quite *other* modes of expression than the verbal one. Knowledge of this kind is literally ascribed to different parts of the body. He puts the point like this:

> Knowledge is contained in the ability to perform special tasks. A dancer has knowledge in her limbs, an experimentalist in hands and eyes, a singer in the tongue, the throat, the diaphragm (p. 159).

---

5 Johannessen, K.S. (1981) 'Language, Art and Aesthetic Practice', in Johannessen, K.S. and Nordenstam, T., (eds.), *Wittgenstein – Aesthetics and Transcendental Philosophy*, Hölder-Pichler-Tempsky, Vienna, 108–26.

6 See Feyerabend, P.K., 'Knowledge and the Role of Theories' (1988) *Philosophy of the Social Sciences*, 157–78. In the following page references to this article are inserted in the text.

Something similar is also the case with the relation between language and knowledge. Knowledge does not exist in a nebulous medium independent of language. 'Knowledge resides in the ways we speak, the flexibility inherent in linguistic behaviour included' (p. 159). And the flexibility of the linguistic behaviour that Feyerabend has in mind is essentially bound up with the limitless amount of figurative expressions that the language is capable of forming. The examples he gives are ambiguities, analogies and patterns of analogical reasoning. The very possibility of being able to work with analogies and patterns of analogical reasoning is a means for reworking already existing concepts as well as forming new ones. Accordingly these elements are said to constitute a destabilising element of permanent nature in every natural language. This is for Feyerabend how new sense is formed in language.

Professional Knowledge as a Species of Analogical Thinking

As we noted Feyerabend touches upon the role of language in connection with matters of tacit knowing. The points concerning analogies and patterns of analogical reasoning are extremely important as they are usually overlooked or deliberately left out when the resources constitutive of sense making are described in the received view. The nature and use of metaphors and analogies is an intriguing matter that has attracted quite a few philosophers and literary scholars, including myself.[7] A lot has been written on this subject without any palpable success. The mist surrounding matters of metaphor is still awaiting its dissipation. Regrettably few have, however, approached these questions from an epistemological point of view.

Analogical reasoning is much less often treated, but Aristotle described one pattern relevant for an epistemological approach: reasoning by examples. In *The Prior Analytics* he notes that we from time to time try to establish a point by using examples. And this is different both from inductive as well as deductive reasoning. Aristotle puts the difference this way:

> Clearly then to argue by example is neither like reasoning from part to whole (the inductive pattern), nor like reasoning from whole to part (the deductive pattern), but rather reasoning from part to part when both particulars are subordinate to the same term and one of them is known (69a).

---

7 See Johannessen, K.S., 'Metaphor and Science', in Åhlberg, L.-O. and Zaine, T. (eds) (1994) *Aesthetic Matters. Essays presented to Göran Sörbom on his 60th birthday*, Uppsala, 53–66.

What Aristotle here describes is one kind of *analogical* reasoning, a kind of reasoning that is sorely wanted when one is facing a difficult task where none of the established principles and methods seem to apply. It is most interesting to find that Aristotle's perceptiveness made him record this as a third kind of reasoning. That is, however, also its limitation. His observation concerns a *pattern* of reasoning with the help of which we may establish a valid point in a discussion. It is not a remark on *analogical* thinking in general. Aristotle sticks to an intellectual operation where thought moves from one particular to another and both are said to be 'subordinate to the same term'. It is also assumed that the first particular is known. And the particulars are thought of as *examples* and not as *particular cases*. The difference is huge. Examples get their status as examples from some universal or concept which is already fairly well established. Examples are examples *of* some principle, concept, norm, rule, law. It is its relation to the already existing universal which establishes something as an example at all. That is why one of the particulars has to be known. It is known to exemplify the universal.

What Aristotle leaves out in this case is the fact that some *judgement* is needed to decide if there exists a sufficient similarity between the two particulars to subsume them under the same term. And if he had had the intention of characterising something like analogical thinking in general he would no doubt have wanted to start with particular cases and not with examples. Particular cases are so to speak in search of a universal, a concept. Particular cases are not yet conceptually determined. They invite *reflection*.

Professional Knowledge and Judgement

Kant's mature view of judgement takes care of the distinction just sketched. Late in life he came to realise that judgement is needed in more than one way. But even discovering that there was a need for some ability to judge in connection with the use of concepts was an achievement in itself. And his reasoning on this point seems strikingly like something we are accustomed to ascribe to Wittgenstein. Concepts, Kant argued, are best thought of as *rules*. Thus the concept 'chair' should be construed as the rule we employ for classifying certain things as chairs. But, he argued, an understanding of how to apply that rule cannot consist merely in the mastery of further rules, since that would transform the problem into one of how those further rules were to be applied. The ability to apply rules, i.e. concepts, must rest ultimately, he insisted, on a different kind of ability, itself *not* a rule-governed procedure. It has to be an ability by which we simply *see* that a thing falls within the scope of a rule. This sort of knack Kant called judgement. To him it was an inborn talent which could only be practiced but not taught. You are badly off if you lack this ability, according to Kant, and he describes the situation this way: 'Deficiency in judgment is just what is ordinarily called stupidity, and for such a failing there is no remedy'.[8]

On the other hand, if you possessed judgement it could be improved through the use of examples: examples of the rules being applied on particular occasions. 'Examples are thus the go-cart of judgement; and those who are lacking in the natural talent [of applying rules] can never dispense with them' (p. 178). Thus we see that according to this conception judgement is an ability concerned with the appropriate application of rules to particular situations. It is, however, exclusively conceived of from the point of view of the universal. But when you face some totally unexpected natural phenomenon in your research, a radically new work of art or some unheard of action which by common consent is experienced as a grave felony but hardly covered by the existing system of laws as currently practiced, there is no ready-made universal, principle or concept to be consulted. You simply do not know what to say or do. All the established ways of proceeding fail you. You cannot expect a universal to 'be pulled out of a hat in some magical way', as Kjell Winbladh puts it in the report from the Combitech Software project (p. 60). Kant eventually realised that a different sort of judgement was needed in this type of situation. And in his work *The Critique of Judgement* he expresses the difference this way:

> Judgement in general is the faculty of thinking the particular as contained under the universal. If the universal (the rule, principle, or law) is given, then the judgement which subsumes the particular under it is determinant... If, however, only the particular is given and the universal has to be found for it, then the judgement is simply reflective.[9]

This aptly sums up the predicament in which we find ourselves when the established repertoire of concepts and theories fails us. We somehow have to draw on our experience to produce something analogous to a universal, for instance produce a simplifying picture with a deliberately open-ended and manifold application or develop a repertoire of family-like particular cases to be used as objects of comparisons, or something

---

8 Kant, I. (1963) *Critique of Pure Reason*, translated by N.K. Smith, London: Macmillan & Co Ltd, 178.

9 Kant, I. (1952) *The Critique of Judgement*, translated by J.C. Meredith, London: Oxford University Press, 18.

similar. This is a creative response, of course, but we see now that some sort of judgement is unavoidably put to use in a reflective way.

In passing we should note that both the *determinant* and the *reflective* judgement is in operation when we, for instance, compare one particular case with another in order to spot traits of similarities sufficient to subsume them under the same term. Spotting something involves a process of seeking, and that is the task of the reflective judgement. Deciding if the similarity is sufficient for subsumption can only be done by the determinant judgement. This may then be one way of pinpointing the complexity of putting experience based knowledge to use in situations where reflection and creativity are required.

Kant's way of talking may nevertheless feel a bit awkward and old-fashioned. And we certainly no longer believe in faculties of the mind, as Kant did. It is, of course, not my intention to suggest that we should take over the Kantian terminology. But as we do work with metaphors and analogies, make comparisons, pass judgements on the basis of experience and are notoriously puzzled by the tacit component in our knowledgeable hold on the world, we should, in my opinion, take a good look at what the classic masters have to offer us in this respect. It is certainly not sufficient for our purposes, but it is a promising start. And we need such a point of departure to be able to develop a deeper understanding of the complexity of the problems involved.

The Constitutive Role of Particular Cases in Professional Knowledge

A quite striking and instructive analysis of analogical thinking is written by the American lawyer, Edward H. Levi. In a book called *An Introduction to Legal Reasoning* (1948) he discusses the role of the judge operating within a case-law system. In such a system, the rules of law are to some extent created by the judges themselves through the precedence-creating decisions in particular cases. According to Levi case-law situations of this kind have the following properties:[10] (1) Important similarities are discerned between previous cases and the present one. (2) The legal rule which is embedded in the previous case(s) is formulated. (3) And then it is applied to the new case. But other judges do not have to feel bound later by the judgement in the present case. On principle at least, one is free to stress other aspects of the cases.

---

10 Levi, E.H. (1948) *An Introduction to Legal Reasoning*, Chicago & London, 1–2.

Concerning this analysis I would like to emphasise three things. First, the arguments necessarily involve comparisons between *particular* cases – the precedent(s) and the present case. Thus we find here a genuine case of analogical thinking. Secondly, the case-law principle opens up the possibility that the rules of law are discovered and formulated as a result of the comparisons made. Reflections taking the form of working out concrete comparisons are thus the very means of developing the legal system as such – both in scope and in depth. Thirdly, the entire legal system is in a sort of constant flux since old paradigms are always prone to be replaced by new ones. And it is impossible to anticipate or predict the new paradigms on the basis of the existing system of laws. Each new application has to grow out of the belabouring of a given set of precedents judged to be relevant to a given case being tried before the court.

And for our purpose the whole of this mechanism may function as an object of comparison in Wittgenstein's sense[11] to throw light on similarities as well as on differences concerning our attempts at coming to grips with various aspects of the experience based knowledge. In any case we should definitely not do what the Dreyfus brothers do – hide all the complexity behind the term 'intuition'.[12] When they characterise the transition from novice to expert as a movement from rule dependence to intuitive acting, this tends to hide one of the most basic aspects of operating with experience based knowledge. What I have in mind is Kant's (and Wittgenstein's) observation that *all* knowledgeable acting in the last instance has to be *ruleless* acting. Missing this we risk overlooking another potentially fruitful circumstance in this matter: the interesting parallel between the mastery of language and the use of professional knowledge. In the field of language there is of necessity a kind of ruleless acting when a new situation presents itself to the language user. In such a case he is literally forced to respond in a *creative* manner; otherwise he will fail to cope with the newness of the situation. In this respect we may even consider the use of language and concept formation as one of the large looming paradigms of professional knowledge. But that is another story to be told on a different occasion.

---

11 In *Philosophical Investigations* Wittgenstein says that language games are to be considered as objects of comparison (§130) intended to 'throw light on the facts of our language' by way of similarities as well as dissimilarities.

12 See Dreyfus, H.L. and Dreyfus, S.E. (1986) *Mind over Machine. The Power of Human Intuition and Expertise in the Era of the Computer*, Oxford: Basil Blackwell, especially Chapter 1 where they describe the acquiring of experience from novice to expert and stress how the experts act non-reflectively.

16 Dialogue, Depth, and Life Inside Responsive Orders: From External Observation to Participatory Understanding

John Shotter

The aspects of things that are most important for us are hidden because of their simplicity and familiarity. (One is unable to notice something – because it is always before one's eyes.) The real foundations of his enquiry do not strike a man at all. Unless that fact has at some time struck him. – And this means; we fail to be struck by what, once seen, is most striking and most powerful (Wittgenstein, 1953, §129).[1]

Truth is not born nor is it to be found inside the head of an individual person, it is born between people collectively searching for truth, in the process of their dialogic interaction (Bakhtin, 1984, 110).

Rules of correct reasoning were first extracted by Aristotle, yet men knew how to avoid and detect fallacies before they learned his lessons, just as men since Aristotle, and including Aristotle, ordinarily conduct their arguments without making any internal reference to his formulae...Indeed if they had to plan what to think before thinking it they would never think at all; for this planning would itself be unplanned. Efficient practice precedes the theory of it; methodologies presuppose the application of the methods, of the critical investigation of which they are the products (Ryle, 1949, 30–1).

In this chapter, I want to explore the relevance of the methods Wittgenstein used in his later philosophy, in attempting to gain an understanding of some of the crucial 'practicalities' of performing, i.e., of expressing,

---

1 All date only citations are to Wittgenstein's works.

knowledge in dialogues. In doing this, I want to emphasise, like Johannessen (this volume, and 1994), not only the primacy of our practices, but also the importance within them of our living, embodied, expressive-responsive reactions to the others and othernesses[2] in our surroundings. As Johannessen points out, following Wittgenstein (1974), such spontaneous reactions can give rise to *intransitive understandings*, i.e., unique, only once-occurrent understandings, that not only allow us to understand the concrete, detailed particularities of our surroundings in their *own* terms, but also as we shall see, makes the intrinsic creativity of dialogue possible.

The nature of the dialogical is alien and strange to our modern, western sensibilities. Schooled, as we have been ever since the Greeks, in the value of individual contemplative thought prior to planned and effortful action, rather than in the worth of socially refined and sensitive ways of acting effortlessly (as in gaining at least a first understanding of the words in such a text as this, for instance), we fail to notice its existence. In the past, it has remained ignored in background to all our activities together. However, an awareness of the strange and amazing nature of the dialogical will help us, not only to conduct ourselves in many of our current social activities in a much more well oriented, less trial-and-error fashion, but it will also help us to understand the new learning that must also occur between us if we are to create such effortless forms of coordinated action in other spheres of our lives.

Central to an understanding of our effortless, dialogically-structured, jointly executed everyday activities, will be the idea of a 'responsive order' (Gendlin, 1997). This is the idea, articulated also by the other thinkers to whom I refer below, e.g., Bakhtin, Wittgenstein, and Merleau-Ponty, that as living, embodied beings we are all always already embedded in an intricate flow of complexly intertwined relationally-responsive activities between ourselves and the others and othernesses around us. Wittgenstein (1980) puts it thus: 'Only in the stream of thought and life do words have meaning' (No. 173). Indeed, as many who must read this chapter as written in not in their own language are aware, reading (or listening) to a foreign language is not easy. The very nature of our everyday social lives with

---

2 In choosing to talk of both others and of *othernesses* here (rather than of other *persons* and of *objects* or *things*), I mean to signal a distinction which will become of increasing importance in the course of this chapter. The distinction is to do with the way in which we deal with our sense of how something is *real* for us, of how its nature is not just open to any interpretation we wish to put upon it. Scientific or object *realism* wants to talk of things in our surroundings as having a life of their own *independent* of us. I want, following Rudd (2003), to talk of them as having a life of their own *in relation* to us. Rudd (2003) calls this 'expressive realism,' and as I see it, it is quite consistent to hold to an *expressive realism* within the context of a thoroughgoing *social constructionism* (Shotter, 1984, 1993a and b).

each other is such that, as Johannessen (in this volume) puts it: 'It is required of us that we not only react unreflectively towards certain features in our surroundings, we also have to react in the same way towards them. There must be a level in our sense-making activities where our reactions do not spring from any kind of reflection or reasoning. They have to be immediate responses to the world around us. And this is another aspect of the phenomenon of intransitive understanding' (see p. 290). Without these immediate, unreflective understandings, our everyday lives with each other would be impossible. As living, embodied beings (as 'open' systems) we cannot help but be spontaneously responsive to events occurring around us. In being responsive in this bodily way, a complex intertwining of our own outgoing responsive activities with those coming into us from others and othernesses 'out there' occurs, and this is where all the strangeness of the dialogical begins.

As soon as two or more different forms of life meet, another shared or collective form of life within which both participate, with its own unique world and character (a culture?) emerges between them. More than merely an averaged or quantitatively shared world emerges, a world with a new dimension of connectedness results, a qualitatively new world opens up at the point of contact between them. Just as the two 2-D monocular points of view from our two eyes are not merged into each other to produce an 'averaged' 2-D view, but somehow work together to create a binocular 3-D 'space' with an extra dimension of 'depth' to it – so other such extra-dimensioned 'world-spaces' are created in all our relationally responsive practices. Indeed, as Bakhtin (1984) remarks, it is only in the meeting of 'unmerged consciousnesses' (p. 9), each also with its own world, that such a dialogically-structured space is created, a dynamic unity in plurality.

This, then, is what is so special about our embedding within such responsive orders. New relations that matter to us, new features requiring our evaluative judgements, new dimensions that both offer us certain opportunities for action while also exerting certain calls upon us to which we must respond, are continually created, unnoticed, in our dialogically-structured meetings. Although we usually remain unaware of always being situated within such a dialogically structured space, although the created sense of a 'depth' usually remains unnoticed in the background to our lives together, it is always from within such a space, in 'answer' to the 'calls' it exerts upon us, that we responsively perform our actions. The unique nature of such spaces can only be studied from within the practices in which they are created. To investigate their nature, their structure, the calls they can exert on us, what is possible for us within them and what is not, we need some utterly new methods of investigation, quite different from the 'onlooker' methods inherited from the natural sciences.

Science and Art – an Interplay Across the Boundaries

Central both to my Wittgensteinian account, and to Johannessen's, is the role of concrete examples in our making clear the nature of our practices, not only in our teaching them to others, but in our intellectual inquiries into their very nature. Indeed, the examples I describe below are central to *the style* of my whole account. Thus it is important for us to be aware of what is being done in such an activity. It is easy to misunderstand their role. For it is only too easy to take it for granted that, as intellectuals, our prime task is that of formulating laws, rules, or principles in propositional form, with the idea that practical activities consist in 'the putting of theories into practice'. In this context, examples are taken as being exemplary, as being merely illustrations of a principle. But in teaching (and understanding) a practice, examples are crucial, it cannot be done just by stating and teaching rules or principles. Why? Because the development of a responsive order between us, must begin with events to which we all spontaneously *respond in the same way*. As Wittgenstein (1969) puts it, 'our rules leave loop-holes open, and the practice has to speak for itself' (§139). In other words, here, in the teaching of a practice, examples do not serve an *illustrative role*, the proof of the correctness of a theory, but a *constitutive role*, i.e., they work to inaugurate in us, practically and responsively, new, never before performed, ways of seeing and acting. Hence, we should see the use of *striking* examples, as provocative of new reactions, as one of Wittgenstein's central methods in his attempt to teach us the *practicalities* of doing his kind of philosophical investigation into our practices, examples we can 'get into'.

Wittgenstein (1980) comments on the originary importance of such spontaneous reactions as follows: 'The origin and the primitive form of the language game is a reaction: only from this can more complicated forms develop. Language, I want to say, is refinement, "in the beginning was the deed" [Goethe].' By the word 'primitive' here, Wittgenstein (1980) wants to make it clear that he does not mean something historically primitive, back in humankind's early times, but 'that this sort of behavior is pre-linguistic: that a language-game is based on it, that it is the prototype of a way of thinking and not the result of thought' (§541). These shared understandings that begin with our bodily reactions, can then be progressively refined as our practical involvements with the others around us continue to unfold. We should think of this as occurring, not only in our early lives as we begin to learn to be language users, but ceaselessly throughout our lives, in all our involvements with the others around us. To understand something new is to learn something new.

We are not, however, very practiced in either noticing the important 'practicalities' involved in our dialogically-structured activities, or in noticing their 'magical' nature. As we understand the practicalities of the more informal aspects of our institutional forms of intellectual inquiry more, we will see how important all the preparations for and preliminaries to them are: the informal conversations, the orienting remarks, the looking at and discussion of examples, the comparisons with other practices, and so on: the kind of things that go on in apprenticeships! As Wittgenstein (1953) remarks about the activity of naming things: 'One forgets that a great deal of stage-setting in language is presupposed if the mere act of naming is to make sense' (§257), and it is just the as yet unnoticed and unremarked upon nature of this stage-setting that I want to bring out into the open.

Given the emphasis on detailed examples in the teaching of a practice, I would now like to turn to the chapter by Karl Duner, Lucas Ekeroth, and Mats Hanson. For, as Mats Hanson remarks about the designing of the Masters' course in engineering at KTH, the aim was to transform the course into 'a stage for the learning process' (see p. 176), and to organise it as 'a project with the aim of developing an actual product, an artefact, in co-operation with an external partner' (see p. 177).

Depicted here is a project within which a stage, a space of possibilities, is created upon which 'interaction across traditional and cultural boundaries' (see p. 175) can occur, the project combines the arts and humanities with the natural sciences and technology. All these features will be important to us. Let us first do some stage-setting: Karl Dunér, the director at the Royal Dramatic Theatre, was the 'external partner' in this project. As one consciousness among the plurality of unmerged consciousnesses involved in it, he had envisioned a dynamic sculpture/picture of seven moving, box-like forms he called Company I-VII. His main purpose in devising such a piece of 'performing' art was to create unexpected events – for, as he rightly remarks, unprepared events can often give much more powerful feelings than prepared ones. We might go further, and note Janik's remark (Janik, 1990), that practical philosophy does not begin with a problem as an obstacle to be surmounted, but 'with a surprise. The contrary of what our paradigm has led us to expect, the impossible, as it were, occurs' (see p. 57). Thus the task faced by the plurality of consciousnesses here is not just a simple engineering problem of creating artefactual forms that correspond externally to the forms on a blueprint. It is a special one that requires talk and other forms of communication 'about' something which does not yet exist, to which one cannot refer directly, which exists only in Dunér's mind or imagination. They must create an entity that has a 'presence', a 'way of being in the world', an 'inner form' of the kind Dunér imagines. To do this, they must all intertwine their activities in such a fashion: Dunér, the engineering students, the professor, so as to bring what was at first only implicit in Dunér's gestures, drawings, utterances, and other expressions out explicitly into a shared public space.

As Janik remarks about problems of this kind, let us call them 'bewilderments', for they are more to do with us not yet knowing an overall way to which to turn, than with merely overcoming a barrier along a way already being followed, they have 'the character of a riddle inasmuch as everything that we need to understand is before us and not hidden to view' (Janik 1990, 44). This is exactly right. Janik then goes on to suggest that the task is akin to that of getting what is in view before us into focus, of finding a new perspective on it, something which a new paradigm case can give us. Here I disagree. The paradigm of 'a perspective' here is misleading. It is too implicated in our current, modernist, centralised ways of thinking and acting. It not only gives rise to a formal ordering of events in our surroundings, to a one-eyed, single order of connectedness from a single, static point of view. It plays down the element of surprise, or spontaneity, that both Janik and Dunér bring to our attention, as well as the importance of the dialogically-structured nature of such events, the fact that it is not just a one-eyed individual's way of seeing a logical order that is at issue, but the creation of an utterly new dimension of relatedness by the coordinated, unmerged intertwining of the activities of a plurality of consciousnesses.

Although we can, as Janik remarks, only escape bewilderments by 'changing the way we live' (Janik, 1990), the kind of change we need involves much more than a changed perspective or changed point of view. We need to change the very way we 'look over' what is visible before us, the way we look expectantly from each place upon which we focus, and our two eyes converge, to the next. A good paradigm for some important aspects of what is involved here, is provided by the 3-D virtual realities seemingly present 'in' the random-dot auto-stereograms popular a few years ago. (Another paradigm, of course, is that of 'seeing' meaning in the array of print spread out on this page.) If we are to 'see' what is 'hidden' in such displays, it is not a new way of thinking we have to learn: being told theories or principles, or about what is supposedly 'there' before us, will not help us at all in actually seeing it! To 'see' the 3-D shape, we will have to try to provoke ourselves to adopt new 'ways of looking' until our bodies, suddenly, spontaneously, create the new way of looking required to see the holistic vision we seek. To this end, various indirect hints – such as 'try crossing your eyes', 'start with the display touching your nose and move it away slowly', 'look at a pencil point halfway between the display and your eyes, and try to notice what is occurring beyond it!' and so on – might be of some help.

For we need to induce our two eyes to both focus and converge, not on the 2-D surface of the page containing the random dots, but '*out there*' in the space of the 3-D display 'hidden' in the dots. Once we 'see' the 'object' in the display, we 'see' it, not by now being able to '*think it out*' as one might solve a problem, but in terms of a whole specific range of spontaneously occurring, bodily reactions and anticipatory responses, for instance, we see the near parts of the 'object' at a distance near to us and the far parts as far from us, not just as large and small as in a 2-D display. Once in possession of the appropriate 'way of looking,' we can automatically 'look from' one part of the display, having allowed it to '*call out*' a certain response from us, while 'looking toward' another with a certain adjustive anticipation, and so on, and so on (Shotter, 1996a). Our bodies create in us qualitatively new relational dimensions, joining retrospective experience to prospective anticipations. Indeed, it is as if each element we encounter and respond to, 'tells us' how to be prepared to '*go out to meet*' the next, so that, as it were, we can turn toward it with our hand already raised to shake its hand.

I have considered some of the deep and crucial differences between the overcoming of bewilderments and the solving of problems, because this is what is demonstrated in the example of performing knowledge presented here, in the mechatronics Masters' course at the KTH. The Company I-VII project required the coming together of 28 engineers (represented here by Lucas Ekeroth), their teachers (represented by Mats Hanson), and Dunér. What I see as standing out in its presentation are the following points (listed in order of their appearance in the presentation):

(1)   the construction of new knowledge on the basis of an individual's former knowledge and experience (Hanson);
(2)   the necessity for knowledge to be operational, to be usable in work involving an interplay between different people (Hanson);
(3)   the surprise of the engineers at the lack of association between the order in their 'high tech' products and Dunér's 'half-finished', artistic use of them (Dunér);
(4)   the 'translation' of Dunér's artistic requirements into measurable specifications (Ekeroth);
(5)   their division into specific functions and interfaces (Ekeroth);
(6)   the ongoing modification of existing designs in the step from specification to construction (Ekeroth);
(7)   the re-using of already existing things as a part of creativity (Hanson);
(8)   the ease with which details can be overlooked (Ekeroth) – this emphasis on details is very important, and I shall return to it;
(9)   mechatronics is an interplay requiring the involvement of many figures (Hanson);

(10) Dunér operated as a director in mise en scene just as in the theater (Dunér);

(11) the way in which the tacking back and forth between envisaged whole and what has so far been developed works to modify further development (Ekeroth);

(12) dealing with the unclear and ambiguous by 'getting into' the developing situation – which can be done by, among other things, 'living with one's examples, the masters . . . [by] apprenticeship' (Hanson, see p. 183);

(13) the emergence of possibilities of thinking differently arising from the group's dialogues: 'an engineer shared a wild and "impossible" idea' (Ekeroth, see p. 184);

(14) the use of gestures and many other means than just words – Dunér's demonstration of how slowly a figure should move by his movement of a tin along a ruler (Ekeroth);

(15) Dunér finding that his original envisioning of Company I-VII could be embellished as new technological possibilities merged (Dunér);

(16) finding that what many of the engineers at first thought easy was (with artistic criteria to satisfy) more difficult to achieve than originally thought.

I listed all these features of the Company I-VII project because we are not very good at noticing the 'practicalities' involved in our practices. These are just some of the important details involved in a group of very different people coming together to form between them, a resourceful, self-reflective, self-developing community of learners. Central to them all coming together in this way was not, as Mats Hanson emphasises right at the start, the one-way transferral of principles from teacher to student in lectures. People work in living contact with each other, reacting and responding to each other's actions; they function within a responsive order. In so doing, they exhibit a kind of active, practical understanding very different from the passive intellectual understanding we are used to discussing in our current philosophical theories of knowledge and understanding. As Bakhtin (1986) describes it: 'All real and integral understanding is actively responsive, and constitutes nothing more than the initial preparatory stage of a response (in what ever form it may be actualized). The speaker himself is oriented precisely toward such an actively responsive understanding' (p. 69). To contrast with the representational-referential kind of understanding we are used to discussing in our current philosophies, we might call this kind of more practical understanding, understanding of a relational-responsive kind. For, rather than an inner picture or representation of a state of affairs, it gives us an understanding, a sense, of how, within an ongoing practice with others, to 'go on' to relate ourselves responsively to what might next occur. Indeed, to repeat what has already been said above, with such an understanding, it is as if each element we encounter, 'tells us' how to prepare ourselves to 'go out to meet' the next, so that we can, as it were, turn toward it with our hand already raised to greet its coming.

Rather than reflect further on these details here, it will be more useful to link them in my discussion of the other two examples below, for, as Wittgenstein (1953) remarks, it is in the very nature of this kind of understanding that it 'consists in "seeing connections"' (§122). As we gradually find our 'way about' inside such dialogically-structured practices, as they become more familiar to us, as we come to feel more 'at home' within them, just as with those of our dwelling places already familiar to us, which contain different spaces for different uses at different times, so we can begin to specify their 'ecology', i.e., the whole set of internally related, interdependent, regions (spaces) and moments (times) making up the interconnected flow of a practice. What is crucial about our practices, is that they are held together by us all being immersed within a shared and sharable responsive order.

To repeat, Wittgenstein's (1969) insistence on the constitutive importance of examples in this process is important. In being obsessed with objectivity, with only ever being outside observers of repetitive forms or patterns, we have ignored unique, novel, fleeting, first-time events. Not only have we dismissed their occurrence, thinking of them as inessential variations in underlying, hidden ideal forms, but we have also ignored the 'inner sense' we have of their dynamic structure, the shaped and vectored sense of the openings they offer us for our practical movements within them. Intellectually, we have persisted in acting as if we are mere spectators of a world 'over there', open only indirectly to our one-way manipulative activities, rather than participants in a world around us 'here', to which we must spontaneously and responsively relate if we are to be 'answerable' to its 'calls' upon us. Fleeting though its calls may be, 'once-occurrent events of Being,' Bakhtin (1993) calls them, as both he and Wittgenstein (1953) show, they each have their own unique, and very complex, inner structure.

Precision and Improvisation – Characterising Half-finished, Still-developing Knowledge

The presentation of examples, not as passive forms but as active, ongoing, happening events, draws out certain spontaneous responses from us, which, although vague and seemingly indefinite in themselves (imageless), form in fact a highly specific sensible basis, i.e., 'an inner standard', against which our more explicit expressions and formulations (images) can be judged as to their adequacy or not. What is important about them is the intricacy of the responsive interplay between ourselves and our surroundings they provoke in us: the moment of their presentation consists in a complex mixture of influences, from us and from whatever the example is. The mixture is not just a matter of so much flour and so much butter and milk, a mixing of quantities, but a complex and intricate intertwining of noticing, acting, talking, remembering, focusing here, focusing there, moving around, relating to others, closing off to outside influences, and so on, with all the component activities occurring in appropriate spatial and temporal relations, and coming also from the different positions occupied by all the people involved. A space with a multiplicity of relational dimensions comes into existence. We can think of the dialogically structured intertwining that occurs as an 'orchestration', a complex, polyphonic unfolding of many interwoven, co-responsive functions. Thus any event in which an example is used not only has its own quite unique character, but has a kind of 'fullness' to it, in that a number of different orders may originate from it. About the 'fullness' possible in the utterance of a single word, Wittgenstein (1980) notes that we can say of the expression 'Fare well!,' that 'A whole world of pain is contained in these words.' 'How can it be contained in them?' he asks, 'It is bound up with them. The words are like an acorn from which an oak tree can grow,' he replies (p. 52). The different examples we use in our discussions are just like the seeds of different varieties of plant; while the actual plant to emerge will be influenced by the interactive conditions during its growth, oak trees can never grow from apple seeds. To grow the right kind of plant we need the right kind of seed. The jointly shared moments which 'set the scene' (provide a shared sensible basis) for the rest of our shared talk, seem crucial. Elsewhere, I have described the kind of specificity here, in such jointly shared moments, as 'already specified further specifiability' (Shotter, 1984, 187).

The specificity, and fullness, of the shared sense that can arise in such jointly shared moments is relevant to the question posed at the start of the chapter by Niclas Fock and Christer Hoberg: 'How do we find a way to develop the knowledge of system developers?' (see p. 110). How can an expertise, a skill, be developed in a never stable, never finalised sphere of activity? The question is very similar to the question of how can we develop a skill with language in our everyday lives; for our use of words is also a matter of skillful improvisation. Are there any rules or methods that might be of any help?

The project Fock and Hoberg outline is aimed at promoting the growth of professional expertise among a group of software engineers in the Combitech Software company (a consultancy company with more than 100 engineers creating software for real-time systems). Central to the project is 'the dialogue seminar' (designed in conjunction with Bo Göranzon and Maria Hammarén); but it is worth drawing out the parallels here to the use of 'Dialogue Conferences' in the Swedish 'Learning Regions' project (Gustavsen, 1992; Shotter and Gustavsen, 1999). For, just as a central concern in the Learning Regions project is with all involved coming to share a scenic-sense of the region they all occupy as a dynamic arena full of developmental resources (cf. the idea of a 'stage' in the previous Company I-VII example), so here too is the same concern with all involved developing 'a common view' (see p. 92). What is it to have such a view, and how is it that dialogues are crucial to its development?

To give answers to these questions, we must study the strange nature of joint, dialogically structured activities more closely. They are quite unlike the actions of an individual, which can be explained by giving the individual's reasons for acting, or the behaviours of an individual, which can be explained by giving their causes. As I have shown elsewhere (Shotter, 1984, 1993), such joint activities constitute a distinct, third realm, sui generis, of activity. Its characteristics are perhaps best listed:

The Third Realm

- To the extent that everything done by any of the individuals involved in it is done in spontaneous response to the others or othernesses around them, we cannot (as we have seen) hold any of them individually responsible for its outcome: thus it lacks a reason.
- Yet it is not brought about by any causes external to them either: it is produced only by 'their' activity, and 'they' collectively are responsible for it.
- It has its origins in the fact that, as living beings, we cannot not be spontaneously responsive to each other and to other 'othernesses' in our surroundings.
- As soon as a second living human being responds to the activities of a first, then what the second does cannot be accounted as wholly their own activity, for the second acts in a way that is partly 'shaped' by the first (and the first's acts were responsive also)...this is where all the strangeness of dialogical activity or 'joint action' (Shotter, 1984, 1993a and b) begins.

A Complex, Intertwined Mixture, an Invisible Whole or Unseparated Multiplicity

- What the participants produce between them is a very complex mixture of not wholly reconcilable influences; as Bakhtin (1981) remarks, at work within it are both 'centripetal' tendencies (inward toward order and unity), as well as 'centrifugal' ones (outward toward diversity and difference).
- Influences from vision, touch, hearing, taste, and smell, as well as our body senses, our own and our responses to those of others, are all mixed in together.[3]
- Joint action is in fact a complex mixture of many different kinds of influences.
- This makes it very difficult for us to characterise its nature: it has neither a fully orderly nor a fully disorderly structure, a neither completely stable nor an easily changed organisation, a neither fully subjective nor fully objective character.
- Indeed, we could say that it is its very lack of specificity, its lack of any pre-determined human order, and thus its openness to being specified or determined yet further by those involved in it, in practice, that is its central defining feature.
- Indeed, relying on the directionality inherent in the temporal unfolding of living activities, we are able at certain crucial moments in our exchanges with others, to use such expressions as 'Look at *that*', 'Listen to *this*', 'Do like *this*', '*This* is what I meant', and so on.[4]
- However, it is not wholly unspecified. The 'dialogical reality or space' people spontaneously construct in their joint actions is experienced

---

3 Merleau-Ponty (1964) talks of the intertwining that occurs thus: 'It is a marvel too little noticed that every movement of my eyes – even more, every displacement of my body – has its place in the same visible universe that I itemize and explore with them, as, conversely, every vision takes place somewhere in tactile space. There is double and crossed situating of the visible in the tangible and of the tangible in the visible; the two maps are complete yet they do not merge into one. The two parts are total parts and yet are not superposable' (p. 134).

4 The crucial nature of the *moment of utterance* cannot be over-emphasised: in coming at a particular moment in the already ongoing flow of contingently intertwined activity occurring between them and us, in pointing in their gestural expressiveness from '*this* past' toward '*that* kind of future'. People's activities allow us to intervene at *this* or *that* moment, and in doing so, to point them toward '*another kind* of future', toward seeing a connection between events of a previously unnoticed kind. Wittgenstein (1953) calls these the 'essential references' of an utterance: 'In saying "When I heard this word, it meant...to me" one refers to a *point in time* and to a *way of using the word*...And the expression "I was then going to say..." refers to a *point of time* and an *action*. I speak of the essential *references* of the utterance in order to distinguish them from other peculiarities of the expression we use' (1953, p. 175).

(sensed) as a 'third agency', with its own specific demands and requirements: 'Each dialogue takes place as if against the background of an invisible third party [an "it"] who stands above all the participants in the dialogue (partners)' (Bakhtin, 1986, 126).

What is so special about dialogically structured activities, is that the very responsive nature of the activity between us makes it impossible to say which aspect of it is due to you and which to me. An 'it' emerges between us with its own requirements, a responsive order, which we are both a part of and participants in, and which as such can make calls upon us both.

Fock and Hoberg give a very nice example of the gradual emergence of such a shared 'dialogical reality or space', a shared 'it', among a group of eight software engineers in a 'dialogue seminar' meeting to discuss whether there are any 'methods' of use to them in their development work. I list what seem to be the crucial events:

- Mike agrees to take the minutes.
- Johan begins by reading a prepared text on methods, he is critical of too much analysis of demands, wants more prototypes, and mentions the danger of ignoring details.
- Tomas adds that prototypes can be used for testing at an early stage in development.
- The others agree.
- Tomas then says: 'The architect must be strong and know what he is doing.'
- Johan responds: 'It is easy for the architect to stop acting as a mentor and begin to overrule people.'

The two statements are opposites of each other...energy is created in the group...tension, movement...what Arlene Katz and I would call an 'arresting moment' has occurred (Shotter and Katz, 1996; Katz and Shotter, 1996b); the two statements seem opposed, yet they are based on concrete experiences shared by all members in the group...clearly their 'reality' can be ordered explicitly in a number of ways:

- Tomas now says: 'The role of the architect is often too strong in the organisation, and he may be difficult to put in his place.'
- Although almost a complete contradiction of his earlier statement, this is not a change in Tomas's viewpoint, but a broadening to take into account other aspects of the dialogue.
- They circle around...they refer to each other's examples...it feels as if participants' experiences begin to find one another...

- But there is a feeling too, that there is something they are failing to get to...there is not yet an 'it' between, a shared sensibility, a shared sense that 'calls' unconfused actions from them.
- Kjell, well-known for his use of certain methods, then reads his text and points to problems associated with different viewpoints.
- Odd responds: 'It is interesting with your experience you are critical of methods.'
- Kjell answers: 'It depends on how they are used. I want a method that structures what I have arrived at...[But] when one reaches difficult areas, producing objects and creating systems...it is here that experience comes into play and you get no help from methods here.'
- There is a moment's silence...Kjell's statement creates another 'arresting, moving, or striking moment.'

(Pause, silence)

- Somehow, Kjell's statement 'said it all'...there was nothing more to say about the role of methods.
- A new topic suddenly emerged: the role of the software architect... 'How does the systems architect build up an overall view?'
- The idea of an 'architect' does not provide any new information, but re-orients the whole group toward a new way of looking at their activities.
- Kjell answers: By first making a detailed study of conditions and then, by drawing on experience, seeing a way forward.
- 'I believe that is how an architect works when designing a house,' says Key.
- Everyone had become so involved in this formulation of a new way of working that they had forgotten the time...now there is a common 'it', a topic (topos=place), a 'scene' toward which all can orient, within which all can play a part...it is not only recorded in the minutes, but also 'resides' with the participants.

I have focused on this episode because I want to suggest, in line with Wittgenstein's (1980) claim that the origin of a new language-game is in a new reaction, which is not the result of thought but the prototype for a new way of thinking, that the arresting moment created by Kjell's statement was crucial to the emergence of 'a common view.' Irrespective of any ideas as such they might have had in their heads, in all spontaneously responding in the same way to Kjell's statement, that methods work *after* the creative fact, but not *before*, the members of the group created between them jointly a shared, sensible basis of a new kind (a new space between them with a 'depth' to it) to serve as a 'standard' against which all could make sense of and judge each other's further contributions. Such striking moments have that quality of 'fullness' to them, the intricate,

intertwined complexity mentioned above as a central property of dialogically structured activity in the third realm, possessed by good examples.

I began by pointing out the (rational) invisibility of those aspects of
our lives together in which we interact with and understand each other
effortlessly, and how such unreflective, effortless ways of coordinating
our acting are a necessary prerequisite to all our more planned, reflective,
and effortful activities. I went on to outline their relationally-responsive
nature, and how, although they might seem so orderly that the following of
rules, or the use of methods, was behind them in some way, they gave
rise to a sense of ordered spaces with 'a depth of possibilities' to them.[5]
In other words, as Kjell put it above, while such spaces are amenable to
further ordering by explicit rules or methods, such rules or methods are
only of use for that kind of structuring once one has already arrived at
such a space, an 'it', their initial creation must be achieved by other
means. They are created in the living, responsive meeting of two or
more different forms of life, who cannot avoid responding to each other.
It is in such meetings that we can find the source of human creativity, not
somewhere mysteriously hidden inside the human mind. Voloshinov
(1986) puts it this way: 'The experiential, expressible element and its
outward objectification are created...out of one and the same material.
After all, there is no such thing as experience outside of its embodiment in
signs. Consequently, the very notion of a fundamental, qualitative difference
between the inner and outer element is invalid to begin with. Furthermore,
the location of the organizing and formative center is not within (i.e., not in
the material of inner signs) but outside. It is not experience that organizes
expression, but the other way around – expression organizes experience.
Expression is what first gives experience its form and specificity of
direction' (p. 85). It is in certain of our dialogically structured responsive
expressions that our new ways of going on begin, in those moments when
an event strikes us, when something happens that matters to us (Katz and
Shotter, 1996a; Shotter and Katz, 1996; and Katz and Shotter, 1996b).

Training in Forms of Life – Setting the Scene for our Language-games

At the foundation of our lives together is a community of shared sensibilities and shared reactions, not an identity of ideas, inner pictures, and

---

5 Fock and Hoberg note that 'great complexity has great depth, but not a great surface'
(see p. 125) – again, we may take Kjell's account of the limited help offered by methods in
creating new system architectures, as an example here: it has great depth but little appears
on the surface.

claimed beliefs. It is a community of effortless, responsive expression and understanding that grows from 'seeds' created in shared moments to which all involved spontaneously react in a somewhat similar manner. Thus important in us coming to such a set of shared sensibilities and reactions, and then going on to refine and elaborate them, is something theatrical, a certain staging or dramatisation of our performances seems to be required from time to time. For three things must occur in such moments: new shared reactions must first spontaneously occur; then all must notice the circumstances of their occurrence, i.e., what it is in our surroundings that 'calls out' such reactions from us; and then once we understand the dependence of our reactions on their surroundings, we can begin to arrange for their occurrence under our own control. Crucial in this activity, as Vygotsky (1986) points out, are what we might call our 'directive', 'instructive', and 'organisational' forms of talk in everyday life work. For example, we 'give commands' ('Do this,' 'Don't do that'); we 'point things out' to people ('Look at this!'); 'remind' them ('Think what happened last time'); 'change their perspective' ('Look at it like this'); 'place' or 'give order' to their experience ('You were very cool... you acted like a madman'); 'organise' their behaviour ('First, take a right, then... ask again...'); and so on. We spontaneously respond to all these instructive forms of talk. They 'move' us, in practice, to do something we would not otherwise do: in 'gesturing' or 'pointing' toward something in our circumstances, they cause us to relate ourselves to our circumstances in a different way – as if we are continually being 'educated' into new ways. Indeed, the utterances of others can seem so central to the structuring of our performances, that it is as if a set of rules stated in words underlies what we must learn. Let us repeat here Wittgenstein's (1953) remark quoted above, that 'one forgets that a great deal of stage setting in language is presupposed if the mere act of naming is to make sense' (§257).

If we are to understand how to construct ourselves into communities of shared sensibilities and shared reactions in certain professional spheres, then we need more than a set of verbally stated rules, we need the initial training that makes it possible for us to follow such rules effortlessly. We need an inner 'at homeness' with 'all the circumstances which constitute the scene for our language-game[s]' (§179). We need a scenic-sense of the space of possibilities within which the emergence of such a community can occur.

Above, in the KTH example, I mentioned Dunér's gestures, and in many such practical situations, the use of gestures toward common features, acknowledged as such by all in a shared situation, is commonplace, but nonetheless, of crucial importance. Indeed, we can note here Wittgenstein's (1966) remark, that when we are first being taught the use of certain words, 'one thing that is immensely important in teaching is exaggerated gestures and facial expressions' (p. 2), that emphasise the 'characteristic part [they play in]...a large group of activities...the occasions on which they are said...' (p. 2). It is the gestural function of these instructive forms of talk that is their key feature, that gives them their life: for they 'point beyond' themselves to features in the momentary context of their utterance. It is the way in which we do this, i.e., 'show' our possible connections to our circumstances in their voicing, that makes such talk revealing of our individual 'inner lives'.[6] This is the function of all the extra 'staging', the theatricality, of their expression, in voicing all our words in the same flat tone, we too easily forget that they owe their life to their intertwining with our communally shared embodied responsiveness to our surroundings. As a result, we try to explain their functioning by linking them to mysterious events inside us somewhere: in our 'minds' we say. The theatricality of our expressions prevents us from making that mistake.

I want to mention the structure of the 'dialogue seminars' used 'as a tool of knowledge theory' in the Saab-Combitech case above. They have a certain theatricality about them; they work by dramatising certain events in such a way as to help create a responsively ordered community. Let me turn to the seminars first.

The Dialogue Seminars

They have a shared, three part structure: preparation, the seminar itself, and the writing of minutes. First, we can note that the activity of *preparation* is quite different from that of *planning*. Planning is a matter of deciding on a schematism in terms of which to sequence an already well practiced set of routine activities, and nothing to do with creating a community. Preparation is different. It is to do with orienting ourselves toward attending to appropriate details, sensitising ourselves to be responsive to certain kinds of events, participating in those kinds of events that will bring us into responsive contact with those around us in our community. Whorf (1956) describes the nature of these activities among the native-American Hopi Indians, a community much more directly oriented

---

6 Our 'inner worlds' and 'mental lives' are not, so to speak, geographically within us; they are grammatically *in* the responsive ways in which we live out our lives together. The complex 'shape' of our activities and their relation to their circumstances may give rise to talk of inner mental states, but: 'It is misleading to talk of thinking as "mental activity". We may say that thinking is essentially the activity of operating with signs' (Wittgenstein, 1965, p. 6) – which is an activity out in the world between us. Wittgenstein's stance toward our mental activities here is clearly shared by Vygotsky, Bakhtin, and Voloshinov.

and sensitive to its responsive relations with its surroundings than we westerners. He describes both inner and outer preparing. While outer preparing includes such activities as announcing the event, so that all in the community know of it, and other such activities as ordinary practicing, rehearsing, getting resources and implements ready, introductory formalities, preparing special food, and other such activities as ceremonies and dances, inner preparation is a matter of prayer, meditation, good wishes, good will. But how can prayer and meditation make a real, concrete difference in people's conduct of their lives? While we think in terms of, as Whorf puts it, inner 'mental surrogates', the Hopi think much more in terms of their responsive contacts with their surroundings. Thus in their preparing activities, in prayer and meditation, they mentally rehearse their contacts with, their relations to, the actual, concrete details of their surroundings: 'Though to be most effective should be vivid in consciousness, definite, steady, sustained, charged with felt good intentions. They render the idea in English as "concentrating, holding in your heart, putting your mind on it, earnestly hoping". Thought power is the force behind ceremonies, prayer sticks, ritual smoking, etc. The prayer pipe is regarded as an aid to "concentrating" (so said my informant). Its name na'twanpi, means "instrument of preparing"' (p. 150).

As those in a peace negotiation silently hand the pipe to each other, look into each other's eyes, gesture kindly toward one another, they all respond to each other with trust and care, from which the peace negotiation takes its beginnings. Whorf goes on to comment: 'Against the tendency of social integration is such a small, isolated group, the theory of "preparing" by the power of thought, logically leading to the great power of the combined, intensified, and harmonized thought of the whole community, must help vastly toward the rather remarkable degree of cooperation that, in spite of much private bickering, the Hopi village displays on all important cultural activities' (p. 151). Hopi preparing activities then, are to do with getting ready to be sensitive to crucial details in one's surroundings. The preparing activities devised for the dialogue seminars: the reading and the writing assignments, would seem to be aimed at very similar goals: the reading 'to shape concentration' (see p. 96, and writing as 'a way of associating with one's material, one's thoughts and experiences, and consciously putting them in a particular order' (see p. 99).

The seminar is conducted in two parts: reading one's writing assignment aloud, and collective reflections. The voicing of words is important in two ways: one is that it returns us to the sensuous situation in which we responsively use and understand words, rather than reacting to them representationally; the other is the benefit that 'one "perceives" the reactions of the group' (see p. 99), and what is shared and what is not shared becomes apparent. 'Reading aloud is also a way of focusing, it is collective concentration on something that is shared' (see p. 100).

After the reading, there is collective reflection. This is the moment when 'thoughts are to meet' (see p. 101). It is in these 'meetings', these moments of dialogical contact, as also in the Saab-Combitech Systems case above, when two very different expressions, which point to very different (often seemingly conflicting) features in the topic under discussion, are nonetheless responsively connected to each other, that creative things happen. Indeed, we might call such moments, poetic moments: for, as long as the gap created by the juxtaposition of the two different thoughts is not too great, as with the monocular views from our two eyes, our bodies will responsively create (Gr: poiesis = creation, making) ways to bridge them, to create a view in depth which accommodates both. This is the power of our dialogically structured, living, responsive understandings, they create ordered spaces of possibilities between us prior to the existence of any rules.

The final stage in the dialogue seminars, the writing of minutes, 'fixes' or 'captures' these new developments which otherwise might pass by unnoticed. '[We] see what one had not been aware of at the time,' writes Maria Hammarén (see p. 213). Indeed, the lived experience of the moments when juxtaposed thoughts meet in a dialogue seminar are extremely rich; they have a kind of 'fractal fullness' in that as one looks into their ordering one can see endless further orderings. Written minutes give intelligibility, i.e., an agreed and shared structure to such otherwise 'endlessly full' experiences, thus to set the stage for everyone's next step, but the fact of their 'fullness' or 'depth' should give us pause in the realisation that no written formulation is ever adequate to its capture. To claim to have achieved a 'final codification' of such activities is a great mistake.

Concluding Comments

Rather than socially refined and sensitive ways of acting effortlessly (as in Confucianism), ever since the Greeks, we in the West have valued individual, reflective thought prior to planned and effortful action. We have thus had an obsession with theories and theorising, with the belief that only true theories can give rise to right action. However, in recent times, as Toulmin (1990) points out, 'the problems that have challenged reflective thinkers on a deep philosophical level, with the same urgency that cosmology and cosmopolis had in the 17th century, are matters of practice: including matters of life and death...The "modern" focus on the written, the universal, the general, and the timeless – which monopolized the work of most philosophers after 1630 – is being broadened to include once again the oral, the particular, the local, and the timely' (p. 186). We are now beginning to see the recovery of a Practical Philosophy of practices (which needs a theory-centered philosophy to be interwoven into it).

Philosophy seeks a comprehensive view, a sense of how things hang together as a whole, a view that we can hold in common with others. We now realise that there are two quite distinct ways in which we can approach this task, two quite distinct forms of comprehensive understanding with two quite distinct motives:

- One approach is from the outside as observers of formal patterns. It aims at the form of understanding we seek in our traditional theory centred philosophy, an understanding of a representational-referential kind. It aims at 'fixing' the object of one's understanding within a medium of representation, usually, in written language. The urge to express our knowledge (especially of human affairs) in this way, in terms of hierarchically ordered schemes of logically interlinked propositions, a system, although rhetorically justified by appeals to equality and the disinterested objectivity of science, leads, as both Foucault (1977) and Scott (1998) show, to just those kinds of 'regimes of knowledge' required in administering a State centrally. The synoptic 'view(s)' of the affairs of State such a philosophy provides, are not got by attending to local details, but exist in terms of single, complete and closed orders of connectedness represented in various schematic artefacts in such a control room.

- The other way in which we can arrive at a comprehensive view, a scenic-sense, of the whole responsive order within which we live and share our lives with others, is through participating with them all in creating that order, but participating in it in certain special ways that help us to acquire a reflexive awareness of some aspects at least of its nature. Our explorations here have been aimed at increasing our awareness of our own involvements in creating, elaborating, and refining such an order. The form of understanding to which involvements give rise is that of a relationally-responsive kind. Unlike the view from the centre, it is a kind of understanding democratically distributed throughout the whole order within which it has its being. It is an understanding of a much 'fuller' or 'deeper', i.e., more ordered kind, than that given by a system of propositions imposed upon it, externally.

Until recently, our participation in such communities of shared sensibilities and shared reactions has remained unnoticed in the background of our lives together, and as a consequence, ignored in our theory-centered philosophies. It is only after a group has developed a responsive order within itself that its members can all understand each other's claims to knowledge, expressed in terms of systems of propositional forms, and agree upon how to respond to them, without this kind of relational-responsive understanding of a shared responsive order, formal systems become unintelligible. Indeed, we might even go so far as to say that the systems of propositions we invent to articulate aspects of its orderly nature are, as products, after the fact, and, as forms or shapes, beside the point. They are only of retrospective worth. More than that, insistence on understanding everything from within formal systems works to render both the continuously creative nature of the present moment rationally-invisible to us, and also the value of the first-time, constitutive events that can occur within it. The amazing creativity occurring in front of our eyes every moment is excluded from our discussions by the disciplinary rules we feel we must follow in them, if we are to be properly professional academics.

Thus, rather than celebrating its existence as a real aspect of the circumstances within which we act our acts and live our lives, we misinterpret its meaning. Rather than accepting the real possibility of the emergence into existence, in our dialogically structured activities, of previously inconceivable, new possibilities, we assume that all such newness can only result from the discovery of something in fact already in existence, but radically hidden from us, i.e., hidden in the sense of it only being possible to understand it indirectly, through manipulations suggested to us by the use of theories. The doctrine of radical hiddenness thus works both to licence yet more research disciplined by formal systems, and to depreciate the value of our seemingly undisciplined, unsystematic, ways of being creative between us. Everywhere, we seek to replace our informal ways of making sense with each other, with supposed 'better' more formal ways, thus tending to destroy the very responsive orders sustaining their intelligibility. Yet, strangely, every human group creates such an order amongst its participants spontaneously, effortlessly. Embedded in our ordinary everyday activities, out in the world between us, not hidden behind appearances, are the methods we need. Just as Aristotle extracted the methods of logic from our everyday forms of reasoning, so Wittgenstein (1953), among others, has begun to supply us with the methods we need for arriving at the comprehensive, synoptic sense we require, if we are know our 'way about' better inside the responsive order we all share in our lives together (Shotter, 1996b). As Toulmin (1990) remarks, under the influence of this work: 'The idea that handling problems rationally means making a totally fresh start [was] a mistake all along. All we can be called upon to

do is to take a start from where we are, at the time we are there... There
is no way of cutting ourselves free of our conceptual inheritance; all we
are required to do is to use our experience critically and discriminat-
ingly, refining and improving our inherited ideas, and determining more
exactly the limits of their scope' (p. 179).

References

Bakhtin, M.M. (1981) *The Dialogical Imagination*. Edited by M. Holquist, trans.
by C. Emerson and M. Holquist. Austin, Tx: University of Texas Press.
Bakhtin, M.M. (1984) *Problems of Dostoevsky's Poetics*. Edited and trans. by Caryl
Emerson. Minneapolis: University of Minnesota Press.
Bakhtin, M.M. (1986) *Speech Genres and Other Late Essays*. Trans. by Vern
W. McGee. Austin, Tx: University of Texas Press.
Bakhtin, M.M. (1993) *Toward a Philosophy of the Act*, with translation and notes
by Vadim Lianpov, edited by M. Holquist. Austin, TX: University of Texas
Press.
Foucault, M. (1979) *Discipline and Punish: the Birth of the Prison*. trans. A.M.
Sheridan, Harmondsworth: Penguin Books.
Gendlin, G. (1997) The responsive order: a new empricism. *Man and World*,
30, 383–411.
Gustavsen, B. (1992) *Dialogue and Development: Theory of Communication,
Action Research and the Restructuring of Working Life*. Van Assen, Netherlands:
Gorcum.
Janik A. (1990) Tacit Knowledge, Rule Following and Learning. In eds
B. Göranzon and M. Florin, *Artificial Intelligence, Culture and Language: On
Education and Work*. Springer Verlag, London.
Johannessen, K. S. (1994) Philosophy, art, and intransitive understanding. In
K.S. Johannessen, R. Larsen, and K.O. Amas (eds) *Wittgenstein and Norway*.
Oslo: Solum Forlag.
Katz, A.M. and Shotter, J. (1996a) Hearing the patient's voice: toward a 'social
poetics' in diagnostic interviews. *Social Science and Medicine, 46*, 919–31.
Katz, A.M. (1996b) Resonances from within the practice: social poetics in a
mentorship program. *Concepts and Transformation, 2*, 97–105.
Merleau-Ponty, M. (1968) *The Visible and the Invisible*. Evanston, Il: North-
western University Press.
Rudd, A. (2003) *Expressing the World: Skepticism, Wittgenstein, and Heidegger*.
Chicago and La Salle: Open Court.
Ryle, G. (1949) *The Concept of Mind*. London: Methuen.
Scott, J.C. (1998) *Seeing Like a State: How Certain Schemes to Improve the
Human Condition Have Failed*. New Haven and London.
Shotter, J. (1993a) *Cultural Politics of Everyday Life: Social Constructionism,
Rhetoric, and Knowing of the Third Kind*. Milton Keynes: Open University
Press.
Shotter, J. (1993b) *Conversational Realities: Constructing Life through Language*.
London: Sage.
Shotter, J. (1996a) Living in a Wittgensteinian world: beyond theory to a poetics
of practices. *Journal for the Theory of Social Behavior, 26*, 293–311.

Shotter, J. (1996b) 'Now I can go on': Wittgenstein and our embodied embeddedness in the 'hurly-burly' of life. *Human Studies, 19,* 385–407.

Shotter, J. and Katz, A.M. (1996) Articulating a practice from within the practice itself: establishing formative dialogues by the use of a 'social poetics' *Concepts and Transformations, 2,* 71–95.

Shotter, J. and Gustavsen, B. (1999) *The Role of Dialogue Conferences in the Development of 'Learning Regions': doing 'from within' our lives together what we cannot do apart.* Stockholm: Center for Advanced Studies in Leadership, Stockholm School of Economics.

Toulmin, S. (1992) *Cosmopolis: The Hidden Agenda of Modernity.* Chicago: University of Chicago Press.

Voloshinov, V.N. (1986) *Marxism and the Philosophy of Language.* Trans. by L. Matejka and I.R. Titunik. Cambridge, MA: Harvard University Press, first pub. 1929.

Vygotsky, L.S. (1986) *Thought and Language.* Translation newly revised by Alex Kozulin. Cambridge, MA: MIT Press.

Whorf, B.L. (1956) *Language, Thought and Reality: Selected Writings of Benjamin Lee Whorf. Ed. J.B. Carroll.* Cambridge, Mass.: M.I.T. Press.

Wittgenstein, L. (1953) *Philosophical Investigations.* Oxford: Blackwell.

Wittgenstein, L. (1965) *The Blue and the Brown Books.* New York: Harper Torch Books.

Wittgenstein, L. (1966) *Lectures and Conversations on Aesthetics, Psychology and Religious Belief,* ed. Cyril Barrett. Oxford: Blackwell.

Wittgenstein, L. (1969) *On Certainty.* Oxford: Blackwell.

Wittgenstein, L. (1974) *Philosophical Grammar,* ed. Rush Rhees, trans by A. Kenny. Oxford: Blackwell.

Wittgenstein, L. (1980) *Culture and Value,* introduction by G. Von Wright, and translated by P. Winch. Oxford: Blackwell.

17 Rule Following, Intransitive Understanding and Tacit Knowledge: An Investigation of the Wittgensteinian Concept of Practice as Regards Tacit Knowing

Kjell S. Johannessen

Imagine the following situation. A scientist claims to have made an important discovery in chemistry. In turns out, however, that he is not capable of articulating the exact character of the discovery in a verbally precise manner. Neither is he able to support his knowledge claim by the traditionally accepted methods. If this should ever happen, we could be quite certain that his alleged discovery would not be taken seriously by the scientific community, even if formerly he was a well-renowned researcher. Why is it that we can be so confident about the outcome of this claim to knowledge? In the first place there is the lack of precision in his description of the possible discovery. This creates unclarity about how it relates to the already established knowledge in the field. Does the contended discovery represent a further development of principles and ideas already in use or does it involve some new principle necessitating the rejection of any of the older ones? In the second place there is the lack of empirical support of the traditional and well-known kind.

This is a quite natural way of reasoning. Scientific knowledge certainly should be clearly formulatable in words or symbols and convincingly backed up by empirical evidence. Otherwise there is no legitimate claim to *know* something. When knowledge is thought of in this way, however, we simply take it for granted that if we are justified in maintaining that we know something, the following conditions at least must be fulfilled:

1. Our knowledge must be capable of formulation in some language or other.
2. Our linguistically articulated knowledge must be supported by experience or be proven by formal means.

These, in themselves quite reasonable requirements, were combined with the verification theory of meaning and turned into a dogma by the logical positivists, thus making scientific knowledge the paradigm of knowledge *simpliciter*. The idea of there being different kinds of knowledge, or at least different contexts and thus different constraints on the claims to know something, is by implication characterised as a piece of traditional rubbish of no intellectual value whatsoever. Considered in the light of the customary ways of talking and thinking about knowledge, the logical positivist way of understanding it represents a significant narrowing down of the field in which we can legitimately maintain that we know something. Part of what this fairly narrow conception of knowledge was supposed to accomplish was to provide us with a clear-cut distinction between fact and value. If we possess anything that properly could be termed moral knowledge it consists wholly in the knowing of moral *facts*, whatever that may be. Moral *values* are necessarily beyond the reach of this conception of knowledge, as it is the hallmark of values that they can neither be empirically justified nor formally proved. The same goes for any other kind of value. We cannot be said to *know* aesthetic, religious, legal or any other sort of human values.

Wittgenstein drew the only possible conclusion in the *Tractatus* when he said: 'In the world everything is as it is, and everything happens as it does happen: in it no value exists; and if it did, it would have no value. If there is any value that does have value, it must lie outside the whole sphere of what happens and is the case' (T 6.41). This is a rather dismal picture of the human world. It is, however, what we have to accept if we grant the adequacy of the positivist paradigm.

Its adequacy, though, is what could reasonably be doubted since it makes us face the following dilemma: either we resign ourselves to the mere travesties of moral and aesthetic knowledge that result from conforming to the paradigm and hurry to convince ourselves that the whole European culture has been on the wrong track all along, as it has been perfectly natural to speak about knowledge in these contexts, or else we start wondering about its status.

If we stick to the second alternative, we soon discover that the positivist conception of knowledge is in no sense the proper expression of the one and only genuine insight into the nature of knowledge. This follows from the fact that such an insight can neither be empirically established nor formally proven. On the empirical side it simply flies in the face of the established use of the terms 'know', 'knowing', and 'knowledge'. On the formal side it becomes a matter of how to secure the adequacy and reliability of the chosen axioms. *That* cannot be done by formal means alone. Therefore it is not a matter of insight into, or adequate analysis of, the concept of knowledge at all. It is rather a question of producing a persuasive definition of the terms mentioned for any future use in intellectually responsible contexts. Realising this, it becomes quite in order to try to decide if there is any point in depriving ourselves of the right to talk about knowledge in moral, aesthetic, legal, and religious contexts or whether we are better off by producing a more adequate grasp of the ways we in fact use the terms in question in the different kinds of contexts. Such a reflection might proceed in various ways. I consider it profitable first to produce a reminder of one of the most influential conceptions of knowledge in our culture, and then take a closer look at the premises of the persuasive definition that the positivists put forward, attending especially to the possibility of tacit knowing.

The Aristotelian Analysis of Knowledge

In the ancient tradition we find no objections to talking about knowledge in the most varied fields of experience. Aristotle is an example in this respect. In his analysis of man as a moral being the intellectual virtues play a central role. As is well known, they are threefold, comprising not only *episteme* (scientific knowledge in the strict sense) but also *phronesis* (practical wisdom) and *techne* (craftsmanship).[1] They are all constitutive of man as a moral being. Deprived of any one of them we should not be able to cope with the demands of the moral aspect of human existence. This becomes clear as soon as we realise the very limited scope of what Aristotle called scientific knowledge (*episteme*). This kind of knowledge deals only with strictly necessary conditions. Such conditions are said to be eternal and unalterable. This trait distinguishes *episteme* from *phronesis* and *techne*. For the two latter both deal with changeable conditions. *Techne* however, is the sort of thing that can be thought and can be forgotten. This is not the case with *phronesis*. In a fundamental sense it can neither be learnt nor forgotten, even if it can be improved upon. If one should happen to 'forget' one's practical wisdom, that would mean nothing less

---

1 Aristotle discusses this threefold division in *The Nichomachean Ethics* Book VI.

than ceasing to exist as a moral being, and therefore as a responsible *human* being. A severe fit of madness would probably illustrate what is at stake here. A loss of one's practical wisdom, in Aristotle's sense, would mean loss of contact with the human world, and thus fatally affect the very essence of humanity in man. The nature of practical wisdom is consequently said to consist in *knowing* what is the morally right action in a concrete situation. Such knowledge is an end in itself, in the same way that knowledge about the eternal and unalterable is an end in itself. This does not, however, apply to the possession of *techne*, as it is said to have its goal outside itself. To have *techne* is to be able to make something with a correct understanding of the principle involved. Knowledge of this kind is primarily expressed in the choice of suitable materials and in the handling of them. It is thus basically conceived as various forms of skill. For Aristotle that does not depreciate its character and status as knowledge in any way. One reason for this is that one can have a satisfactory knowledge of the thing which is to be made quite independently of actually making it in any concrete case. This is not so with practical wisdom, since it is displayed in the determination of the morally right action in a concrete situation. Such a determination is always a matter of reflecting upon the interplay between possible norms of action that might apply to the present case and the special features of the particular situation confronting us. Practical wisdom is thus the ability to mediate between general moral principles and the multiplicity of the possible courses of action that uniformity and consistency in the life of action must take into account when facing any particular situation. Moral knowledge embraces, in other words, not only the norm which is right in a given situation, but also how it can best be applied in the concrete case. And this is why Aristotle includes in his conception of this kind of knowledge both a discretional component and a non-eliminative reflection with respect to the special character of the particular situation.

The Method of Language Construction and its Presuppositions

All this complexity in the concept of knowledge is missing in the logical positivists. We should, however, remember that they are by no means alone in maintaining such a conception of knowledge. The view of the logical positivists represents only the end point of a development which began as early as the Renaissance with the new scientific age. Galileo asserted that the book of nature is written in the language of mathematics. And from here it is not a long leap to the dream of the exact language in which all scientific knowledge can be formulated in an unambiguous way. The idea of the universal language, set forth by the logical positivists, is merely the modern version of this old Leibnizian dream. Within this framework knowledge and language are woven together in an indissoluble bond. The requirement that knowledge should have a linguistic articulation becomes an unconditional demand. The possibility of possessing knowledge that cannot be wholly articulated by linguistic means emerges, against such a background, as completely unintelligible.

Nevertheless it is the possibility of just such various kinds of tacit knowing that is presently being explored in certain quarters concerned with the philosophy of science. It has in fact been recognised in various camps that *propositional* knowledge, i.e. knowledge expressible by some kind of linguistic or notational means in a propositional form, is not the only type of knowledge that is scientifically relevant.[2] Some have, therefore, even if somewhat reluctantly, accepted that it might be legitimate to talk about knowledge also in cases where it is not possible to articulate it in full measure by proper linguistic or notational means. In the following I will refer to such cases of knowledge as *tacit* knowledge.

Here it is important to realise that the 'not possible'-clause is a *logical* one. Tacit knowledge is thus knowledge which, for logical reasons, cannot be adequately articulated by linguistic or notational means. The discretionary component in the Aristotelian conception of moral knowledge would be a case in point, as there are no established principles for the *application* of moral principles. This example indicates that there might be something to gain from reflecting rather persistently on the *application* of different sorts of language rules if our aim is to clarify the specified idea of tacit knowledge. By this I do not mean the tacit knowledge of the system of rules that any competent user of a natural language is supposed to have, according to Chomsky and his followers. This kind of tacit knowledge can be completely articulated by a generative theory of the language in question. This is fairly easily achieved because such a theory is restricted to the aspect of sentence-formation. But when it comes to explicating or establishing the conceptual content of a given

---

2 In particular I am here thinking of various philosophers in the hermeneutical tradition widely understood, for instance people like Hubert Dreyfus, Charles Taylor, and Isaiah Berlin. All three of them have worked out alternative conceptions of the nature of knowledge in which there feature elements that are not completely expressible by verbal means alone. Berlin, for instance, points to what he terms 'knowledge of life', a kind of knowledge which is said to consist of 'general laws which cannot possibly all be rendered explicit'. A historian that is short of this kind of knowledge is a poor historian, according to Berlin. See his rightly famous article 'The Concept of Scientific History', reprinted in Berlin, *Concepts and Categories*, Oxford (1980). The quotation is to be found on p. 128.

But I also have in mind people from the Wittgenstein tradition in the philosophy of science, Thomas S. Kuhn, Georg Henrik von Wright, and Allan Janik. In addition there are, of course, Michael Polanyi and his adherents, the man who coined the term 'tacit knowing' in his main epistemological work, *Personal Knowledge*, London and Chicago (1958).

sign in some language the case is different. Here there might be something like tacit knowledge in our sense at work that cannot be completely captured by the so-called semantical rules that are used for this purpose.

The logical positivists, however, saw no problem in formulating a language which could articulate in a completely perspicuous way all the knowledge that a given scientific discipline considered as established. According to Carnap and his adherents this could in fact be done very easily by specifying a language S.[3] In a simplified version such a language consists, in the first place, of a vocabulary which contains both logical constants and empirical variables. In the second place, it consists of a very small number of formation rules or syntactic rules that unambiguously lay down the class of well-formed sentences in S. In the third place, it consists of a very small number of transformation rules which specify in an unambiguous way how to move from one well-formed sentence to another in S. Fourthly, there is a quite small class of rules which connects some of the empirical variables with a fairly clearly circumscribed segment of discernible reality. These rules make up the semantic rules. Carnap termed them correspondence rules since they performed the task of connecting the otherwise completely formal system of signs with slices of empirical reality.

It is this third class of correspondence rules that interest us in this connection. They are usually said to have the following form:

The sign 'T' can be justifiably applied if and only if the observable properties P_1 & P_2 & $P_3 \ldots P_n$ are simultaneously present in the perceived state of affairs.

Disagreement concerning the correct form of the rule is presently of no significance. What matters is the fact that a correspondence rule in effect represents a linguistic articulation of the conceptual content which the sign T has in the language S.

This completes the formal specification of S. But what about the *application* of S? What is presupposed concerning the mastery of language S? It seems that mastering S is, essentially, assumed to consist in two different though interrelated operations: (a) being able to form well-formed sentences in S on a given segment of the empirical reality, and (b) being able to derive one well-formed sentence from another. And if one wonders what is involved in understanding a sentence in S, there is a definite answer to that: understanding a sentence in S means to know what is the case if the sentence expresses a true proposition. We thus realise that S is required to be a consistent extensional language where the (cognitive) meaning of an individual sentence can be specified

---

3 See, for example, Rudolf Carnap, *Introduction to Semantics*, Cambridge, Mass., Chaps. II and III. My presentation here is substantially simplified but I hope correct in essentials.

quite independently of any context of use. The correspondence rules will consequently be the only link between language and reality. These days it is no news for us that the language S is radically incomplete if it is regarded as an analysis of the core of a natural language. But that is not the point in our context. I have sketched this logical-positivist interpretation of the nature of language as a reminder of how central a role the concept of a *rule* has for traditional philosophical analysis of language. It was in fact theories of this nature which constituted the philosophical context of Ludwig Wittgenstein's endeavour in the 1930s to find the way to a more adequate analysis of the factors that are involved when a sentence is used meaningfully on a certain occasion. An especially important fruit of these endeavours was what I would like to call the rediscovery of the kind of intransitive understanding and judgmental power that are necessarily tied to the competent use of language.

I prefer to talk about rediscovery since Aristotle a long time ago had already tracked down something very similar in his analysis of moral knowledge. The intransitive understanding and the judgmental power in question may, as I intend to show, quite legitimately be said to involve certain types of *tacit* knowing. Wittgenstein concentrated his attention on various aspects of the application of natural language in different situations. Reflections on the user's relationship to language and use situations are conspicuous by their absence in the conception of language that the logical positivists stood up for. In their way of thinking the logical form of the language system was the sole feature of language that mattered. This can be seen with reference to the idea of a correspondence rule sketched above. It has the form of a definition. The sign T is the *definiendum* of the definition while the specification of the observable properties represents the defining expression, the *definiens*. The definiens lays down the only legitimate set of necessary and sufficient conditions for the use of the sign T. The occasion on which the definition is to be used, the purpose of the activity in which the definition has a point, etc. are not to be taken into consideration. The definitional strategy pursued makes no reference to any form of context whatsoever. It is merely the equivalence between *definiendum* and *definiens* that in the end is of interest. A definition thus turns out to be a rule of substitution in disguise, a purely formal affair.

Around 1930, Wittgenstein was for a short period attracted to such an idea of the nature of language and how it is connected with reality. He discussed them with great care in his conversations with Waismann and Schlick.[4] Fairly soon, however, he came to realise that this

---

4 See in this connection, Waismann, F. (1979) *Ludwig Wittgenstein and the Vienna Circle*, Oxford: Blackwell.

view represented a blind alley. Too much is left in the dark if one thinks of language along these lines. We might get a glimpse of the surface of the hidden dimension if we reflect a little on the act of formulating a formal language of type S. One of the things we immediately discover is that we have to do with a certain type of human *action*. It is something we do with a particular aim in mind. In this respect the construction of a formal language is no different from all other uses of language, it is developed and applied on certain occasions for certain purposes.

The positivists decided that this was too obvious to be philosophically relevant. But it is extremely important for an adequate understanding of how language and reality is related to realise that language and human action are intimately interwoven, especially if we consider it to be of the greatest importance to understand how it was possible to form, apply, and transmit the conceptual resources contained in S in the first place. Actions involving the use of language have, like all other human actions, both definite aims and various kinds of presuppositions. Sometimes the aims are misconceived and the presuppositions forgotten. That is certainly what did happen in this case. Naturally, it is not in itself a misconception to attempt to improve our understanding of the nature of natural languages. But when this attempt is seen in the light of the character of the approach and its presuppositions, it becomes more than a bit peculiar, as you have to draw on conceptual resources already at hand to construct a language of type S. These resources are what we need to understand better, and they have no obvious similarity to the constructed languages and the way they are made to connect with reality in the form of correspondence rules. To analyse a constructed language with the aim of increasing our understanding of the essence of natural languages is thus the equivalent of studying the cart in the hope of learning something of importance about the horse which pulls it. The method of construction, however, gives the impression of being both scientific and reliable. In addition it has a certain rationale in so far as one wishes to investigate foundational problems in mathematics and their relevance for an axiomatic ordering of the already established scientific knowledge in a given discipline.

This approach thus holds no promise whatsoever when it is a question of understanding the nature of natural languages and how they are related to reality. In this respect it is definitely abortive. Wittgenstein spends quite a lot of time and intellectual energy, as can be seen in the first part of his *Philosophical Investigations*, trying to spell out its misbegotten character. This is not, however, the place to develop his criticism on a larger scale; I have done that elsewhere.[5] For our purposes it is enough to concentrate on the problems connected with the idea of correspondence (semantic) rules and the uncovering of the hidden presuppositions. Especial emphasis will be given to the question of spotting the phenomena of intransitive understanding and the exercise of judgmental power as the expression of tacit knowledge when rule-following behaviour comes up for scrutiny.

To save space and make the presentation more efficient it will be convenient to enumerate what I consider to be the most significant points in his alternative position:

1. To formulate a correspondence rule is to carry out a definitional action which makes use of conceptual resources that have already been developed.
2. If one is to hope to understand the specific character of natural languages, one must investigate the conditions for forming the original conceptual tools to be found in them.
3. This is best done by studying the situations where teaching and explaining of the concepts occur. This is the key to uncovering the basic clues which the competent language-user draws on when employing the acquired concepts.
4. A definition or a semantic rule can be applied in different ways. Even a flawless definition gives no recipe as to how it should be used.
5. We must make a fairly sharp distinction between the definition itself (or the rule understood as a logical form) and the *application* it is possible to make of it.
6. Each and every definition is always applied in a space of presuppositions which are not themselves traceable in the linguistic expression of the definition. This is due to the fact that the very act of applying the definition springs from a much richer source than the understanding of the isolated verbal expression of the particular definition. It is done on the basis of a more or less holistic understanding of language.
7. The totality of these presuppositions cannot itself assume the form of a definition or set of definitions. The vantage-point for carrying out the definitional action would then be eliminated and would in its turn make such actions impossible.
8. In the final instance there cannot be rules that lay down how a semantic rule or a definition should be applied. The application of

---

5 Cf. my study *Wittgensteins senfilosofi. En skisse av noen hovedtrekk* (Wittgenstein's Later Philosophy. A Sketch of Some Main Features), Stencil Series No. 42, Department of Philosophy, University of Bergen, Bergen (1994), Chap. I and II.
  The salient implications of Wittgenstein's pragmatic turn for the philosophy of science are outlined in my book, *Tradisjoner og skoler i moderne vitenskapsfilosofi* (Traditions and Schools in Modern Philosophy of science), Bergen (1985), Chap. IV.

a definition (semantic rule) is and must necessarily be performed without the support of any further rules.

9. The application of semantic rules and definitions is not, however, a completely spontaneous and unfounded reaction. It is not only anchored in drill-like training from childhood on; it is also rooted in the kind of experience resulting from this training: an experience involving, as we shall see, intransitive understanding and judgmental power which in a logical sense cannot be cast in the form of propositional knowledge or articulated as a system of rules.

10. This aspect of our grasp of a natural language is thus said to have a tacit dimension that should not be overlooked when scrutinising Wittgenstein's view of the relationship between language and world. Wittgenstein is in fact using the concept of practice to underline this very element in our linguistic handling of reality.

This summary of some of the main traits of Wittgenstein's views on rule-following as they pertain to the problem of tacit knowing, gives a certain indication as to the direction his later philosophy was taking.

What is most striking in Wittgenstein's later philosophy is perhaps his turning away from dealing with rules and their logical form to investigating what it means to *follow* rules. In this way the application of the rule and the very nature of the situation of the user become the focus of his philosophical interest. This is sometimes called 'the pragmatic turn'. Since one and the same rule can be followed in different ways, the correspondence rules cannot do what was asked of them: constitute the meaning of the empirical concepts and thus mediate between language and reality. What guarantees that a rule is followed in the same way time after time cannot itself be a rule at all. It must in the end depend upon our actions and different kinds of spontaneous reactions giving rise to what Wittgenstein once himself called *intransitive* understanding.[6]

---

6 The expression 'intransitive understanding' is used in *Philosophical Grammar* (PG), p. 79, where Wittgenstein tries to make up his mind about how to characterise the understanding of a picture. He gives us the following options: 'If I say "I understand this picture" the question arises: do I mean "I understand it *like that?*" With the "*like that*" standing for a translation of what I understand into a different expression? Or is it a sort of intransitive understanding?' If the latter is the case, 'then what is understood is as it were autonomous, and the understanding of it is comparable to the understanding of a melody'. He gives us to understand that he goes for the second alternative. Thus we see that understanding a picture or a melody has an intransitive character in the indicated sense. This also applies to the understanding of poetry where we are said to understand 'something that is expressed only by these words in these positions', *Philosophical Investigations* (PI, §531). In this context it is once more a question of having an alternative expression for what is understood or not: 'We speak of understanding a sentence in the sense in which it can be replaced by another which says the same; but also in the sense in which it cannot be replaced by any other. (Any more than one musical theme can be replaced by another.)' *ibid.*

This is the deeper significance of his remark that rule-following is a *practice*.[7]

This concept is one of the key concepts in his later philosophy. We meet here most of the themes that dominated his thinking during this period. It is therefore not unreasonable to consider his later philosophy as a kind of practice philosophy, if by this term we mean a philosophy that operates from the insight that there exists a complicated network of mutually constitutive relations between concept formation, human reactions and activities, and what we call our reality. To learn to master a natural language is, in this perspective, not to learn how to formulate well-formed sentences on the basis of syntactical rules and with the help of language signs, which are tied via correspondence rules (semantic rules) to a certain segment of reality. It is, instead, to learn to master an enormously large repertoire of situations where use of language is included in an exceedingly varied, but non-eliminable way. In other words, it is a matter of mastering human reality in all its complexity. It is a matter of learning to adopt an attitude towards it in established ways, reflecting over it, investigating it, gaining a foothold in it, and becoming familiar with it. This is accomplished mainly because we are born into it, grow up in it, and eventually are trained in the practices of linguistic involvement. This, then, is the background for maintaining that there exists an internal relationship between concept formation, forms of human reactions and activities, and the reality which emerges as *our* reality by virtue of the concepts we have formed on this basis about it.

In the sequel I am going to use the following abbreviations to refer to central writings from Wittgenstein's *Nachlass* that have been edited and published as separate books:

PI = *Philosophical Investigations*, Blackwell, Oxford (1953).
OC = *On Certainty*, Blackwell, Oxford (1969).
PG = *Philosophical Grammar*, Blackwell, Oxford (1974).
RC = *Remarks on Colour*, Blackwell, Oxford (1977).
RFM = *Remarks on the Foundations of Mathematics*, Blackwell, Oxford, 3rd revised edition (1978).
C&V = *Culture and Value*, Blackwell, Oxford (1980).

References to these works will in the following be included in the text.
7 The concept of practice is introduced in the middle of his discussion of rule following in PI, §202, to emphasise its most fundamental aspect. It articulates the observation that there exists a way of understanding a rule that is not an interpretation, an understanding that is expressed in ways of acting. Its character as intransitive understanding is fairly clearly indicated in OC, §139, where Wittgenstein says that 'the practice has to speak for itself'. I return to this question and elaborate upon it below.

Practice as the Expression of Intransitive Understanding and Judgmental Power

If this interpretative sketch is pointing in the right direction, and I am quite convinced it does, it will obviously pay to take a closer look at Wittgenstein's concept of practice and what goes with it. But first we must note that a much wider concept of language is at work here than the one we have met with in the logical positivists. Wittgenstein includes such things as gestures, facial expressions, posture, the atmosphere of the situation, as well as such situationally determined actions as, for example, smiling and nodding to an acquaintance as we are passing, turning one's back on somebody and going off without saying a word, standing on the quay and waving goodbye to friends, sitting in a restaurant and making a discreet sign that the waiter's presence is desired, attending an auction and making an offer with a little hand movement, etc. This extended concept of language is aimed at capturing all the means we make use of in our day-by-day situations to make ourselves understood. In the pragmatic perspective it is quite natural to make such things part of the concept of language, since they are all sense-making means in the situations in which we use or react to a sentence with understanding. If this seems far-fetched you just need to remind yourself of the fact that a sentence does not say, of itself, that it is to be taken as, say, an assertion. Other elements in the situation must be understood in a certain way if this is to be the natural response to it. The very same sentence could in different contexts express quite another thought content. Take for instance the sentence: 'Laurence Olivier was convincing as Hamlet'. It may be used to convey many different types of thought content depending upon the wider context in which it is employed. Let me just indicate a few of them:

1. It could be used to convey a description of his interpretation of the Hamlet role in the contextually implied production.
2. It could be used to give expression to a certain interpretation of his performance in a naturalistic perspective.
3. It could be used to evaluate both his interpretation of the role and his performance of it.

These are logically speaking very different types of thought content that must be kept apart lest confusion should arise. But if we do not know the closer details of the current use-situation, we will not be able to make up our minds about what is actually said. From this it follows that our mastery of a natural language must include a kind of grasp or practical understanding of an enormously large repertoire of situations involving the use of language. One must know what is going on in a concrete case, and that kind of knowledge cannot be had from any sort of linguistic inventory. The adequate use of pieces of language, and the appropriate response to it, requires a situational understanding and a judgmental power that by far transcends what can be derived from the meaning immanent in the sentence alone. This is one of the reasons why Wittgenstein urges us to investigate the use of language. That will lead us to the discovery of the necessary interplay between the sentence form and the character of the situation in which it is applied.

This reminder brings us back to Wittgenstein's conception of practice which incorporates what he considers to be of importance in the analysis of rule-following activities. His conception draws attention precisely to the factors that are constitutive of meaning in situations involving the use of language in a non-eliminable way. One of the more surprising things that surfaces in this perspective is that the very exercise of an activity might be a constitutive part of the formation of concepts. The content of a concept can thus be regarded as a function of the established use of its expression.[8] The exercise of a given practice is consequently to be taken as a necessary element as regards the expression of a concept. To document that one does in fact master a given concept one has to be accepted as a competent performer of the series of established activities or practices which incorporates the concept. The practice can thus be said to represent the *application* of the concept. This yields the following principle of conceptual mastery:

> The grasp a given concept gives us on the relevant aspect of the world is basically and most adequately expressed in the *exercise* of the practices in which it is incorporated.

---

8 There is some need for caution in the way of expressing this point, since the traditional understanding of rules and concepts takes it for granted that the rules or the concepts can be articulated in their entirety. When, in the previous text, I have put rule and formulatable conceptual content more or less on an equal basis, this has been a concession to the tradition in the name of convenience. At this point in my presentation it is therefore incumbent on me to call attention to the fact that for Wittgenstein there is also such a thing as a rule that can only be partially articulated. Accordingly we can talk about rules and thus about rule-following activities also when it is a matter of being incapable of articulating the rule itself completely by verbal means, and not only when it concerns the very performing of the practice in question. Consequently we shall have to distinguish between that type of intransitive understanding which in general is attached to the application of concepts and the one that is a function of the logical character of the rule or concept itself. There exists a kind of family resemblance between these two types of intransitive understanding, but they have different sources and are thus different in kind.

It is thus our application or practice which shows how we understand something. That is what Wittgenstein has in mind when in his lapidary style he maintains that '*practices give words their meaning*' (RC, § 317).

This point gives us an opportunity to make some fairly basic observations. The first concerns the problem of how *the identity of rules* is secured over time. What guarantees that a principle, a law, a norm, a concept, in short everything which Wittgenstein calls a rule, is applied in the same way from one time to another and from one person to another? We have already seen that the rule itself cannot give such a guarantee. According to Wittgenstein it is the exercise of the established set of practices that gives this guarantee. The identity is secured through the application in so far as it has the character of an established practice. And the requisite mastery of the application can only be acquired through a guided exercise of the established set of activities that make up the accepted use of the rule.

The second observation which can be made in connection with Wittgenstein's conception of the established practices as constitutive of meaning has to do with the main theme of this chapter: forms of intransitive understanding and their expression of tacit knowledge in the sense sketched. Against the outlined background it should no longer represent a problem to talk about rules or concepts which can be formulated only incompletely as regards content, at least when it is a question of formulating the content by verbal means. We have just noted that the criterion for their adequate mastery lies primarily in their application. The knowledge which is built into that mastery can consequently be considered to have a partial and non-reducible expression in action. Therefore it is not possible to put into words this aspect of action in which the intellectually explicable part of the concept is necessarily embedded. There is, however, no need to be alarmed by this observation as regards the means for checking that a person does in fact possess an adequate grasp of a given concept. Since it is always possible to instruct and guide the person who tries gropingly to acquire an acceptable mastery of the practices in which the concept in question is embedded, we also have at all times sufficient intellectual control both of the possession and of the conceptual content. It is therefore neither outrageous nor shocking to maintain that concepts, as well as other forms of rules, exist which can only be articulated incompletely by verbal means, but which nevertheless are fully usable tools both in our scientific investigation of reality and in ordinary communication.

Concepts of this kind can be demonstrated in a number of different contexts. They are, however, more easily spotted in some contexts than in others. In particular I have in mind the aesthetic, moral, and legal fields of experience. Here it is easier than elsewhere to come to see how different situational elements turn out to be constitutive of the meaning that we attribute to a certain sentence used on a given occasion. Let us pick aesthetics as a particularly well-suited area for illustrative purposes. It is, for example, not possible to formulate necessary and sufficient conditions for the use of the linguistic expression of a certain concept of artistic style. The term 'mannerism' will do as an example. We can only learn to master this term in an adequate way if we obtain a broad first-hand experience of typical instances of mannerist paintings at the same time as we learn through expert guidance to recognise the visual physiognomy that characterises them. Here, then, we cannot manage without the requisite first-hand experience. Nor can we free ourselves from the proto-typical examples, because they provide us with the paradigmatic physiognomy that constitutes a non-eliminable part of the concept of mannerism. No description can take the place of the first-hand experience of the paradigm cases of the mannerist physiognomy. *Examples* and *first-hand experience* are thus shown to be constitutive elements in the formation of the concept of mannerism.

   To be able to spot a judgmental component we can simply develop this example a bit further. Let us say that you have proved, to the community of art historians, that you have a sufficient grasp of the concept of mannerism, as it is developed on the basis of the chosen paradigmatic paintings, and the accompanying commentaries from the experts, that make you perceive the physiognomy of the paintings in the intended way. And you have got a job in a museum where you have to act in the capacity of an expert on mannerist paintings if required. Then somebody presents you with a totally unknown painting from the period in question (Italian painting between 1520 and 1600) which in some respects seems to you to be quite similar to the physiognomy of the paradigms that make up your first-hand perceptual knowledge of what a mannerist painting is. Some of the less salient features are, on the other hand, not particularly reminiscent of the constitutive paradigmatic examples. Furthermore, it is beyond reasonable doubt that the painting stems from the right period, it has an unquestionable Italian look, but it turns out to be impossible to attribute it to any of the well-known mannerist painters. The task at hand is now to decide whether it can justifiably be called mannerist or not. Whatever decision you make, there will always be a judgmental component at work when applying concepts in this kind of context. The concept in question is inherently dependent on such a component in this sort of application as there does not exist a list of descriptions that is both necessary and sufficient for deciding the matter. A given application is therefore bound to be contestable as W.B. Gallie pointed out a long time ago concerning the concept of art.[9] But that does not depreciate its value as a tool of research

9 Gallie, W.B. 'Art as an Essentially Contested Concept', *The Philosophical Quarterly*, Volume 6, No. 23, April 1956.

in art history. Everything relevant to its application lies open to view. It can be checked at any time by those who have acquired the relevant kind of experience, i.e. the experience you gather by being exposed to the paradigmatic paintings and equipped with the expert commentaries. The decision actually made will, however, substantially affect any future application of the concept. If accepted, it gets the character of a correct judgement and as such it will be incorporated in the research tradition as a possible object of comparison on future occasions of applying the concept of mannerism. In this way the correct judgement has become one of the means by which the art historians steer their course through the ocean of renaissance paintings. It has thus become constitutive of the sense of the concept.

But what about the *activity aspect* that we stressed rather heavily earlier on? That can be seen in such things as correctly identifying the paintings in question, making the right sort of commentary about them, producing enlightening comparisons if asked, etc. This is the kind of activity that necessarily involves application of the acquired concept of mannerism. It has in fact very little to do with forming syntactically well-formed sentences in which the term 'mannerism' occurs in non-eliminable ways. Part of what you learnt when acquiring the concept of mannerism is thus not susceptible to articulation by verbal means. It has to be conveyed by examples and by expert guidance during an extended period of training.

The importance of examples, correct judgements, and first-hand experience whose role can be only partially articulated is, however, not confined to the fields of aesthetics, morals, and jurisprudence. We also find it where the logical positivists felt most at home, that is to say in physics. When Thomas S. Kuhn maintains that a paradigm, in the limited sense of 'exemplary past achievements', can guide research without the existence of formulated theories, general laws or rules of method, it is this very aspect of the possession of a concept that he has in mind.[10] In his own opinion it belongs to 'the most novel and least understood aspect' of his book.[11] And that is no doubt an apt judgement. Let us see if it is possible to substantiate the above account on the basis of what Kuhn has to say on this matter. To accomplish that within a reasonable space I have to presuppose a general knowledge of his position.

Kuhn has taken the application aspect of concepts very seriously, probably inspired by his many, long, and intricate discussions with Stanley Cavell concerning these matters. That resulted in a pragmatic conception of the growth of scientific knowledge that emphasises the

---

10 Kuhn, T.S. (1970) *The Structure of Scientific Revolutions*, revised edition with Postscript, Chicago, 42. My references in the following are to the revised edition.

11 Kuhn, *op. cit.*, 187.

unavoidable presence of a tacit component in our grasp of reality. This comes about in the following way. A model solution to a basic scientific problem represents, according to Kuhn, an application of a scientific theory or law. Independently of this application neither theories nor laws have any concrete meaning. The model problem-solutions, by virtue of being examples of applications of theories and laws, lay down the specific kind of cognitive content that pertain to them alone. Accordingly both theories and laws are primarily understood in terms of their applications and cannot be wholly understood independently of them. This makes the model problem-solutions constitutive of the adequate understanding of scientific theories and laws. They represent in short the use-situations for any kind of universal statement in a given scientific discipline. As such they also give promise that the same kind of procedure can be used to solve pressing problems elsewhere in the same or related fields of research. But in no way does there exist any identity between the original problem-situation, where the model solution is found, and the undetermined area of possible future applications. This relation is more a matter of a kind of homogeneity, which according to Kuhn can best be characterised as a *family resemblance*, a term he borrows from Wittgenstein. Consequently the applied theories and laws cannot be regarded as completely finished scientific products; they must rather be considered as kinds of schemata which are bearers of an indeterminate number of future applications. Kuhn uses here, as an example, Newton's second law, 'f=ma', and shows how it is given different formulations when working with mutually different but nevertheless related problems. We thus realise that, even here, articulation is necessarily a partial matter. It turns out that there is no such thing as a complete formulation of the conditions for the use of scientific theories and laws, not even in relation to a given application of them, since here we shall have to take into account the tacit components embedded in the existing research tradition to which the individual researcher belongs. And that indicates the next step in our investigations. What is involved in the competent exercise of the established research tradition, besides learning by heart a series of formulae and abstract symbolic expressions?

Kuhn's viewpoint gives us the opportunity to scrutinise this question in a more thorough way than we have done so far. The crux of the matter is his explanation of how researchers are enabled to recognise the family resemblance that is said to exist between different problem situations. The answer, he gives us to understand, lies in looking closer at the role the model problem-solutions play in the training of researchers. In passing we may note that this strategy is completely in keeping with Wittgenstein's advice to deal with the situations where the teaching or explaining of concepts takes place. When looking at what is going on here we discover, according to Kuhn, that students acquire the relevant scientific concepts by learning to carry out experiments which either are part of or are decided by the model solutions. This is how they get to know nature's behaviour in the field of research in question. Expert knowledge and linguistic knowledge, are thus necessarily intertwined and emerge as two sides of the same coin in the pragmatic perspective as developed here by Kuhn. And I certainly subscribe to that part of it which concerns the nature and mode of operation of our concepts in scientific contexts. To acquire a concept is to develop a certain grasp of a slice of reality. A gradual and simultaneous acquiring of both aspects takes place. In the course of this learning process the students build up a certain familiarity with the discipline's approaches to problems as they appear in the light of the reigning model for problem-solving in the research field in question. This familiarity is a fruit of experience. It also comprises training in a certain aptitude for seeing the similarities between different kinds of problem-situations, even if on many points they are quite different. Thus likenesses of this sort may be said to have an *analogical* character. The initial problem-solutions which the newcomers to the discipline are exposed to have as their goal, we may say, the building up of the sort of experience and problem familiarity which later make it possible for the ready-trained researcher to function adequately on the research front. But the ability to display reactions which are adequate to the situation and develop an eye for the analogous features in the new problem situation, and this is, of course, my main point here, cannot be put into rules of method or in any other way established or articulated by verbal means. The receptiveness to new applications of the shared paradigm represents a form of competence which is inextricably linked with acquiring the particular discipline's concepts, theories, and laws. This sort of competence cannot be established independently of learning to master them. It is, however, made invisible when one keeps attention focused very one-sidedly on the *de facto* articulated concepts, theories, and laws and forgets to ask what it takes to be a competent user of them. That is why it is important to keep insisting on the need to investigate the application of concepts and theories. It is here that the interesting stuff lies buried.

Further Aspects of the Mastery of Practices and Tacit Knowing

We have now elaborated a little on the question of what role experience plays in connection with the application of concepts in various fields. It has also been shown that there is much more to the competent handling of concepts than is included in the sheer grasping of their intellectual or verbally articulatable content. But the mode of presentation may have given the impression that the previous remarks mainly concern singular concepts considered in isolation from the rest of the language. That is not intended, and what is said in the sequel is partly meant to prove that impression wrong and partly aims at commenting more in detail on that very fertile concept of practice that is gradually coming to the fore in Wittgenstein's latest writings.

We have already more than once hinted at a much wider perspective, for instance in the point-by-point summary of Wittgenstein's criticism of the logical positivist conception of language and meaning (cf. points (6) and (7)). We have also indicated that human reactions, as well as established human activities, are in general to be considered as the context and background for the formation and development of the conceptual resources in natural languages. This is where it may be profitable to start elaborating upon the question of the interrelatedness of practices and what goes with that. A point of departure as good as any is the earlier remark that the offering as well as the application of a definition take place in a space of presuppositions that has a holistic character. Wittgenstein puts this point in a completely general way by saying that '(t)o understand a sentence means to understand a language' (PI, §199). Language is here thought of as a kind of integrated whole in which a particular sentence gets its meaning. Understanding a sentence cannot be any isolated or chance happening. One must have a certain understanding of the language as a whole to be able to grasp the meaning of a particular sentence in a given situation. In fact Wittgenstein himself suggests, even if somewhat hesitantly, that this overarching understanding of language is constitutive of the very meaningfulness of the individual sentence: 'The understanding of language…seems like a background against which a particular sentence acquires meaning' (PG, p. 50). To the conventionally minded this understanding has, however, a most peculiar character. The following comparison is made by Wittgenstein to emphasise its most salient feature: 'The understanding of language… is…of the same kind as the understanding or mastery of a calculus, something like the ability to multiply' (ibid.). To understand a language is thus said to consist in a preparedness to *act* with words in certain ways on particular occasions.

Once more we get an indication that there is a kind of understanding that is an integrated part of being a competent user of language, but which cannot be expressed *by* language. This is what I have chosen to call *intransitive* understanding. It is internally related to this overarching grasp of language that is only adequately expressed in the competent exercise of the manifold of practices that constitute human language.

Only by having a sufficient mastery of this manifold can one be said to understand the particular rules that could be abstracted from the various practices.

From this it follows that a given practice cannot be thought of as an isolated monad, such as Karl Otto Apel and Jürgen Habermas presuppose in their criticism of Wittgenstein.[12] One cannot, after all, decide the identity of a given practice exclusively from the rules that it was possible to formulate on the basis of observing the linguistic habits of people who successfully participate in the established manifold of practices. If we come to a foreign culture and see two persons seated on each side of a quadrangular board which is divided into 64 squares and on the board there are placed pieces resembling chessmen, we cannot for this reason conclude that these people are playing chess. What they are doing could just as well be part of a religious or magical ritual. It is only when we see what happens, let us say, at the outcome of the activity that it is possible to decide with a certain reasonableness that it is a game or not. Practices with the character of games are integrated in the culture in ways quite different from religious and magical practices. By virtue of these contextual relations all practices are shown to be necessarily integrated entities. To establish the identity of a particular practice cannot be done solely, therefore, on the basis of the semantic rules assumed to be immanent in it. Its relations to the surrounding practices have to be included in any reliable procedure for establishing the identity of practices. We thus see that the interrelated manifold of widely different practices makes up one single though variegated whole. Mastery of a particular practice can therefore be regarded as a fragmentary expression of an overarching and comprehensive understanding of reality, which is common to the participants of the language community. And to have a common language is for Wittgenstein to share a form of life, because 'to imagine a language is to imagine a form of life' (PI, §199).

The expression 'form of life' is, as is by now well known, one of the quasi-technical terms in Wittgenstein's later philosophy.[13] But it does not mean anything obscurely deep or hidden. It is just one of many literary means he is using to make us look in a certain direction when reflecting upon the character and function of natural languages. It signifies what

---

12 Cf. Apel, K.-O. (1967) *Analytic Philosophy of Language and the Geisteswissenschaften*, Dordrecht, and Habermas, J. (1967) *Zur Logik der Kulturwissenschaften*, Frankfurt.

13 Even if it has been very much discussed it occurs only five times in PI. In keeping with his philosophical method he does not give it any kind of definition either. Still there seems to be some need for a quasi-technical vocabulary even in his way of doing philosophy. That is most clearly seen in the second part of PI where he starts talking about 'picture-object', 'the dawning of an aspect', 'noticing an aspect', 'organisation', 'internal relation', etc.

he regards as the rock bottom of such reflections, what has to be accepted as the given.[14] It is a matter of making us realise that there is such a thing as a right place for the human language, amidst the human tasks and activities with their accompanying expectations and disappointments.

The idea of there being a right *place* for something he also uses in another connection where he makes the striking aphoristic remark: 'A smiling mouth *smiles* only in a human face' (PI, §583). A smile is a smile only in the context of a human face. In this way he makes the point that hoping is a phenomenon which can only occur in human life. Essentially the same point is made concerning language in general by talking about forms of life. He is just gesturing towards something fundamental in giving sense to linguistic signs. Similar expressions would have done equally well. This is seen from his remark that 'language, I should like to say, relates to a way of living' (RFM, VI, §34). The same basic point is being made. Beyond the totality of established practices there exists no meaningful relationship about which we can have an understanding.

It seems, however, that this is a difficult point to grasp, especially for his philosophical antagonists. It has been taken to imply that language is a kind of cultural prison-house from which it is impossible to escape, in the sense that no contact with different cultural prison-houses can be established, and thus making trans-cultural and historical knowledge unattainable in principle. This is, though, a complete misunderstanding. Certainly, the human form of life as a complex totality of variegated but interrelated practices does develop and change. It is historically situated and in continual movement in the sense that coinage of new concepts unceasingly continues. This means, admittedly, a definite limit to attempts at understanding foreign cultures, but only in the sense that it reminds you that no intellectual endeavour to understand something foreign to our own culture is without its presuppositions.

All this is, however, beside the point Wittgenstein is making. For he is talking about what goes into making sense in general, in any kind of cultural context. That is why he is most anxious to insist that 'language did not emerge from some kind of ratiocination' (OC, §475). It has no rational foundation. It is in fact founded in various forms of human *reactions*, according to Wittgenstein. That becomes clear from his often quoted remark: 'The origin and the primitive form of the language game is a reaction; only from this can more complicated forms develop. Language I want to say is a refinement, "in the beginning was the deed"' (C&V, p. 31).

---

14 At the end of PI Wittgenstein in effect says that '(w)hat has to be accepted, the given, is so one could say – *forms of life*', p. 226. (Original emphasis.)

This remark can be interpreted in very different ways: (a) as a comment on the origin and development of language; and (b) as a logico-grammatical remark concerning the nature of human language. Only the second one is in keeping with Wittgenstein's philosophical method. That is a sufficient reason for preferring it to the first. On the second interpretation this remark is directed to the role reactions play in making various kinds of signs meaningful vehicles of human communication. It is required of us that we not only react unreflectively towards certain features in our surroundings, we also have to react in the *same* way to them. There must be a level in our sense-making activities where our reactions do not spring from any kind of reflection or reasoning. They have to be *immediate* responses to the world surrounding us. And this is another aspect of the phenomenon of intransitive understanding. It is normally expressed in the sureness with which we act in a particular case. Our reactions to human faces, sources of sounds, and the direction of a pointing finger are examples Wittgenstein himself uses in this connection. We have already met with one version of this idea when we investigated the example of forming the concept of mannerism in art history. Here it was said that one could not do without a first-hand exposure to the paintings chosen accompanied by the guiding commentaries from an expert. In the first-hand exposure we were supposed to respond to the physiognomy of the particular mannerist paintings. Without this element of experience the guiding commentaries from the experts make no sense at all. Our reactions become more and more refined as time goes by, but the immediate and unreflective familiarity with the particular physiognomies of the various mannerist paintings can never be dropped. If our memory of them, through some accident or other, should happen to be erased, talk about such paintings will no longer mean anything to us.

This point does not, however, apply only to concepts employed in the aesthetic area. According to Wittgenstein the same holds, *mutatis mutandis*, for the application, i.e. the understanding, of all kinds of empirical concepts. There is an element of immediacy and unreflective familiarity connected with the application of concepts in all the variegated fields of experience. Without this inborn responsiveness to the empirical surroundings we would not be able to develop a stable and consistent system of meaningful signs. There would be nothing to mediate between the abstract and verbally articulatable content of the concept and the particular and concrete case which is a probable candidate for being subsumed under it. Wittgenstein more than once complained about 'the contemptuous attitude towards the particular case' in contemporary philosophy.[15]

---

15 See Wittgenstein, L. (1956) *The Blue and Brown Books*, Oxford: Blackwell, 18.

The point just sketched is one of the things that get overlooked if one assumes this attitude and pays no heed to anything but the rule or the intellectual content of the concept. In a fundamental sense works of art are also particular cases. That is why they are of such unique philosophical interest to him. To reflect upon our responses to works of art makes it possible to point out in a very obvious way what goes on when we confront particulars. This explains his frequent and little-understood comparisons between understanding a sentence and understanding a work of art; a melody, a painting and a poem are the examples he uses. And he gives us to understand that the similarities between these two types of understanding are much more extensive than we are ordinarily inclined to believe.

Furthermore, reflections on the particular case are also internally related to the teaching of concepts since, in the ultimate case, there is nothing else to go by except our own immediate and unreflective responses to the examples given. We have already had occasion to see that examples are indispensable in the *forming* of a concept. Something similar is the case also in *teaching* them. There is an obvious limit to how far it is possible for us to explain the meaning of a word with the help of other words. We come in fact quite quickly to a point where we are forced to explain the word's meaning through examples and training in its use. Here at this rock-bottom level the appropriateness of the examples and the character of our responses are non-eliminable. The interplay between them is providing something that descriptions or rules are incapable of doing. This is why Wittgenstein says that 'not only rules, but also examples are needed for establishing a practice. Our rules leave loop-holes open, and the practice has to speak for itself' (OC, §139). But examples could not accomplish what is here expected of them if there were not a kind of agreement in our reactions to them, as noted earlier. That is an important part of the point he is making when he says that 'there must be agreement not only in definitions but also (queer as this may sound) in judgements' if language is going to be a means of communication (PI, §242). The term 'agreement in judgement' covers a series of different but interrelated cases from instinctive and spontaneous to more refined and developed reactions towards the empirical world, the common element being the fundamental fact that there are no rules or principles to go by when we react.

This point has also been put by Wittgenstein as an argument against the possibility of formulating rules for the application of rules. The idea is simple, but indeed basic. We have already seen that a definition or the expression of a rule cannot itself determine how it is to be applied, as it can be interpreted in various ways. From this it follows that there can be no point in formulating a new rule that lays down how the first is to be applied. For then the same problem will arise once more in connection with the expression of the new rule. It, again, can be taken or understood in various ways. And thus it will go on *ad infinitum* if we try to escape from the tangle by this route. This is, in other words, a dead end.

At one stage there thus have to be cases of rule-application which are not determined by other rules. The application of rules is accordingly in principle rule-less. That is what stops us from 'establishing a practice by rules alone'. The examples are indeed indispensable; and they must function by virtue of themselves, for they must show what the rules cannot state, how they are to be reacted to or handled, i.e. understood as expressed in practice. There is in fact nothing else one can use for help in those basic situations where one learns language, apart from the guidance which is given in connection with the examples. This is the deeper reason for regarding our agreement in reactions as a necessary condition for giving sense to various kinds of signs in human communication.

But this point has also another and for our purposes rather interesting aspect. This concerns the intransitive understanding that is acquired by getting the knack in rule following. For what we know when we know how to apply a given rule can, in its turn, only be conveyed to others by the help of examples and hints about how they should be handled. If a practice is dependent on our reacting adequately to the given examples for it to be established at all, there must be certain forms of reaction which in themselves are not of an intellectual nature, but which are a necessary part of the formation of concepts in all fields of experience. It is thus an essential part of sense-making in general.

But let us now change from examples to ways of understanding, i.e. following rules. Approaching it from this angle it is also possible to locate an element of immediacy and unreflective familiarity. Here the determination of sense will come to the fore and thus document how basic Wittgenstein considers the practice-aspect of rules to be. In the middle of his discussion of rule-following in *Philosophical Investigations* he sketches a tangle that results if one gives in to the temptation to look upon rules as something that in the end determine our ways of acting. Then a particular action must be regarded as an expression of the way in which we in fact interpret the rule in question, and we may truly be said to act according to rules. This yields, however, a conceptual conflict that is described in the following way:

> No course of action could be determined by a rule, because every course of action can be made out to accord with the rule ... If everything can be made out to accord with a rule, it can also be made to conflict with it. And so there would be neither accord nor conflict here (PI, § 201).

This shows the full extent of the predicament we find ourselves in if acting according to rules is thought to involve an understanding of the rules which has the character of interpretation. In a concrete situation the following would be the case: whatever we do is, on one interpretation, in accord with the rule, and on another interpretation it is in conflict with the very same rule. Such an outcome is, of course, intolerable. Wittgenstein's way out of the quandary is to insist that 'there is a way of grasping a rule which is not an interpretation, but which is exhibited in what we call "obeying a rule" and "going against it" in actual cases' (ibid.). Hence we must resist the temptation to think that every kind of action according to rules is a matter of interpretative understanding of the rules, since this creates a logically impossible situation.

Wittgenstein's alternative is a kind of understanding that is expressed in acting in concrete cases. That is why in the following paragraph he concludes that 'hence also "following a rule" is a practice' (PI, §202). This argument is placed at the end of a series of logico-grammatical remarks concerning different aspects of rule-following activities, most of which we have to leave untouched here. Our aim is to see what kind of role the concept of practice is made to play in this context, and how that is related to the question of intransitive understanding. For this purpose it is to the point to note that interpretation and practice are in fact made out by Wittgenstein to be opposites. Interpretation is to him something that involves conscious intellectual activity. To interpret is to form a hypothesis. But such a hypothesis or interpretation can in no way be said to *determine* meaning since qua hypothesis it must be given an explicit verbal form and as such is liable to various interpretations.

At some point, though, it must be possible to indicate what in fact does determine meaning, otherwise we are caught in a circle with no escape, a really vicious one. It is exactly at this point that the concept of practice is called upon to do its job. In one place Wittgenstein remarks, as already noted, that 'practice gives words their meaning' (RC, §317). That is why 'the practice has to speak for itself'. There can be no question of *articulating* that particular aspect of rule-following which simply consists in *performing* the set of activities that make up the established practice. And the acceptable performance is a fruit primarily of the response elicited by the examples used when the concept in question was first acquired and the kind of training that the learner was exposed to. We have, however, noted earlier that acquiring the mastery of a conceptual practice also involves acquiring a certain kind of experience that plays a guiding role in new cases of applying the concept. We are, so to speak, able to perceive that the standard conditions for the use of a given concept are present without being able completely to account for this skill by verbal means only. This is at least part of what

Wittgenstein has in mind when in *On Certainty* he remarks that 'we recognize normal circumstances but cannot precisely describe them' (OC, §27).

In none of these situations, however, is there any need for the presence of an interpretation of the rule to explain why we go on acting or applying the concept in question in the intended way. We both can and do manage quite well without such an interpretation. Still, there is a sort of understanding involved in these cases. We *do* in fact notice that the standard conditions for the application of a given concept are present. We would not have been able to do that if we had not been equipped with the responsiveness to the surroundings that we indeed do possess, and had not had the occasion to profit from the training given.

This intransitive understanding expressed in the proper performance of the established practices of a language-society might thus, not inappropriately, be looked upon as a sort of *tacit* knowing, a way of knowing how to recognise conditions for the use of a concept, how to respond to them, how to develop the use on the basis of them, how to abstain from the application of the concept in certain cases, etc. In many respects this tacit knowledge element, embedded in our conceptual competence, is similar to what Kant pointed out and called a talent. It was why I permitted myself to talk about judgmental power earlier on. But the talk about judgement in the traditional sense is prone to produce mental barriers in people and thus put an end to the discussion before it has come off the ground. It is Wittgenstein's merit to have made us look once more at this most peculiar phenomenon of mastering a human language and what goes with that. In the process we have been able to make one or two discoveries that may improve our understanding of what is involved here, especially as concerns intransitive understanding and tacit knowing.

Part 5

TACIT KNOWLEDGE AND LITERATURE

Henrik Ibsen: Why We Need Him More Than Ever

18

Allan Janik

Although I am by no means an expert on Ibsen, I do consider that we have a lot to learn from him, and I would like to explain why. I do not harbour any illusions that I shall say anything radically new about Ibsen, rather, I hope to provoke *reflection* upon certain aspects of Ibsen's art that I find particularly relevant for a critical understanding of the current state of culture. In insisting that Ibsen challenges us today just as much as he did 100 years ago, I am not claiming that he and he alone does so, but that I find his peculiar way of criticising modernity particularly relevant to understanding what is disturbing in contemporary western society.

Ibsen is one of those artists, like Jacques Offenbach, with whom he shares more than you might think, who has fascinated me personally from my very first encounter with him. That was with *Hedda Gabler*, a play which I still find difficult to overrate. The world of Ibsen's dramas is one which I recognised immediately at my first exposure to them, although not without a certain puzzlement and discomfort, as the world in which I live. Whatever I may have found confusing or disquieting in Ibsen, I recognised the problems that he so grippingly presents as somehow or other *ours*.

My scholarly interest in Ibsen was aroused later in the course of inquiries into the intellectual origins of Ludwig Wittgenstein's concept of philosophy, specifically while investigating Otto Weininger's crucial influence upon Wittgenstein. The need to assess Weininger's enthusiastic essay on *Peer Gynt* involved immersing myself more and more deeply in that play, and in Ibsen generally. The result was an increasing sense of Ibsen's importance, not simply for Wittgenstein, for whom he was important enough (as we shall see), but for coming to grips with one of the *philosophically* most distressing aspects of modern life: our tendency to seek gratification rather than knowledge from the arts.

Be that as it may, as dramaturge at a small theatre in Innsbruck I had the possibility to combine my scholarly interests with my personal ones by organising an adaptation of *Little Eyolf* in 1995. Confronting the difficulties that the characters and plot of this extraordinary play present as a dramaturge for Innsbruck's Kellertheater further deepened my respect for, and fascination with, Ibsen's art, especially his extraordinary dialogue and his much neglected wit.

Increasingly I found myself growing aware of something that I take to be emblematic of nearly everything relating to him, namely, that theatre people as well as Ibsen scholars have to face the difficulty that he is both cleverer than they tend to assume, and concerned with a wider range of intellectual, moral and social problems than they normally are today. In many respects he is a philosopher's playwright, in whose works the great ideas and aspirations of the nineteenth century, liberalism, progress, evolution, faith, the press, etc. are subjected to critical scrutiny. No small part of Ibsen's importance today attaches to the profundity of his analyses of that taboo topic failure, which is, after all, only the reverse side of the coin of aspiration. His explorations of what children expect from their parents are positively extraordinary. Moreover, there is little wonder that Freud would admire his ability to trace the embeddedness of our present problems deep in our personal past. For all these reasons I take it to be a crucial fact about Ibsen that we can only understand the intentions he built into his plays, their structure and substance, with difficulty, and that said difficulty is tied to the necessity to re-examine the presuppositions *we* bring to discussions of his plays. Moreover, precisely that difficulty has a lot to do with making Ibsen so important today: he forces us to reflect upon ourselves. It is, in fact, worth reflecting a bit upon how scholars treat historical personalities generally.

A funny notion of progress has been instilled into us, according to which we assume that, because we live later than the past masters, that we know more than people in the past. That may be true in a sense, but it is deceptively false with respect to the history of ideas. Every high school student of physics knows more about the subject than Aristotle did, but we should not on that account let ourselves be conned into thinking that the high school kids are better physicists than he was. Yet, something like that seems to happen all the time. In her brilliant novel *Possession* Antonia Byatt has penetratingly satirised the fallacies surrounding scholars' arrogance with respect to the figures they study from the cultural past. Byatt portrays a group of literary historians trying condescendingly to reconstruct the intellectual and personal relationships of nineteenth century people, who were in fact infinitely more subtle and sensitive than the people who study them, whose apparent quaintness and familiarity tempts scholars to project a non-existent naïveté upon the subjects of their research. I have encountered this phenomenon continually among people writing about Otto Weininger over the past 30 years. Indeed, until the path-breaking researches of Hannelore Rodlauer, Waltraud Hirsch and Steven Beller in the late 1980s and early 1990s, it was safe to say that the literature on Weininger was getting worse rather than better, so deeply anachronistic are the approaches of scholars to Weininger. The idea that we are smarter, simply because we come later, is a scholarly form of *hubris* and no less self-destructive with respect to our cultural heritage. The dubious assumptions of earlier generations of Ibsen enthusiasts: Shaw, who was by no means silly, comes immediately to mind, have introduced a healthy scepticism about interpreting his texts. In any case, our very familiarity with Ibsen, and he is not alone in this, tempts us to consider that he is easier to understand than is the case. In fact, his art militates against easy understanding, and that is one very important reason why I think he deserves our attention today.

What is it, then, that makes Ibsen so important today? Briefly, his art is the polar opposite of the typical Hollywood film. In the latter everything is laid out in black and white. There are no gray tones. The characters are good or bad, weak or strong, ugly or handsome, sympathetic or repulsive with very little in between. In fact a typical Hollywood film presents a Manichean struggle between the forces of light and those of darkness, in which the latter have the upper hand up to the last three minutes of the film when good violently trounces evil. The aim is to amuse, enchant, thrill, shock, above all, to entertain the viewer. I am informed that some Hollywood script contracts actually specify that there should be an explosion in the film every 10 minutes. Technically the films are perfect, and perfectly suited to seducing and sedating any viewer who happens to start watching. Little wonder that outside the United States from France to India there is a movement among cineastes to liberate themselves from American dominance. However, the very difficulties involved in doing that are perhaps even more telling about the state of culture today than the desire itself. It is only seldom that Hollywood ventures to provoke reflection, challenge accepted views or problematise difficult situations in life as it does in films like *The Ox Bow Incident, Gentleman's Agreement, Twelve Angry Men* or *Philadelphia*, to name but a few random counterexamples which prove that Hollywood does not necessarily have to be stupid. Make no mistake: I have nothing against Hollywood as such, except perhaps disappointment at its superficiality. My disappointment is rooted in the conviction that in our world our self-image and therefore our identity is formed on the basis of narrative models that we find in the media. When these models are superficial and tawdry, how can we expect to be anything but superficial and tawdry ourselves?

Instead Hollywood deals in gross feelings, peddling cheap thrills in our cinemas, and perhaps even more significantly, in our homes on television. More than 40 years ago John Kennedy's media advisor Newton Minnow had already condemned television as a 'wasteland'; clearly, things have not changed in the least. The language of television is the language of the movies. It is the exaggerated rhetoric of melodrama. It is precisely that fact which makes Ibsen, as the subverter of melodrama, its antipode.

In contrast to his two great contemporaries Chekhov and Strindberg, Ibsen is *full* of melodrama as the Norwegian Ibsen scholar and media expert Helge Rønning has pointed out. When I first heard Professor Rønning discuss the theme, I have to admit I was puzzled by that claim. However, upon reflection I began to realise that he had put his finger on something crucial to Ibsen's art, and to his importance today: it was precisely Ibsen's great talent for relativising the exaggerated emotions and actions typical of melodrama as well as its basic sentimentality that makes him especially relevant as the antipode, or better antidote, to Hollywood.

I find this thesis relatively easy to verify. Showing *The Wild Duck* to a group of students in my seminar on theatre as knowledge, with a view to bringing out the contrast between Ibsen's drama and Hollywood, they were not only profoundly moved, but surprised and *intrigued* by the complexity of the characters. You could not pigeonhole them. Those students actually took obvious delight in exploring and debating the moral qualities and motivations of the characters, as well as their own problems involved in evaluating them. At first glance Ibsen's characters seem to fit a familiar sentimental mould, but in fact they do not. The more we discuss them, the more elusive and therefore fascinating they seem to become, as my students discovered.

This is where Ibsen, perhaps better than his contemporaries, speaks to us. He speaks the language of our time in many respects better than his contemporaries, and ours. Analogous to contemporary painters such as James McNeill Whistler and Vilhelm Hammershøi, he discovered the colour gray in his dramas. To pursue the analogy a bit further, he produces the illusion that he paints in the black and white of melodrama, when in fact he paints in subtle shades of gray that confer a provocative opacity upon his characters and ultimately, the notion of tragedy itself. He turns the stereotyped conventions of *la pièce bien faite* with its clearly delineated plot: exposition, crisis, resolution, and equally clearly identifiable characters: heroes and antagonists, against themselves to explore a deeper dimension of human action where suffering takes on a poetic character; in *The Pretenders to the Crown* suffering is, after all, the source of the poet's gift. *John Gabriel Borkmann* is a case in point here. Be that as it may, Ibsen understands that melodrama is part and parcel of modern life and how melodrama can move us without gripping us. His plays exploit that understanding. For that reason mediocre productions hardly rise above melodrama. In contrast to Scribe and Co., his plays, peopled with weak, wavering characters, so difficult for nineteenth century actors to play, always puzzlingly other than they present themselves, offer little by way of resolution to the action. Viewed superficially, it is as if they were badly written on purpose.

Yet, they incorporate a profound understanding of the difference between mere sadness and genuine tragedy, which is foreign to conventional ways of thinking then and now. Ibsen's ability to move from mere sadness, the sense that I am being ill-treated by fate and my fellows, to genuine tragedy, the realisation that my being who I am *necessitates* my sufferings, is the very core of his art. Catharsis, not gratification, is its aim. The very effort of turning the tables on the conventions of nineteenth century theatre, which entails employing melodrama masterfully for non-sentimental goals, often makes it difficult for directors to realise that goal today, when theatre people are more concerned about how to play than *what* to play. If we consider how he manages to educe tragic monumentality from melodrama, we move yet closer to appreciating his special place among the critics of modernity.

Ibsen ruthlessly exploits the potential of ambiguity to deconstruct the clichéd conventions of everyday life. That ambiguity, extending to a lack of resolution in his plays, lends them a positively *uncanny* character that all of the explosions and shocks that Hollywood produces cannot begin to evoke. The depth of Ibsen's confrontation with the 'Lebenslüge' bears directly upon the resulting complexity of his drama. Indeed, we might here compare his greatness to Gigli's singing: Gigli's greatness, we are sometimes told, lies in the fact that, he went up when other tenors went down, similarly, Ibsen got more complex when others got simpler. The complexity in question is almost always a matter of increasing ambiguity. None of this is a secret. All of these themes are stock-in-trade for Ibsen scholars.

Ibsen's metaphors are a case in point. In his seminal study of *Peer Gynt*, Asbørn Aarseth, for example, has given us a rich description of the way that Peer's character is revealed in terms of the animal metaphors he uses to describe himself: the reindeer buck, the horse, the tomcat, the falcon, the cock, the bear, the donkey, and the mouse and those that the people around him employ to describe him, swine, donkey, beast, mad dog. Ibsen's metaphors introduce colour and variety into his plays but they do more than that. In a sense they function like leitmotifs, directing our attention and accentuating the mood of the action. No one who has ever experienced *Brand* can forget the power that the phrase 'the ice church' conveys. In his later plays, Ibsen's metaphors increasingly have an uncanny way of turning into mysterious symbols that are emblematic of a character's destiny. The eyes and the water as they function in *Eyolf* or *The Lady from the Sea*, for example, not to mention the 'white horses' of *Rosmersholm*, are images that immediately come to mind. Ibsen uses them to strike our fancy, to intrigue us and to puzzle and distress us. The use of such images is a prime reason for considering Ibsen a symbolist. Their foreboding way of evoking the supernatural without ever mentioning it can hardly be described as anything but uncanny. Briefly, Ibsen's metaphors are a source of creative ambiguity in his drama.

The role of ambiguity in Ibsen's concept of character is antithetical to our conventional understanding of personality, and especially important for understanding his significance for our culture. Ironically, it is his antagonist, at once mentor and disciple, August Strindberg, who offers us the most succinct account of Ibsen's creative exploitation of ambiguity in the preface to *Miss Julie*:

> What will offend simple minds is that my plot is not simple, nor is its point of view single. In real life an action...is generally caused by a whole series of motives, more or less fundamental, but as a rule the spectator chooses just one of them – the one which his mind can most easily grasp or that does most credit to his intelligence.

The point is that Ibsen's drama (and Strindberg's) incorporates a crucial insight into what is perhaps the most vexing problem in our world, that of human identity, namely, the insight that it can only be captured in a dramatic situation because it has to be seen simultaneously from several perspectives. Thus Brand is at once the complete Christian and the total anti-Christian, an idealist and a prig. Stockmann is simultaneously a paragon of civil courage and a kind of madman, and Hedda Gabler is at once a decadent aristocrat unable to reconcile herself with a boring middle class marriage, and a profoundly neurotic woman torn between sexual desire and frigidity. The examples could easily be multiplied. The point is that it is central to Ibsen's art that both of these interpretations and others as well be simultaneously present in the character. The more we reflect upon what we have experienced in following the action of the play, the more we are *puzzled*, not merely confused, but provocatively vexed and amazed by the characters, as my students discovered. Ibsen stimulates wonder in us and wonder is, after all, the great stimulus to philosophy, as thinkers as different as Aristotle and Wittgenstein maintain.

Nobody has grasped the centrality of wonder in Ibsen better than the 18 year old James Joyce (!) in his essay 'Ibsen's New Drama' in 1900:

> Ibsen's plays do not depend for their interest on the action, or the incidents. Even the characters, faultlessly drawn though they be, are not the first thing in his plays. But the naked drama – either the perception of a great truth, or the opening up of a great question, or a great conflict which is almost independent of the conflicting actors, and has been and is of far-reaching importance – this is what primarily rivets our attention.

Thus Joyce considers Ibsen's dramas to be monumental but he hastily adds this monumentality emerges from the lives of ordinary people. The source of our wonderment is how he raises their experiment to the sort of *Ereignis* (happening) that Nietzsche considered to be the very essence of Greek tragedy.

It seems that Ibsen and Strindberg were playing analogous roles to Cézanne and Picasso in the invention of cubism. Like Cézanne, Ibsen was presenting seemingly innocuous melodramatic moments from life, but simultaneously making us look at his characters from a plurality of angles; whereas Strindberg, like Picasso, was separating the depiction of solid forms from familiar linear perspectives, and thus driving a wedge between the dramatic character and the kinds of dramatic narratives in which actions are conventionally situated. Although, Ibsen, like Cézanne, could introduce a multiplicity of perspectives into a single picture, it was left to Strindberg to make the full break with tradition in his expressionist works.

Be that as it may, the melodramatic situations that the characters find themselves enmeshed in induce us to identify with them and thus to enter upon the road to catharsis. However, the more we follow up that process of identification through comparison between ourselves and the figures in an Ibsen play, the more the ambiguities in the character force us to a radical reconsideration of what is transpiring before us. The identity of the characters, as well as our own, is continually being called into question. Thus the reflection that catharsis demands with its moments of identification and comparison has a way of jolting us out of the comfortable certainties of the everyday and leading us to a new critical perspective where we come to realise how difficult solutions to real problems are to obtain.

Moreover, what is true of character is equally true of plot. It is not for nothing that the conclusions to Ibsen's last dramas, think of *The Lady from the Sea, Eyolf, Rosmersholm* or *When We Dead Awaken*, leave us with a highly disquieting sense of unreality and frustration. What transpires does not really amount to a resolution of the conflicts that we have experienced. By the way, Ibsen's curious sense of an ending is something that he shares with Jacques Offenbach. His *Le Périchole* and *Bluebeard* are two cases in point. It is as if Ibsen was parodying the happy ending in *The Lady from the Sea*, inverting it in *Rosmersholm* and *When We Dead Awaken* and affirming it as anguishing implausibility in *Eyolf*. In no case does Ibsen make it easy for us to follow him, for the play does not end when the curtain goes down. His endings too are uncanny and this too is a source of wonder.

Indeed, his very relation to the classical conception of tragedy is itself uncanny. The question of that nature of tragedy in Ibsen is a perplexing one, whose very problematic character tells us a lot about him. In terming *Ghosts*, a 'family drama' he clearly associates himself with bourgeois melodrama: family secrets, parenthood, love/hate for children/spouses are all over the place in Ibsen, but at the same time this is grafted on to classical tragedy. Ibsen, as we have seen, well understood the structure of the *pièce bien faite*: a hero or heroine with something to achieve, or hide, protagonist and antagonist move systematically to foil one another, an unanticipated change in the action just past the play's midpoint, leading to a resolution at the finale. All of these features are presupposed by Ibsen. However, he superimposes the structures of classical tragedy's ironic reversal of (family) relationships and recognition scenes upon bourgeois melodrama to transform its tragic potential. He seems to move in a theatrical space between the two.

Just as Ibsen sought to incorporate the archaic 'Viking' values into his modern characters, he sought to incorporate Greek tragedy into his plays, which might be seen as having a number of 'layers' of significance. In any case, his characters certainly suffer simply by being who they are. As a man of his age Ibsen asks the question whether it is heredity or environment, inherited weakness or faulty upbringing, nature or the human will that necessitates their actions. Ambiguity enters into the picture once more because, while it is clear in every case that all of these factors are at work, it is never clear which is decisive. Just as much as Sophocles, Ibsen is convinced that character is fate. However, Ibsen seems to flaunt simple explanations of how human identity is formed suggesting different possibilities without affirming any one of them absolutely. Thus there is tragedy within the great sadness that Ibsen's protagonists experience but it lurks elusively beneath the surface, again, in an uncanny way. The parallels with *Antigone* and *Lear* are clearly suggested, but they are anything but direct or univocal. Brand and Borkman strive after monumentality but they never achieve it. Ibsen seems to be posing the question, is *anybody* in *our* world really *majestic* enough to bear tragic suffering and guilt? The plays are highly suggestive but silent. Their silence suggests that Ibsen's answer is 'no'. However, the fact is that he remains silent.

Let me conclude with some reflections upon Ibsen's metaphor, according to which we are 'dead' in our everydayness, to speak with Heidegger. This metaphor is one we find throughout Ibsen's oeuvre from *Peer Gynt* to the title of the 'epilogue' to his last cycle of plays *When We Dead Awaken*. Under the rubric of being dead he thinks of nothing less than failing to live an examined life. Peer strives his whole life for an identity, as Hollywood understands the notion, but, in the end, has none. His story could be the prelude to C.G. Jung's *Modern Man in Search of a Soul*. It is certainly absolutely central to the human drama in our society especially since World War I when the comfortable certainties of the nineteenth century were swept away once and for all. The resultant *anomie*, that social disequilibrium in which our hierarchy of values disintegrates, is what we have had to live with since then. Our confused search for a soul is a response. Hollywood's contribution to that search is a model at best hysterical, at worst cynical, of what it is to be human. Ibsen's depiction of what happens when our conventional images of each other, and ourselves, are effaced pre-empts this theme and has only become more important since his death; for we are still living with that heritage, whatever we might think subjectively. In fact our self images are shallow and labile but profoundly intertwined with one another in their superficiality. Everywhere in Ibsen the fragility of identity is exposed. Ibsen, contrary to Hollywood, steadfastly refuses to give us a simple account of identity. Heredity, social circumstances, intrigue, weakness, arrogance are all determining factors in his dramas but there is no resolution concerning which is the crucial determinant. Instead we have to reflect on the matter. We have to take a hard look at ourselves. In order to do that, we need a mirror. Hollywood's simple and straight-forward image of what we are is, in fact, a distorting mirror; whereas, paradoxically, Ibsen's tragedies, for all their ambiguities and uncanniness, presented us with a straight-forward view of ourselves. Remember that *theoria* in Greek originally meant to take a look for yourself, as opposed to accepting things on the basis of hearsay. Moreover, the *theatron*, the theatre, was the place where we could take that hard look. Ibsen's renewal of the theatre has everything to do with that understanding. He refuses to allow us cheap answers. He does not tell us how to find a soul but shows why it is so difficult to do so. His challenge is that of Socrates, who insisted that the unexamined life is not worth living. It has never been more relevant than in the age of the media.

19 Theatre and Workplace Actors

Richard Ennals

Introduction

While working with Bo Göranzon and Maria Hammarén since 1987, I have also been involved with collaborations, on research and practical cases, with other partners around Europe, within and across a number of disciplines. In this chapter I hope to suggest how apparently different lines of research and practice can converge, share insights, and give rise to new 'hybrids'. In particular, I hope to provide a broader context for the final chapter by Bo Göranzon, Maria Hammarén and Adrian Ratkic, 'The Dialogue Seminar Method: Training in Analogical Thinking' (this volume). Their work reflects the emergence of a radical new sustainable practice.

Bridging Gaps

The Dialogue Seminar, hosted by the Royal Dramatic Theatre since 1987, has bridged gaps between arts and sciences, and echoed pioneering ventures by Richard Demarco at the Edinburgh Festival Fringe, linking Arts and Sciences, East and West. Richard Demarco celebrates connections, and 'boldly goes where none have gone before', for example inviting the first Head of Government of newly independent Lithuania to give a piano recital in Dundee, Scotland.

The Edinburgh Festival is annual, brief but frenetic, and the connections are typically transient, based on performance. We may see the Festival, with the Fringe, as an extension of the Scottish Enlightenment, and with ambitions to have a sustained impact on cultural and working life. This ambition is reflected in the sixth volume of the 'Skill and Technology' series edited by Bo Göranzon. *Skill, Technology and Enlightenment: On Practical Philosophy*, was published in 1995, and included philosophical dialogues as well as more conventional accounts. 'Beyond all Certainty', by Bo Göranzon and Anders Karlqvist, (Göranzon and Karlqvist, 1995) was performed at the Edinburgh Festival, as well as at numerous other venues around Europe, including the annual conference of the Swedish Association of Graduate Engineers. The experience stimulated an international competition for philosophical dialogues, which attracted numerous entries. My own entry (Ennals, 1997) was a dialogue, on 'Art and Wealth', between Adam Smith, Joseph Beuys and Paul Fentener van Vlissingen. It was set in the Edinburgh Poorhouse, familiar to Adam Smith, which later became an Edinburgh Festival Fringe Venue, where Beuys and van Vlissingen presented their work. The setting and words are authentic, but the synthesised dialogue provides a summary of the industrial period, introducing the concept of social sculpture.

Dialogue and Work Organisation

Similar generalisations could be made about a series of Dialogue Workshops, in the apparently different field of work organisation. I have worked with Björn Gustavsen since 1988, in both Sweden and Norway. We have been identifying coalitions of researchers and practitioners, often supported by social partners, engaged in practical development work in regions around Europe. On a number of occasions we have brought together groups from several countries (Sweden, Italy, Germany, UK, Norway, Belarus, France) and explored the kind of connections and communication which are possible (Ennals and Gustavsen, 1999; Fricke and Totterdill, 2004; Gustavsen and Ennals, 2006). Despite the lack of a common language, we find practical points of contact, and shared experience of practice. New business opportunities, and new ways of working, have resulted.

The award-winning Dialogue Seminar has continued since 1987, weaving an intellectual tapestry which has enriched the culture of Stockholm, and has permeated through to the wider world through issues of 'Dialoger'. Similarly, seminars, journals, and books describing national programmes of enterprise development, have flowed from the tradition of research on work organisation. In both traditions there had been a concern to develop ongoing live cases, demonstrating the approaches which are being developed, and contributing to the enrichment of organisational cultures. This has also led to the enhancement of innovative activities.

In this book we have illustrated a series of practical cases, with particular emphasis on the organisational culture change at Combitech

Systems, through the introduction of the Dialogue Seminar Method. The cases have been presented against the philosophical background of practical philosophy, with frequent reference to the work of Wittgenstein. One criticism could be that considerable effort was involved in developing relatively few cases; however, that laid the foundations for the new broad-based practice taken forward by the early pioneers. Another is that the Method depends very much on the expertise, experience and presence of the originators, Bo Göranzon and Maria Hammarén. This dependency has been reduced as the flow of completed doctorates and documented cases enables the work to be accessible to a wider audience, such as the readers of this book.

Programmes

I want to suggest further possible suitable practical cases for treatment, which have arisen from the tradition of work organisation, taken forward in the Norwegian national enterprise development programmes 'Enterprise Development 2000' and 'Value Creation 2010' (Gustavsen et al., 2001; Levin, 2002). The associated doctoral programme, 'Enterprise Development and Working Life' (EDWOR), is unique in being based on the methodology of action research (Greenwood and Levin, 1998) and organisational renewal. Research is no longer separate from practice, but involves reflecting on practice, writing from within the form of life under study.

There was an intermediate link. From 1997 to 2001 the Swedish National Institute for Working Life (where Bo Göranzon and Björn Gustavsen formerly worked) organised a series of 64 international workshops, with the theme 'Work Life 2000: Quality in Work', culminating in a conference as part of the Swedish Presidency of the European Union (Wennberg, 2000; Skiöld, 2000). I was rapporteur, working with a total cast of 1,000 workplace research actors. In each workshop the cast contributed to dialogue, drawing on their own expertise and experience, and I provided the script from a simultaneous transcript of the discourse (Ennals, 1999, 2000, 2001). The work was taken forward in a new programme with the applicant countries to the European Union 'Work Life and EU Enlargement', and in summaries of research reports produced by the Swedish-led SALTSA programme of international research into changes in working life.

Since 2003, the EDWOR doctoral programme has been meeting for four intensive teaching weeks per year, in different locations. It is run as a 'travelling circus', taking full advantage of mobile and wireless technologies. Ten international faculty work with 20 doctoral students, all practitioners in enterprise development and regional development. They come together on a regular basis to make direct contact, and to learn from encounters in what Gustavsen has termed a 'development organisation' (Gustavsen, 1992; Ennals and Gustavsen, 1999). They then return to their 'production organisations', their usual projects, as part of regional development programmes based on action research, hoping to apply what they have learned.

Learning from Cases

How do we learn? I was asked by Bo Göranzon to speak about practical problems of the transfer of skills, at a Swedish seminar in London in 1987. I chose to cite the work of Wittgenstein, which I had studied as a philosophy student at King's College Cambridge. I talked about following rules, the culture of work, and tacit knowledge. This talk became a chapter (Ennals, 1988) in *Knowledge, Skill and Artificial Intelligence* (Göranzon and Josefson, 1988), the first of the six volume 'Skill and Technology' series, published for the Stockholm conference on 'Culture, Language and Artificial Intelligence' in 1988.

Many research and development projects have produced sets of good practice case studies, as if these provided, in themselves, the basis for diffusion, innovation and change. Björn Gustavsen, speaking at the Stockholm conference in 1988 (Gustavsen, 1988), was critical of reliance on 'star cases'. Despite the assembly of numerous collections, he argued that there is little evidence that such cases in themselves lead to learning. The focus needs to be on process, not products. From experience of one case, one can begin to describe it against the background of others, and learn from differences. He has continued to develop the argument (Gustavsen, 1992, 1997; Ennals and Gustavsen, 1999; Gustavsen et al., 2001; Gustaven and Ennals, 2006).

The present book provides a manual for the Dialogue Seminar Method. It is intended for immediate use in support of a doctoral programme at the Swedish Royal Institute of Technology. It should also contribute to other doctoral programmes, such as at the Norwegian University of Science and Technology and Kingston Business School. In each case, the focus of attention is on practice, and the book is intended to be read and used by reflective practitioners.

Doctoral students on the Norwegian EDWOR programme receive two years of taught courses from the international faculty, and then focus on their own individual doctoral projects. Having encountered the intellectual underpinnings of action research, and located their own projects in the context of Nordic and Norwegian working life research, they face what is essentially the same question. Given that they have seen star cases, and have become familiar with the work of the leading authorities in their field, how can they move on to apply what they have learned in their own practice?

The students have been encouraged to be critical, and have developed their writing skills, already achieving international publication. They can describe their chosen cases, and they are familiar with the classic methods of bringing participants together. As their taught courses end, they seek to gain experience of Dialogue Conferences, and other tools such as Search Conferences. Each method has become associated with particular proponents. In each case, the tacit knowledge of the proponent can be neglected: it could not achieve full documentation in a practitioner manual.

Suitable Cases for Treatment

There are new cases where the Dialogue Seminar Method may have a key role to play. However, successful use of the method will depend on understanding the cultural context, and particular knowledge issues.

In Eastern Norway, the town of Raufoss has been successful in converting from reliance on defence industries, to a new engagement in civil production. The former one-company town was transformed into a host of a constellation of Small and Medium-Sized Enterprises. They are now coming together in networks and coalitions, with action research interventions seeking to build awareness of shared traditions of skill, and potential joint future agendas. The research tools in regular use include Dialogue Conferences (Leirvik, 2005), and there has been work on writing a shared history, reconstructing a tradition of skilled artisanship, which preceded the dominance of defence industrial work. This is reminiscent of Bo Göranzon's work on Diderot and the Enlightenment (Göranzon, 1995).

In Northern Norway, business parks in the Tromso region are seen as a way of developing employment opportunities, adding to a local economy that has been dependent on fisheries. Small companies, sharing common premises, need to develop a common identity in a business park, if the parks are to become a viable new form of work organisation (Holen, 2005). The business parks operate as networks, rather than with hierarchical management. New ways of thinking, and new working relationships, are needed.

A Choice of Methods

What does the Dialogue Seminar Method offer in such cases? It has become commonplace to argue that people need to be brought together, to engage in dialogue. Perceptive doctoral students raise difficult issues of power, participation, legitimacy and democracy (Normann, 2005; Fosse, 2005), which may have become accepted by the previous generation of action researchers. It is easy to see why they are concerned. There can be no one simple formulaic approach: one size does not fit all. What is more, as action researchers, committed to interventions, they are aware of the importance of their own engagement.

At this point, some students, and their academic advisors, are tempted to revert to traditional solutions from applied social science. They may feel reassured by quantification, by the feeling of objective detachment, and by the prospect of publication in respected journals. By comparison, action research methods can seem uncertain and unfamiliar.

Theatre and Catharsis

Each EDWOR teaching week, for this writer, has taken the form of a five act play in the tradition of Henrik Ibsen, spread over five days. Participants arrive full of idealism, and with particular intended tasks in mind, typically related to their individual cases and dissertations. They join a structured learning community, with a negotiated programme. Typically, in each week some form of intellectual crisis has erupted late in the third act, on Wednesday. This has to be confronted on the Thursday, before the protagonists depart on the Friday. The pattern has become almost routine, and the power of catharsis is understood.

Students do not willingly return to their action research projects determined to provoke crises and experience catharsis. However, they recognise the need for common experiences, from which learning can be derived. At the first teaching week I introduced exercises from the UNESCO 'Experience Centred Curriculum' (Wolsk, 1975). These were initially used as ice-breaking exercises, and did not depend on deep insights into shared experience with the group: however, they have provided a valuable reference point over the subsequent two years.

There are ways of linking the work on dialogue by Göranzon with that of Gustavsen and Levin. This is not done by proclamation or assertion, within what is already a crowded and contested field (Reason and Bradbury, 2001), but by moving sideways and making connections, using the grammar and vocabulary of the local language game. Theatre provides a vital link. The doctoral students are now facing the question of what to do when they have brought the workplace actors together. The answer now seems obvious: set the scene, and then 'rehearse'. This constitutes a paradigm shift, involving a new set of metaphors.

Motivation for the Dialogue Seminar Method

Before we re-introduce the Dialogue Seminar Method, we must re-establish the motivation. There are limits to the extent to which conventional social scientific analysis, drilling down through data, can deliver. Once we recognise that only a minority of overall knowledge is explicit, that a further fraction is implicit, but that the bulk is tacit, then we have a problem. Drilling down will not give us reliable access to tacit knowledge.

We need to step sideways, to engage in analogical thinking. That is, of course, the skill of the stand up comedian, who makes us think by making us laugh. In order to take this sideways step, we need confidence and competence, including in the art and practice of communication in the form of life of the local culture.

Once we enter the realms of humour as analogical reasoning, there is a great deal to enjoy, including the range of world literature and live performance. Humour is a way of overcoming conceptual hurdles, moving sideways. One can defy Piagetian analysis with the right joke. Humour cannot be automated. It depends on deploying insights into two rationalities at once. Think of the process of osmosis, through semi-permeable membranes, then try to do it with words. Perhaps Wittgenstein, Austin and Searle should have said more about humour when developing their accounts of speech acts. I tried to make this point in my chapter in 1988 (Ennals, 1988a), and was of course required by the publishers to provide references for my jokes.

The playwright Tom Stoppard, born in the Czech Republic, has been a pioneer of humour and analogical reasoning. See his version of the origins of language use in *Dogg's Hamlet* and his exploration of ambiguity in *Rosencrantz and Guildenstern are Dead* and *Jumpers.* 'Dogg's Hamlet', as the Preface explains, is derived from a section of Wittgenstein's *Philosophical Investigations.* Stoppard said 'The appeal to me consisted in the possibility of writing a play which had to teach the audience the language the play is written in' (Stoppard, 1980). That is, in essence, what we are also trying to do, in practical philosophy.

I trace Stoppard's style of thinking, in terms of intellectual gymnastics, back to John Donne, and then of course to Shakespeare. The remarkable feature of Shakespeare is that each generation finds new analogies, and the text provides a reference point. At the 1988 Stockholm conference 'Culture, Language and Artificial Intelligence', I was asked to consider 'The Tempest' in the context of 'Star Wars' (Ennals, 1988b).

As someone who writes for therapy, I find that analogical reasoning has a particular function. Once I have captured the essence of a problem in writing, in a metaphorical style to which others can relate, I am free to move on. Ideally, as a teacher, I can enable my students to move on. I relate this to Wittgenstein's account of explanation as the process which precedes the ability to move on. Let me take one example, from Tam Dalyell MP's cover comments on my book 'Star Wars: A Question of Initiative' (Ennals, 1986): 'Star Wars is, as Richard Ennals has put it, a game of celestial snooker, a load of balls intended to fill American pockets. In the absence of a spare planet, there is no way of testing the system'. I had found a way of making peace campaigners laugh. It would have been more impressive, of course, to have found a way of enabling their campaign to succeed.

Healthy Working Centres: Dealing with Disaster

When projects encounter problems, the capacity to reflect and think analogically can be crucial. Disasters cannot necessarily be prevented, but they can be turned into learning opportunities. Bo Göranzon, who was researching leadership issues (Göranzon, 1997) asked me to explore this theme in the opening lecture for the Centre for Advanced Studies on Leadership (Ennals, 1996).

In South East England, congested roads and public transport have led the regional development agency SEEDA to explore the feasibility of a new form of work organisation. In the Healthy Working Centre, employees of two or more organisations would share a workplace close to home (McEwan and Ennals, 2005). Apart from challenging conventional approaches to employment and management, and raising questions about autonomous working and trust, Healthy Working Centres, like the Norwegian Business Park, face the challenge of developing new social capital. The research team at the Centre for Working Life Research submitted an ambitious tender bid, but found their aspirations converted into binding performance targets, with stringent financial penalties for any shortfalls, despite the fact that the specified objectives had been achieved.

It became essential to stand back, and find new metaphors with which to make sense of the demanding situation which the team faced, struggling for survival despite the acknowledged success of their work.

For the first impulse text, the inspiration came from Lewis Carroll:

DODO are a young regional development agency, who are still trying to learn to fly. Using money from Europe, they have been commissioning research projects, and gaining experience in contracting and monitoring. They have explained to their inexperienced contract executives that advanced literacy skills are not required, as they will not be expected to read any of the reports which are produced as a result of the projects. The crucial skill involves the use of a pencil to tick boxes which are shown on the official spreadsheet. Virtual reality monitoring is, after all, the most reliable approach, as it is not open to annoying distractions from the outside world.

DODO have an exciting vision of the future. They know that the way forward is through Business Links, and that their proposed new forms of work organisation are sure to succeed as long as the message is delivered to employers. When they commission a feasibility study on the subject, the question is therefore not whether to jump, but how high. It is entirely reasonable therefore to remunerate the researchers on the basis of the number of employers who jump. That principle is enshrined in the contract, and is not open to negotiation.

Suggestions that there could be other futures than are captured on the DODO spreadsheet are of course preposterous. The best response is to disregard such views, treating them with the contempt that they deserve. This approach is adopted by other creatures in the region who wish to benefit from DODO in the future. It would not be diplomatically prudent to express doubts regarding the flight capabilities of the DODO. It is much wiser to keep one's corporate head in the sand. This has been the policy of Ostrich University.

We predict a long and glorious future for DODO, as it learns to fly, and amazes the world with the grace of its movements. Their renown is sure to spread through the literature, as contract executives ensure that all providers collect all droppings, to be audited, evaluated, and preserved as evidence for future generations. Meanwhile, ongoing regional development activities are being outsourced to other organisations in the virtual region, where effective flight capabilities are well established.

This first impulse text could be seen as highlighting issues which set the researchers against the regional development agency. Further discussion, as official decisions were taken to appeal, revealed that possibly both 'sides' were victims of a structural situation that was out of control. This prompted a second impulse text, drawn from the genre of disaster movies:

The crew and passengers on the Titanic maiden voyage were full of confidence. They had set ambitious targets in terms of luxury and speed, and launched on time, to great acclaim. The weather was good, and all seemed to be on schedule. The dance band was playing. Champagne was being poured. Suddenly, there was a shock. Those looking through the portholes saw an iceberg. . . .

Watching the DVD of the movie, in the comfort of our homes, we know what is going to happen, with the story told as by a survivor, decades later, and with documents from the wreckage. We know that, time after time, we are watching the inevitable turn of events. We cannot wind back the clock, adjust the script, and change matters. Still, we watch. It was not just a matter of surface damage by an iceberg. There were fundamental flaws in the design of the ship, which meant that, once disaster struck, there was no chance of recovery. The design could not be changed. It was, we can say, a disaster waiting to happen.

Looking back on the traumatic events of that day in the Atlantic, those who survived have been able to make some sense of the story. They remember the dance band who continued to play 'Nearer my God to Thee', the affluent first class passengers who ensured their own survival at the expense of others who were travelling steerage class, and the captain who went down with his ship. There will doubtless have been romances and other personal relationships. At the time, the situation was clearly an unimaginable nightmare for all concerned. Years later, it has been possible to learn lessons. However, there is no substitute for experience.

The argument of this book is that there are limits to what can be achieved by analytical thinking alone. If we want to gain access to tacit knowledge, this cannot be done simply by 'drilling down'. This works only with explicit codified knowledge, which is merely the tip of the iceberg of knowledge which needs to be managed. We need to develop analogical thinking, by which we mean the capacity to reflect on our own experience with reference to other cases, including 'Living Labs', or external stimuli.

Reflecting on Earlier Disasters

Earlier cases were set out in *Executive Guide to Preventing IT Disasters* (Ennals, 1995). The opening example was the Tay Bridge Rail Disaster as described by William McGonagall:

> Beautiful Railway Bridge of the Silv'ry Tay!
> Alas, I am very sorry to say
> That ninety lives have been taken away

On the last Sabbath day of 1879
Which will be remember'd for a very long time.

Another classic disaster story in the same book, from the 1990s, came from the Wessex Regional Health Authority:

> It was an attractive idea to develop a single information system to link the different hospitals, services and units across a region: if the system succeeded it could serve as a model for other regions, with considerable commercial benefits for the partners. Budgets and timescales were conditioned by this objective, imposing pressure on individual professionals to support the project and avoid action that might be prejudicial to its success.
>
> In the light of day, in the dispassionate account of a television documentary, the project seems fatally flawed. Strategic managers appear to have had little idea of the technical complexity of the task to which they were committed, and gave short shrift to those who recommended caution. The outcome was a working system in only one small part of the region, and national questions about the costs incurred: money allocated for the National Health Service had been used to pay consultants and vendors, many of whom also acted as advisers for the Authority.

Being aware of previous disasters does not provide a guarantee of protection from any new disasters, whether on the railways or with information systems, but it can help us in our reflections as we try to make sense of our experience. We learn from encounters with the unexpected.

The Dialogue Seminar Method

The Dialogue Seminar Method offers both a possible way forward in developing sustainable dialogue, and a means of enhancing professional skills of facilitation in the action research tradition. Now is the time to add the Dialogue Seminar Method to the repertoire of tools for action research, in enterprise and regional development. We have a new generation of critical students and practitioners, who are becoming leaders.

There will doubtless be alternative schools of Dialogue Seminar Method direction, as there are in theatre direction and literary criticism. We are entering the fields of what Stephen Toulmin called casuistry and rhetoric, where he found the theatre provided a powerful context for the exploration of intellectual dialogue in 'Imaginary Confessions' (Toulmin, 1995). What is more, we may identify existing practical approaches which can be regarded as consistent with the Dialogue Seminar Method. This breaks new ground in linking previously separate traditions of research and practice.

The theatre is the key, with the metaphor of theatrical rehearsals. Theatre is not simply a spectator sport. At its heart is the performance of knowledge, which has been a neglected dimension of knowledge society.

References

Ennals, R. (1986) *Star Wars: A Question of Initiative*, Chichester: John Wiley.

Ennals, R. (1987) 'Socially Useful Artificial Intelligence', *AI & Society* 1.1. 5–16.

Ennals, R. (1988) 'Can Skills be Transferable?' In Göranzon, B. and Josefson, I. eds *Knowledge, Skill and Artificial Intelligence*, London: Springer Verlag.

Ennals, R. 'Star Wars: A Modern Version of Shakespeare's "The Tempest"'. Presentation at 'Culture, Language and Artificial Intelligence' conference, Stockholm, May 1988.

Ennals, R. (1995) *Executive Guide to Preventing IT Disasters*, London: Springer Verlag.

Ennals, R. 'Can Disasters be Prevented?' Lecture at the Centre for Advanced Studies on Leadership, Stockholm, 1996.

Ennals, R. (1997) 'Art, Artificial Intelligence and Wealth: Dialogue with Adam Smith'. *AI & Society* 11.3–4, 247–63.

Ennals, R. (1999) *Work Life 2000: Yearbook 1: 1999*, London: Springer Verlag.

Ennals, R. (2000) *Work Life 2000: Yearbook 2: 2000*, London: Springer Verlag.

Ennals, R. (2001) *Work Life 2000: Yearbook 3: 2001*, London: Springer Verlag.

Ennals, R. and Gustavsen, B. (1999) *Work Organisation and Europe as a Development Coalition*. Dialogues on Work and Innovation 7, Amsterdam: John Benjamins.

Fosse, J.-K. (2005) 'The potential of dialogue in a municipal development project: Action research and planning practice'. *AI & Society* 19.4.

Fricke, W. and Totterdill, P. (eds) (2004) *Action Research in Workplace Innovation and Regional Development*. Dialogues on Work and Innovation 15, Amsterdam: John Benjamins.

Göranzon, B. (1987) 'The Practice of the Use of the Computer'. *AI & Society* 1.1. 25–36.

Göranzon, B. (ed.) (1995) *Skill, Technology and Enlightenment: On Practical Philosophy*, London: Springer Verlag.

Göranzon, B. (1997) 'Leadership: Implementation of Theory or Development of Practical Skills?' *AI & Society* 11.3–4 166–76.

Göranzon, B. and Hammarén, M. 'The Methodology of the Dialogue Seminar: Guidelines', 2005 (this volume).

Göranzon, B., Hammarén, M. and Ratkic, A. 'The Dialogue Seminar Method: Training in Analogical Thinking', 2005 (this volume).

Göranzon, B. and Josefson, I. (eds) (1988) *Knowledge, Skill and Artificial Intelligence*, London: Springer Verlag.

Göranzon, B. and Karlqvist, A. (1995) 'Beyond all Certainty'. In Göranzon, B. ed. *Skill, Technology and Enlightenment: On Practical Philosophy*, London: Springer Verlag.

Greenwood, D. and Levin, M. (1998) *Introduction to Action Research*, Thousand Oaks: Sage.

Gustavsen, B. 'Action Research Case Studies'. Presentation at 'Culture, Language and Artificial Intelligence' conference, Stockholm, May 1988.

Gustavsen, B. (1992) *Dialogue and Development*. Social Science for Social Action: toward organizational renewal. Vol. 1, Maastricht: Van Gorcum.

Gustavsen, B. (1997) 'Organisation as Development Coalition'. *AI & Society* 11.3–4 177–201.

Gustavsen, B. and Ennals, R. (eds) *Learning together for Local Innovation: Promoting Learning Regions*. CEDEFOP, 2006 (in preparation).

Gustavsen, B., Finn, H., and Oscarsson, B. (eds) (2001) *Creating Connectedness: The role of social research in innovation policy*. Dialogues on Work and Innovation 13, Amsterdam: John Benjamins.

Holen, F. (2005) 'Organisational identity in business parks'. Working paper, EDWOR programme, Norwegian University of Science and Technology, Trondheim.

Leirvik, B. (2005) 'Dialogue and power: The use of dialogue for participatory change'. *AI & Society* 19 April.

Levin, M. (ed.) (2002) *Researching Enterprise Development: Action Research on the cooperation between management and labour in Norway*. Dialogues on Work and Innovation 14, Amsterdam: John Benjamins.

McEwan, A.-M. and Ennals, R. (2005) 'Building Social Capital and Regional Innovation through Healthy Working Centres? An Investigation in the South East of England'. AI & Society 19 April.

Normann, R. (2005) 'Can Regions Learn? Critical Assessment of Regions as Arenas for Regional Development'. *AI & Society* 19 April.

Reason, P. and Bradbury, H. (eds) (2001) *Handbook of Action Research*, Thousand Oaks: Sage.

Skiöld, L. (ed.) (2000) *A Look into Modern Working Life*. Swedish National Institute for Working Life, Stockholm.

Stoppard, T. (1980) *Dogg's Hamlet, Cahoot's Macbeth*, London: Faber and Faber.

Toulmin, S. (1995) 'Imaginary Confessions'. In Göranzon, B. ed. *Skill, Technology and Enlightenment: On Practical Philosophy*, London: Springer Verlag.

Wennberg, A. (2000) *Work Life 2000 Quality in Work: Scientific Reports from the Workshops*. Swedish National Institute for Working Life, Stockholm.

Wolsk, D. (ed.) (1975) *The Experience-Centred Curriculum*. UNESCO, Copenhagen.

Part 6

CONCLUSIONS

20 Training in Analogical Thinking: The Dialogue Seminar Method in Basic Education, Further Education and Graduate Studies

Bo Göranzon, Maria Hammarén, Adrian Ratkic

Summary

The dialogue seminar method was developed to facilitate experience transfer in Combitech Systems, a specialised and knowledge-intensive Swedish enterprise. As a whole the dialogue seminar method, which includes reading, writing and advanced forms of dialogue, may be regarded as a framework for the process of reflection. Each part of the method is based on analogical thinking. Analogical thinking involves reflection on the similarities and differences between various objects. It is a dominant activity in judgement and action: whether the judgement or action be expressed in academic research, in industrial development projects or in traditional 'practical' occupations. Further, analogical thinking is important in all problem solving, in the arts and in those stages of research work that include inventiveness and imagination. For several years the dialogue seminar method has been applied in graduate education at the Royal Institute of Technology in Stockholm, and may soon become an essential part of a range of educational programmes in the network of our partners. The dialogue seminar method has already proved to be a powerful tool in the continuing professional development of music teachers at the Royal College of Music in Stockholm. We aim to explore the potential of the dialogue seminar method in giving systematic support to analogical thinking. Research on skills and technology has shown that the arts may be seen as a source of powerful, paradigmatic examples of practical knowledge. For that reason, work continues, together with the Collegium Musicum department of the Royal College of Music in Stockholm.

Specific Goals

- To develop research that is closely allied to practice by means of a variety of applications of the dialogue seminar method.
- To examine the role of reflection in basic education, further education and graduate studies.
- To examine the dialogue seminar method as an alternative to traditional master-apprentice teaching as a method of exchanging experience in training for professions.
- To examine the nature of analogical thinking (digression in conversation) by connecting with the classic fundamental texts of the philosophy of science.

A Review of the Subject Area, Theory, Methods, and Preliminary Results

A Review of the Subject Area, Theory and Methods

Skill and Technology was introduced as a graduate programme at the Royal Institute of Technology, Stockholm, in 1995. The subject area, which evolved from long-term case studies on skills from the end of the 1970s, established its profile through basic research studies on the epistemology of practical knowledge. The tradition of passing on knowledge and skills was a key issue from the outset. Bo Göranzon's dissertation, *The Practical Intellect* (1990) and Maja Lisa Perby's dissertation, *The Art of Mastering a Process* (1995) demonstrated that the concept of tacit knowledge was central to our understanding of practical knowledge. Reflection on the experience of practitioners emerged as a vital element. Both in the research project and the graduate studies programme, Maria Hammarén's book, *Writing: A Method for Reflection* (Skriva – en metod för reflektion) (Utbildningsförlaget, 1995) was the inspiration for the introduction of a component of self-assessment through writing. In his book Bo Göranzon demonstrated that reflection on experience required 'masks' through which to reflect. He identified four fruitful sources: texts from the period of transition in the history of ideas, Wittgenstein's philosophy of language, qualitative case studies with concrete examples from different occupational practices, and the classical literature of the theatre. From Hammarén and Göranzon's combined perspective came the *dialogue seminar method*. Today, the view of teaching and the development of ideas, seen from an epistemological perspective, lies at the core of this subject.

In recent years the development of methods for experience transfer has been a priority task for skills research. Preliminary findings were presented in Maria Hammarén's dissertation *Ledtråd i förvandling — om att skapa en reflekterande praxis* (Clues in Transformation: on Creating a Reflective Practice) which mainly examines a project on experience transfer in Combitech Systems. This work was carried out from 1996 to 1999 by Maria Hammarén and Bo Göranzon. The task of the development project was to produce a systematised path to experts' familiarity with a large number of language games, i.e., by focusing more on the communicative aspects of language than on its dead-ends. The communicative possibilities were to be found in stories, examples and indirect representation. The conversational form itself, with its often drastic associations with the world of perception, linked language action/language use and the world in a way that set imagination and analogical thinking in motion.

The work at Combitech Systems resulted in the company setting up a 'learning lab', with the dialogue seminar method a cornerstone of this learning organisation. Six of the company's consultants continued their studies of the method and its epistemological background as graduate students in skill and technology. The first dissertation from this group is Jan Sjunnesson's *Spindeln i nätet: om ledarskap och analogiskt tänkande: en studie i ledarskap och analogiskt seende* (The Spider in the Web: on leadership and analogical thinking: a study in leadership and analogical perception) (2003). Niclas Fock's dissertation was presented in June 2004, and the others later the same a year. Two of the graduate students in the group intend to take doctor's degrees.

The experience gained from the programme at Combitech Systems has now been further developed through the creation of the *KTH Advanced Programme in Reflective Practice*, a graduate studies programme for practising graduate engineers, economists, people in the artistic professions and others. The dialogue seminar method is used both as a pedagogical basis in the programme's courses and as a research method in the graduate student case studies on skills. Adrian Ratkic's dissertation for the Licentiate in Skill and Technology, *Avvikelsens konst* (The Art of Digression) (2004), describes and discusses the use of the dialogue seminar method in the research programme.

Essays on this research are published regularly in the journal *Dialoger* (which received the Cultural Journal of the Year award in 1996) and the journal *Spelplats*. The first issue of *Dialoger* was published in 1986, and at the time of writing 72 issues have been published. The journal *Spelplats* is a forum for the publication of reflective texts that are produced in the course of work using the dialogue seminar method. Ten issues of *Spelplats* have been published to date. Information on the Dialoger publishing house publications which, in addition to the journals *Dialoger* and *Spelplats* also include books, may be found at: www.dialoger.se.

Theory and Methods

The role of the researcher in skill and technology is related to aspects of action research. In this tradition, research and the application of research findings are not two separate phases of the task. While the researcher aims to improve the practice of the subject of the study, at the same time he allows himself to be influenced by what he learns in interacting with the subject of his research, whether this may involve a readiness to revise his own theoretical assumptions or to modify the method during an ongoing investigation. We see the dialogue seminar method as an extension of research that is closely allied to professional practice, on which the research area of skill and technology has been based for close to 30 years. An important assumption in the theoretical background of the dialogue seminar method is that thinking takes place in a community, as part of historically established practices. Similar perspectives: that thinking does not occur exclusively in the head of an individual; that it takes place between people and with the help of physical and cultural tools that develop in an historical context, are discussed in Roger Säljö's book *Lärande i praktiken: ett sociokulturellt perspektiv* (Learning in Practice: a socio-cultural perspective) (2000). In his book, *Genom huvudet* (*Through the Head*) (2002) Johan Asplund also argues in support of the theory that thinking and learning is something that takes place principally between people.

Furthermore, several decades of research on skill have shown that it is extremely difficult through direct questioning, for example in the form of questionnaires or interviews, to arrive at the core of the professional's skills, where, not least, attempts to create so-called expert systems have run into considerable difficulties (Göranzon and Josefson, 1988). Dialogue-inspired methods, in which conversations between researcher and professional continue over a longer period of time, have proved to be more accessible (Göranzon, 1990 and Perby, 1995). We have called such methods indirect, because both the responses and the researcher's questions emerged gradually, in the course of many conversations that may span several years, and whose purpose is for the researcher to develop his ability to identify the interaction of dynamic skill with a changing context. This gradual emergence of appropriate interpretations and composite pictures is different to responses given to direct questions. The dialogue seminar method, which is described below, falls into the category of indirect methods.

The core of skills was gradually identified under the heading of tacit knowledge. Tacit knowledge is linked to earlier experience. Experience-based knowledge is separate from other, more theoretically oriented knowledge because it is context-dependent, i.e. its expression is always connected to situations in which it is visible in the form of actions, gestures and reactions, such as the practice of a profession. Therefore, experience-based knowledge is difficult to deal with in theoretical education. At an early stage in the evolution of this research area, attention was drawn to the need for reflection as an alternative way of 'theorising' about experience-based knowledge. Support was found in Hubert and Stuart Dreyfus' model of the way knowledge acquired through practice is developed. To achieve competence, which in Dreyfus' model is equivalent to resolving a known problem by the rigorous application of explicit rules, was of little relevance in this research area, where interest has always focused on the dynamic aspects of skill, what is expressed in inventiveness and imagination: the qualitative aspects to be found in artistic work processes and elsewhere. There are two more stages in Dreyfus' knowledge model: skill and expertise. These are the two aspects of professional practice on which the research area concentrates. There is less and less interest in producing more of the same: the development of the community is dependent on good judgement in new situations and in a reality that is dynamic, i.e. in development work of all kinds. No process automatically leads a person forward from competence to skill. To move beyond the competence stage requires risk and reflection on concrete examples and sequences of events that had developed in unexpected directions. This means that one has to think *analogically*, to search, and to see similarities and differences between paradigmatic examples and examples of topical situations that call for a solution. In this perspective, for example, a researcher gains knowledge from learning by example rather than from instructions, and through personal contact with prominent researchers rather than reading books. The classic studies of a researcher's knowledge by Ludwik Fleck, Michael Polanyi and Thomas Kuhn point in the same direction. A well-known example from the humanities is Hans Georg Gadamer's *Philosophische Lehrjahre*, an autobiographical work in which he describes his experience of informal and personal learning in his association with his teachers.

Is not speaking of tacit knowledge a contradiction? How, for example, can one describe 'the essence of Picasso's painting in his blue period without showing any pictures'? It cannot be done. On the other hand, one may ask: how can the greatness of Picasso's painting from his blue period be explained to someone who has contemplated these works for years but not understood why these scribbles and daubs are considered to be great art, without speaking about and commenting on these pictures? (Sällström, 1989). The answer is that the path to comprehension must involve both illustration and verbal tutoring on the subject. In the words of Kjell S. Johannessen, aesthetic practice is, after all, a mode of behaviour that involves language. Comments and verbal direction occur in the process of learning tacit knowledge, whether it be sport, music, glassblowing, knowledge of the human condition, an engineer's assessment of a project's timeframe and budget limits, or a researcher's expertise in handling laboratory equipment. To be unable to capture the tacit dimension in words is a question of being unable to capture it exclusively and precisely in the form of statements. But this is different than saying that it is unnecessary and even impossible to speak of it. The question of the connection between tacit knowledge and language does not condemn us to silence. Rather, it is a question of the kind of language we can use to identify the tacit aspects of our knowledge, and gain access to them.

The Dialogue Seminar Method

The dialogue seminar method uses external impulses to bring experiences to life. These experiences are then represented in stories. The source of the external impulses is found in literature and essays on knowledge. The method is founded on humanistic traditions and traditional humanistic reflection: reading slowly and constantly making notes in the margin. There is also the challenge of having the notes act as a record of the connections to examples that reading the texts may produce. In preparation for each seminar, the participants read the same texts. Slow writing, which includes a process of examination and reappraisal, is just as important as reading. Taking their notes as a basis, the participants paste together a new story, a written reflection. Interweaving reading and writing in this way impels the people in the group to reflect. The reflection, which works on the group members' individual experiences, is then shared with the group by reading aloud. Thus some important qualifications have been made to the conversation that this process produces, and this qualified conversation is then set out in the minutes, a permanent record of what has been said. Different language games are brought into play, and nuances and contrasts stand out in a detail that is not possible in an ordinary conversation.

The flow of thought in the dialogue seminars is anything but straight, and it should be noted that this is a deliberate choice. The participants are invited to give free rein to their thoughts, to seek examples and examine the area of thinking that is the theme of the session. This makes special demands of the person leading the seminars and of the person appointed to record the 'minutes of ideas'. An example of the occurrence of digressions and side-tracking with a programmatic consequence is the writings of Denis Diderot. Marian Hobson, Professor of French, says that Diderot's digressive tactics are related to his perception of the role of analogy in the development of experience-based knowledge (Hobson, 1994). Diderot's work stands out as a precursor of both Kant's thinking on the concept of experience analogy, and on the thinking of our time on the connections between the way of reasoning in professional contexts, and in artistic and aesthetic contexts. Skill research has demonstrated that arguments and conversations on experience in occupational contexts are of necessity analogical, i.e. based on examples on which we reflect by means of comparative analysis (Johannessen, 1999a).

The systematic digressions in the conversation are also linked to the idea of what reflection in general means. We may regard reflection as an essentially comparative activity. Reflection on skill that takes place through all four of Bo Göranzon's 'masks': the philosophy of language, the history of ideas, analogies to other occupation-based examples, and classic literature and drama, is precisely a comparative activity. Take, for example, some analogies whose systematic examination plays an important part in postgraduate education in the KTH Advanced Programme in Reflective Practice. Contemporary attempts to question experts on the kind of knowledge they possess, in the hope of being able to upload this knowledge into a computer memory, may be seen as analogous to Socrates' attempts to question the prophet Euthyphro about his expert knowledge of the piety of man. One may also see Leibniz's 'characteristica universalis' as analogous to our contemporary dream of intelligent computers, or Diderot's description of the mind, the body and thinking as interwoven in a net-like structure as analogous to ideas circulating in the forefront of contemporary research on consciousness.

A Wide Range of Applications

Today, the dialogue seminar method is used in three kinds of situation:

1. as a method of using narrative form to portray and convey experience-based knowledge;
2. in the education and group instruction of graduate students; and
3. as a method for gathering empirical data in research on skill.

What separates the application of the method in situation (1) from the application of the method in situation (2)? The framework of the seminars is the same: reading and writing assignments, reading the writing assignments aloud, dialogue, and minutes-taking. The difference lies in the way of reflecting, both in the writing assignments, and on them. The graduate student chooses an aspect of a classical text on the philosophy of science, and reflects on the relevance of the text and its possible application in the dissertation work, rather than responding to the text with a story that depicts experience.

Let us take an illustrative example. There are similarities between what we want to achieve in training our graduate students, and problems in the practice of performing music. The study of the practice of performing music addresses the question of the performance of music from earlier times, and the related problems of the creativity of the musicians. Earlier composers' music was performed over and over again. A common way of dealing with the need for creative performances in such a situation is to give the musicians a free hand to do whatever they want. The paradox is that at that point the performances begin to be similar. One performer produces an outstanding interpretation, and others gradually begin to imitate that performance. The reproductive aspect of the performances tends to overshadow the creative aspect. This is in conflict with the idea that great creativity comes from unlimited freedom.

One of a number of ways for musicians to avoid the problem was to study historical source material in the form of notes, information about the composer's life, writings left by the composer, contemporary history, etc. The result of these deliberate efforts to carry on a dialogue with the historical source material was that the individual performances became more creative and began to differ from one another, despite the fact that the musicians drew on the same historical sources.

Today, we can see similar problems in the interpretation of classic texts on the philosophy of science. René Descartes, for example, is often arbitrarily classified as the philosopher of abstract doubt. If one goes back to the source and reads his *Discourse on Method*, a different picture emerges. There, Descartes stands out as a person who is fully aware of the importance of practical experience (Göranzon, 2001; Molander, 2001). In the programme of graduate studies, the KTH Advanced Programme in Reflective Practice, we have done exactly that: put graduate students into direct contact with Descartes' text to stimulate their own creative thinking on the concept of method and to encourage them to find a personal voice as a researcher. In addition to Descartes, we also read source texts by Plato, Galileo, Leibniz, d'Alembert, Diderot and Gadamer. This is in line with what Sir Peter Medawar, who was awarded the Nobel Prize in Medicine in 1960, says in the introduction to his book *The Limits of Science* (1985), that what he finds most rewarding in the philosophy of science is short texts, often not more than essays, that open the eyes to new perspectives and empower the imagination. The texts he names include Descartes' *Discours de la Méthode* (1637), Samuel Taylor Coleridge's *A Preliminary Treatise on Method* (1818) and Shelley's *Defence of Poetry* (1821).

The Dialogue Seminar at the Royal Dramatic Theatre, Stockholm

Over the years, the Dialogue Seminar at the Royal Dramatic Theatre, Stockholm has gained an important position in this sphere of research. We see its work as a laboratory for basic research in the humanities. At the moment, dialogue seminars are held twice a term at the Royal Dramatic Theatre, Stockholm. From these sessions, which are recorded on videotape, come articles and books. It may be mentioned here that the result of the Dialogue Seminar's work is inculcated in various ways into graduate studies. Texts that have proved to be inspirational in the seminars at the Royal Dramatic Theatre are included in the dialogue seminar method in various educational contexts. The seminars at the Royal Dramatic Theatre are usually developed into articles in the journal *Dialoger*, but they may also contain the seeds of books. At present, books are being published in the form of double issues of *Dialoger*. The most recent examples are Allan Janik's *The Use and Abuse of Metaphors* (2003) and Gunnar Bergendal's *Ansvarig handling: uppsatser om yrkeskunnande, vetenskap och bildning* (Responsible Action: Essays on Skills, Science and Education) (2003). The next book, to be published in 2005, is Tore Nordenstam's *Exemplets makt* (The Power of Example). Today, the Dialogue Seminar at the Royal Dramatic Theatre is part of a symposium on R&D in the arts that is funded by the Swedish Research Council.

Project Description

How can analogical thinking be promoted, and what part can it play in different kinds of education? In this present project we want to examine the potential of the dialogue seminar method for providing systematic support to analogical thinking. Further research is required into the various components of the method.

Regarding *writing*, a special kind of writing, as we have called it, several important areas call for further examination, where each component can be rooted in a philosophical/literary tradition.

1. Walter Benjamin's, *Paris, Capital of the Nineteenth Century*, in *The Arcades Project* examines the emergence of the moderns. He speaks of the 'epic' sides of the truth and relates them to the form of communication used in the crafts. He sets information, which corresponds to the industrial work process and sensation, against epic narrative representation. With the sensation, 'whatever still resembles wisdom, oral tradition or the epic side of truth is razed to the ground'. However, it is easy to allow oneself to become engrossed on far too simple grounds by the narrative, by the dramatological devices. In the modern industrial society, how do we produce stories that create a new relationship with imagination and reflection?

2. In paragraph 122 of his *Philosophical Investigations*, Ludwig Wittgenstein writes that a perspicuous representation produces just that understanding which consists in 'seeing connections'. Seeing appropriate and relevant connections is essential in the transfer of experience from a number of unique cases to a new situation. In her English translation of paragraph 122 G.E.M. Anscombe uses the word 'earmark' to underscore that in a representation that is visible it is possible to identify the form of report we are making – which language game is expressed in what is represented. The activity consists of finding and discovering cases that have the ability to transfer. All that remains for a person who wants to communicate clearly at a given point in time is, strictly speaking, the word woven into the fabric of an action. How do we arrive at the stage that 'earmarks' relevant connections and that leads us on to a new, different use of our experience?

3. In the dialogue seminar method, reading is also an indispensable part of writing. Jean Starobinski's penetrating study, *Montaigne in Movement*, draws attention to the very form of writing that is interwoven and immersed in reading. Montaigne's essays are full of references and quotes, mainly from his readings of classic thinkers. Starobinski brings to the fore Montaigne's broad consciousness, which he sets against consciousness in our own times. 'In Montaigne, consciousness is in a constant dialogue with images from the past, but many present-day devotees of immediate existence reject both the cultural heritage as ingenuous submission to the siren song from future communities: their present is then so narrow that it becomes identical with that of the animals, . . . '. To extend consciousness by indicating texts that maintain a standard of literary quality, and that speak to us from another time or another horizon, is an important objective. But what texts could form a canon? And what criteria must be met if the students themselves are to reflect in greater depth?

4.   Regarding an intensification of the *management* of the Dialogue Seminar, the tradition of the philosophy of science offers an important area with which to establish connections. In his *Dialogue on the Two Chief World Systems* Galileo Galilei presents an ideal argument for the dialogue seminar method as such. He emphasises that he wants to explain the ideas in the form of dialogues because they will then not be limited by 'a strict application of mathematical laws'. The dialogues provide scope for digressions that are sometimes at least as interesting as the main issue. Digression is a central factor in Galileo (as it is in Diderot). To direct a dialogue seminar requires a sophisticated approach to the abundance of digressions and the variety of experience the participants present, both in their texts and in conversation. The digressions that create the scarlet thread, the central theme, are so many and so extensive that it becomes necessary to grasp, to earmark, those that may be fruitful connections. In Galileo's dialogue, the interaction between the roles of directing a dialogue seminar and writing the 'minutes of ideas' has an ideal model. *Dialogue on the Two Chief World Systems* is an example of a possible connection to classic texts on the philosophy of science. To establish stronger connections with classic texts on the philosophy of science is an important part of developing the training of analogical thinking.

5.   The role of analogical thinking need not be limited to reflection on experience-based knowledge. An ongoing project is examining the role of reflection in graduate studies. Adrian Ratkić has emphasised that scientific and philosophical reflection in the KTH Advanced Programme in Reflective Practice has been deliberately carried on through analogies. The graduate students who have completed the programme have, in one way or another, had skill as a theme in their dissertations. In the past year, two musicians and teachers from the Royal College of Music, Stockholm, and Clas Pehrsson, a Professor at that College, have been associated with the programme. In the future we want to continue to widen the circle of participants by including graduate students from other disciplines and with other research interests, and have the entire group, through dialogue seminars, to examine one another's scientific models, theories and methods. To acquire a scientific education will, in this sense, be to gain an overall view of the limits of one's own field of knowledge, not through a course in the modern philosophy of science, but through reflection inspired by close reading of classic texts on the philosophy of science and the humanities. The project refers to what is now a more than century-old debate on the two cultures, the scientific and the

humanistic, and raises the issue of possible points of contact between the two in the context of Swedish education.

6. From the spring term of 2003, work with the dialogue seminar method in co-operation with Collegium Musicum at the Royal College of Music, Stockholm and the Institution for Skills and Technology at KTH has included activities in the Collegium Musicum's teaching group. Based on earlier experience from similar work at KTH, we confronted the problem that the musician, like other artists in non-verbal disciplines, is usually less inclined, and less in the habit of, expressing verbally his most important thoughts on skill, and that music college teachers therefore largely base the structure of their teaching on non-verbal methods. It is therefore often difficult to steer teachers' discussions of concrete teaching issues towards important matters. This problem is accentuated by the teachers usually being alone in the teaching situation, for which reason genuine common empirical data are difficult to build up.

These problems have resulted in a review of some aspects of the method, and have given rise to a further development of the method. Inspirational materials such as film and pictorial material have proved to be promising alternatives to the written text in encouraging the emergence of analogically-based reflections. Minutes of ideas produced in different layers, with the most recent layer reflecting on the previous layer, have also made it easier to record conceptual issues of general interest.

In preparation for continued work we therefore plan to proceed with this kind of further development of the method, which is expected to lead to clearer presentations of quality criteria for inspirational material, and documentation. All this work will be put in the larger context at the Royal College of Music, dealt with in 'A Research Strategy for the Royal College of Music', the official report the College submitted to the Ministry of Education in November 2003, in which co-operation with external research schools and institutions similar to that with KTH is identified as an indispensable feature of the Royal College of Music's current and future research.

7. We want to initiate a processing of the documentation from the previous eighteen years of the Dialogue Seminar's activities, to make it available to a wider circle of teachers, graduate students, people in the artistic professions, and other interested parties in the educational system. Today, the Dialogue Seminar's archive has about 250 videocassette tapes, a total of about 500 hrs of playing time. It will be possible to include the processed material in the dialogue seminar method, see point (6) above.

Significance

The role of analogical thinking in the transfer of experience-based knowledge has long been given attention in this research area, but thus far has not been examined in sufficient depth. In this project we broaden the knowledge of the connection between analogical thinking and different kinds of reflection: scientific and philosophical, aesthetic, and reflection on practical knowledge. This makes it possible to build a better platform in different kinds of education for training in the two leadership roles in the dialogue seminar: dialogue seminar director and minutes-taker. This in its turn is important for the possibilities of future modification of the method to suit different kinds of education, such as teacher training.

References

Asplund, J. (2002) *Genom huvudet*, (Through the Head) Göteborg: Korpen.

Bergendal, G. (2003) *Ansvarig handling: uppsatser om yrkeskunnande, vetenskap och bildning*, (Responsible Action: Essays on Skill, Science and Education) Stockholm: Dialoger.

Civilingenjörernas yrkeskunnande: arbetsbok för reflektion (1994) (The Engineer's Skill, a workbook for reflection) Civilingenjörsförbundet.

Coleridge, S.T. (1957) *Selected Poetry and Prose*, Penguin books.

Dreyfus, Hubut L. and Dreyfus, Stuart E. (1986) *Mind Over Machine: The Power of Human Intuition and Expertise in the Era of the Computer*, Oxford: Blackwell.

Forskning av denna världen: praxisnära forskning inom utbildningsvetenskap (2003) (Research of This World: Practice-related research in the science of education) Stockholm: Scientific Council, Scientific Council Report 2.

Göranzon, B. and Josefson, I. (eds) (1988) *Knowledge, Skill and Artificial Intelligence*, London: Springer Verlag.

Göranzon, B. (1990) *Det praktiska intellektet* (The Practical Intellect) Carlssons.

Göranzon, B. (2001) *Spelregler – om gränsöverskridande* (Rules of the Game – on exceeding the limits) Stockholm: Dialoger.

Hammarén, Maria: *Skriva – en metod för reflektion* (1995) (Writing – a method for reflection) Stockholm: Utbildningsförlaget.

Hammarén, Maria: *Ledtråd i förvandling – om att skapa en reflekterande praxis* (1999) (Clues in Transformation: On creating a reflective practice) Stockholm: Dialoger.

Hammarén, Maria, 'Yrkeskunnande, berättelser och språk' (Skill, Stories and Language) in *Dialoger* 61/2002: Minne och fantasi (Memory and Imagination).

Hoberg, C. (ed.) (1998) *Precision och improvisation: om systemutvecklarnas yrkeskunnande* (Precision and Improvisation. On the Skills of the Systems Engineer) Stockholm: Dialoger.

Hobson, M. (1994) 'Diderot, Implicit Knowledge and Architecture: Perceived Analogies' *Dialoger* 30–32.

References

Janik, A. (1991) *Cordelias tystnad: om reflektionens kunskapsteori*, Cordelia's Silence: On the Epistemology of Reflection) Stockholm: Carlssons.

Janik, A. (2003) *The Use and Abuse of Metaphor*, Stockholm: Dialoger.

Johannessen, K.S. (1999) *Praxis och tyst kunnande*, (Praxis and Tacit Knowledge) Stockholm: Dialoger.

Johannessen, K.S. (1999a) 'Det analogiska tänkandet', (Analogical Thinking) in *Dialoger* 50–51: Vetenskap och konst.

Medawar, P. (1985) *The Limits of Science*, Oxford: Oxford University Press.

Molander, B. (2001) 'Osäkerheten i samtalet' (Uncertainty in Conversation), in *Herr Bos akademi*, bilaga till *Dialoger* 58–59.

Nielsen, K. and Kvale, Steinar (ed.) (2000) *Mästarlära: lärande som social praxis* (Master and Apprentice: learning as a social practice) Lund: Studentlitteratur.

Nordenstam, T. (1968) *Sudanese Ethics*, Uppsala: Nordiska Afrikainstitutet.

Pauli, J. (2003) 'Dialogen förenar de två filurerna' (Dialogue Unites Two Sly Dogs) in *Dagens forskning*, 3–4 March.

Pehrsson, C. (2000) 'Musikalisk uppförandepraxis' (The Practice of Performing Music) in *Dialoger* 55. Descartes and Galileo.

Pehrsson, C. (2001) 'I en död mästares sällskap' (In the Company of a Dead Master) in *Dialoger* 60: Uppförandepraxis.

Perby, M.J. (1995) *Konsten att bemästra en process: om att förvalta yrkeskunnande*, (The Art of Mastering a Process: on the management of skill), Gidlunds.

Ratkić, A. (2001) 'Analogi och musik' (Analogy and Music) in *Dialoger* 60.

Ratkić, A. (2004) *Avvikelsens konst: metod och analogiskt tänkande*, (The Art of Digression: Method and Analogical Thinking), Stockholm: KTH-INDEK.

Schön, D.A. (1991) *The Reflective Practitioner: How professionals think in action*, Aldershot: Ashgate (1st edition 1983).

Szlezák, T.A. (1999) *Platon och läsaren* (Plato and the Reader) Stockholm: Atlantis (Original Title: *Platon läsen*).

Sällström, P. (1989) *En kommentar rörande den tysta kunskapen och språkets gränser*, (A Comment on Tacit Knowledge and the Limits of Language) *Dialoger* 9.

Säljö, R. (2000) *Lärande i praktiken: ett sociokulturellt perspektiv* (Learning in Practice: a sociocultural perspective) Stockholm: Prisma.

Tillberg, P. (ed.) (2002) *Dialoger om yrkeskunnande och teknologi* (Dialogues on Skill and Technology) Stockholm: Dialoger.

Index

Index compiled by Terry Halliday